Environments
and Behavior

Proceedings of the conference, The Impact of Specific Settings on the Development and Behavior of Mentally Retarded Persons, held at the University of California, Los Angeles.

Jointly sponsored by the National Institute of Child Health and Human Development of the United States Public Health Service, and by the Mental Retardation Research Center of the University of California, Los Angeles.

Environments and Behavior

The Adaptation of Mentally Retarded Persons

Edited by

Keith T. Kernan, Ph.D.
Associate Professor
Department of Psychiatry and Biobehavioral Sciences
Mental Retardation Research Center
University of California, Los Angeles

Michael J. Begab, Ph.D.
Former Head, Mental Retardation Research Centers Program
National Institute of Child Health and Human Development
Bethesda, Maryland

Special Consultant to the President
University Park Press

Robert B. Edgerton, Ph.D.
Professor
Departments of Psychiatry and Biobehavioral Sciences
    and Anthropology
Mental Retardation Research Center
University of California, Los Angeles

University Park Press
Baltimore

UNIVERSITY PARK PRESS
International Publishers in Medicine and Human Services
300 North Charles Street
Baltimore, Maryland 21201

Typeset by Brushwood Graphics
Manufactured in the United States of America by The Maple Press Company

Library of Congress Cataloging in Publication Data
Main entry under title:

Environments and behavior.

Papers presented at a conference held at the University of California, Los Angeles, in Sept. 1979, sponsored by the National Institute of Child Health and Human Development.
Includes index.
1. Mentally handicapped—Congresses. 2. Man—Influence of environment—Congresses. I. Kernan, Keith T. II. Begab, Michael Jay, 1918- III. Edgerton, Robert B., 1931- . IV. National Institute of Child Health and Human Development (U.S.)
HV1568.E55 1983   362.3   83-1204

ISBN 0-8391-1781-7

Contents

Methods and Models

Residential and Community Settings

Work Settings

Educational Settings

Language and Setting

Training and Placement

Contributors and Conference Participants

Henry A. Alker, Ph.D.
Saybrook Institute
1772 Vallejo Street
San Francisco, California 94123

Donald M. Baer, Ph.D.
Department of Human Development
  and Family Life
Bureau of Child Research
University of Kansas
Lawrence, Kansas 66044

Bruce L. Baker, Ph.D.
Department of Psychology
University of California, Los Angeles
Los Angeles, California 90024

Michael J. Begab, Ph.D.
Special Consultant to the President
University Park Press
300 N. Charles Street
Baltimore, Maryland 21201

John M. Belmont, Ph.D.
Associate Professor
Department of Pediatrics
University of Kansas Medical Center
39th and Rainbow Boulevard
Kansas City, Kansas 66103

Sylvia Bercovici, Ph.D.
Center for the Study of Human Rights
Columbia University
New York, New York 10027

Gershon Berkson, Ph.D.
Illinois State Pediatric Institute
1640 West Roosevelt Road
Chicago, Illinois 60608

Arne T. Bjaanes
The Center for the Study of Community
  Perspectives
P.O. Box 64
Patton, California 92369

Don Brenneis, Ph.D.
Department of Anthropology
Pitzer College
Claremont, California 91711

Edgar W. Butler, Ph.D.
Department of Sociology
University of California
Riverside, California 92502

Duncan B. Clark
University of California, Los Angeles
Los Angeles, California 90024

Ralph P. Ferretti, Ph.D.
Cognitive Studies
University of Washington
Seattle, Washington 98195

James J. Gallagher, Ph.D.
Director
Frank Porter Graham Child Development
  Center
University of North Carolina
Highway 54, By-Pass West
Chapel Hill, North Carolina 27514

Ronald Gallimore, Ph.D.
Mental Retardation Research Center
Neuropsychiatric Institute
Center for Health Services
760 Westwood Plaza
Los Angeles, California 90024

Jay Gottlieb, Ph.D.
Department of Educational Psychology
Shimkin Hall
New York University
New York, New York 10003

James Intagliata, Ph.D.
Division of Community Psychiatry
Department of Psychiatry
School of Medicine
State University of New York at Buffalo

2111 Main Street, Building E
Buffalo, New York 14214

Mindy Katz, M.S.
Albert Einstein College of Medicine
Yeshiva University
1300 Morris Park Avenue
Bronx, New York 10461

Paul Koegel, Ph.D.
Mental Retardation Research Center
Neuropsychiatric Institute
Center for Health Sciences
760 Westwood Plaza
University of California, Los Angeles
Los Angeles, California 90024

Helene Koller, M.P.H.
Albert Einstein College of Medicine
Yeshiva University
1300 Morris Park Avenue
Bronx, New York 10461

Sharon Landesman-Dwyer, Ph.D.
Child Development and Mental Retardation
  Center
WJ-10
University of Washington
Seattle, Washington 98195

Lewis L. Langness, Ph.D.
Mental Retardation Research Center
Neuropsychiatric Institute
University of California, Los Angeles
Center for Health Sciences
760 Westwood Plaza
Los Angeles, California 90024

Elliot Lessen, Ph.D.
Department of Learning, Development
  and Special Education
Northern Illinois University
DeKalb, Illinois 60115

Harold Levine, Ph.D.
School of Education
University of California, Los Angeles
Los Angeles, California 90024

D. L. MacMillan, Ph.D.
School of Education
University of California
Riverside, California 92502

Janice McLaren
MRC Medical Sociology Unit
Institute of Medical Sociology
Westburn Road
Aberdeen AB9 22E
Scotland

C. Edward Meyers, Ph.D.
Lanterman State Hospital
Research Department
P.O. Box 100-R
Pomona, California 91767

Gale M. Morrison
Department of Special Education
Graduate School of Education
University of California
Santa Barbara, California 93106

J. R. Newbrough, Ph.D.
Director
Center for Community Studies
John F. Kennedy Center for Research in
  Education and Human Development
George Peabody College
Nashville, Tennessee 37203

Nathaniel Owings, Ph.D.
Gallatin Easter Seal Speech and Hearing Clinic
Department of Speech Communication
Montana State University
Bozeman, Montana 59717

Stephen A. Richardson, Ph.D.
Department of Pediatrics
Albert Einstein College of Medicine
Yeshiva University
1300 Morris Park Avenue
Bronx, New York 10461

Ann K. Rogers-Warren, Ph.D.
Department of Special Education
Peabody College of Vanderbilt University
Nashville, Tennessee 37203

Terry L. Rose, Ph.D.
College of Human Development and Learning
University of North Carolina
Charlotte, North Carolina 28223

Frank R. Rusch, Ph.D.
Department of Special Education
University of Illinois at Urbana-Champaign
Urbana, Illinois 61801

Sharon Sabsay, Ph.D.
Socio-Behavioral Research Group
Mental Retardation Research Center
Neuropsychiatric Institute
University of California, Los Angeles
Center for Health Sciences
760 Westwood Plaza
Los Angeles, California 90024

Robert L. Schalock, Ph.D.
Mid-Nebraska Mental Retardation Services
522 Eastside Boulevard

P.O. Box 1146
Hastings, Nebraska 68901

Nancy Scherer, Ph.D.
CDMRC
University of Washington
Seattle, Washington 98195

Richard P. Schultz
University of Illinois at Urbana-Champaign
Urbana, Illinois 68101

Gary B. Seltzer, Ph.D.
Program in Medicine
Brown University
Providence, Rhode Island 02912

Marsha Mailick Seltzer, Ph.D.
School of Social Work
Boston University
264 Bay State Road
Boston, Massachusetts 02215

Clarence C. Sherwood, Ph.D.
School of Social Work
Boston University
264 Bay State Road
Boston, Massachusetts 02215

Paul E. Stucky, M.S.
John F. Kennedy Center for Research in
    Education and Human Development

George Peabody College
Nashville, Tennessee 37203

Jim L. Turner, Ph.D.
Socio-Behavioral Research Group
Mental Retardation Research Center
Neuropsychiatric Institute
University of California, Los Angeles
Center for Health Services
760 Westwood Plaza
Los Angeles, California 90024

Steven F. Warren, Ph.D.
Department of Special Education
Peabody College of Vanderbilt University
Nashville, Tennessee 37203

Barry Willer, Ph.D.
Division of Community Psychiatry
School of Medicine
State University of New York
2211 Main Street, Building E
Buffalo, New York 14214

Andrea Zetlin, Ed.D.
Socio-Behavioral Research Group
Mental Retardation Research Center
Neuropsychiatric Institute
University of California, Los Angeles
Center for Health Sciences
760 Westwood Plaza
Los Angeles, California 90024

Foreword

In her famous book *Coming of Age in Samoa,* Margaret Mead commented on the situation of the handicapped as follows:

> ...Samoa's lack of difficult situations of conflicting choice, of situations in which fear or pain or anxiety are sharpened to a knife edge will probably account for a large part of the absence of psychological maladjustment. Just as a low-grade moron would not be hopelessly handicapped in Samoa, although he would be a public charge in a large American city, so individuals with slight nervous instability have a much more favorable chance in Samoa than in America. Furthermore, the amount of individualisation, the range of variation, is much smaller in Samoa. Within our wider limits of deviation there are inevitably found weak and non-resistant temperaments. And just as our society shows a greater development of personality, so also it shows a larger proportion of individuals who have succumbed before the complicated exactions of modern life (p. 207).

The whole thrust of Mead's early work in Samoa was to demonstrate that the Samoan *cultural setting* did not bring about the same "problems" for adolescents that appeared so predictably in the more complicated American setting. It is, of course, a widely shared belief that presumed "simple peoples" fare much better in "simpler societies." Yet there is surprisingly little information available on the effects of settings on the lives of mentally retarded persons. As far as I know, the conference held at the University of California, Los Angeles, in 1979, sponsored by the National Institute of Child Health and Development, from which this collection of papers was put together, was the first attempt to deal seriously with this question.

It would seem obvious, perhaps even self-evident, that the setting in which one finds oneself affects one's behavior. It might seem equally obvious that this would be true for the mentally retarded population. However, we simply do not know very much about the life situations and settings the handicapped person must deal with in everyday life. We do not understand the demands made by such settings. We believe that certain kinds of environmental settings should reinforce social skills, whereas others must inhibit the development of such skills, but the process by which this occurs is not well documented. We know that there are few useful roles provided for retarded citizens living in the wider community and that roles can be setting-specific, but we do not well understand the implications of this for their adaptation and well-being. We would quite naturally like to believe that some settings might help to bring forth improvements in behavior and performances. There is, unfortunately, some reason to believe that certain roles and settings actually demand "retarded" behavior, even though that may not be intended. In any case, we also believe, as Mead remarked, that our lives in the modern industrial world are inordinately complicated and difficult. If that is truly the case, the lives of the slow, the deviant, and the exceptional must be rendered all the more difficult. These are difficult questions to research, and a useful methodology is only just now being developed. Although the papers collected together here may actually pose more problems than they solve, that is true of all pioneering efforts. While on this frontier the authors should be commended for their insights and encouraged to build further on what they have so diligently begun. Insofar as handicapped persons suffer simply from our ignorance, we can surely make their lives easier and more productive.

L.L. Langness, Ph.D.
University of California, Los Angeles

Environments
and Behavior

Introduction

Robert B. Edgerton and
Keith T. Kernan

The diaspora of mentally retarded persons from large institutions to various community settings as a consequence of deinstitutionalization has been well underway for more than a decade, and studies of selected cohorts of mentally retarded adults who were released from large residential institutions have accumulated since around World War I. Yet, it is undeniably the case that the great weight of research in mental retardation has concentrated on the measurement of attributes of mentally retarded individuals to the neglect of the social settings and contexts in which they live. Michael Begab (1978) summarized this history:

> Much of the past and current research in mental retardation has relied on standard psychometric instruments, task performance tests, questionnaires, interviews, adaptive behavior measures, and clinical judgments. Although of unquestionable value for certain purposes, these approaches tell us little about the process of adaptation or how the retarded individual applies his learning, communicative, and interpersonal skills to real life situations. Furthermore, they do not assess the setting-specific nature of most behavior nor specify the environmental context in which behavior is shaped (p. xi).

Recognizing the same pattern, Carl Haywood (1977) called for more research ". . . on the characteristics of various settings in which mentally retarded persons reside and function, and we need research on the influence of those settings on the behavior and development of retarded persons. Further, we need intensive research on person-setting interaction to determine the differential effects of various environments upon the behavior and development of different individuals.''

From the perspective of experimental psychology, Penelope Brooks and Alfred Baumeister have reached similar conclusions. Expressing the same dissatisfaction with experimental strategies and the need for the study of people in their natural settings articulated earlier by such leaders in psychological research methodology as Donald Campbell, Lee Cronbach, and Walter Mischel, Brooks and Baumeister (1977) made these observations:

> Our understanding of retarded behavior is only as good as the understanding of the context in which the behavior is observed. When the investigator observes subjects' performance on a highly contrived task, administered by strange adults, in a completely atypical environment for those subjects, he must insure that the measurements obtained under these conditions relate, in some meaningful and direct way to the natural circumstances of those individuals. As it is now,

1

we experimental psychologists seem to be more concerned with precise measurements than with important ones. Perhaps we are seeking generalizations where there are not any. We emphatically do not recommend discarding the experimental method. Nevertheless, we are suggesting that experimenters may be forced to leave the security of laboratories, tolerate greater ambiguity, and go where people actually live in order to analyze adaptive behavior into components that perhaps could then become the basis for development of dependent measures and theories for further experimental study. We are concerned that the laboratory analysis of retarded behavior is proceeding along the course of least resistance and that this stream may become so far removed from its original source that it is in danger of losing its identity, fragmented into complex irrelevancies and meaningless epiphenomena (p. 415).

THE STUDY OF BEHAVIOR IN SETTINGS

Recognition that human behavior is greatly influenced by the setting or context in which it occurs has been slow to take hold in the field of mental retardation, yet it has long been a truism in many fields of social inquiry. More than 50 years ago, for example, sociologist W. I. Thomas said what was to become an aphorism: "If men define situations as real, they are real in their consequences." Sociology went on to focus much of its research on the ways in which people define situations and then behave in concert with those definitions (McHugh, 1968). Even before Thomas, anthropologists recognized the central importance of different settings or contexts, and they too have concentrated on the setting-specific character of human behavior.

Yet perhaps the most systematic study of the behavior of persons in particular settings has developed in psychology. Egon Brunswik (1952) was an important pioneer but the most influential approaches have probably come from Roger Barker and his associates. As Jerome Bruner (1965) wrote: "I am still struck by Roger Barker's ironic truism that the best way to predict the behavior of a human being is to know where he is: in a post office he behaves post office, at church he behaves church." Borrowing from ecology and ethology, an ecological psychology has developed around a naturalistic perspective. Sometimes called "environmental psychology," this perspective has developed new and useful concepts about behavior in settings based on the measurement of a setting's "information load," or its novelty and complexity (Mehrabian, 1976), and has created a technology for observing and recording behavior in various settings. Phil Schoggen, who has himself contributed a great deal to this perspective, provided an excellent summary of its history, methods, and implications for mental retardation (1978). Schoggen has these cautionary words about progress:

> But in mental retardation, as elsewhere in behavioral science, methods of studying behavior in real life situations are, despite encouraging progress in recent years, still in a rather primitive stage of development relative to the sophisticated tools of experimental, personality, and social psychology. Methods for describing, classifying, and conceptualizing the ecological environments of behavior are even less well developed . . . we know little more about how to do this than we did when Brunswik suggested it about 20 years ago. Researchers in mental retardation as well as in psychology and other behavioral sciences who take the ecological perspective seriously should give high priority to the development of methods for studying environments of behavior (p. 57).

Some might object that this assessment of methods for the study of settings is too dismal, but few could argue with the conclusion that little progress has been achieved in applying these methods in the study of mental retardation. One line of research, from the ethnographic methods of sociology and anthropology, has made contributions to the description of setting-specific behavior (Edgerton and Langness, 1978), but this approach has not yet systematically described the characteristics of settings themselves. When settings have been described or classified, as by Moos (1974) or Balla (1976), these have typically been restricted residential settings, and even within these kinds of settings, research is at a preliminary stage. Nevertheless, as we have pointed out, it is recognized that the study of settings, as well as the behavior that occurs in them and is produced by them, is essential if we are to better understand the lives of mentally retarded persons, the effects of setting on behavior and development, the effectiveness of training programs, and the nature of mental retardation itself.

Settings may be viewed as culturally defined and as requiring culturally appropriate behavior—"at church he behaves church." If mentally retarded persons do not recognize settings for what they are or are unaware of the behavior appropriate to them, then the way in which they are viewed and treated, and consequently the quality of their lives will be affected. For example, one of the mildly retarded young adults we have been studying participates in a men's discussion group at his church. He often introduces topics that are not appropriate to the discussion. At one meeting, for example, during a discussion of spiritual crises, he told of how he felt when he had to wipe up spilled coffee twice for the same customer at the cafeteria where he works. Repeated instances of similarly inappropriate behavior have resulted in condescending attitudes and treatment of him by other members of the group. Although the effect of such treatment on the quality of his life as he perceives it may be subtle or, indeed, not perceived at all, it is nevertheless real. He is not treated as a person who behaves appropriately is treated, that is, as the other members of the group are treated. The social interaction in which he engages, in this setting as well as others, is altered with unknown, but undoubtedly profound, consequences for his self-image and his future development.

Behavior that is inappropriate to the setting may have less subtle and more direct impact upon the lives of mentally retarded persons. This is particularly true on those occasions when an individual is attempting to obtain services or provide for personal needs. Inappropriate behavior in an interview with a social worker, in a job interview, or on the job itself can have immediate and negative consequences—consequences that are not at all subtle and that affect the well-being of the individual involved. An expanded knowledge on the part of researchers of what behavior is required in the settings that mentally retarded people are likely to come into contact with and the inappropriate behavior that mentally retarded people exhibit in such settings could form the basis of improved training programs that would be of immediate practical benefit.

A consideration of setting demands and of the skills necessary to recognize and act appropriately in particular settings raises interesting theoretical as well as practical issues. Culturally defined settings require culturally appropriate behavior. To act appropriately in a particular setting, participants must accomplish a number of tasks. They must, of course, be able to recognize settings for what they are. That is, they must have knowledge of the variables that define a setting as a particular type and be able to identify and recognize them. Second, individuals must be aware of appropriate and effective behavior given the setting. Finally, given the ability to recognize settings and knowledge of the behavior appropriate to them, individuals must possess the skills necessary to produce that appropriate behavior and to interpret the behavior of others. These skills are based on areas of competencies—

perceptual, cognitive, behavioral, and linguistic—the impairment of which are the defining features of mental retardation. The study of the behavior of mentally retarded persons in naturally occurring settings is therefore not only of practical import but also has theoretical implications. Not only can the results of more controlled studies be tested for their general applicability but new and otherwise unforeseen hypotheses can be generated for further study in more controlled research situations (Berkson, 1978).

In the studies that have been done of the effect of settings on the behavior and development of mentally retarded persons, the settings are often physical settings as defined by the service delivery system. These are settings as we may typically think of them—family care facilities, board and care facilities, sheltered workshops, wards in institutions, and so on. The dimensions or variables, especially in large-scale studies, are often given, in that some aspect of the system is being evaluated. The size of the facility, the neighborhood context, or the implementation of normalization principles, to cite some of the variables of setting discussed in this volume, are studied for their impact upon the lives and development of individuals.

It should be noted, however, that important as it is to study these central settings, if our knowledge of the community adaptation of mentally retarded people is to be improved, we must resist the temptation to study *only* types of settings such as group residential facilities or sheltered workshops. Mentally retarded persons as well as their parents, spouses, friends, and co-workers live their lives in many settings that have yet to be examined in any systematic way. Where such persons sleep and eat is important, of course, but so are their work places of all sorts as well as the buses, cafes, bowling alleys, markets, movie theaters, sidewalks, and all of the other places—especially public places—where people are expected to behave appropriately and competently. We need to study *all* settings and contexts, including those such as outpatient clinic waiting rooms or social workers' offices. Mentally retarded persons may not behave in these places very often, but when they do, it can be of crucial significance for their future lives. In addition we must take care to think of settings in the total context of a person's life. We need to know what different settings require of mentally retarded persons, but we also need to know how any given person—over the course of time—learns to adapt to the demands of settings. One kind of complex and confusing setting may be adapted to over time; others may be avoided. Of course, this may be true of all people, not just mentally retarded ones. Unless an individual is studied over time, in the full context of his or her life activities, we cannot hope to understand the part that particular settings play in that individual's adaptive success or failures. It is also important to keep in mind that a physically defined setting—a church for example—may offer multiple expectations for proper behavior. The church basement may one night be used for Bible study, on another for a bingo game, and on yet another as an auditorium for a radical political speaker. The same physical environment then (a basement room) in the same socially defined physical structure (a Christian church) may call for markedly different behavior depending on the situation or context. Similarly, the same situation—for example, a going away party for a co-worker—may take place in various physical environments such as a private home, an office, a conference room, or a public park.

Moreover, we must study not just person-setting interactions, but we must carefully determine how alterations in social context or structure may affect those interactions. In some settings, like buses, how a mentally retarded person may cope with the task of riding the correct bus in an appropriate way may depend primarily on the behavior of one person—the bus driver. Whether the driver is friendly and helpful or curt and uncommunicative could make all the difference. In a supermarket, on the other hand, the critical factor might be whether goods on shelves or counters are marked with clearly stamped individual prices. As Brenneis (1982) pointed out, "a complex web of variables—physical, social, cultural, temporal, psychological—is closely intertwined in any setting, and any consideration of the relationship between setting and outcome factors requires a careful untangling of those features."

As we pointed out above, the social and behavioral sciences are becoming increasingly concerned with issues of environment, context, setting, and ecological validity. A general awareness has grown that our attempts to understand human beings and their behavior must consider the interaction of environment and person. Training programs must consider the environments in which the behavior they hope to produce will eventually take place. Laboratory findings must be validated in natural environments. And, finally, our understanding of the relevant dimensions of settings must be sharpened and improved.

This volume represents an initial attempt to address these issues in mental retardation research and program design and evaluation. If our field is ever to improve its understanding of mental retardation and our ability to help mentally retarded persons, this must be only the first of many steps.

REFERENCES

Balla, D. A. Relationships of institution size to quality of care: A review of the literature. *American Journal of Mental Deficiency,* 1976, *81,*117–124.
Begab, M. J. Foreword. In G. P. Sackett (Ed.), *Observing behavior,* (Vol. I). Baltimore: University Park Press, 1978.
Berkson, G. Social ecology and ethology of mental retardation. In G. P. Sackett (Ed.), *Observing behavior,* (Vol. I). Baltimore: University Park Press, 1978.
Brenneis, D. Making sense of settings: An ethnographic approach. Working Paper No. 21. Socio-Behavioral Group of the Mental Retardation Research Center, U.C.L.A., 1982.
Brooks, P. H., & Baumeister, A. A. A plea for consideration of ecological validity in the experimental psychology of mental retardation: A guest editorial. *American Journal of Mental Deficiency,* 1977, *81,*407–416.
Bruner, J. A. The growth of the mind. *American Psychologist,* 1965, *20,*1007–1017.
Brunswik, E. The conceptual framework of psychology. *International Encyclopedia of Unified Science,* (Vol. 1). Pt. 2. Chicago: University of Chicago Press, 1952.
Edgerton, R. B., & Langness, L. L. Observing mentally retarded persons in community settings: An anthropological perspective. In G. P. Sackett (Ed.), *Observing behavior,* (Vol. I). Baltimore: University Park Press, 1978.
Haywood, H. C. The ethics of doing research . . . and of not doing it. *American Journal of Mental Deficiency,* 1977, *81,*311–317.
McHugh, P. *Defining the situation: The organization of meaning in social interaction.* Indianapolis: Bobbs-Merrill, 1968.
Mehrabian, A. *Public places and private spaces: The psychology of work, play and living environments.* New York: Basic Books, 1976.
Moos, R. *Evaluating treatment environments: A social ecological approach.* New York: John Wiley & Sons, 1974.
Schoggen, P. Ecological psychology and mental retardation. In G. P. Sackett (Ed.), *Observing behavior,* (Vol. I). Baltimore: University Park Press, 1978.

METHODS
AND MODELS

Paradigms for Studying Interactional and Environmental Effects with Mentally Retarded Clients

Henry A. Alker

This chapter is an overview of different paradigms for studying situational or contextual variables as they may or may not interact with client characteristics to influence behavior. "Paradigm" in this context is not a grand, revolutionary framework for restructuring knowledge in the manner of a Copernicus, Darwin, or Einstein. Instead, alternative paradigms are simply different procedures for data collection and analysis, that is, different methodologies. Each has its limitations and advantages.

Secure and useful information probably will develop more when investigators choose methodologies that are most suitable for their substantive theories. But interest in promoting one's favored theory is not sufficient reason for preferring a paradigm. Generalizations or new discoveries finding expression in several methodologies rather than one are more likely to modify our limited knowledge in lasting fashion. It is remarkable and at the same time rather disappointing how many investigators within their research careers use so few alternative paradigms. Even groups of affiliated investigators in the aggregate show strongly restricted variability in paradigm selection.

Why are contextual and interactional factors so timely? An historical overview of the last decade or two on the vigorous, increasing interest in these approaches is unnecessary, but two points should be emphasized. First, long-term, careful follow-up studies of treatment outcomes, with various clinical populations (e.g., Edgerton and Bercovici, 1976), have found minimal long-term predictability. Whatever therapy a patient may receive in a hospital, however confident a clinician may be that the patient will survive on the outside, over the long term, predictive accuracy is meager. Psychologists working with nonclinical populations and faced with the responsibility for making long-term predictions of performance have recognized the same point (Stern, Stein, and Bloom, 1956). Environmental events, which the psychologist often cannot predict and even more rarely can control, determine the outcome of interest. And even if it is not the environmental events per se that make the crucial difference, it is some interaction between those events and the person's needs and abilities that explains and determines what happens.

Second, a range of research findings (Mischel, 1964), aided by cultural and ethical supports, have emphasized that psychologists and others too often blame the victim. More neutrally put, causation and responsibility are attributed to the person when scientifically and/or ethically the magnitude or even locus of this causation is otherwise, is in the environment. From these background considerations a central question emerges around which this chapter proceeds. How, if at all, is the person involved with the environmental or contextual events that influence his or her fate?

The most natural and orderly way for a behaviorally trained researcher to organize these issues is in terms of a factorial design that distinguishes person effects from environmental effects and both such effects from their interactions. With analysis of variance or its sometimes more useful regression analogues, the researcher can get right to work using this formulation. Unfortunately, for a variety of reasons (Alker, 1976) this relatively simple and highly overlearned response does not do the job very well. All research designs oversimplify, but this approach has as an unintended consequence that person-environment interaction is somewhat of an afterthought. After the sums of squares for person and environmental factors are removed, then we see what's left for the interaction term. Too many interactions are seen as embarrassing or even evidence that one has not designed the reseach well (Nisbett, 1976). Yet anybody involved with the human predicament who forgets for the moment what professional training has taught, will note that person-situation interactions are rampant.

Attribution theorists, who have repeatedly discussed the error of attributing causation to the person when contextual factors might be more important, themselves are guilty here. Their designs make attribution to an interaction itself an afterthought or even a wastebasket category. These concerns led to the organization of this chapter into two categories: 1) environmental approaches or paradigms that make interaction with the person less explicit, and 2) environmental approaches that make interaction more explicit. Although this organizational device represents as a categorical contrast what is merely a matter of degree, it nonetheless may redeem itself somewhat if the reader thereby sharpens his or her focus on the specific model of interaction at hand. This categorization does not imply, incidentally, that paradigms not focusing explicitly on interaction are of lesser value than those that do. A good environmental conception helps rather than hinders an interactionist perspective.

A final note before proceeding: the author is not an expert on mental retardation. Length limitations obviously mean that this chapter must be highly selective. Selection, consequently, emphasized approaches that do *not* appear frequently in the literature on mental retardation but might be productive if they did. Constructive alternatives do provide a partial basis for a critical review of the existing literature. The intent here, however, is not to provide a critical review but merely to provide some fresh alternatives.

ENVIRONMENTAL APPROACHES
PERIPHERALLY CONCERNED WITH INTERACTION

Barker's Ecology of Behavior Settings

Barker and associates (Barker, 1963, 1968; Barker and Schoggen, 1973) developed the most extensive and systematic approach to characterizing environments as they impinge on people. This relatively well-known approach features as its unit for ecological analysis, the behavior setting. These naturally occurring units are of intermediate size. For example, going through a line to pick up a welfare check, listening to a teacher in a classroom, or playing basketball all involve different behavior settings. Such settings have standard patterns of behavior that involve groups or aggregates of people, not an individual per se. And they have distinctive milieus that circumscribe or contain those behaviors but are nonetheless independent of them.

Particularly interesting is a theory that gradually has emerged about such settings in relation to behaviors taking place therein. This theory, built upon an extensive, painstaking descriptive base, exemplifies a happy congruence between theory and method. In his classic cross-cultural study comparing small towns in Kansas and England, Barker found that although the American town was smaller, its residents were three times more likely to be exhibiting performances for which they could be held responsible than residents in the English town. Because there were, in fact, slightly more behavior settings in the Kansas community than in the English one, a remarkable cross-cultural difference is present. Persons in the Kansas behavior settings are, comparatively speaking, spread thin across those settings. This difference in settings Barker speaks of with the term "undermanned" (Barker, 1960).

Price (1976) reviewed recent developments in the theory of "undermanned" versus "overmanned" settings. This matter warrants some discussion here because it relates to current research interest on treatment settings for the mentally retarded (e.g., Balla, 1970; McCormick, Balla, and Zigler, 1975). When behavior settings are undermanned, a lower level of expectation for maximum performance may be expected. When behavior settings are overmanned, competitive pressures may be much higher. Barker believes (1960) that undermanned settings produce a stronger feeling of self esteem with more opportunities to succeed or fail. Overmanned settings have fewer such opportunities and more demanding standards as well. A major implication of this theory, and research supporting the theory, for example, Barker and Gump (1964), is that size per se as an environmental variable is deeply confounded.

Smaller treatment units may achieve greater success when they provide more under-manned behavior settings for their clients. Larger units could achieve the same gains if a comprehensive survey of behavior settings showed that they did not differ from the smaller units in the extent to which they were undermanned. Likewise the contrast between residentially oriented and institutionally oriented treatment environments may be con-founded with the extent to which these settings are overmanned or undermanned. Policy-oriented research should not overlook the longer-term goal of explaining why residential treatment blending in with the surrounding community (Eyman, Demaine, and Lei, 1979) improves patient adjustment.

The theory of undermanning itself is not static. Although claiming that smaller settings generally are undermanned, this theory in later versions has refined its conception in terms that make sheer physical space logically independent of undermanning and overmanning. Wicker and associates (Wicker, 1968; Wicker, McGrath, and Armstrong, 1972) argued that whether or not a setting is undermanned depends on the number of people who seek to participate and are eligible to do so, the "capacity" of a setting in terms of the different roles performers may play in the setting, and the "maintenance minimum" of the setting—the number of functionaries or performers required for the setting.

The behavior setting approach acknowledges interaction between settings and their inhabitants (Wicker et al., 1972; Wicker and Kirmeyer, 1976). This interaction is dynamic with "a continual interaction between the people in a setting and other aspects of the setting itself" producing a stable behavior pattern (Price, 1976, p. 222). But, for several reasons, the person-situation interaction in this approach has only limited articulation. First, the stubborn fact remains that this approach focuses primarily on settings. Typically, the behavior setting researcher does not follow people around as they travel from one setting to another. Because settings often involve patterns of behavior involving groups of people who may disperse in different directions after leaving the setting, this limitation is understandable. Practically, the researcher may have no other choice. So it is not surprising that the interaction emphasized by workers in the behavior setting approach takes place within the setting itself rather than between different persons and different settings.

Nonetheless, several further limitations need to be pointed out. Even within the reciprocal person-setting interaction, greater precision could be available as to which factor was stronger: the persons or the setting. Just positing that persons interact reciprocally with settings over time doesn't determine whether the casual influence of the setting or the person is stronger. Perhaps some people carry with them a capacity for developing reciprocal interaction with certain settings more than others. And, equally important, perhaps some settings have capacities for engaging certain people in reciprocal interaction much more than others. Anybody who has noticed the extraordinary affinity between certain client populations and bingo games should understand the issue raised here. Would changing the activity taking place during the bingo game—for example, to a token economy—have a massive effect on the involvement produced? Or would changing in some small manner the client population in those contexts overwhelm that difference?

Last, because the behavior setting approach often and even necessarily focuses on groups of interacting actors, it does not often attain clarity with regard to psychological process available from the study of individual persons in varying situations. Very few groups, with the possible exception of the family with young children, remain in cohesive contact with one another as they move through widely varying situations. Consequently, patterns that might emerge in such journeys are lost. Students of person-situation inter-action who focus on individuals often ignore this potential source of information too, but at least in the latter case the practical difficulties are not so difficult to surmount.

In conclusion, the behavior setting approach to assessing environments endures and increases in importance as its substantial empirical base becomes theoretically articulated. With this articulation comes opportunities for explaining results or available and future research on such controversial issues as residential treatment centers versus large, isolated institutional facilities. The analysis of client populations in a variety of natural settings as well could profit from systematic application of the behavior setting approach. The more theoretically explicit, however, the greater the chances are that the theory can be, and probably will be, shown to be limited or even false. Behavior setting theory dwarfs most other approaches to this subject, so the likelihood that it soon will be replaced by a superior approach is small. But its specific focus has limitations, some of which have already been pointed out, and others of which are discussed in what follows.

Assessment Approaches Applied to Environments

Environmental assessment approaches using methods originally developed for personality assessment and now applying them to environments (Craik, 1972; Moos, 1974; Wandersman and Moos, 1979) should be mentioned briefly in this context. Whether the use of rating scales, check lists, and questionnaires applied to environments instead of people will solve all the problems associated with traditional personality assessment's use of such procedures has not yet been determined. For example, we do not know to what extent the social desirability response-set or the acquiescence response-set characterizes response to environments. Nor do we know whether the semantic structure of people's implicit theories about environments partially explains correlations between different aspects of the perceived or judged environment. These problems probably do not seriously interfere with counting the number of tables in a national park or identifying the shade of gray on the walls of a custodial institution. But as soon as one gets into environmental assessment of social climate, institutional morale, and the role demands or norms for autonomy—as environmental assessors do—then these problems are serious. And they have not been resolved or even raised in much research on environmental assessment.

Categorizing this research tradition which, to be sure, has major accomplishments (Moos, 1974) as relatively unarticulated regarding person-situation interaction is somewhat arbitrary. Wandersman and Moos (1979), for example, gave a nice example of how patients' severity of disturbance interacts with the demands for competence characterizing a treatment environment. They did not probe beyond the recognition of this pattern, however.

Persons Characterize Environments

Complementary to an environmental approach that emphasizes actions in a given setting would be a perspective identifying with whom the actor is interacting. The significant other(s) may help characterize the social milieu especially in circumstances in which there is some latitude for departing from the role requirements of the situation. This perspective focuses on the psychological realities of a given situation at a less aggregated level than the behavior-setting approach. The actor or observational subject of particular interest matters as an individual. He or she in most settings is interacting with persons who may be different or similar. For human beings, in contrast to the lonely cityscapes painted by de Chirico, other human beings are often the most significant part of their environment.

Three formal categories help characterize immediate or contemporary human environments. First, the people with whom one is interacting may be described with respect to their average level on some dimension. The level of verbal ability, for instance, of those with whom one regularly interacts may be generally high or generally low. Second, one may characterize those with whom one interacts in terms of their variability on a particular dimension. For example, walking down a busy street in a large city a person encounters an extraordinary variety of people in terms of age, ethnicity, place of origin, wealth, and education. As soon as one steps off the street into some private or commercial setting, the variability is usually sharply reduced. And in even more restrictive or institutional settings, homogeneity may be relatively striking, if not oppressive.

Last, using a multifaceted conception of human beings, one can characterize them in terms of the complementary or discordant relations among their several characteristics. For example, a small group may contain some members emphasizing task leadership while others primarily maintain socio-emotional links within the group. Less happily, a group may contain some members eager to display their competence for public approval while others in the same group fear that their incompetence will be unmasked.

These three formal bases for characterizing significant others apply in two importantly different ways: relative to the actor or in relatively absolute terms independent of the actor. Thus a group may be quite slow in solving certain problems but relative to a particular actor, nonetheless, be very fast. Likewise, variability within a small group or dyad with respect to some given attribute may differ dramatically when the actor is included in the analysis. For example, two younger children placed in interaction with an older adult immediately create a significant heterogeneity. And finally, with complementary or discordant attributes, one can focus on relations with the actor or simply ignore the actor and characterize relevant patterns among only the others present.

Systematic applications of this perspective are still somewhat sparse (see Alker, 1976; Moos, 1976, Chapter 9). Yet sporadic findings about the importance of significant others are sufficiently tantalizing to warrant such an inquiry. Edgerton and Bercovici (1976) reported, for example, that the long-term adjustment of a mildly retarded sample related more to the availability of nonretarded "benefactors" than any other variable. Such benefactors, typically family members, are much more likely to enable mildly retarded persons to attain gainful employment than are social service agency personnel. These benefactors are significant others *par excellence*. One wonders if a group of detractors might also be identified if a comprehensive inventory were made in the lives of clients making poorer adjustments.

Gilbert and Hemming (1979) also reported an encouraging finding. Psycholinguistic ability increases in a mentally retarded sample following interaction with others enjoying greater competence than the client population. These results raise some interesting questions concerning ability-grouping in special education programs. No doubt the story is complex with a host of relevant additional variables such as self-esteem and cooperative versus competitive group norms requiring consideration. The point is that when we think of environmental psychology or situation versus person effects, we tend to lose sight of the fact that situations and environments contain other persons, themselves requiring systematic scrutiny.

This perspective may complement that provided by behavior-setting theory, even though focusing on individual differences seems irrelevant to a perspective emphasizing social structure, role demands, and group norms. The extent to which a setting is overmanned or undermanned in part does reflect the supply in that setting of significant others who are or are not ready and willing to perform the role demands in that setting. Talking about significant others, however, goes beyond behavior setting theory. The variability of others with whom one interacts may be just as crucial as their homogeneity. And it is only the latter case that is focal in behavior setting work. Variability in the extreme can be unpredictable and even overwhelming. And homogeneity among significant others can be stultifying.

Edgerton (1976) gave one example of a failure in long prediction in adjustment that implicates the subtlest kind of significant other effects—complementarity. A mentally retarded woman observed during an early period in longitudinal research was found to be quite dependent and even passive in relation to her husband. She exhibited little autonomy, causing researchers to be quite pessimistic about her long-term adaptation when her husband subsequently passed away. Surprisingly, following this traumatic event, the woman gradually developed increased autonomy and fended much better for herself than any simple exponent of personality consistency might have expected. This kind of prediction also would apparently elude practitioners of behavior-setting theory who are not much interested in the individual case.

What we need to know about this woman, at least to generate a plausible prediction, is how she fared in interaction with significant others not expecting her to be passive and dependent. Perhaps her apparent lack of autonomy was designed to complement her husband's needs or perception of his own role. A capacity to enact a complementary role vis-à-vis a significant other could be a strong basis for encountering and enduring an uncertain future. It is not that one wants to take unfair advantage of the benefits of hindsight in this case. The point is that with a systematic inventory of the significant others with whom this woman interacted, an inventory that characterized their behaviors as well as hers, researchers would be in a better position to formulate serious hypotheses to meet the tests of prediction and explanation.

Characterizing significant others, by itself, does not substantially articulate the structure of person-situation interaction. Like the behavior setting approach, there is no systematic tracking of a given individual from one interpersonal setting to another. So, with this approach, one cannot automatically obtain information on whether a given individual tends to create distinctive interpersonal reactions in the manner of a self-fulfilling prophecy. Or perhaps transitions across various social settings are characterized by an increasing mastery of the subtle cues and performance demands contained therein. This approach is explicitly interactional in only the minimal sense that social interaction constitutes the domain within which data are gathered.

In fact, for the relational sense in which a person's attributes are defined vis-à-vis those of the significant others with whom he or she interacts, a factorial separation of the person from the situation becomes logically impossible. To characterize the person one characterizes those with whom he or she interacts. Much of the literature on person-situation interaction (Magnusson and Endler, 1976) cannot deal with this complexity. But the recent literature on person-situation interaction is undergoing a vigorous and creative ferment, which offers some approaches characterizing person interaction going far beyond the simple factorial designs in which persons are crossed with different situations in a standard analysis of variance design. Those new approaches are discussed below.

PERSON-SITUATION INTERACTIONS

Perhaps the most dramatic advance in recent years toward actually specifying what is going on in a person-situation interaction comes from the work of Daryl Bem (Bem and Funder, 1978; Bem and Lord, 1979). This work explicitly focuses on the meaning of typical or classic laboratory situations. A similar logic can, and has been, applied to elucidate the meaning of field situations (Alker and Wohl, 1972). In Bem's work the key is to characterize what kind of persons should perform in an experimental situation given the prevailing theoretical account of such behavior.

Bem constructs a description of such a person in line with one or more theoretical accounts using a Q-sort (Block, 1978). This description (or descriptions if several alternative theoretical accounts are available) is called a template. Then Bem proceeds to collect Q-sort descriptions of the persons performing in the laboratory from friends or roommates who know them relatively well in a variety of non-laboratory contexts. The third step is to examine empirically the descriptions from the friends or roommates of the persons who yield the expected result in the laboratory setting and those who do not. Finally, one can compare the ideal theory-specified template with the Q-sort description generated by different individuals in the actual laboratory experiment. In this manner not only can the theory about the kind of people who yield the predicted response in the experimental situation be tested, but also the ecological validity of the experimental situation can be assured. Behavior in that setting has meaning in relation to the behaviors of subjects outside that setting on the basis of which friends or roommates provided their Q-sort descriptions. A procedure that allows one to choose between alternative theoretical hypotheses, when available, as well as support the ecological validity of a typical laboratory setting certainly has a lot going for it, given the widely discussed "crisis" in experimental social psychology.

Here the willingness to characterize persons as an aid to characterizing the meaning of behavior in a given standardized situation certainly exploits a direct focus on person-situation interaction rather than treating such an interaction as an afterthought or, even worse, as a nuisance. This focus is a qualitative one seeking to determine who does what and even why. Too much of the work on person-situation interaction (e.g., Magnusson and Endler, 1976) simply is concerned with quantitative estimates of how much variance is due to persons, situations, and their interaction—somewhat arbitrary matters in any case depending on what term goes first in the multiple regression equation.

Alker and Wohl (1972) used a similar logic in explicating the meaning of two different field settings, the suburban and inner city classroom. These investigators characterized differences in the meaning of these two settings by discovering what kinds of persons performed well and poorly in these contexts. The inner city school awarded grades more in line with a person's desire for pleasing evaluative authorities and achieving via conformity.

Both laboratory and field settings frequented by mentally retarded persons invite the application of these designs. The standardized intelligence test setting comes to mind as a case in point. Likewise, the much-debated difference between community-oriented versus institutional treatment settings could be clarified by using a direct focus on who seems to adjust more favorably and who least favorably in each setting. This logic clearly differs from that used by the behavior setting approach because individual differences in behavior in a given setting are essential to defining the meaning of those settings. No such designs have been applied to either the field setting or the standardized testing situation. Again, putting people back into environmental psychology has a lot to be said on its behalf.

For policymakers working with more aggregated data a different approach explicitly focusing on client-environment interaction is available. This approach has a sociological and ultimately econometric ancestry, but it too explicates the nature of person-environment interaction beyond the degree represented in current research.

A two-step multiple regression procedure, advocated by Kohn and Schooler (1973), speaks to a basic ambiguity in all formulations that acknowledge reciprocal interaction between persons and environments. Given such interaction, which partner, as it were, in the interaction carries most of the weight? Specifically, when client characteristics reciprocally interact with environmental characteristics, which member of the interaction is causally more important? Simple path analytic models now coming into vogue (Eyman, Demaine, and Lei, 1979) do not answer this question. The two-step least squares model does.

This data analytic procedure, derived from econometric research, proceeds by finding a set of variables other than those posited to be in reciprocal interaction. Standard demographic variables, and additionally historically antecedent variables, are used in this procedure to develop separate one-way path equation models for each of the two terms in reciprocal interaction. Assuming these demographic variables control a substantial amount of the variance, and that estimation error does not bias the outcome, an estimate is derived from the variance that remains unexplained. This estimate allows researchers to make an inference concerning the relative magnitude of effect each term in the reciprocal interaction carries.

Such a result is more than academic in importance. For example, if we know that certain types of clients are differentially attracted to certain types of treatment facilities, it is impossible to compare the outcome of different types of facility. To be more specific, suppose that more severely disturbed clients more often migrate toward large institutions and more moderately disturbed clients seek out residential treatment facilities. The kind of client and the type of institution interact. Covariance techniques can be applied here but they may not ultimately satisfy the doubts. We really want to know whether it's the more disturbed clients or the putatively more inadequate treatment that accounts for an apparent weakness in treatment outcome data. Two-step least squares speak specifically to this type of problem. Kohn and Schooler (1973) gave a worked-through example of how one actually does the calculations so it is not included here. The conclusion does seem to follow, nonetheless, that in some cases the structure of a client-environment interaction can be articulated beyond merely saying that the interaction is reciprocal.

Before closing, some brief mention must be made of the classically coordinated assessment of persons and environments made in the Henry Murray tradition by Stern et al. (1956). This work has been ignored by most subsequent researchers although it sets a standard of excellence many would do well to emulate. The procedure goes well beyond the conjoint assessment of need and press familiar to most undergraduate students of personality. Perhaps more germane is the possibility, as yet unrealized, that systematic, conjoint assessment of cognitive skills and environmental challenges could be undertaken. Such an endeavor would constitute a substantial advance over where we are now with all of our almost useless taxonomies of cognitive skills and our unrelated taxonomies of various situations.

CONCLUSIONS

The upshot of the various points made in the course of developing the argument in this chapter is that we should bring the person or at least people back into a position of importance within environmental psychology. In a sense this conclusion is more or less an inevitable consequence of structuring the argument around the topic of interaction of client characteristics with environmental variables.

To this conclusion the reader may reply that one is merely dragging environmental psychology backward. The apparent controversies inundating the study of persons have been documented by Mischel (1964) and reared their not so lovely head in the more recent literature on the personal adjustment of the mentally retarded (Sternlicht, 1976; Garrison, 1976).

Without rehashing this vast and multifaceted controversy two points should be made. Protagonists in this controversy have virtually all agreed (Magnusson and Endler, 1976) that, substantively, interaction between persons and situations is the order of the day. When it comes to the methodology of person assessment, convergence on a single preference is less complete, but some consensus is emerging. Alker and Owen (1977), for example, argued that it is ultimately silly to maintain that behavioral sampling assessment methodology is always superior to a trait approach or even a biographical approach. The criterion researchers are trying to predict in real life situations is often multifaceted in nature with specific behaviors in specific situations being a part, but only a part. Often more global judgments are part of the criterion itself as are the attainment of certain biographic milestones during one's journey through life. These different criteria each invite the application of different assessment methodologies. Controversies between different approaches that beg the criterion question by employing only one type of criterion and then claiming that a given methodology is superior regardless of what criterion is employed create more heat than light.

Alker and Owen (1977) demonstrated in an exploratory study that behavior samples are most likely to predict other behavior samples, traits are more likely to predict other traits, and biographical statuses do the best job of predicting future biographical status. So putting the person back into environmental psychology within an explicit interactional framework may not be as regressive a step as it seems. People make the environments that matter.

REFERENCES

Alker, H. A. Beyond ANOVA psychology in the study of person situation interactions. In D. Magnusson and N. Endler (Eds.), *Personality at the crossroads*. New York: Wiley Inter-science, 1976.

Alker, H. A., & Owen, D. Biographical, trait, and behavioral sampling predictions of performance in a stressful life setting. *Journal of Personality and Social Psychology*, 1977, *10*, 717–723.

Alker, H. A., & Wohl, J. Personality and achievement in a suburban and an inner city school. *Journal of Social Issues*, 1972, *28*, 101–114.

Balla, D. Relationship of institution size to quality of care: A review of the literature. *American Journal of Mental Deficiency*, 1976, *81*, 117–124.

Barker, R. G. Ecology and motivation. In M. R. Jones (Ed.), *Nebraska symposium on motivation*. Lincoln: Univ. of Nebraska Press, 1960, pp. 1–49.

Barker, R. G. (Ed.) *The stream of behavior*. New York: Appleton-Century-Crofts, 1963.

Barker, R. G. *Ecological psychology*. Stanford, Calif.: Stanford University Press, 1968.

Barker, R., & Gump, P. *Big school, small school*. Stanford, Calif.: Stanford University Press, 1964.

Barker, R., & Schoggen, P. *Qualities of community life*. San Francisco: Jossey-Bass, 1973.

Bem, D. J., & Funder, D. C. Predicting more of the people more of the time: Assessing the personality of situations. *Psychological Review*, 1978, *85*, 485–501.

Bem, D. J., & Lord, C. G. Template matching: A proposal for probing the ecological validity of experimental settings in social psychology. *Journal of Personality and Social Psychology*, 1979, *37*, 833–896.

Block, J. *The Q-Sort method in personality assessment and psychiatric research*. Palo Alto, Calif.: Consulting Psychologists Press, 1978.

Craik, K. Assessing environments. In P. McReynolds (Ed.), *Advances in psychological assessment*, (Vol. II). San Francisco: Jossey-Bass, 1972.

Edgerton, R. B., & Bercovici, S. M. The cloak of competence: 10 years later. *American Journal of Mental Deficiency*, 1976, *80*, 485–497.

Eyman, R. K., Demaine, G. C., & Lei, T. Relationship between community environments and resident changes in adaptive behavior: A path model. *American Journal of Mental Deficiency*, 1979, *83*, 330–338.

Garrison, M. Personality: Another view. In J. Wortis (Ed.), *Mental retardation and developmental disabilities*, (Vol. 8). New York: Brunner/Mazel, 1976.

Gilbert, K.A., & Hemmins, H. Environmental changes and psycholinguistic ability of mentally retarded adults. *American Journal of Mental Deficiency*, 1979, *83*, 453–459.

Kohn, M., & Schooler, C. Personality and occupations: Their mutual interaction. *American Sociological Review*, 1973, *38*, 97–118.

Magnusson, D., & Endler, N. *Personality at the crossroads* (Eds.), New York: Wiley Interscience, 1976.

McCormick, M., Balla, D., & Zigler, E. Resident-care practices in institutions for retarded persons: A cross-institutional, cross-cultural study. *American Journal of Mental Deficiency*, 1975, *80*, 1–17.

Moos, R. *Evaluating treatment environments: A social ecological approach*. New York: John Wiley & Sons, 1974.

Moos, R. *The human context: Environmental determinants of behavior*. New York: John Wiley & Sons, 1976.

Mischel, W. *Personality and assessment*. New York: John Wiley & Sons, 1964.

Nisbett, R. Interactions or main effects? In D. Magnusson and N. Endler (Eds.), *Personality at the crossroads*. New York: Wiley Interscience, 1976.

Price, R. Behavior setting theory and research. In R. Moos (Ed.), *The human context: Environmental determinants of behavior*. New York: John Wiley & Sons, 1976, 213–247.

Stern, G., Stein, M., & Bloom, L. *Methods in personality psychology assessment*. New York: Van Nostrand, 1956.

Sternlicht, M. Personality: One view. In J. Wortis (Ed.), *Mental retardation and developmental disabilities*, (Vol. 8). New York: Brunner/Mazel, 1976.

Wandersman, A., & Moos, R. Evaluating sheltered living environments for retarded people. In C. Haywood and J. R. Newbrough (Eds.), *Living environments for mentally retarded persons*. Baltimore: University Park Press, 1979.

Wicker, A.W. Undermanning, performances and students' subjective experiences in behavior settings of large and small high schools. *Journal of Personality and Social Psychology*, 1968, *10*, 255–261.

Wicker, A.W., McGrath, J.E., and Armstrong, G.E. Organization size and behavior setting capacity as determinants of member participation. *Behavioral Science*, *17*, 1972, 510 ff.

Wicker, A.W., & Kirmeyer, S. From church to laboratory to national park: A program of research on excess and insufficient populations in behavior settings. In S. Wapner, B. Kaplan, and S. Cohen (Eds.), *Experiencing the environment*. New York: Plenum Press, 1976.

Mentally Retarded Persons in the Community

Paul E. Stucky and
J. R. Newbrough

Retarded persons have often been regarded as not being an integral part of the community, although it is probable that not more than 10% of the retarded population has been placed in institutions for retarded persons at any given time (MacMillan, 1977). Their behavior has frequently been perceived as deviant and undesirable, so that until recently, people preferred to segregate them socially or physically from the rest of the community, depriving them of basic human rights and locking them into a particular role. There was little awareness that ''no man is an island, entire of itself. . .'' and that by segregating deviant and handicapped persons, the community was diminishing itself.

The role and place of retarded people are being redefined by two movements that are having a profound effect on the local community: mainstreaming and deinstitutionalization. Mainstreaming is an expression of Public Law 94–142 that all handicapped children must have available to them free appropriate public education that includes supportive services to meet their unique needs and that takes place in the least restrictive environment. In practice, this has meant the incorporation of many retarded children into the regular school system. It has necessitated changes in school policies, in teaching practices, and in the attitudes and experiences of retarded and nonretarded children, their parents, and the community at large (Paul, Turnbull, and Cruickshank, 1977).

Deinstitutionalization grows out of the recognition of the right of retarded persons to live and receive necessary care and habilitation under the least restrictive conditions possible. The deinstitutionalization movement has contributed to a substantial decrease in the number of retarded persons in institutional settings (Bruininks et al., 1980). There has been an increase in the number and variety of alternative living arrangements in the community (Baker, Seltzer, and Seltzer, 1977; Bruininks, Hauber, and Kudla, 1980). In practice, deinstitutionalization has meant physical relocation and administrative changes as well as social changes for both retarded persons and the other people in their environments.

Mainstreaming and deinstitutionalization have led to the resettlement of institutionalized retarded persons or the involvement of those living at home within the larger community. The approach has been, on the one hand, to create systems within the community designed to meet the variety of special needs of retarded persons, including a

21

range of types of care and residential facilities, as well as work, educational, and recreational settings appropriate to different types and severity of handicap. On the other hand, the approach has stressed training programs designed to help retarded persons acquire socially appropriate and useful skills.

The result has often been like mixing oil and water (Edgerton, 1967). Retarded persons can learn to go autonomously about their daily rounds in the community, but their style often does not integrate with middle-class surroundings. They can come to look like other people, but that does not necessarily lead to participation in the lives and activities of their neighbors. They can learn the behavior that corresponds to particular situations, but they have difficulty evaluating the cues of a new situation to determine which is the appropriate behavior (Zipperlen, 1975). This often leads to mistakes and a sense of failure on their part, and to their rejection by other members of the community.

Normalization has been defined by Nirje (1969) as the making available to retarded persons conditions of daily life that are as similar as possible to those of the mainstream of society. Wolfensberger (1972) added the notion of eliciting behavior patterns in retarded persons that were as similar as possible to those of everyone else. If normalization can lead to a process whereby retarded persons and the community become adjusted or adapted to each other, then it can be useful to speak of the creation of normal settings rather than of normal or normative people. Retarded persons can be thought of as part of the overall community, which must be changed and adapted to allow for diversity and participation of all its members, and normalization becomes the process of creating settings that make this possible.

COMMUNITY INTEGRATION: A GAMES METAPHOR

We have chosen to consider community integration from the perspective of ecological psychology and to use a metaphor of team games on a playing field to provide a systems perspective on the dynamics of the matter. Ecological psychology offers the notion of *behavior setting* (a place-time where patterned behavior occurs), which we will use as a basic building block because we see normalization as a process of altering and creating settings. The matrix of change and interrelationships is provided by the game metaphor.

Games and game theory have been used to understand social processes (Schelling, 1963; Shubik, 1964). They provide a way of understanding the flow of social processes beyond a few exchanges or cycles. In social psychology, they have often been used for understanding two or more conflicting or competing interests, where the individuals were seen as deciders in a set of exchanges where gain and loss were the primary concerns (Lyman and Scott, 1970). The paradigm here is of a game of skill or a game of chance, where the individual is the primary subunit of analysis.

We have chosen a team game on a playing field as the analogy to shift the emphasis from the retarded person in conflict with other persons or groups, in which there is strong competition between their interests, to the view of the larger collective (the community, the school, the social matrix of the game) having an interest in the retarded persons being related meaningfully (cooperatively) to some of the games. This also recognizes the particular interests of the person in being accepted, in being a member, and perhaps in being esteemed (Lyman and Scott, 1970). In this more macroscopic view, we can illustrate 1) the complex and rule-governed activity in which mentally retarded persons participate, and 2) the value position that includes retarded persons as necessary to the functioning of the community, not surplus to it.

Behavior Settings

The behavior setting was one of the basic units developed by R. G. Barker and his colleagues for studying the ecology of behavior in a small town (Barker, 1968). The study by R. G. Barker and Wright (1955) was the first total community study. R. G. Barker and Schoggen (1973) followed that up and compared it to a village in England. In these studies, it was observed that many kinds of actions tended to occur only within particular kinds of settings, so that there were quite stable behavior and milieu patterns, independent of the presence or absence of particular individuals. As an example, people got their hair cut at the barber shop, not in church, and they threw the bowling ball in the bowling alley, not in the bank. Each setting had a boundary, it existed in a given space and time framework, and it included both people and things that may have been dissimilar but were interdependent. Within a particular setting, people performed different functions that contributed (to a greater or lesser extent) to the existence of the setting.

Behavior settings can be classified according to the similarity of their behavior-milieu patterns into genotypes. If two behavior settings are of the same genotype, people can carry out the same behavior patterns in both without appreciably disturbing the functioning of either one. An employee at McDonald's can go to work at Burger King without significantly affecting the functioning of the latter. Behavior settings create and limit types of behavior, and opportunities for experience. Given particular resources, a setting will tend to produce behavior appropriate to those resources. If people in different settings behave differently, it is not merely because there is some psychological difference between them. It is because the combined behavior and milieu pattern is different.

Behavior settings collectively make up the habitat of a community. The amount of diversity of behavior that is possible and acceptable in a habitat depends on the variety of available behavior settings. Thus, differentiation of the community into a variety of settings allows for the integration of very different behavioral styles in a normal and acceptable fashion. This permits more participation, which can contribute to a sense of satisfaction with the community (Ahlbrandt and Cunningham, 1979).

Because behavior settings require the performance of particular tasks in order to exist, they exert pressure on people to enter and take part, or to leave if their behavior is not functional. This claim that behavior settings make on people describes the dynamic process that determines integration and participation in the community. If the number and diversity of behavior settings and of functions that need to be performed is great in proportion to the available population, there will be a greater possibility and demand for people to become involved.

The Community as an Ecology of Games

Long (1958) described the community as an ecology of games in which the community functions by the interaction of players sharing a common playing field but playing different games. The players in one game make use of the players in another so that people share in a number of games. For each person, however, one particular game always takes priority over the rest.

Warren (1973) talked of community as being locality based. Long (1958) identified the overall locality as the territory, but observed that there was generally no overall territorial game that ordered the various games in the system. Thus, there is no mechanism for reorganizing existing games or creating different ones to incorporate new elements, such as retarded persons, which enter a community. Current interest in community and neighborhood organization (cf. Warren and Warren, 1977) represents a recognition of the importance of taking responsibility for the territorial game. In urban settings, however, the games are played over such a wide area that the territorial game can easily seem unmanageable, particularly to local neighborhood groups.

The implications of the theory of behavior settings for understanding retarded persons in the community can be illustrated by using the game metaphor. In a game, if we are to understand the behavior of persons and judge whether it is appropriate, we must first know what the game is. It makes a difference whether the persons throwing and catching a ball are playing football, basketball, or baseball, or whether they are playing a game of their own invention. If we conclude that the game is baseball and the persons are the pitcher and the catcher, it is still not enough to watch them alone. The moment at which the pitcher throws the ball depends on the signal from the catcher, the readiness of the batter, and on all the other players occupying their respective positions. So all the players must be watched.

It is important to note what roles people are playing. Sometimes they are fielders, sometimes they are batters, and sometimes they are relegated to the bench. Baseball may not be their only game. They may be the guards on a basketball team and cheerleaders for a football team. There are many games going on in the community. There is the school game, the work game, the civic game, the political game, and many others. Some people play in many games, others in only a few. To be fully understood, they must be observed in all the games and roles they play.

When retarded persons arrive in the community, they are generally assigned to certain games and excluded from others. There is a work game, which might be played at a sheltered workshop or in a factory. There is a leisure time game in which the active players are most often the retarded persons themselves and in which members of the service professions act as trainers and coaches to assist them in acquiring the necessary behavioral skills to play properly. Retarded persons often seem to be playing in a different league from everybody else, a sort of little league.

Retarded persons may arrive in the community with behavioral styles and social skills that are not suitable for the new games they will be encountering (Birenbaum and Seiffer, 1976; Rosen et al., 1970). Their experience is not unlike that of any other group of immigrants into a community with a lifestyle different from its own. They may have unfamiliar and annoying habits. They may have trouble finding the playing field or locating the players. Those already playing may not be willing to allow them to join the game, or there may be no positions open. Liaison persons or organizations (such as a Newcomers Club) can be of vital importance. The liaison role (Dokecki, 1977; Newbrough, 1977; Williams, 1977) provides for socializing settings for newcomers and linkages between the newcomer and the existing games (and among the games themselves), thus helping to integrate the community. This role emphasizes the importance of the territorial game in which the function of the liaison specialist is to enable the games to function for the well-being of all involved.

Attributes of Games

There are certain attributes that are common to almost all games: 1) a place and time for playing; 2) playing material and equipment; 3) players and other participants; and 4) rules and objectives. Although the thrust of this chapter is to consider community integration, the game metaphor applies to total care institutions as well. In fact, the attributes of games, discussed below, can be more carefully identified there.

Place and Time   The place of the game is where the players interact. It may be an informal place like a living room, a backyard, or a city street. Or it may be some place that is formally constituted as a playing area, like a gym, a park, a factory, a school, or a store. It often includes not only the playing field itself, but also an area for support personnel and for spectators.

A boundary of some sort generally sets off the game area. The boundary may be informal and scarcely recognizable, such as an alley or a hallway between the living room and the kitchen. Other places have formally constituted barriers with gates to control who comes in and goes out. Either way, a boundary sets off those who are taking part from those who are not, and it serves as a territorial standard to identify which behavior is appropriate.

Games (like behavior settings) take place at specific times, and they generally have a specific duration. To properly play the game, people have to be at the right place at the right time, and they have to know when to start and when to stop. For retarded persons in particular, this requires training in sorting relevant cues from irrelevant, and in the use of reasoning and of strategies to interpret and resolve problems encountered in new situations (Goldstein, 1974, 1977). This will enable them to better judge what game is being played and what skills and behavior are appropriate.

Playing Materials and Equipment   The playing materials and equipment are of various types. One type is *functional:* it is that with which the game is played (a ball, a bat, a pencil, or a hammer). A second type represents *authority* and is used by those who determine whether people are playing the game right or if they get to play at all. A whistle and a siren are symbols of this type. A third type denotes *membership*. It includes the shirts and hats that distinguish those who are a part of the game from those who are not. The fourth type is that which provides for the *enjoyment and smooth functioning* of the game. It includes the popcorn and the drinks, and also the janitor's broom.

When training programs teach retarded persons to dress and groom appropriately to their age, they are equipping them to take part in community games. The same is true when they teach them to use public transportation, to get around by themselves, and to manage their money. This has to be done, sometimes, in the face of "institutional behavior" that the person has already learned—certain ways of walking, looking, talking, standing, etc. Such behavior is similar to equipping the retarded person with a T-shirt that reads *I am retarded. Treat me differently* (Willer, personal communication).

Players and Other Participants   Games are composed of people who perform a variety of roles; indeed, it is because there are people that the game is played at all. Some of the roles are crucial. The game must have them if it is to go on. Others are not essential, but nevertheless contribute in some way.

The players have ultimate responsibility for making the game happen. There is generally a specific number of players, both a maximum and a minimum, and among them is a hierarchy, with some positions being more crucial than others. Within the community, the players are those actively engaged in running business, church, and civic affairs, as well as those who work in the factories and buy at the stores. Some are, like professional athletes, working for public visibility and a supportive public following.

Working closely with the players are a group of special personnel, coaches and trainers, whose function is to prepare the players for the game. They often decide when players are ready to play or if they get to enter the games at all. People engaged in professional service delivery often perform this function for retarded persons.

A third group is represented by the referees and officials. They commonly determine whether the game is going to take place and how it is going to be played. They are also the ones that get blamed if the outcome is not satisfactory. In the community, this role is often played by government, supervisory agencies, and boards of directors. The media, too, play this role—perhaps more effectively than anyone else. They carry out a determining function directly through editorial opinions, and indirectly by the topics they select and by the way they present them to the public.

A fourth group, which is often the largest, is made up of the spectators. They actively watch the game and know what is happening, but they do not need to be able to play. Some of them are willing spectators, who would rather watch than play. Others are would-be players who were not allowed in. The role of the spectators is very important. Sometimes they are the reason the game is going on at all. In other instances, even if they are not essential to the game, they inject it with meaning. They are the audience in the church, the members of the club, the voters at the meeting, or the neighbors who discuss events over the back fence—as spectators, not direct players.

A fifth group sells the popcorn and handles the equipment. Their functions may be peripheral to the main game, but they are parts of concessions that represent a vitally important infrastructure. Persons in these games often do not understand the main game nor do they need to. Theirs are simpler games that are easy to play and are, at the same time, useful and supportive to the larger game. They are the janitors or those who sell the soft drinks; they are the people who help set up the art show or those who mow the lawns and shovel the snow. Their roles, however, have tended to be eliminated by advancing technology and mechanization, so these people are often left without anything to do, and they become onlookers and uninvolved bystanders.

Onlookers and bystanders do not understand the game nor do they have any part in it. Although they are not aware enough to be spectators, they can appreciate a spectacular event—a fantastic catch or an extraordinary performance. Expert players can create fantastic events, but sometimes unexpected circumstances will put a bystander in a position to do an extraordinary performance or an act of heroism. When that happens, she or he is noticed by everybody and suddenly (and briefly) rises in public esteem.

The last type are those people outside the game who are not allowed to enter and participate. Some may want to watch, but they do not have the money for the ticket. Others may want to play, but they do not have the skill to be on the team. These are the people in institutions: prisons, mental hospitals, and institutions for mentally retarded persons. They are also those who are not institutionalized, but who are thought to be lacking the skills or personal characteristics required for access to the game. Deinstitutionalized persons are often in this position.

Rules and Objectives   Games have rules for the purpose of regulating behavior, defining objectives, and determining who plays each role. These rules initially grow out of social practice, but eventually they become reified and sanctified as "the way things are done," so that they define social practice (Berger and Luckman, 1966). When retarded persons enter a community, they need to learn a complete set of rules, and they have to know when particular rules apply. Having an interested person look out for them is very helpful both for getting started and for learning what is acceptable. They may discover that one of the rules is that retarded persons do not get to play, or that it is fair to take advantage of them in the name of free competition and making a profit. Retarded persons may try to get around these rules by attempting to "pass" as normal people (Edgerton, 1967; Olshansky, 1972). Others try to help by not labeling them (Mercer, 1971). If the community is to be normalized to allow for their integration, however, the rules of exclusion will ultimately have to be changed.

Games and Behavior   The game ultimately determines the specific behavior and objectives of each person, although they are modified by individual differences and competencies. Sometimes it looks like people have different roles when actually they are playing different games. This can be the case between mental health professionals and their patients (Cumming and Cumming, 1962).

People generally take part in a number of different games, and have different roles in each. Shifting from one to the other requires flexibility and good judgment. Reputation often determines which games and roles people will play. Persons who are known to be very good bankers or industrialists may be asked to be trustees of a university — a game they may know nothing about and for which they may be unsuited. The effect of reputation on retarded persons is more pernicious. Retarded persons are known for not being able to play the games well. As a result, they are typically excluded, instead of being assigned appropriate roles. This situation, in which attitudes affect assignment, is one of the major hurdles to normalization. Often only when there are not enough persons to perform all the necessary roles will people attempt to figure out an assignment for a retarded person.

People derive satisfaction from playing the game and producing products (Long, 1958). Well-being, then, depends on having access to the game (J. S. Barker, cited in Barker and Schoggen, 1973) and participation in a personally meaningful and fulfilling role. Retardation often means lack of access to the game; poor mental health often derives from lack of meaning in playing the game.

Getting into the Game   Games have admission criteria: they require a ticket. A specific skill can be a ticket: knowing how to operate a lathe may gain entry into a factory; being poised and articulate may gain entry to social games. But for a skill to be a valid ticket, it must be known that one has that skill. People make their skills known either by demonstrating them or by being vouched for. Often the skills of retarded persons are not known, and they do not know how to present themselves except, perhaps, by saying, "I want." Hence the critical importance of the person that Edgerton (1967) described as the benefactor, a person without stigma in the community who can vouch for the retarded person. Because staff of mental retardation facilities typically do not see their role as that of voucher, it is the natural social support network that most often serves this function.

In addition to meeting admission criteria for getting into the game, there must be a role to play. This is frequently a problem for retarded persons. Often, for the games in which they are permitted to play, the only role available is that of bystander.

People are included or excluded from the playing field depending on the structure of the game and the attitudes of the other participants. If the structure of a game no longer calls for a particular role, like that of the office messenger, the person performing that task can be relocated or simply expelled. Often, however, the structure of the game is not defined beforehand, but gets determined by the attitudes of the other participants, as acted out either by someone in an authority role, such as a manager, a coach, or a foreman, or by someone who takes the initiative at the moment, such as a player, a spectator, or a bystander. Kohn and Williams (1956) discovered, in their attempt to understand restaurant desegregation, that if ambiguous situations could be defined and structured at the outset, persons would be admitted who might otherwise have been barred. The application to retarded persons is that if agreements can be made in advance that mentally retarded and handicapped persons will be allowed into the community games and will be provided with special coaching as needed, then when the situation arises, a spokesperson can probably ensure that they will be granted access. Whether they can remain in the game depends on their abilities, the tolerance, the sponsorship, or some combination.

Learning the Game   People can learn new games by going to training centers or by taking part in practice games. Residential and work facilities for retarded persons can serve this function if they simulate, as much as possible, the situation the retarded person is likely to encounter in the community. There is a danger, however, that training centers will promote dependence and keep persons from the risk-taking of ordinary life that is necessary for continued growth and development (Perske, 1972). This is often done in the name of protecting the person.

Communities do not generally have practice sessions as part of their games: people learn by doing. For a retarded person, this may mean starting out as a bystander who hangs around where a game is being played. The bystander watches how others play and, when a role is unoccupied, he or she takes the chance to play a little. This type of situation might still be found in small, and often village-like communities where there are places to hang out (like soda fountains, barber shops, or neighborhood stores) and where the environment is simple enough to allow for running errands and performing simple tasks. More urban settings often lack such places, have more skilled persons also hanging around, or have hazardous surroundings. This may require that more structured training settings and more formal coaching staff be provided for the retarded to learn the community games and that more assumption of the role of sponsor be undertaken.

Getting to Play: The Understaffed Game   If a game is to go on, certain roles must be filled. If one such role becomes vacant, an opportunity to play is created. Someone who was not playing will have to be drawn in.

Barker and Schoggen (1973), in their discussion of behavior setting theory, observed that the force on townspeople to participate and maintain a particular behavior setting varied inversely with the number of available inhabitants. This has a number of implications for an understaffed setting in which there are not enough people to fill all the roles. There will tend to be more frequent and serious deficiencies that need attention. There will be more efforts to counter deviation, but people will be expelled less and the barriers between roles will tend to become more permeable. Most importantly, each person will be called upon to perform more actions, more roles. There will be increased variety in the actions they perform, and these actions will generally require a higher level of responsibility and skill. As a result, people will perform closer to the top of their ability or even learn new skills. Thus, an understaffed game will draw people in, and those persons will be challenged, sometimes stretched, into growth.

Games can be deliberately understaffed so that retarded persons are drawn in and become essential parts of the game. This is what has happened in sheltered villages like Camphill (Baker et al., 1977; Davis, 1978; Zipperlen, 1975). A Camphill community is a partially self-supporting village in which nonretarded staff (called co-workers) and their families represent at most 50% of the population, the rest being mentally retarded persons, called villagers. (In the village described by Baker et al. (1977), the co-workers and their families constituted about 40% of the combined population.) Of necessity, the normal and handicapped people must be interdependent if the maintenance and production tasks are to be accomplished so that the community can survive economically. The village is generally set in a rural environment, and a number of the tasks may be done by hand instead of using sophisticated equipment. The tasks include farming, gardening, woodworking, weaving, baking, and housework. Villagers and co-workers alike are given their assignments daily by a Works Group on the basis of what the community needs, so that no member of the village is busy with any job that is not truly needed by the village.

The village is divided into four neighborhoods, each carrying out its own local governmental functions. Co-workers and villagers together determine expenditures for food, household, and entertainment. Villagers live together with co-workers and their families, sharing in the household tasks and in the social life. Thus, villagers and co-workers are playing the same games and the village is experienced as community by both — neither of which tends to be true in most institutional or group home settings in which nonretarded people are the staff who work a shift in return for a wage.

COMMUNITY PSYCHOLOGY AND COMMUNITY DEVELOPMENT

Together with other professionals, community psychologists have become concerned about the coping and adaptation of persons living in environments that can be altered to remove hazards and enhance their lives. As a field, it has been traditionally oriented to intervention approaches, whether for mental health or social amelioration reasons (Bloom, 1980; Cowen, 1973; Kelly, Snowden, and Muñoz, 1977).

This chapter is to develop the point that the design of appropriate living environments is essential to the attainment of integration and well-being. Such environments must be designed to include places, times, and projects that promote the natural involvement and participation of all members of the community. For retarded persons, this means that the environment must be designed to allow and, if necessary, compensate for organismic and socialization deficits, to provide for participation in community projects, and to provide support—both ongoing as well as in crisis.

The absence of integration into a community is a problem for most North Americans, except perhaps for those living in small, stable, well elaborated towns and neighborhoods (Nisbet, 1953; Warren and Warren, 1977). In fact, the lack of community life and the awareness of its crucial importance for personal and social well-being have contributed to the development of the community approach to psychology and to interest in neighborhood and community revitalization. Both of these can be useful as models for the integration of retarded persons into the community, but, perhaps more significantly, they are important for the creation and maintenance of communities into which retarded persons can be integrated.

Social and Community Intervention

The primary objective of social and community intervention is to promote and increase the well-being of defined population groups. This objective is implemented by means of a two-fold focus. The first calls for intervention and support of individuals in need. This can be an ongoing or an emergency service and is generally community-based, such as a comprehensive community mental health center or a Crisis Center. The availability of an accessible place where people know they can turn in need is an important aspect of this focus. In most communities, there is no analogous place designed to meet the needs of retarded persons, although the California Regional Centers and the Direction Centers founded by the Bureau of Education for the Handicapped are important steps in that direction.

The second part of community intervention is the focus on prevention programming designed to eliminate hazards to mental health and to strengthen coping resources both in individuals and in group structures. Here the emphasis has been on competency building and early intervention in children, and in populations at risk, and on attempts to affect the social environment through consultation, mental health education, public policy, or by promoting natural support resources. The analogous movement for prevention of mental retardation is becoming increasingly important.

Social Supports A significant result of the community intervention and mental health movement has been the discovery of social supports as a major resource for coping with stress (Caplan and Killilea, 1976; Cobb, 1976; Gore, 1978; Warren, 1977). One type of social support, described by Warren (1977), is the informal support network, which refers to the people we turn to for coping with the vicissitudes of daily living, large or small. The network is not a group; in fact, its members may not know each other. They constitute a network by their relation to a particular person. A network might include a spouse, siblings, friends, neighbors, relatives, and co-workers. According to Warren, research shows that informal support networks provide for as much as 80% of coping with problems for the average person, compared to only 20% by formal support persons such as social workers, doctors, clergy, police, teachers, and mental health professionals. Informal support networks are used for help in depression and loneliness, in finding a job, in locating educational opportunities, in dealing with fears, or in getting a lift downtown. They function as people listen and give emotional support, provide specific information, perform concrete helpful tasks, help identify professional helping resources, or serve in place of professionals when the latter are not available or not trusted (Warren, 1977).

A second and related type of social support is the self-help group. Katz and Bender (1976) described a self-help group as a small group of people who have come together voluntarily for mutual aid in satisfying a common need, overcoming a common handicap or problem in living, and bringing about personal and/or social changes. Gartner and Riessman (1977) noted that a self-help group provides people with a reference group and a base for activity. It is characterized by face-to-face interaction, and there is an emphasis on participation and action by the members. Alcoholics Anonymous is the largest and perhaps the best known self-help organization, but the range of self-help groups covers all aspects of human need and concern. Within mental health, self-help groups include Recovery, Inc., made up of ex-patients, and Parents Without Partners, for single parents. Within the area of mental retardation, there are numerous self-help groups for relatives of retarded persons, including the National Association for Retarded Citizens and groups of parents of children with particular problems (Katz and Bender, 1976). There is also the self-advocacy group of retarded persons themselves, called People First (Posner, 1977; Schaaf et al., 1977).

Prevention   Preventive interventions (called primary prevention) have two objectives: to reduce the rate of occurrence of dysfunctions and disorders in the populations and to promote optimal mental health and well-being (Cowen, 1973; Goldston, 1977). The accomplishment of these objectives requires a long-term commitment to intervention in people's habitats (Kelly et al., 1977). Prevention is based on the recognition that adaptation and well-being depend on the quality of the living environment as well as on people's ability to cope successfully with it.

Klein and Goldston (1977) identified essential elements of prevention activities. First, they should focus on a condition that can be precisely observed and recorded. Second, they should be directed toward specific population groups identified as being at risk for that condition. Third, a clearly defined intervention plan should be used. Fourth, the incidence of the condition should be measured before and after the intervention. In addition, the use of control groups would be valuable. This would permit a more precise evaluation of the effectiveness of the intervention.

Kelly (1971) described three approaches to preventive intervention. The clinical approach, as illustrated by consultation, aims to improve the functioning of individuals rather than altering their personality structure or self-concept. Their improved functioning changes their relationships and helps bring about change in other people. In an organizational approach, interventions aim to restructure environments, such as neighborhoods, so that organizations can better deal with crises. The third approach is through community development, whereby communities are helped to mobilize their resources and plan their own changes and future directions.

Within the field of mental retardation, prevention is beginning to be directed at reducing the incidence of mental retardation itself (California Association for the Retarded, 1979; Fotheringham and Morrison, 1976). Within this direction, activities are focused on reducing the incidence of retardation that results from factors in the social and physical environment, genetic disorders, problems related to pregnancy, and accidents, disease, and nutritional problems in childhood.

A second focus in prevention programming for retarded persons is suggested here. This is the reduction of the incidence of behavioral and emotional dysfunctions and disorders and the enhancement of coping and well-being. This can take place through enhancement of retarded persons' competency and of the quality and supportiveness of the living environment. This will require an understanding of the daily events and risks encountered by retarded persons in their ongoing life in the community and of the resources with which they attempt to cope.

A Science of Everyday Life   Everyday life has become a focus of the social sciences. Truzzi (1968) in sociology and Barker (1963) in psychology illustrated very clearly that more is known about human behavior in special settings than in the daily rounds. The approach used by anthropologists for the study of everyday life of other cultures has become important and is gaining in being acceptable as a scientific approach. Community psychology as an intervention-oriented science needs as careful an understanding of the daily rounds as possible, and some ways of understanding how changes in those rounds affect people in their settings (as the social situations, themselves). The science of everyday life needs to be developed in such a way that social and community actions can be seen as interventions into the games of daily living as well as the creation of new games in which more people can play.

NEIGHBORHOOD AND COMMUNITY REVITALIZATION

The neighborhood revitalization movement is an important contemporary social movement that relates directly to the recovery and creation of communities as living environments. It addresses the concern of psychologists and other social scientists for the alienation and social isolation that are believed to be associated with the loss of community (Nisbet, 1953) or of the psychological sense of community (Sarason, 1974).

Sense of community has been variously described as "the sense that one was part of a readily available, mutually supportive network of relationships upon which one could depend and as a result of which one did not experience sustained feelings of loneliness..."(Sarason, 1974, p. 1), or as "a feeling that members have of belonging, of members' mattering to each other, and a shared faith that members' needs will be met through their commitment to be together" (McMillan, 1976, pp. 10-11). It has often been associated with villages and rural communities where there were harvesting events, barnraisings, and quilting bees, where men gathered in taverns to discuss community affairs, and where merchants and consumers were on a first name basis (Glynn, 1978). Tönnies (1957) described it in terms of *Gemeinschaft,* characterized by small, intimate social units, such as the family or the tribe, in which communication between persons was informal and intimate. The recovery of neighborhood life and the strengthening of mediating structures (Berger and Neuhaus, 1977) — schools, families, civic organizations, and churches — have been seen as ways to return the sense of community to people's lives. Activity patterns would change as people's daily rounds became more centered in the neighborhood. The streams of behavior would criss-cross more, creating the opportunity for greater interactions and, perhaps, more interest in each other.

Neighborhood revitalization rises out of the convergence of a number of social movements. One movement is described by the history of community development in rural, agricultural areas and of community organizing in urban, generally poor, areas to fight exploitation and urban deterioration. The work of Alinsky (1972) was a part of this beginning with the Back of the Yards movement in Chicago in the 1940s. In the 1960s the poverty program activated a lot of neighborhood level activity (Spiegel, 1968, 1969). A second movement is represented by the history of the local public education in this country which began in the 1930s (Scay, 1974) and has more recently been expanded by the Community Education Act of 1974 to provide for the use of the local school as a center for community activity and ongoing education. A third movement is represented by the history of Housing Acts to establish building and housing codes and to provide for housing rehabilitation. This movement had a culmination in the Housing and Community Development Act of 1974. This act provided for federal funding, but it placed on the local community the responsibility for code enforcement and for developing programs and projects for neighborhood preservation (Ahlbrandt and Brophy, 1975). It is the Housing and Community Development Act of 1974, together with the earlier Model Cities Act of 1966, that framed the neighborhood revitalization movement. The aim of this movement is the preservation of the neighborhood as a living environment by concerning itself with the conservation and rehabilitation of housing and other aspects of the physical environment as well as of the social environment through the action of local citizens in conjunction with the private and public sectors (Ahlbrandt and Brophy, 1975).

The neighborhood revitalization movement has not only led to the recuperation of the environment, but to an emphasis on community participation as an essential part of the process. The Model Cities Act called for "the most feasible participation" of the poor in local community action programs. The 1974 Housing and Community Development Act, through its Block Grant Program, authorized local communities to establish their own development priorities and stipulated that citizens must be given the opportunity to participate in defining their needs and in developing their community's applications for funding. This has led to increased citizen participation in local issues and to the use of local institutions such as the school as centers for people to meet together and initiate projects. Erber (1976) noted that community action proved to be a training ground for people to develop skills in administration and communication, suggesting that people learn primarily by doing. It showed also that there is no type of voluntary action more likely to engage and maintain citizen involvement than that which directly and obviously affects their daily lives.

THE RETARDED PERSON IN THE COMMUNITY

When retarded persons live in a community but are not part of its daily life, the community is fragmented and not fully integrated. In fact, it could be argued that an unintegrated community is not a community at all. Normalization is a process of community integration. It is a process that benefits everybody. It is an individual and a systemic project. It is individual because each person must acquire the necessary skills to be able to participate in the games that link the various members of the community, while at the same time being tolerant of those whose styles are different from his or her own. It is systemic because the games must be adapted and expanded to allow everyone to participate in a meaningful way.

Many existing neighborhood and community games do not have roles for retarded people. The community will need to develop new games, new roles, and playing fields that are accessible to retarded persons. This would be, at the same time, normalization and community revitalization. It would call for an approach to intervention designed to be supportive and enabling to retarded persons as part of a process of revitalization and integration directed at creating community for all. Such a design would, first of all, provide for the creation of games and settings where people could interact and have their physical and emotional needs met. This would include fostering an environment in which self-help could take place and in which retarded persons and their families could find support as part of informal social networks. Second, it would provide for formal support and consultation services that were readily accessible. Third, it would take place in the context of community projects that were seen as vital by all. Unimportant work would not be acceptable, either for retarded persons or for anyone else.

REFERENCES

Ahlbrandt, R. S., Jr., & Brophy, P. C. *Neighborhood revitalization.* Lexington, Mass.: Lexington Books, 1975.

Ahlbrandt, R. S., Jr., & Cunningham, J. V. *A new public policy for neighborhood preservation.* New York: Praeger, 1979.

Alinsky, S. D. *Rules for radicals.* New York: Random House, 1972.

Baker, B. L., Seltzer, G. B., & Seltzer, M. M. *As close as possible: Community residences for retarded adults.* Boston: Little, Brown & Company, 1977.

Barker, R. G. (Ed.). *The stream of behavior.* New York: Appleton-Century-Crofts, 1963.

Barker, R. G. *Ecological psychology.* Stanford, Calif.: Stanford University Press, 1968.

Barker, R. G., & Schoggen, P. *Qualities of community life.* San Francisco: Jossey-Bass, 1973.

Barker, R. G., & Wright, H. F. *Midwest and its children.* New York: Harper & Row, 1955.

Berger, P. L., & Luckman, T. *The social construction of reality.* New York: Doubleday & Company, 1966.

Berger, P. L., & Neuhaus, R. J. *To empower people: The role of mediating structures in public policy.* Washington, D.C.: American Enterprise Institute for Public Policy Research, 1977.

Birenbaum, A., & Seiffer, S. *Resettling retarded adults in a managed community.* New York: Praeger, 1976.

Bloom, B. L. Social and community interventions. *Annual Review of Psychology,* 1980, *31,* 111–142.

Bruininks, R. H., Hauber, F. A., & Kudla, M. J. National survey of community residential facilities: A profile of facilities and residents in 1977. *American Journal of Mental Deficiency,* 1980, *84,* 470–478.

Bruininks, R. H., Thurlow, M. L., Thurman, S. K., & Fiorelli, J. S. Deinstitutionalization and community settings. In J. Wortis (Ed.), *Mental retardation and developmental disabilities: An annual review,* (Vol. 11). New York: Brunner/Mazel, 1980.

Caplan, G., & Killilea, M. (Eds.). *Support systems and mutual help: Multi-disciplinary explorations.* New York: Grune & Stratton, 1976.

California Association for the Retarded. *Agenda for action.* Sacramento: State Council on Developmental Disabilities, 1979.

Cobb, S. Social support as a moderator of life stress. *Psychosomatic Medicine,* 1976, *38*(5), 300–314.

Cowen, E. L. Social and community interventions. *Annual Review of Psychology,* 1973, *24,* 423–472.

Cumming, J., & Cumming, E. *Ego and milieu.* New York: Atherton, 1962.

Davis, S. The life and times of Rudolf Steiner, Part 3: Notes from Camphill Village. *New Age,* 1978, *4*(2), 56–59, 78–79.

Dokecki, P. R. The liaison perspective on the enhancement of human development: Theoretical, historical, and experiential background. *Journal of Community Psychology,* 1977, *5,* 13–17.

Edgerton, R. B. *The cloak of competence*. Berkeley: University of California Press, 1967.

Erber, E. Why citizen participation. *HUD Challenge*, January 1976, pp. 8–9.

Fotheringham, J. B., & Morrison, M. *Prevention of mental retardation*. Toronto: National Institute on Mental Retardation, 1976.

Gartner, A., & Riessman, E. *Self-help in the human services*. San Francisco: Jossey-Bass, 1977.

Glynn, T. J. Community psychology and psychological sense of community: Measurement and application. Paper presented at the 86th annual meeting of the American Psychological Association, Toronto, August 28-September 1, 1978.

Goldstein, H. Social learning: A curriculum element in the education of retarded children. Unpublished manuscript, Curriculum Research and Development Center in Mental Retardation, Yeshiva University, 1974.

Goldstein, H. Reasoning abilities of mildly retarded children. In P. Mittler (Ed.), *Research to practice in mental retardation: Education and training* (Vol. 2). Baltimore: University Park Press, 1977.

Goldston, S. E. An overview of primary prevention programming. In D. C. Klein & S. E. Goldston (Eds.), *Primary prevention: An idea whose time has come* (DHEW Publication No. (ADM) 77–447). Washington, D.C.: U.S. Government Printing Office, 1977.

Gore, S. The effect of social support in moderating the health consequences of unemployment. *Journal of Health and Social Behavior*, 1978, *19*, 157–165.

Katz, A. H., & Bender, E. I. (Eds.). *The strength in us: Self-help groups in the modern world*. New York: New Viewpoints, 1976.

Kelly, J. G. The quest for valid prevention interventions. In Task Force on Community Mental Health, Division 27 of the American Psychological Association, *Issues in community psychology and preventive mental health*. New York: Behavioral Publications, 1971.

Kelly, J. G., Snowden, L. R., & Muñoz, R. F. Social and community interventions. *Annual Review of Psychology*, 1977, *28*, 323–361.

Klein, D. C., & Goldston, S. E. Preface. In D. C. Klein & S. E. Goldston (Eds.), *Primary prevention: An idea whose time has come* (DHEW Publication No. (ADM) 77–447). Washington, D.C.: U.S. Government Printing Office, 1977.

Kohn, M. L., & Williams, R. M. Situational patterning in intergroup relations. *American Sociological Review*, 1956, *21*, 164–174.

Long, N. E. The local community as an ecology of games. *American Journal of Sociology*, 1958, *64*, 251–261.

Lyman, S. M., & Scott, M. B. *A sociology of the absurd*. New York: Appleton-Century-Crofts, 1970.

MacMillan, D. Sense of community: An attempt at definition. Unpublished manuscript, Center for Community Studies, George Peabody College for Teachers of Vanderbilt University, Nashville, Tenn., 1976.

MacMillan, D. L. *Mental retardation in school and society*. Boston: Little, Brown & Company, 1977.

Mercer, J. R. Sociocultural factors in labeling mental retardates. *Peabody Journal of Education*, 1971, *48*, 188–203.

Newbrough, J. R. Liaison services in the community context. *Journal of Community Psychology*, 1977, *5*, 24–27.

Nirje, B. J. The normalization principle and its human management implications. In R. Kugel & W. Wolfensberger (Eds.), *Changing patterns in residential services for the mentally retarded*. Washington, D.C.: President's Committee on Mental Retardation, 1969.

Nisbet, R. A. *The quest for community*. New York: Oxford University Press, 1953.

Olshansky, S. Changing vocational behavior through normalization. In W. Wolfensberger (Ed.), *Normalization: The principle of normalization in human services*. Toronto: National Institute on Mental Retardation, 1972.

Paul, J. L., Turnbull, A. P., & Cruickshank, W. M. *Mainstreaming: A practical guide*. Syracuse: Syracuse University Press, 1977.

Perske, R. The dignity of risk. In W. Wolfensberger (Ed.), *Normalization: The principle of normalization in human services*. Toronto: National Institute on Mental Retardation, 1972.

Posner, B. The pride of work, the pride of being. In P. Mittler (Ed.), *Research to practice in mental retardation: Education and training* (Vol. 2). Baltimore: University Park Press, 1977.

Rosen, M., Kivitz, M. S., Clark, G. R., & Floor, L. Prediction of postinstitutional adjustment of mentally retarded adults. *American Journal of Mental Deficiency,* 1970, *74,* 726–734.

Sarason, S. B. *The psychological sense of community: Perspectives for community psychology.* San Francisco: Jossey-Bass, 1974.

Schaaf, V., Hooten, T., Schwartz, T., Young, C., Kerron, J., & Heath, D. People first: A self-help organization of the retarded. In J. Wortis (Ed.), *Mental retardation and developmental disabilities* (Vol. 9). New York: Brunner/Mazel, 1977.

Schelling, T. C. *Strategy of conflict.* New York: Oxford Galaxy, 1963.

Seay, M. F. *Community education: A developing concept.* Midland, Mich.: Pendell, 1974.

Shubik, M. (Ed.) *Game theory and related approaches to social behavior.* New York: John Wiley & Sons, 1964.

Spiegel, H. B. C. (Ed.) *Citizen participation in urban development: Concepts and issues* (Vol. 1). Washington, D.C.: NTL Institute for Applied Behavioral Science, 1968.

Spiegel, H. B. C. (Ed.) *Citizen participation in urban development: Cases and programs* (Vol. 2). Washington, D.C.: NTL Institute for Applied Behavioral Science, 1969.

Tönnies, F. *Community and society.* (C. P. Loomis, Ed. and trans.). New York: Harper Torchbook, 1957.

Truzzi, M. (Ed.) *Sociology and everyday life.* Englewood Cliffs, N. J.: Prentice-Hall, 1968.

Warren, R. *The community in America.* Chicago: Rand McNally, 1973.

Warren, R. B. The role of neighborhood in a national mental health policy. Testimony before the President's Commission on Mental Health, Nashville, May 25, 1977.

Warren, D. I., & Warren, R. B. *Neighborhood organizer's handbook.* South Bend, Ind. University of Notre Dame Press, 1977.

Williams, J. S. Liaison functions as reflected in a case study. *Journal of Community Psychology,* 1977, *5,* 18–23.

Wolfensberger, W. (Ed.). *Normalization: The principle of normalization in human services.* Toronto: National Institute on Mental Retardation, 1972.

Zipperlen, H.R. Normalization. In J. Wortis (Ed.), *Mental retardation and developmental disabilities* (Vol. 7). New York: Brunner/Mazel, 1975.

The Uses of
Social Policy Analysis
with Mental Retardation

James J. Gallagher

The era from 1950 to 1970 was an important area for program growth for those interested in mentally retarded citizens. Federal legislation, in particular, provided the base for greatly expanded research, leadership training, and demonstration:

1958	PL 88-926	Grants for training leadership personnel in education of the mentally retarded.
1963	PL 88-164	Grants for research and demonstration projects in area of the handicapped.
1966	PL 89-750	Grants to states for preschool elementary and secondary school children.
1975	PL 94-142	Education for All Handicapped Children Act mandating services to all identified handicapped children.

Major federal agencies such as the National Institute for Child Health and Human Development and the Bureau of Education for the Handicapped were established to provide leadership in administering programs for the mentally retarded (Kirk and Gallagher, 1979).

These programs were established in an era of deep concern over the unmet needs of many citizens in the United States, and represented an emotional commitment to do something meaningful for problems that had long been ignored. Such programs were designed out of the best estimates of leaders in the field, but represented hopes more than careful analyses.

This era of concern has now been largely replaced by a new era of program evaluation and accountability (Weiss, 1975). The hard fact of limited program resources has dampened the emotional fervor and caused a reassessment of how professionals and public decision makers can best work together to meet common needs. Nowhere is such reassessment more vigorous than in the area of research and its contributions.

The rapid emergence of the new field of *social policy analysis* should alert us to some major unmet needs in our own professions (Gil, 1973). This chapter lists some of those unmet needs, identifies some of the causes for the emergence of policy analysis, and notes two potential applications of this new field to mental retardation.

Despite the relative affluence of the scientific community today as compared to times past, the modern scientist has to deal with a series of questions never addressed by colleagues of a few generations ago. Then, a fairly simplistic philosophy of scientific activity could be stated in the following syllogism:

> Truth is good.
> The more truth we possess, the better off we will be.
> Therefore, the search for truth should have highest priority.

Such an idea is not totally abandoned today, as typified by a statement by Bronowski (1973): "We are a scientific civilization. That means a civilization in which knowledge and its integrity are crucial. Science is only a Latin word for knowledge...knowledge is our destiny."

The atom bomb, pesticides, pollution, genetic research and the potential for generating uncontrolled viruses, and other "truths," or applications of "truths," have caused modern scientists to become somewhat more cautious. We now recognize the importance of asking such questions as:

How will our truths be used?
Who will decide how they will be used?
What are the likely consequences of the possible uses of our "truths?"
Should we attempt to *do* everything that we can to human beings? If not, what are the rules to govern our choices? The emergence of a new set of procedures called social policy analysis comes from progressive dissatisfaction with the uncertain communications channels between the *keepers of knowledge*, the scientists, and the *keepers of power*, the politicians.

The current interest of scientists in public affairs seems to be made up of equal parts of guilt over some unforseen consequence of their past work and dismay and horror over what happens to their ideas once those ideas get into the public domain. Also, the scientist's curiosity can be piqued just as much by the mystery of "why government doesn't work," or "what forces influence communication between scientist and policymaker" as by the mysteries of the cell or brain functioning. The concern of the scientists is well stated by Sagan (1979):

> As a consequence of the enormous social and technological changes of the last few centuries, the world is not working well. We do not live in traditional and static societies. But our governments, in resisting change, act as if we did. Unless we destroy ourselves utterly, the future belongs to those societies that, while not ignoring the reptilian and mammalian parts of our being, enable the characteristically human components of our nature to flourish; to those societies that encourage diversity rather than conformity; to those societies willing to invest resources in a variety of social, political, economic, and cultural experiments . . . to those societies that treat new ideas as delicate, fragile, and immensely valuable pathways to the future.

The translation of research into a practical product has been complicated enough. Table 1 shows an analysis of how long scientific ideas take to get translated into a viable application. The extended length of time to translate knowledge to action gives one clue to

Table 1. Time lapse between discovery and implementation

Innovation	Year of first conception	Year of first realization	Time (in years) from conception to realization
Heart pacemaker	1928	1960	32
Input-output economic analysis	1936	1964	28
Hybrid corn	1908	1933	25
Electrophotography	1937	1959	22
Magnetic ferrites	1933	1955	22
Hybrid small grains	1937	1956	19
Green revolution: Wheat	1950	1966	16
Organophosphorus insecticides	1934	1947	13
Oral contraceptive	1951	1960	9
Video tape recorder	1950	1956	6
Average time elapsed			19.2

Adapted from Glaser, 1976.

the impatience of policymakers with research. Table 1 also shows that we are learning how to reduce that time lag in recent years.

If we learn more about the process of communication between the academic and political worlds, we may have similar success in reducing the time it takes to make the translation of knowledge to public policy more accurate and more faithful to what we know.

Two major strategies can be identified as having served the function and purpose of sharing wisdom from academia to policymakers for the last couple of decades. The first of these could be labeled the "Blue Ribbon Commission approach." In this instance, a particular social issue such as delinquency, or the state of the American family, or child-care needs is identified, and a commission composed of the most distinguished individuals available is brought together and asked to give their best counsel and advice to the government on the true nature of the problem and their suggestions for ways to remediate the problem. Some recent examples of this strategy is the Carnegie report on the family (Keniston, 1977), the National Academy of Sciences report "Toward a National Policy for Children and Families" (Aldrich, 1976), and the latest report of the Presidential Commission on Mental Health (1978).

The flaws in this approach lie in the difficulty of moving from what the experts know about the problem (a substantial amount) to some feasible strategy or manageable government program (about which they know very little). Not infrequently, commissions would make recommendations that were so impractical, or so costly, that the recommendations would be rejected out of hand by the public policymakers. Nor was there often any serious consideration given to the additional problem of effectively inserting the recommended new program into an already existing resource network.

In general, the commissions have served admirably to summarize the problems, but have rarely provided suggestions for new policies that were practical or capable of being implemented. Indeed, some cagey administrators or legislators have been accused of establishing study commissions in order to delay effective decision making on important, but painful, political issues.

An exception to the problem is noted in the work of the Commission on Labeling of Exceptional Children, established by Hobbs (1976). With the help of over 50 professionals who wrote on various aspects of the topic, Hobbs produced a scholarly state-of-the-art report on this particular topic, and a thoughtful consideration of alternative strategies, with the pluses and minuses of each of those strategies. Most commissions have neither the time nor the resources for such careful study and result only in the restatement of the obvious.

A second major strategy that has been used in the past to bridge the gap between academia and policy is the guru approach. A particular agency or legislative committee would identify a distinguished academician whose judgment they trusted to advise them on policy directions in a particular field of expertise. Thus, one would find the same professionals testifying over and over again before congressional committees on major issues of health or education or appearing on key study panels.

Other professional gurus would be found on advisory councils of the various agencies or such bodies as the National Academy of Sciences, and would bring their consultation and advice to bear in this fashion. The limitations of this approach were that it depended on the gurus adequately reflecting the more general consensus of their professional colleagues *and* upon the guru's ability to make the required translation between what we know and what we should do.

What the public policymakers often found, to their dismay, was that their particular guru did not reflect a consensus, but instead a highly personal and individualistic attitude toward a given policy. These experts, even the commissions, proved incapable of making the translation from adademic knowledge to workable public implementation.

Neither the commission nor the guru approach was particularly strong on the future implications of policy in terms of cost or personnel needs. Gallagher (1972), for example, pointed out (see Table 2) that the most popular model for educating children who were emotionally disturbed or learning disabled resulted in personnel needs that could not be met under any conceivable support of training facilities for the next few hundred years, if ever. A simple calculation of the personnel needed, based upon the number of unserved children and the favorite model of service delivery, yielded an impossible result.

Sarason et al. (1977) in discussing human services and resource networks stated:

> We have never known of a human service agency of any kind that asserted that it had the resources to accomplish its goals (p. 19).

The reason for this event, they explain, is that the definition of the solution auto-matically places the solution out of reach. If physicians are necessary to the delivery of health care, or teachers with masters' degrees necessary to the education of handicapped children, then we have made certain that the goal of full service will never be reached because there never will be sufficient physicians or specially trained teachers, nor the training facilities to train them, to enable the society to reach the goal of full service.

At the University of North Carolina at Chapel Hill, we have embarked on a program of policy analyses that tries to systematize the gathering of essential data, the assembling of possible action alternatives, and recommendations based upon the application of explicit criteria.

Table 2.   Special education manpower needs — estimation

Needed information		National current model emotionally disturbed	National current model learning disabilities
Children needing services (ages 5–19)		2%	1%
Children now receiving special services		1,200,000	600,000
Trained professionals available		90,000	120,000
Professionals needed to meet 60% of need		11,000	9,000
		79,000	14,000
		(8:1 ratio)	(20:1 ratio)
Existing training institutions		About 40	About 30
Current output of training institutions		About 500	About 400
Maximum capacity of training institutions		About 1000	About 800
Years to criterion—maximum capacity		79 years	33 years
		Year – 2049	Year – 2003
Years to criterion	Current support	Never	Never
(8% attrition)	Maximum support	Over 800 years	Over 200 years

Adapted from Gallagher, 1972.

There are two types of policy analyses, each of which requires a different approach. The first type of analysis begins from an accumulation of data or scientific information that would lead those concerned with the applications of public policy to consider various alternatives to current practice.

The second analysis stems from concern over existing policy where questions have been raised on how effective such a policy is. An example is given for each type of analysis.

The policy analysis model adopted by the Bush Institute for Child and Family Policy (Gallagher, 1979) follows a sequence of six steps.

A.   Restatement of the problem
B.   Criteria for analysis
C.   Synthesis of information
D.   Alternative strategies
E.   Criteria for strategy choice
F.   Implementation strategies

POLICY ISSUE: LANGUAGE DEVELOPMENT AND MENTAL RETARDATION

Over the past two decades data have accumulated from social science research and theory regarding early language development and its relationship to mental retardation. This knowledge and its implication for child development seem to call for public policy attention.

Restatement of the problem:

1.   Can we modify the linguistic environment of young, potentially retarded children in ways that will result in better development for these children?
2.   Can public policy initiatives enhance the application of such strategies?

Why is normal language development important? The important literature summary by MacNeill (1970) brought to the attention of many social scientists the theoretical work of Chomsky (1965) on linguistic structure and the incredible linguistic rule-mastering ability of the young child. When the child makes mistakes, such as "Bobby goed across the street," he or she reveals a rule consistency for past tenses that the English language itself doesn't have. So a built-in system capable of reception, interaction, and expression of verbal symbols is obviously present in the developing child. Some of the linguistic principles that seem now accepted would be:

1.   Normal 4-year-olds have operationally nearly mastered the syntactic structure of the English language—they operate with rules which they, or their parents, would be unable to name or define.
2.   The full development of cognitive abilities will not be accomplished without the effective development of linguistic abilities.
3.   The child without operative verbal systems tends to be "present" oriented. Both past experiences and future rewards or punishment appear to have less meaning and influence.

Werner (1979), in reviewing cross-cultural findings on language, concluded:

Every language, no matter in what culture it is spoken has universals that describe its basic
syntactic structure such as noun phrases and verb phrases . . . every language of the world
also uses the same grammatical relations, subjects, and predicates, verbs and objects (p. 195).

When this linguistic system does not develop as expected, for whatever reason, the
problems in this linguistic dimension often create problems in other developmental areas as
well. The full potential of the intellect may be unattainable without the verbal symbol
system, even as advanced thinking in mathematics relies on the mastery of mathematic
symbolic systems. The progressive mastery of a system of verbal symbols allows us to
communicate past experiences to others and project future alternatives. It allows us to
discuss causality, as Blank (1974) pointed out. Finally, it changes the probability of various
responses. If a child can use verbal responses, for example, it lowers the probability of a
physical response to social stress.

It has been suggested that the lack of adaptive responses in the mentally retarded
individual is due to the inability to store, interrelate, or express ideas. This deficit seems
attributable, in part, to the inability to utilize fully this linguistic symbol system (Robinson
and Robinson, 1976; Schiefelbusch, 1972).

Analysis of Criteria

This step in the analysis focuses upon making explicit the dimensions upon which the policy
analysis will be conducted. Programs receiving public policy support for enhancing
linguistic abilities should evidence positive findings on:

1. Increased ability of mentally retarded children to adapt to regular school program.
2. Demonstrable ability of mentally retarded children to use language for classification
    and interpretation.
3. An increased motivation and interest in learning on part of mentally retarded children.
4. A program design in harmony with existing cultural and institutional operations.

Synthesis of Information

This stage in the analysis is designed to draw together information that would 1) confirm the
nature of the problem, 2) identify important elements of proposed programs, and 3) give
evidence on the likelihood of success of proposed policies.

Is the problem of language development of children with mild mental retardation a
serious one? Language reception and expression seem closely linked to early intellectual
development, which in turn is linked to social class.

Kushlik and Blienden (1974) described the relationship between social class and
retardation as being so strong that no children of higher socioeconomic status parents are
found to obtain an IQ score of less than 80 unless they have a pathological condition. This
phenomenon has been demonstrated cross-culturally in a series of large and small epidemiologic studies: in Hawaii (Werner et al., 1967), in the Netherlands (Stein, Susser, and
Soenger, 1977; Zachaw-Christiansen and Ross, 1975), in Scotland (Birch et al., 1970), in
England (Hindley, 1968; Walberg and Marjoribanks, 1976), and in the United States
(Broman, Nichols, and Kennedy, 1975; Richardson, Higgins, and Ames, 1965). But social
class is not an explanatory variable, merely a cluster of various lifestyles related strongly to

family income. The low-income family environment from which emerges almost the total population of children with mild mental retardation does reveal different parent-child interactions or styles of communication. Middle-class mothers vocalize more to their babies under 1 year of age than do lower-class mothers (Kilbride, Johnson, and Streissguth, 1977; Ramey, Farran, and Campbell, 1979).

In free-play interactions, low-income mothers more frequently allow their children to play alone (Snow et al., 1979). This withdrawal from interaction seems to begin when the child becomes a toddler; as the growing child makes greater demands on his or her mother, middle-class mothers tend to increase the level of their interactions; lower-class mothers decrease theirs (Farran and Ramey, 1979).

In a structured situation such as teaching the child how to accomplish a specific task, low-income mothers more frequently than middle-income mothers rely on physical intrusion (Hess and Shipman, 1965), offer litle positive reinforcement (Feshback, 1973), and rarely communicate to the child the goal of the activity (Brophy, 1970; Steward and Steward, 1973). In addition, low-income mothers have been portrayed as providing a deficient linguistic environment for their children (Hurley, 1969). They use more "administrative" speech (Ward, 1971), issue more commands, and ask fewer questions (Snow et al., 1979; Streissguth and Bee, 1972; Zegiob and Forehand, 1975).

Important experiences for language development are either missing or present in diminished amounts in families whose socioeconomic status is low. Even when simple labeling of objects seems to be mastered by the low-income child, there are marked difficulties in helping them establish logical chains of events or in transforming information from one situation to another through the use of language. An example of this discrepancy is provided by data from a recent study at the Mental Retardation Center at the University of North Carolina in which preschool children were read stories to determine the child's skill in comprehending and communicating thematically related material. The child first demonstrated an understanding of the story by acting it out with toys and props.

Even though all of the children in the study could act out all of the episodes of the story, the children from low-income families lost twice as many information units as the middle-class children on all stories in verbal recall. Children from poverty homes also made many more errors, producing 15 times the amount of irrelevant information as the middle-class children (Feagans and Farran, 1981).

In another task, which required children to tell others how to open a puzzle box with an invariant sequence of steps, poverty children provided less information in verbal communication than middle-class children. Although they were able to demonstrate their understanding, it was clear that poverty children had difficulty "putting into words" information that they understood (Feagans and Farran, 1981).

One remaining question is whether intervention programs designed to stimulate language reception and expression show promise of improving the developmental status of children, particularly children at-risk for mental retardation. Several summaries of a very substantial literature suggest that such intervention can be productive. Karnes and Teska (1975) reached the following conclusion:

> Can the developmental status of children be changed through deliberate programming? The answer to that from the available research is, Yes. It is possible to move groups of children from one-half to one standard deviation higher on measures of intellectual ability (p. 219).

Stedman (1977) reviewed over 40 longitudinal intervention research programs for children at-risk for developmental programs and concluded that where access to children can be gained in the early years, preferably during the language-emergent years, 1 to 2 years of age, intervention programs will be more effective than those begun at later ages.

The following summary of principles would seem to be defensible within the context of what we now know about general language development:

1. Language acquisition and use are dependent upon an internal system that is triggered by childhood experiences.
2. Some relevant factors that influence the full development of language are: A) the nature of adult stimulation, B) the amount of stimulation, and C) the timing of the stimulation (when in the development flow it occurs).
3. A distinction can be made between *descriptive* language that is used for labeling and simple classification, and *interpretive* language used for delineating logical sequences, the drawing of implications, transformation of ideas, etc.
4. Interpretive language facility depends on social modeling and extensive practice.
5. Language development appears to facilitate the full growth of most of the other developmental channels (cognitive, social, adaptive, etc.).
6. Language development, in turn, is affected by many factors in different life domains. Family interactions, cultural values, and social experience clearly impact on linguistic form and expression.
7. Attempts to intervene to improve language performance can yield definable results. Programs that have clear and specific linguistic objectives appear to have more effect than those with a broad, undifferentiated goal to "improve language."

Alternative Strategies

The next stage in the process is designed to generate viable alternative strategies based upon what we know. There are a variety of alternative strategies that might be entertained that could stimulate language development and prevent the undesirable consequences noted above. Some major candidates for policy are:

1. *Parental education.* Teams of paraprofessionals, supervised by professionals to develop language and communication skills, could provide the home training for parents to help them stimulate early language development in their preschool children.
2. *The establishment of developmental day-care programs for children ages 0–3.* This strategy could be especially useful for working parents if it includes specific programs focused upon language skills development.
3. *Stimulation through media.* Such TV programs as "Sesame Street" and "Mister Rogers' Neighborhood" can provide stimulation through the communication media. We know that many children and their families watch such programs. Again, there should be specific instructional goals which the video material is designed to reach (i.e., language usage).
4. *Guaranteed annual income.* Some type of negative income tax that would lighten the burden on the family and would presumably bring more parental attention and positive interaction with their children.

Criteria for choice	Parental education	Child stimulation	Media programs	Guaranteed annual income	Status quo
Cost					
Past effectiveness					
Personnel needs					
Public support					
Fit with existing programs					

Figure 1.   Matrix for decision-making — language stimulation.

Figure 1 shows the decision matrix out of which a strategy or combination of strategies might be selected. It also illustrates why different persons using their own value base may arrive at different conclusions by either placing greater or lesser weight on the relative importance of cost as a criteria, for example, or disagreeing with the weighted values inserted in the table. The final aid that policy analysts can be to the policymaker would be to assemble data relevant to the matrix. They can assemble cost figures, review past history of the alternative strategies, analyze the potential effect of new programs on existing operations, and gather data on public interest and support. In the end, policymakers will place their weights in this matrix and will arrive at some decision based on their own judgments. One can note the status quo as one of the strategies, since one of the possible decisions can be to leave things pretty much as they are now. One should not ignore the importance of weighing that strategy against the others and provide weights for the decision just as for any other strategy.

Criteria for Choice

The next phase in policy analysis is to array those criteria that will determine how the decision maker will make a choice between these or other alternative strategies. It is often based on implicit or explicit values. Data can be collected on the following dimensions that can be used to compare the relative merits of the strategies.

1.   How much will the strategy cost?
2.   How do we know the strategy will work? Is there evidence of its past performance on relevant groups?
3.   Do we have available personnel, or must we engage in a major new training effort to have them prepared to carry out the strategy?
4.   How does such a strategy fit into an already existing program and organizational structure?
5.   Does the new strategy have public support and political viability?

Policy Implementation

The final step in the analysis is to review some of the issues facing the implementation of the chosen strategy. There are probably three major ingredients to the successful implementation of policy:

1.   Strong emotional commitment on the part of a significant public.
2.   Demonstrable professional competence to carry out the policy.
3.   The ability to integrate new programs with existing programs and services.

The emotional commitment is important because it will determine, in the end, the level of resources to be provided to the program. Without the strong political support of organized parents' groups, the level of funding for program elements identified with mental retardation would undoubtedly be far less than current levels.

The decade or so of work on the stimulation of language does encourage the notion of available professional competence to carry out language programs if the conditions are right.

The final requirement of easily fitting the new objectives into existing services may be more difficult. It would require some readjustment of programs, increased emphasis on language in day care or the home, and perhaps both parental and professional reeducation.

The end product of policy analysis is action (or the deliberate decision to not take action), and so the nature of implementation becomes critical as will be seen in the second example.

POLICY ISSUE: COMPETENCY TESTING AND MENTAL RETARDATION

The following discussion illustrates a policy analysis approach to an issue of current concern, namely, what policy should be followed regarding the special issues of competency testing and its application to mentally retarded students. In this instance, competency testing, the policy is a strategy that has already been put into effect, but we wish to determine whether its application in this special area is appropriate, or requires modification.

Restatement of the problem:

1.   Should educable mentally retarded students be judged by the same standards as average students?
2.   Should there be adaptations in the measures used for assessment of competency of educable retarded students?
3.   Should there be different documents than diplomas used to mark secondary school accomplishments?

Competency testing has become a major factor in the educational system of practically every state. In this instance, the educable mentally retarded student and other categories of exceptional students have become caught in an educational wave of major proportions without much prior attention being paid to the consequences of these policies for them.

A thorough policy analysis must begin with an understanding of where the existing policy, competency testing, came from in the first place. In this case, the basic motivation seems clear. The obvious reason for this widespread testing movement is public concern over the state of the public schools. This concern comes from observation of the number of high school graduates who lack even the most basic skills, and the conclusion that "social promotion" has gotten out of hand. A recent survey of 17-year-olds by the National Assessment of Educational Progress showed:

More than 12% were functionally illiterate.
Only 34% could determine the most economical size of a product.

Only 10% could calculate a simple taxi fare.

Only 53% were aware that the President does not appoint members of Congress.

Extensive data are now available on the impact such a program has on the educable mentally retarded in one Southern state (Gallagher and Ramsbotham, 1978) and can be of substantial assistance in the policy analysis. In June, 1977, the North Carolina General Assembly passed a minimum competency law that required secondary students to show some evidence of minimum competency in basic skills, such as reading and mathematics, before being awarded a diploma. The role played currently by exceptional children is spelled out by State Board of Education guidelines as follows:

1. All exceptional children, excluding the trainably retarded or severely retarded, shall take the tests.
2. Test adaptations or modifications in test administration will be developed where needed (e.g., blind children).
3. A parent may apply for exemption to the local school board for the exceptional child on the grounds that the test might be harmful.

Exemption from the test administration does not mean that a regular diploma will be granted. The Division of Exceptional Children in the State Department of Public Instruction is developing alternative procedures for testing handicapped children (i.e., braille tests for blind children, instructions given in sign language for deaf children).

These decisions, which result in including the mildly retarded child, were taken in the context of recent policy decisions on education of handicapped children. There is a clearly observed trend over the past half-century to help the mentally retarded individual become a more active partner in the total society. Such a trend is illustrated by concepts such as *deinstitutionalization*, *least restrictive alternatives*, and culminating in the present strategy of *mainstreaming*, or bringing mildly mentally retarded children back into regular educational programs to the maximum extent possible (Baroff, 1974). The recent strong move toward mainstreaming seems to be made up of several major dissatisfactions with the alternative strategy of special education classes for the retarded child.

1. Special classes have failed to show beneficial results that were hoped for them.
2. Special classes for the mentally retarded had become the dumping ground for problem children, rather than being unique and offering special opportunities for learning.
3. Many minority children were misclassified as mentally retarded children through inappropriate use of intelligence tests (Kirk and Gallagher, 1979).

Table 3 shows the contrasting assumption chains that underlie these differing public policy approaches to mildly retarded persons. One assumption chain gives the rationale for institutionalization, and the second is the current assumption chain regarding mainstreaming. Underlying the switch from a policy of institutionalization for the mildly retarded to a policy of mainstreaming is a change in assumption about the development of intelligence itself. The modern concept about intelligence is that it is plastic and can be modified by experience. A mentally retarded individual child does not necessarily have to grow up to be a mentally retarded adult, given proper education and experience.

With the shift to mainstreaming, there is the additional assumption that the mentally retarded individual will benefit by experiencing the same program as the other childen of the same age.

Criteria for Analysis

The dimensions along which such a policy decision should be reached are determined by two contrasting value positions. The first is that mentally retarded children will always be in a partially dependent state and should not be expected to reach the same standards of performance as average children. Furthermore, they should not be penalized for that failure. If they are able to master a program of study designed by special educators in an individualized education plan (IEP), then they will have accomplished what educators have deemed to be within their capabilities and should be rewarded for proper performance by a diploma, as the average or bright student is awarded a diploma for his or her accomplishments.

The opposing argument is that there should be one standard minimum performance for academic recognition, and that standard should be applied equally to all students who are in the regular education program. If a retarded child is mainstreamed, then there is an expectation that he or she will be able to perform at some level of competence within that program. It is a deception to mentally retarded students and their parents to pretend they have reached some acceptable standard of performance when they have not. Some alternative recognition for accomplishments would serve the necessary purposes of recognition without allowing mentally retarded individuals to pretend they have achieved goals that they have not.

Criteria for special study would be:

1. How well do educable retarded persons do on measures of basic skills?
2. Can special remediation aid them to reach acceptable standards?
3. What are the consequences for educable mentally retarded persons of not reaching such a level?

Synthesis of Information

Because the emergence of competency tests is relatively recent, data are not in great supply. We do know from past research that many educable retarded persons can master basic learning skills and adapt effectively as adults once they have completed their schooling.

In one state, North Carolina, data directly relevant to this issue have been collected. Tables 4 and 5 show the results obtained. Twelve percent of educable mentally retarded persons passed the competency test in reading in the fall of 1978 and another 18% of those retarded students who had originally failed passed in the spring of 1979 following a period of remediation. In mathematics, 7% of the educable mentally retarded youngsters passed in the fall of 1978. Of those who took the test the second time, following the remedial program, 15% passed.

There are several pieces of information that are important to a final policy determination that are not yet available. Are the educable mentally retarded youngsters who passed really culturally disadvantaged youngsters who have been misclassified or mis-

Table 3.   Assumption chains for policy (mild mental retardation)

Institutionalization	Mainstreaming
Mentally retarded children will always be retarded and dependent.	Mental retardation, without organic origin, is due, in part, to poor or inadequate experiences.
The purpose of education is to help these handicapped children adapt to their handicap.	Mental retardation can be improved with early and continuous educational contact with normal children.
Mentally retarded individuals must be trained in a protected environment where they can't be hurt.	Mentally retarded children will learn good social habits by emulating children of average development.
Mentally retarded individuals can be trained to be apprentices and helpers—nothing independent.	The mentally retarded child will best be able to cope in the normal world by learning to adapt in a normal school environment.
Mentally retarded individuals cannot form independent, personal relation-ships—will be taken advantage of, if allowed total freedom.	Lesson assignments will not be made too simple or easy for them, and their abilities will not be underestimated.

diagnosed? Perhaps successful performance was due to the direct relationship of the special educational program to the test content emphasizing learning of basic skills in reading and mathematics, and that aided some retarded children in passing the examination.

It may be noted that of all 11th grade students, 90% passed reading in the fall and 85% passed mathematics. Of those who took the test again in the spring, approximately half of the students passed the test. Of all students, approximately 7% have not yet passed the competency exams after the first year of their administration, and the educable mentally retarded students make up a proportion of those. It is likely that a majority of educable retarded youngsters will not, in fact, pass a competency test; therefore, any policy analysis must pursue the alternatives that face these students in terms of the diploma issue.

Alternative Strategies

There are a large number of variations on the themes; one has a choice of modifying the test, the passing standards, or the nature of the end document, noting program completion in secondary school. Some of the major strategies that are currently under consideration are listed below.

1. *Modify test administration.* One level of adaptation would be to use the same test and passing standards, but modify the way in which the test was administered. This would ensure that the retarded students' tendency to become confused and their inability to grasp instructions would not cause them not to give their best performance.
    In this case, test administration in small groups with extended instruction periods on how to take the test, and even large print tests, have been suggested.
2. *Lower passing standards.* The basis for this strategy is that many schools modify their passing grade standards for retarded students to take into account their limited ability. Thus, if the student is judged as capable of doing what is expected, then the student is passed. Here, some alternative standard for test performance would be applied. How to achieve that standard is a key question.

Table 4. Performance EMR students on North Carolina competency tests (reading) (1978-79)

Group	Fall testing			Spring testing			
	Number tested	Number passed	% passed	Number tested	% tested	Number passed	% passed
EMR	1,890	219	12	1,517	90.78	287	18.92
All students	81,353	73,264	90	6,674	82.51	3,425	51.32

Table 5. Performance EMR students on North Carolina competency tests (math) (1978-79)

Group	Fall testing			Spring testing			
	Number tested	Number passed	% passed	Number tested	% tested	Number passed	% passed
EMR	1,887	134	7	1,586	90.47	248	15.64
All students	81,322	69,465	85	9,838	82.97	5,169	52.54

3. *Different competence measure*. In this strategy, it is proposed that we take advantage of the extensive work done on developing individualized education plan for exceptional children, and use them as criteria for competency (i.e., if the student successfully meets the objectives of the IEP, he or she would be considered passing the competency requirements).

4. *Different end documents*. In this version, the modification comes at the end of the process where the retarded student who was unable to pass the competency test would be awarded a document other than a diploma to mark his or her school accomplishments. Participation in graduation ceremonies and other important details would be left to the option of local school districts.

The status quo option in this instance means that nothing special would be done, and the retarded student would be treated as other students.

Criteria for Selection

In this instance, as in the previous analysis, the weighting given to the various strategies will depend upon attitudes of parents, teachers, and the general public, as well as the technical ability to carry out the various strategies. Any strategy, as shown in Figure 2, that would be seen as undermining the integrity of the competency program itself would no doubt be seen as negative by the general public that has so far been positively disposed to the program. The continuing data on the level of success of EMR students on the tests will no doubt change the weights placed in the matrix by decision makers.

Implementation

As in the previous analysis on language development, the three criteria to successful implementation are:

1. Strong emotional commitment on the part of a significant public.
2. Demonstrable professional competence to carry out the policy.
3. The ability to integrate policy modification with existing programs and services.

In the analysis of policies already in existence, one of the implementation decisions is not just to modify existing policies, but to consider whether the basic strategy deserves change. Is competency testing the method of choice to deal with the issue of poor school

Criteria for selection	Modify test administration — Standards and documents same	Same test — Lower standards	Different measure of competence	Same test — Different document	Status quo
Past experience					
Public acceptance					
Remedial potential					
Parental acceptance					
School personnel attitude					
Fit with existing programs					

Figure 2. Decision matrix — competency testing projected strategies.

performance? In this case, it is unlikely that any dissatisfaction with the special problems of exceptional children would change the basic strategy, in the absence of dissatisfaction on the general program.

This chapter presents an evolving model of policy analysis that is designed to aid in translating scientific knowledge and experience to public action. It will not bring rationality to an irrational decision process, but it will arm the decisionmakers with a more explicit understanding of the program options available and the criteria base for making decisions.

REFERENCES

Aldrich, R. (Ed.) *Toward a natural policy for children and families.* Washington, D.C.: National Academy of Sciences, 1976.

Baroff, G. *Mental retardation: Nature, cause, and management.* Washington, D.C.: Hemisphere Publishing Corporation, 1974.

Birch, H., Richardson, S., Baird, D., Horobin, G., & Illsley, R. *Mental subnormality in the community.* Baltimore: Williams & Wilkins, 1970.

Blank, M. Cognitive functions of language in the preschool years. *Developmental Psychology,* 1974, *10,* 229–245.

Broman, S., Nichols, P., & Kennedy, W. *Preschool IQ prenatal and early developmental correlates.* Hillsdale, N. J.: Lawrence Erlbaum Associates, 1975.

Bronowski, J. *The ascent of man.* Boston: Little, Brown & Company, 1973.

Brophy, J. Mothers as teachers of their own preschool children: The influence of socioeconomic status and task structure on teaching specificity. *Child Development,* 1970, *41,* 79–94.

Chomsky, N. *Aspects of the theory of syntax.* Cambridge, Mass.: MIT Press, 1965.

Farran, D., & Ramey, C. Social class differences in dyadic influences during infancy. Unpublished manuscript, University of North Carolina, 1979.

Feagans, L., & Farran, D. How demonstrated comprehension can get muddled in production: An hypothesis. Developmental Psychology, 1981, *17,* 718–727.

Feshback, N. Cross-cultural studies of teaching styles in four year olds and their mothers. In A. D. Pick (Ed.), *Minnesota symposia on child psychology* (Vol. 7). Minneapolis: University of Minnesota Press, 1973.

Gallagher, J. J. The origins of social planning strategies and policy. Unpublished manuscript, 1979. (Available from Dr. James J. Gallagher, Director, Frank Porter Graham Child Development Center, Highway 54 Bypass-West, Chapel Hill, North Carolina 27514).

Gallagher, J. J. The special education contract for mildly handicapped children. *Exceptional Children,* 1972, *38,* 527–535.

Gallagher, J. J., & Ramsbotham, A. Developing North Carolina's competency testing program. *School Law Bulletin,* 1978, *9*(4), 1: 9–14.

Gil, D. *Unravelling social policy.* Cambridge, Mass.: Schenkman Publishing Company, 1973.

Glaser, E. (Ed.) *Putting knowledge to use.* Los Angeles: Human Interaction Research Institute, 1976.

Hess, R., & Shipman, V. Early experience and the socialization of cognitive modes in children. *Child Development,* 1965, *36,* 869–886.

Hindley, C. Growing up in five countries: A comparison of data on weaning, elimination training, age of walking, and IQ in relation to social class from European longitudinal studies. *Developmental Medicine and Child Neurology,* 1968, *10,* 715–724.

Hobbs, N. *The futures of children.* San Francisco: Jossey-Bass Publishers, 1976.

Hurley, R. *Poverty and mental retardation: A causal relationship.* New York: Random House, 1969.

Karnes, M., & Teska, J. The effects of early intervention programs. In J. Gallagher (Ed.), *The applications of child development research with exceptional children.* Reston, Va.: Council for Exceptional Children, 1975.

Keniston, K. (Ed.). *All our children.* New York: Harcourt Brace Jovanovich, 1977.

Kilbride, H., Johnson, D., & Streissguth, A. Social class, birth order, and newborn experience. *Child Development,* 1977, *48,* 1686–1688.

Kirk, S. A., & Gallagher, J. J. *Educating exceptional children* (3rd ed.). Boston: Houghton Mifflin Company, 1979.

Kushlik, A., & Blienden, R. The epidemiology of mental subnormality. In A. Clark & A.D.B. Clarke (Eds.), *Mental deficiency: The changing outlook*. London: Methuen, 1974.

MacNeill, D. The development of language. In P. Mussen (Ed.), *Carmichael's manual of child psychology*. Chicago: Rand McNally, 1970.

President's Commission on Mental Health. *Task panel report* (Vol. I). Washington, D.C.: U. S. Government Printing Office, 1978.

Ramey, C., Farran, D., & Campbell, F. Predicting IQ from mother-infant interactions. *Child Development*. In press.

Richardson, W., Higgins, A., & Ames, R. *The handicapped children of Alamance County of North Carolina*. Wilmington, Del.: Nemours Foundation, 1965.

Robinson, H., & Robinson, N. *The mentally retarded child* (2nd ed.). New York: McGraw-Hill, 1976.

Sagan, C. *Broca's brain*. New York: Random House, 1979.

Sarason, S., Carroll, C., Maton, K., Cohen, S., & Lorentz, E. *Human services and resource networks*. San Francisco: Jossey-Bass, 1977.

Schiefelbusch, R. L. (Ed.). *Language of the mentally retarded*. Baltimore: University Park Press, 1972.

Snow, C., Arlman-Rupp, A., Hassing, Y., Jobse, J., Joosten, J., & Vorster, J. Mother's speech in three social classes. *Journal of Psycholinguistic Research*, 1979, *5*, 1–20.

Stedman, D. Early childhood intervention programs. In B. Caldwell & D. Stedman (Eds.), *Infant education: A guide for helping handicapped children in the first three years*. New York: Walker & Co., 1977.

Stein, Z., Susser, M., & Soenger, G. Mental retardation in a national population of young men in the Netherlands, II: Prevalence of mild mental retardation. *American Journal of Epidemiology*, 1977, *104*, 367–404.

Steward, M., & Steward, D. The observation of Anglo-, Mexican-, and Chinese-American mothers teaching their young sons. *Child Development*, 1973, *44*, 329–337.

Streissguth, A., & Bee, H. Mother-child interaction and cognitive development in children. In W. W. Hartup (Ed.), *The young child: Review of research*. Washington, D.C.: National Association for the Education of Young Children, 1972.

Walberg, H., & Marjoribanks, R. Family environmental cognitive development: Twelve analytic models. *Review of Education Research*, 1976, *46*, 526–551.

Ward, M. *Them children*. New York: Holt, Rinehart & Winston, 1971.

Weiss, C. Evaluation research in the political context. In E. Struening & M. Guttentog (Eds.), *Handbook of evaluation research*. Beverly Hills, Calif.: Sage Publications, 1975.

Werner, E. *Cross cultural child development*. Monterey, Calif.: Brooks/Cole Publishing, 1979.

Werner, E., Simonian, K., Bierman, J., & French, F. Cumulative effect of perinatal complications and deprived environment on physical, intellectual, and social development of preschool children. *Pediatrics*, 1967, *39*, 490–504.

Zachaw-Christiansen, B., & Ross, E. *Babies: Human development during the first year*. London: John Wiley & Sons, 1975.

Zegiob, L., & Forehand, R. Maternal interactive behavior as a function of race, socioeconomic status, and sex of the child. *Child Development*, 1975, *46*, 564–568.

Intelligence, Adaptation, and Problem Solving

Ralph P. Ferretti and
John M. Belmont

Specific settings vary greatly for retarded and normal people, and it is quite unthinkable to compile a comprehensive list of settings for either population, much less a correlated set of influences on thinking, or the development of thinking. Somebody may someday accurately predict cognitive growth in view of just a few measures of the individual and the environment, but so far the field lacks the theory that must underlie such a formula. What does exist, however, is a promising focus for organizing research on cognitive development, an idea with respectable ancestry in the evolutionary and psychometric schools, yet also appealing to the modern cognitivist.

The focus is problem solving, and it is a fair bet that any research program aimed at understanding environmental influences on retarded persons will greatly increase its scientific payoff by including problem solving among its organizing principles. For the laboratory psychologist, a useful exercise is to view one's laboratory tasks not as tests of specific functions, but rather as tools for triangulating a global function. Thus, the memory task is not a tool for studying the child's memory, nor is the balance scale a tool for studying his or her understanding of torque, but rather both tasks may be seen as potential tools, as potentially useful problems for studying the child's general approach to thinking. This shift in perspective has led to some novel approaches to the study of intelligence and the specific conditions under which children of a given age will or will not think productively. Some of this progress is reviewed here because it bears directly on this volume's main topic. First, however, as background, it will be helpful to frame out our view of the field, and review some history that invites new MR research approaches.

INDUCTIVE SCIENCE LACKS DIRECTION

Behavioral research in mental retardation is largely inductive, is usually motivated by technicalities, and is sometimes interesting only in its methodological novelty and sophisti-

The preparation of this chapter was supported by Grants HD-00870, HD-08911, and HD-13029 from the National Institute of Child Health and Human Development.

cation. For 20 years there has been an outpouring of instruments and methods to measure various specific aspects of retarded persons' thinking. The quality of the numbers is foremost in this field, hungry for theory, but often driven by narrow definitional and technical concerns. It grapples with measurement, repeatability, and cross-validation, often guided by factor analysis and other weakly analytical inductive statistics. Large theoretical issues are often ignored because too much energy is consumed in the laboratory or in the field, harvesting, organizing, cataloging facts, and confirming findings. As a collective enterprise, MR psychology has hobbled along in this data-oriented way, with little common direction. It is time to stop collecting data for just a moment, and try to view the work in a theoretical light. To begin with, it is instantly sobering, and wonderfully instructive to ask: What is intelligence, and where in this conundrum of cognitive, social, economic (and now political) issues does the work fit in?

INTELLIGENCE THEORY AND PSYCHOMETRY

Consider the etymology of "intelligence." Its primal ancestor is *intelligere,* which means to choose, to decide, to discriminate. The emphasis is on active evaluation of options, and this sense is present more or less completely in all latter-day definitions. For research purposes the modern concerns are the *mechanisms* by which people choose, and the *conditions* under which choice is necessitated. The concept thus relates the presenting conditions and the thinking that subserves choice, and together the ideas suggest problem solving and adaptation (Charlesworth, 1978). Hold the problem solving for a moment and look at adaptation.

The most influential ideas during the late 19th century were biological determinism, the survival of the fittest, and adaptation, deriving from Darwin's naturalism (Tyler, 1976) and it may be added, his good sense. One can hardly exaggerate the power of these concepts as applied to the problem of individual differences in thinking. Darwinian survival and adaptation of species naturally emphasized environmental press over individual activity, but the latter could not and cannot be ignored by psychometric theorists. Thus, Binet and Simon (1916) recognized " . . . there is a fundamental faculty, the alteration or lack of which is of the utmost importance for practical life. The faculty is *judgment* . . . practical sense, intuition, the faculty of *adapting oneself to circumstances.* To judge well, to comprehend well, to reason well, these are the essential activities of intelligence'' (p. 42). Wechsler (1958) likewise viewed intelligence as the " . . . aggregate or global capacity of the individual to act purposefully, to think rationally, and to deal effectively with the environment'' (p. 7). And of course the AAMD itself (Grossman, 1973) includes "deficits in adaptive behavior" along with "subaverage general intellectual functioning" in its definition of mental retardation. In light of the Binet and Wechsler quotes, this AAMD statement is somewhat jarring because, to be sure, it deals with adaptive behavior as though it were some individual quality apart from general intellectual functioning. In the context of modern thinking about mental retardation, however, the distinction makes sense, in a curious manner. The fact is that what AAMD meant by "general intellectual functioning" was actually "general psychometric functioning." AAMD was acting to legitimize psychometric thinking at the highest level of institutional authority, and it is important to understand how that psychometric thinking arrived in modern times bereft of intelligence qua adaptation. How, that is, can there be such a sharp disjunction between the psychometric pioneers' broad characterizations of intelligence and today's practicing psycho-metrists' stark theoretical neutrality and narrow focus on test performance?

Look again at history. The most powerful early influence on psychometry was the very reason for Binet's own investigations, namely, universal compulsory education (Edwards and Richey, 1963). For the first time, a huge range of actual abilities was formally represented in a social institution. This burden required mass assessments of children's potential academic achievements in order to rationalize educational decisions. Then, personnel selection pressures during World War I greatly increased the demands on the test-makers, who reacted by stepping into the arena of group testing, and hence further than ever away from the individual and all hope of assessing personal adaptive functions. The desired result was predictive validity; the focus was on unidimensional ranking of indi-viduals. The dependent variable was the product rather than the process of thought (Tyler, 1976), yet the word *intelligence* was retained as an arrogant misnomer for terms such as "academic prospects," and "leadership prospects." The momentum of these historical choices has impeded development of analytic tools capable of revealing the processes of intelligent adaptation. Having ignored adaptation, having ignored the presenting conditions and the thinking underlying problem solving, the psychometrists nevertheless claimed intelligence as the domain of differential, or correlational psychology, with its heavy reliance on intuition and induction as a vehicle for theoretical construction (Resnick, 1976). The factor-analytic studies of Spearman (1927) and Thurstone (1938) substantially re-inforced psychometry's hold on intelligence, with its definition as activity required by tests of mental ability (Robb, Bernardoni, and Johnson, 1972). Even Guilford's (1967) structure-of-intellect model, with its *operation* dimension, did little to salvage active adaptive thinking. The modal psychometric definition thus attempts to account for a particular dispositional characteristic of an individual as measured by tests (Charlesworth, 1978), and the movement's insistence on such operational thinking spells its demise. The field has neglected to seek rigorous external criteria for validating its constructs, and this "theoretical nihilism and analytic barbarism" (Butterfield, 1978) will ultimately destroy traditional psychometry's position in contemporary cognitive science.

And how about its practical survival? Could this highly empirical approach not at least be vindicated on pragmatic grounds? Evidently not. At least for practitioners in mental retardation, a vexing problem with psychometry has been the intelligence test's poor prediction of retarded persons' institutional and community adjustment (McCarver and Craig, 1974). This failure is not surprising because intelligence tests were originally constructed not to assess life prospects, but only academic prospects. Granted, IQ is the best tool devised for the latter purposes; it is still disconcerting, however, that a diagnosis of low "intelligence" during childhood accounts poorly for adult adjustment. What's yet more disconcerting is that recently developed measures of "adaptability" have fared little better (Leland et al., 1967), and the relationship between IQ and measured adaptability is modest at best. Cobb (1972), in a comprehensive critical review of the relevant follow-up literature, discussed the many conceptual and methodological reasons for these predictive failures. His conclusion on the practical use of IQ:

> The evidence suggests that for a difference in general intelligence to have an appreciable effect on the practical handling of an individual case, the difference must be sufficiently obvious that no refined instruments of measurement will be needed (Cobb, 1972, p. 146).

THE STUDY OF PROBLEM SOLVING
AS AN ALTERNATIVE TO THE PSYCHOMETRIC APPROACH

It is no surprise that contemporary efforts to understand intelligence have led to a rediscovery of adaptation and problem solving. This conceptual shift resulted largely from common concerns about the practical utility of psychometrically assessed intelligence (cf. Brown and French, 1979). More importantly, the study of problem solving focuses research attention on the most widely accepted characteristics of intelligent behavior: the mechanisms and processes by which people adapt and the presenting conditions that require adaptation.

Two distinct approaches have emerged in the study of problem solving (Klahr, 1978). The first approach, whose historical roots are most firmly planted in information-processing psychology (Newell and Simon, 1972), examines strategic processes in formal tasks with well-defined structures that can be readily analyzed. Some of the tasks come from traditional educational curricula and are instructionally relevant. For example, predicting the behavior of a balance-scale was studied by Klahr and Siegler (1978) and Siegler (1976); the motion of objects in a straight line by Simon and Simon (1978). Instructional relevance is not, however, a precondition for adopting a task as a research tool. For example, some workers have argued that the study of intelligence will be best advanced by a thorough analysis of information-processing requirements of tasks found in standardized intelligence tests (e.g., Estes, 1970; Hunt, 1974). Consequently, complex models have been developed to describe people's solutions to tasks such as series completion (Simon and Kotovsky, 1963), memory span (Butterfield and Belmont, 1971), and Raven's Progressive Matrix Test (Hunt, 1974). Finally, some workers have used "puzzles" or games, such as Tower of Hanoi (Byrnes and Spitz, 1977; Klahr and Robinson, 1981), as heuristics for characterizing task solutions. Regardless of their derivation, most tasks studied in the information-processing tradition are relatively well-defined (Newell and Simon, 1972), in the sense that there exists a clear definition of an initial state, an end state or goal, and a series of permissible operations for transforming the initial state into the end state.

The second approach, espoused most articulately by Charlesworth (1976, 1978), focuses on solutions to everyday tasks. This approach is ethological: It is meant to yield a comprehensive account of people's development of adaptations to challenging environments. To date, however, the ethologists have put forth very few accounts of problem solving per se (Levine, 1978) and no solid conceptual foundation for generating testable hypotheses about the role of problem solving in intelligent adaptation (Charlesworth, 1979). This has led to an energetic inductive enterprise of collecting descriptive information about naturally problematic environments and solutions (Levine, Zetlin, and Langness, 1980).

The remainder of this chapter discusses the methods and findings of both approaches—information-processing psychology and problem-oriented ethology—and concludes by discussing the peculiarities of each approach that impede progress in areas of common concern. A perspective is offered from which a combination of experimentation and fine-grained observation can illuminate problem solving and adaptation.

The Information-Processing Approach to Problem Solving

Models of Performance   Here is a brief sketch of problem solving as viewed from the perspective of information-processing theory (Greeno, 1973; Newell and Simon, 1972).

Problem solving involves an environment, which is the objective task as specified by the person who presents it. The task always embodies an explicit goal, and sometimes materials that might be used to reach the goal. A description of the task environment is usually straightforward: a detailed account of the instructions about goals and any accompanying materials is sufficient to permit independent replication.

Besides the task environment, there is the problem solver's subjective understanding of the task, that is, his or her internal representations of the goal and any associated materials (whether or not they are presented in the task environment). Two orders of subjective operations—modes of thought—are believed to operate on the internal task representation. One is the solution proper, that is, the computational method by which materials might be manipulated to satisfy the goal. The other is the problem-solving procedure that yields the solution.

The task is not a problem if the problem solver's first potential solution turns out to meet the explicit goal. The task is a problem only if the final proposed solution (whether or not it actually works) is a modification or a replacement for an earlier one.

The problem solver's internal representation of the task environment, along with problem-solving procedures and existing potential solutions, make up the problem space. The task environment is the objective part of problem solving. It is all that we make it. The problem space is all that we do not see, but can only infer. From the information-processing viewpoint, the problem space is the all-important determinant of problem solution. The scientific challenge is to get a solid inferential grasp on it, and this is done by modeling. Sufficient models of the problem space will accurately predict individual differences in performance within a range of task environments. Current models take many forms, such as *flow diagrams* (Butterfield, Siladi, and Belmont, 1980), *decision trees* (Siegler, 1976), and *production systems* (Klahr, 1978).

Klahr and Siegler (1978) established criteria for choosing among various types of models, and those criteria are worth considering here because of their wide applicability. Within the overarching requirement that a model account for the actually observed behavior, it must be general, it must reflect developmental changes and account for developmental differences in problem solutions ("developmental tractability"), and it must reflect what is already known about the system being modeled—in the current case, human information processing.

In practice, these criteria have never been met, even for a single well-specified task environment (Butterfield et al., 1980). This should come as no surprise. Engineers who must build in the jungle can depend very little on textbook formulae. They must simply hack away. Likewise we must hack away at the vagaries of individual human performance and less-than-perfect measures of it. The sharpest approach, we believe, is to engage in a vigorous invention of unobtrusive, well-validated direct measures of our subjects' internal representations of task environments, their stores of potential solutions, and their problem-solving procedures. Without such assessment tools it will be impossible to account for the normal and abnormal development of problem solving. Process measures inform developmental models.

Developmental Models, Instruction, and Task Analysis   The point is illustrated by Siegler and Richards' (1979) analysis of the development of children's concept of time. The background for this study came from Piaget (1969), according to whom children progress through three distinct knowledge states in their understanding of time. In the first, they judge relative time solely in terms of the spatial stopping points of objects. If two objects were in parallel motion, the one that stops farther ahead is judged to have traveled for the longer time. In the second state, children begin to consider other factors, but Piaget was vague as to what they might be. Finally, at mastery, succession in space is dissociated from time, and correct judgments about time are always made. On the basis of these observations, Siegler and Richards used the rule-assessment methodology (Siegler, 1981) to design tasks that would reveal the course of development for the time concept. Their process analyses generally confirm Piaget's description. They found that in the transition between the first and third states, however, children use a distance rule to judge time. They evidently think that the object that travels the longer distance always travels the longer time. This rule was not predicted from Piaget's observations. Without careful process measurement it would never have come to light.

Information-processing researchers are increasingly advocating instruction as a method for validating their models (Belmont and Butterfield, 1977; Butterfield et al., 1980; Resnick, 1976). Successful instruction of specific task solutions demonstrates the plausibility of the hypothetical processes that underlie the instructed solution. Moreover, in its ideal form, the instruction mimics normal development. This point is illustrated by Butterfield and Ferretti's (1980) experiment involving a graded instructional sequence corresponding to Siegler's (1976) model of development on the balance-scale task. Each instructional unit taught skills that were expected to advance children through the developmental sequence. Four young normal children, all of whom based their pre-instruction predictions on weight alone, were successfully advanced by instruction through each level of the model. The instruction yielded performance not usually achieved by adults. At the completion of instruction, all children accurately used a variant of the torque rule to predict the behavior of the balance scale. To a degree, the results of instruction validate the developmental model.

The design of instruction of any kind always depends on task analysis. In its general form, the analysis might take these steps: First, the task environment is described. A model of the development of performance on the task is then proposed, and empirical analyses (ideally involving unobtrusive measures) are undertaken to substantiate the model. Finally, instructions that guide the child through the developmental model are prepared and administered. To the degree that the model accounts for development on the task, and to the degree that the instructions map onto the model, development will be recapitulated through instructional intervention.

Such an attack is rarely mounted in purely applied settings, although the products of empirical task analyses sometimes resemble those of the rational analyses typically made by applied workers (Resnick, Wang, and Kaplan, 1973). Rational task analyses are descriptions of successful responses to task demands; that is, ideal solutions that do not necessarily correspond to those actually used by people to perform the tasks (Resnick, 1976). In the rational approach, curriculum objectives are defined. A set of component skills and their assumed prerequisites are identified. The child's deficiencies in the use of these skills are then diagnosed, and finally, training is undertaken to remedy these deficiencies. For the cognitive theorist, this procedure is incomplete because it includes no explicit model, yet the model from which the instruction originates is the central theoretical concern. When the purpose is to develop a model of the solutions that people use for a task, we cannot do without detailed empirical task analyses based on human performance.

   Problem-Solving Procedures and Potential Solutions   So far this chapter has discussed the study of developmental changes in people's solutions to given tasks, as they might be understood by highly particularized models. Any model of the problem space must include such solutions, certainly, but will be incomplete if it does not also address the realm of problem-solving procedures, and internal representations generally. In the developmental arena much attention has been given to how internal representations and problem-solving procedures bear on the acquisition, maintenance, and transfer of specifically trained solutions (Borkowski and Cavanaugh, 1979; Brown, 1975; Butterfield et al., 1980; Flavell and Wellman, 1977; Resnick and Glaser, 1976). From these studies we learn that under proper conditions, trained solutions do transfer, in a manner of speaking, to task environments other than the one used in the original training regimen. But we also learn that training often does not transfer, indeed does not even carry over from one encounter with a particular task to another encounter with the same task. Such failures have been attributed to faulty problem-solving procedures, and it seems that the conditions under which successful maintenance and transfer are achieved add not only to the child's fund of potential solutions, but as well must be adding to the store of problem-solving procedures and influencing internal representations as a whole.

   There are many theories of how specific experiences might come to have such broad influence on general cognition (Greeno, 1974; Hayes and Simon, 1977; Norman, Gentner, and Stevens, 1976; Thorndyke and Hayes-Roth, 1979; Sternberg, in press). From these works, one is led to view the influence of specific environments on children's general cognitive growth as a matter of guiding children through a series of not quite identical examples of adaptive thinking. Such training presumably leads the child to abstract the important common elements, not only of the situations, but also of whatever solutions he or she might have brought to bear. By what means new situations are then mapped onto those abstracted commonalities of the previous experiences (the very essence of invention) is unknown, but analogical reasoning might provide a useful model. For present purposes, it is hopeful to assume that instruction in adaptive thinking might best be designed with the properties of tasks in mind.

The Ethological Approach to Problem Solving

The ethologists are motivated by two concerns. First, they note the psychometrists' failure to predict adaptation outside of school settings. Charlesworth (1978) attributed this failure to their narrow focus on dispositional properties of intelligence to the neglect of environmental conditions that elicit intelligent behavior. A second concern is the lack of practical significance of the tasks typically used by cognitive researchers (Brooks and Baumeister, 1977; Sternberg, in press). The question is whether " . . . the structure of tasks and behaviors in the laboratory is representative of the tasks and behaviors in other environments'' (Cole, Hood, and McDermott, 1978, p. 36). This issue arises from the recognition that unlike everyday problems, most tasks used in the laboratory are well defined. They have fixed structures, fixed goals, and well-analyzed solutions. In contrast, many problems in people's everyday environments are embedded in open systems with loosely defined structures and uncertain goals. Moreover, responses are often characterized at least as much by affective investment as by intelligent analysis (Brown and French, 1979; Collins, 1976; Neisser, 1976).

The ethologists' goal is to develop a theory of mundane cognition, a naturalistically based theory of problem solving (Brown and French, 1979; Levine, 1978). They have invested heavily in the naturalistic observation of intelligent behavior (Charlesworth, 1976) in order to produce the descriptive foundation on which such a theory must rest. At present, however, that foundation is still, at best, fragmented (Levine et al., 1980).

Notwithstanding their reservations about the tasks used in psychometry and information-processing research, the ethologists have a solid commitment to study problem solving, which is, in fact, a central feature of their definition of intelligence. This owes to the ethological significance of adaptation, both biological and behavioral. In their view, adaptation links an organism to the requirements of its environment (Charlesworth, 1978). In the grand scheme, the traditional ethologist strives to understand the evolutionary significance of adaptive behavior and the morphological changes that underlie it. In human problem solving, this challenge is particularly severe because the complexity and variability of human behavior, as well as its intergenerational (rather than specific genetic) acquisition, obliges the ethologist to apply naturalistic methods to observe what must seem to be essentially hidden intellectual processes. These cognitive processes are believed to be acquired, yet dependent upon inherited, albeit specialized, abilities (Lorenz, 1971).

Charlesworth (1978) defined a problem as a situation in which ongoing behavior is either externally or internally blocked. Particular environments are not necessarily problematic. Rather, problems are inferred from temporary or permanent interruptions in ongoing behavior. These interruptions arise from the presence of blocking conditions in either the environment (physical or social) or in the head of the problem-solver (cognitive). Thus, the identification of a problem depends upon an observed break in a steady stream of behavior and an observed or inferred condition responsible for the break.

There are two notable characteristics of this approach. First, it is exclusively behavioral. Cognitive processes are not measured, but the observer *infers* their controlling role in determining the problem solver's response to blocking conditions. Second, the ethologist does not distinguish between a blocking condition for which the person already has a solution and one that requires invention or reorganization of previously acquired solutions. This contrasts with most working definitions of problems, but Charlesworth (1978) believes that most situations that elicit adaptation elicit well-learned rather than novel responses. By removing the distinction, the ethologist hopes to develop more comprehensive and representative developmental and environmental norms for problem solving.

In three studies, Charlesworth's research strategy called for observing samples of responses to problematic and nonproblematic situations. This was done in order to catalog the number and kinds of blocking conditions, successful and unsuccessful responses to these conditions, and the contexts in which the blocking conditions occurred. The conditions and responses were classified as being cognitive, social, and physical.

One study of particular note was done with a normal and a Down's syndrome infant. These children were nearly 2 years old and were reared in middle-class families with no siblings. Each child was observed for 16 hours spread over 45 weeks. Charlesworth expected that the majority of blocking conditions experienced by children age 2 would require novel solutions. He observed, to the contrary, that these children encountered cognitive problems only infrequently, and these required only ordinary solutions. Charlesworth acknowledged, however, that his observational methods may have been insensitive to " . . . valid behavioral correlates of cognitive processes involved in problem solving" (p. 28). Physical problems were also infrequent and usually resulted from the absence of a desired object. Nearly 90% of the problems encountered by both children were social in origin, resulting from parental demands. The two children did not generally differ in their distributions of problem types, but the normal child had more *frequent* problems, and these usually involved multiple blocking conditions. The normal child's problems also seemed to be more difficult than the retarded child's. Finally, there were no differences between these children's distributions of response types, or their relative successes in removing the associated blocking conditions.

This study shows naturalistic observation's potential for establishing a data base from which testable hypotheses about real-life problem solving can be drawn. For instance, Charlesworth (1978) noted that the retarded child's problems seemed to be less demanding than those of the normal child. Recall that the majority of both children's problems were occasioned by parental requests. Perhaps it is now reasonable to ask if Down's children's cognitive deficiencies are related, at least in part, to the requirements of the tasks and the quality of instruction to which these children are exposed. That is, can we infer from the co-occurrence of tasks and solutions a relationship between a property of the retarded child's environment and the resulting behavior?

To do so convincingly requires a much firmer grasp of the concept of "task" than Charlesworth (1978) had in his rather general observational studies. Moreover, it requires some understanding of the child's conception of the task (Levine, 1978). The task need not be well defined in the sense of the information-processing usage, and the subject need not have all the operations and knowledge necessary for its solution. But we must know these things because, to the degree that we fail to assess the subject's knowledge, we will have an incomplete description of his or her representation of the task. On this point ethologists and psychologists agree. Certainly, many naturally occurring problems seem to be highly variable in form, structure, response requirement, and frequency, and in the contexts within which they are imbedded. This variability increases the difficulty of describing the objective task environments and the subject's representation of them. We know that in face of great variability in the appearance of laboratory problems, however, subjects sometimes adopt consistent approaches based upon the problems' formal properties (Butterfield and Ferretti, 1980; Siegler, 1978). It is reasonable to assume that something similar occurs in the face of the great variability encountered in natural problem situations. People evidently perceive common properties in their environments that permit solid adaptive responding. The scientist's job is to confirm and characterize those perceptions and to understand their role in problem solving.

One approach to such an enterprise is to narrow one's observational focus to include a single class of problems, broadly defined (Longabaugh, 1980). For example, Levine, Zetlin, and Langness (1980) studied memory tasks that retarded children encountered in the everyday classroom environment. Levine et al. established two criteria for counting a situation/response occurrence. First, the child had to show a compulsion to act, as evidenced by something he or she said or some other confirmable behavior. Then, there had to be a setting condition and a goal, between which the child's actions were clearly meant to fall. On the basis of hundreds of hours of classroom observations, memory tasks were classified along five dimensions: 1) The agent who presented the task, 2) the kind of memory requirement, 3) the frequency of occurrence, 4) the variability in response requirement, and 5) the type of feedback.

Two results are important to the discussion here. First, a single type of response was suitable for the great majority of memory tasks. Thus, the task environments of these children were highly routinized. Second, most responses were not readily scored as either correct or incorrect. Rather, they were evaluated according to a criterion of ''acceptability'' that emerged through something of a negotiation between teacher and child. Levine et al. concluded that the poor classroom performance of educable retarded children might be attributed to their exposure to highly routinized tasks for which more emphasis is placed on appropriateness of a response rather than on its correctness. This conclusion suggests support for the general hypothesis that environmental conditions (task environments) determine, at least to some degree, the quality of retarded children's cognitive deficits. It also points to probable preventative environmental engineering, for example, increasing the variety and reshaping the goal properties of the tasks given. The success of preventative measures would validate the hypothesis, although it is well to bear in mind that failure might be viewed as support for the bland, unchallenging practices observed by Levine et al. to be the retarded child's standard fare. Such an outcome would perhaps be distasteful to some, but it is nevertheless encouraging to be at a juncture where one can even imagine a practical study with implications for policy being informed by ethological methodology. The jump from imagination to implementation will be a long one, however, for there are still some wrinkles to be ironed out of the methods themselves. Here is a brief review of some of them.

ETHOLOGICAL VERSUS PSYCHOLOGICAL METHODS

The ethologist strives to study everyday behavior by naturalistic observation. Longabaugh (1980) advocated that three criteria be met before observational studies are undertaken: 1) the focal phenomena should be easily observable, 2) a human being (rather than an adjunct instrument) should do the observing, and 3) the observations should be made on uncontrolled events.

In the domain of problem solving it seems that these criteria cannot be met, primarily because without instrumentation it is exceedingly difficult to observe cognition during problem solving. That is why, perhaps, the ethologists have ignored cognition (Charlesworth, 1979), despite their belief in its importance. This omission probably contributes to their difficulty in validating cognitive blocking conditions and children's associated responses (cf. Charlesworth, 1978). It may also prevent discovery of conditions that foster the development of effective problem solving because, as we know, enduring cognitive changes happen when experience is only slightly discrepant from existing cognitive structures (Kohlberg, 1969; Piaget, 1972). Uncontrolled, unaided observations may be insensitive to subtle alterations in task environments and behavioral responses that signify important cognitive growth.

The difficulty in meeting the criterion of observing only uncontrolled environments is fully recognized by the ethologists. The identification of tasks, their associated demands, and their internal representations all prove impossible in the face of the great natural environmental variability. As a consequence, order must be imposed at some point in the observation of everyday problem solving. Levine (1978) proposed two "quasi-naturalistic" methods to cope with this difficulty. In one, called the method of open-ended problems, a task is suggested to the subject and the response is observed. Unique to this method is the goal's ambiguity, which permits a wide range of possible solutions depending upon the subject's representation of task requirements.

In the second method, called the method of increased specificity of context, one begins as in the previous method: an ill-defined task is presented for the subject's consideration. The agent now, however, has in mind (but does not at first reveal) a correct response to the requirements of the task. The correct response is based on an analysis of the objective structure of the task. Over time the covert goal is slowly revealed in order to determine the degree of specificity required for the child to adopt that goal.

In aggregate, these methods have much in common with the Soviets' assessment of a child's zone of potential intellectual development (as discussed by Brown and French, 1979). The Soviets distinguish between developmental level versus learning potential, the former being indexed by performance on standardized tests, the latter by capacity to profit from external aids. Initial testing is done under standard instructional conditions. A problem is posed by the tester. If the child is unsuccessful, increasingly specific prompts are administered until success on the problem is attained. Following solution of this problem, additional problems are presented, some of which depend upon the solution used in the previous problem, and some of which require new solutions. As before, increasingly specific prompts are given as needed to achieve success. The test-prompt sequence is repeated across a number of problem domains, producing rich information about responsivity to instructional assistance, ease of transfer, and the generality of problem-solving effectiveness.

The convergence of Levine's and the Soviets' methods represents a shared commitment to these principles, which are also held by the laboratory-based information-processing researcher: 1) children's observable problem solving is cognitively mediated, 2) the child's internal representation of the task environment critically influences behavior in that environment, 3) effective problem solvers succeed in both well-defined and ill-defined task environments, and 4) intelligence is related to success under conditions of incomplete instruction (Resnick and Glaser, 1976). The convergence of the ethological, the Soviet psychometric, and the laboratory-based psychological approaches, as illustrated by their agreement on this slate of principles, seems to provide rich grounds for a fruitful collaborative study of intelligence qua problem solving. It is important to understand why the partnership is only just now flowering.

OBSTACLES TO COLLABORATIVE STUDIES OF PROBLEM SOLVING

Perhaps the greatest impediment to collaboration is the novelty of naturalistic observation in studies of problem solving. Ethologists have until recently avoided the study of cognitively mediated behavior; in fact, they have not yet organized descriptive accounts on which laboratory findings can hope to depend for external validation. This is an enormous barrier that will be difficult and expensive to overcome, but it will yield to sustained research attention.

There are, in addition, some deeply rooted, generally unrecognized, and therefore more insidious, reasons for the paucity of collaborative progress. They reside in the traditions of information-processing psychology and ethological anthropology, and are discussed by Cole and Scribner (1975) in the context of each discipline's beliefs about cultural influences on cognition. The issues are germane to the study of problem solving.

First, anthropologists stress content, and psychologists stress process. The psychologist strives to neutralize cultural influences and isolate a nucleus of universal "content-free" processes. The anthropologist disdains this practice exactly because of the futility of assessing process in culturally meaningless contexts.

Second, the psychologist depends upon carefully structured situations to reveal processes that have wide generality outside the experimental setting. The anthropologist, in contrast, is committed to the observation of naturally occurring phenomena because the imposition of structure renders things hopelessly artificial.

Finally, to generate and confirm hypotheses about cognition, the psychologist uses a manipulative methodology, while the anthropologist uses the unobtrusive methodology of naturalistic and participant observation.

Even given this span of conflicting methods, attitudes, and presuppositions, we can see some points of possible compromise which, if made with reasonable sensitivity to both sides' concerns, would eventually bear fruit. First, there is an increasing understanding in both camps that experimentation and observation can be mutually reinforcing, that content and process can be attended to side-by-side in the study of problem solving (Brown, 1975; Butterfield, 1978; Cole and Scribner, 1975; Levine, 1978). Cole and Scribner made this point very well:

> The psychologist examining any mental mechanism is of necessity examining a mental mechanism with material given in society and culture, and he cannot get away from such 'living contents' even in the artificial isolation of an experiment. Similarly, if anthropologists are concerned with how 'living contents' come into existence and change over history, they need to understand what operations ('processes') individuals bring to the material that is culturally given. (p. 261).

Second, the psychologists will ultimately need to validate their process analyses of laboratory tasks against thorough descriptions of naturally occurring problems and their associated demands. The necessary descriptive and analytic work will also take us a long way toward understanding the apparently adaptive adjustments made by many people who are identified as mentally retarded in their school years. Perhaps the school tasks on which they failed are simply irrelevant to the adult world. Or perhaps there are enough mundane and routinized environments to permit retarded adults to achieve invisibility through modest achievement, or perhaps it will be shown, as Edgerton (1967) observed, that the retarded merely feign competence while in fact chronically failing to meet the requirements of everyday tasks. Disciplined answers to these questions call for disciplined investigations of everyday tasks.

Finally, it is clear that psychologists and ethologists now share a large set of beliefs about the relationship between intelligence and problem solving. Workers in both disciplines are increasingly cognizant of the limitations of their own methods, and have independently proposed arrangements that minimize the variability that is intrinsic to naturalistic observation, and at the same time reduce the artificial constraints imposed in traditional experimentation. The trick has been to view intelligence as an ability to function adaptively with minimal environmental support. We have not yet seen an example of this strategy in practice, but we are working to realize its logic, and would like to believe that the ethologists are inclined toward the same effort. The common enterprise would soon show the way around our current most difficult methodologic and conceptual problems.

REFERENCES

Belmont, J. M., & Butterfield, E. C. The instructional approach to developmental cognitive research. In R. V. Kail & J. W. Hagen (Eds.), *Perspectives on the development of memory and cognition.* Hillsdale, N.J.: Lawrence Erlbaum Associates, 1977.

Binet, A., & Simon, T. *The development of intelligence in children.* Baltimore: Williams & Wilkins, 1916.

Borkowski, J. G., & Cavanaugh, J. C. Maintenance and generalization of skills and strategies by the retarded. In N. R. Ellis (Ed.), *Handbook of mental deficiency. Psychological theory and research* (2nd ed.). Hillsdale, N.J.: Lawrence Erlbaum Associates, 1979.

Brooks, P. H., & Baumeister, A. A. A plea for consideration of ecological validty in the experimental psychology of mental retardation: A guest editorial. *American Journal of Mental Deficiency,* 1977, *81,* 407–416.

Brown, A. L. The development of memory: Knowing, knowing about knowing, and knowing how to know. In H. W. Reese (Ed.), *Advances in child development and behavior* (Vol. 10). New York: Academic Press, 1975.

Brown, A. L., & French, L. A. The zone of potential development: Implications for intelligence testing in the year 2000. *Intelligence,* 1979, *3,* 255–273.

Butterfield, E. C. On studying cognitive development. In G. P. Sackett (Ed.), *Observing behavior* (Vol. 1). Baltimore: University Park Press, 1978.

Butterfield, E. C., & Belmont, J. M. Relations of storage and retrieval strategies as short-term memory processes. *Journal of Experimental Psychology,* 1971, *89,* 319–328.

Butterfield, E. C., & Ferretti, R. P. Toward instructing problem solving: The cases of the balance beam and series completion. Paper presented at the 1980 NICHHD/Vanderbilt Conference on Learning, Cognition, and Mental Retardation, September 16–18, Nashville, Tenn.

Butterfield, E. C., Siladi, D., & Belmont, J. M. Validating theories of intelligence. In H. W. Reese & L. P. Lipsitt (Eds.), *Advances in child development and behavior* (Vol. 15). New York: Academic Press, 1980.

Byrnes, M. M., & Spitz, H. H. Performance of retarded adolescents and non-retarded children on the Tower of Hanoi problem. *American Journal of Mental Deficiency,* 1977, *81,* 561–569.

Charlesworth, W. R. Human intelligence as adaptation: An ethological approach. In L. B. Resnick (Ed.), *The nature of intelligence.* Hillsdale, N.J.: Lawrence Erlbaum Associates, 1976.

Charlesworth, W. R. Ethology: Its relevance for observational studies of human adaptation. In G. P. Sackett (Ed.), *Observing behavior* (Vol. 1). Baltimore: University Park Press, 1978.

Charlesworth, W. R. An ethological approach to studying intelligence. *Human Development,* 1979, *22,* 212–216.

Cobb, H. V. *The forecast of fulfillment: A review of research on predictive assessment of the adult retarded for social and vocational adjustment.* New York: Teachers College Press, Columbia University, 1972.

Cole, M., Hood, L., & McDermott, R. P. Concepts and ecological validity: Their differing implications for comparative cognitive research. *Quarterly Newsletter of the Institute for Comparative Human Development,* 1978, *2,* 34–37.

Cole, M., & Scribner, S. Theorizing about the socialization of cognition. *Ethos,* 1975, *3,* 249–268.

Collins, A. Education and understanding. In D. Klahr (Ed.), *Cognition and instruction*. Hillsdale, N.J.: Lawrence Erlbaum Associates, 1976.

Edgerton, R. B. *The cloak of competence: Stigma in the lives of the mentally retarded*. Berkeley: University of California Press, 1967.

Edwards, N., & Richey, H. G. *The school in the American social order* (2nd ed.). Boston: Houghton Mifflin Company, 1963.

Estes, W. K. *Learning theory and mental development*. New York: Academic Press, 1970.

Flavell, J. H., & Wellman, H. M. Metamemory. In R. V. Kail & J. W. Hagen (Eds.), *Perspectives on the development of memory and cognition*. Hillsdale, N.J.: Lawrence Erlbaum Associates, 1977.

Greeno, J. G. The structure of memory and the process of solving problems. In R. L. Solso (Ed.), *Contemporary issues in cognitive psychology: The Loyola symposium*. Washington, D.C.: Winston and Sons, 1973.

Greeno, J. G. Hobbits and orcs: Acquisition of a sequential concept. *Cognitive Psychology*, 1974, *6*, 270–292.

Grossman, H. J. (Ed.). *Manual of terminology and classification in mental retardation*. Washington, D.C.: American Association on Mental Retardation, 1973.

Guilford, J. P. *The nature of human intelligence*. New York: McGraw-Hill, 1967.

Hayes, J. R., & Simon, H. A. Psychological differences among problem isomorphs. In N.J. Castellan, D. B. Pisoni, & G. R. Potts (Eds.), *Cognitive theory*. Hillsdale, N.J.: Lawrence Erlbaum Associates, 1977.

Hunt, E. Quote the raven? Nevermore! In L. W. Gregg (Ed.), *Knowledge and cognition*. Hillsdale, N.J.: Lawrence Erlbaum Associates, 1974.

Klahr, D. Goal formation, planning, and learning by pre-school problem solvers or: "My socks are in the dryer." In R. S. Siegler (Ed.), *Children's thinking: What develops?* Hillsdale, N.J.: Lawrence Erlbaum Associates, 1978.

Klahr, D., & Robinson, M. Formal assessment of problem-solving and planning processes in preschool children. *Cognitive Psychology*, 1981, *13*, 113–148.

Klahr, D., & Siegler, R. S. The representation of children's knowledge. In H. W. Reese & L. P. Lipsitt (Eds.), *Advances in child development and behavior* (Vol. 12). New York: Academic Press, 1978.

Kohlberg, L. Stage and sequence: The cognitive-developmental approach to socialization. In D. A. Goslin (Ed.), *Handbook of socialization theory and research*. Chicago: Rand McNally, 1969.

Leland, H., Shellhaas, M., Nihira, K., & Foster, R. Adaptive behavior: A new dimension in the classification of the mentally retarded. *Mental Retardation Abstracts*, 1967, *4*, 359–387.

Levine, H. G. Everyday problem-solving in a school for children with moderate retardation. Paper presented at the 77th Annual Meeting of the American Anthropological Association, November 16, 1978, Los Angeles, Calif.

Levine, H. G., Zetlin, A. G., & Langness, L. L. Everyday memory tasks in classrooms for TMR learners. *Quarterly Newsletter of the Institute for Comparative Human Development*, 1980, *2*, 1–6.

Longabaugh, R. The systematic observation of behavior in naturalistic settings. In H. Triandis (Ed.), *Handbook of cross-cultural psychology* (Vol. 2). Boston: Allyn and Bacon, 1980.

Lorenz, K. Psychology and phylogeny. In K. Lorenz (Ed.), *Studies in animal and human behavior* (Vol. 2). Cambridge, Mass.: Harvard University Press, 1971.

McCarver, J. R., & Craig, E. Placement of the retarded in the community: Prognosis and outcome. In N.R. Ellis (Ed.), *International review of research in mental retardation* (Vol. 7). New York: Academic Press, 1974.

Neisser, U. General, academic, and artificial intelligence. In L. B. Resnick (Ed.), *The nature of intelligence*. Hillsdale, N.J.: Lawrence Erlbaum Associates, 1976.

Newell, A., & Simon, H. A. *Human problem solving*. Englewood Cliffs, N.J.: Prentice-Hall, 1972.

Norman, D. A., Gentner, D. R., & Stevens, A. L. Comments on learning schemata and memory representation. In D. Klahr (Eds.), *Cognition and instruction*. Hillsdale, N.J.: Lawrence Erlbaum Associates, 1976.

Piaget, J. *The child's conception of time*. London: Routledge and Kegan Paul, 1969.

Piaget, J. Intellectual development from adolescence to adulthood. *Human Development*, 1972, *15*, 1–12.

Resnick, L. B. Task analysis in instructional design: Some cases from mathematics. In D. Klahr (Ed.), *Cognition and instruction*. Hillsdale, N.J.: Lawrence Erlbaum Associates, 1976.

Resnick, L. B., & Glaser, R. Problem-solving and intelligence. In L. B. Resnick (Ed.), *The nature of intelligence*. Hillsdale, N.J.: Lawrence Erlbaum Associates, 1976.

Resnick, L. B., Wang, M. C., & Kaplan, J. Task analysis in curriculum design: A hierarchically sequenced introductory mathematics curriculum. *Journal of Applied Behavior Analysis*, 1973, *6*, 679–710.

Robb, G. P., Bernardoni, L. C., & Johnson, R. W. *Assessment of individual mental ability*. Scranton, Pa.: International Textbook Company, 1972.

Siegler, R. S. Three aspects of cognitive development. *Cognitive Psychology*, 1976, *4*, 481–520.

Siegler, R. S. The origins of scientific reasoning. In R. S. Siegler (Ed.), *Children's thinking: What develops?* Hillsdale, N.J.: Lawrence Erlbaum Associates, 1978.

Siegler, R. S. Developmental sequences between and within concepts. *Monographs of the Society for Research in Child Development*, 1981, *46* (2, serial no. 189).

Siegler, R. S., & Richards, D. D. Development of time, speed, and distance concepts. *Developmental Psychology*, 1979, *15*, 288–298.

Simon, H. A., & Kotovsky, K. Human acquisition of concepts for sequential patterns. *Psychological Review*, 1963, *70*, 534–546.

Simon, D. P., & Simon, H. A. Individual differences in solving physics problems. In R. S. Siegler (Ed.), *Children's thinking: What develops?* Hillsdale, N.J.: Lawrence Erlbaum Associates, 1978.

Spearman, C. *The abilities of man*. New York: Macmillan, 1927.

Sternberg, R. J. Reasoning, problem solving, and intelligence. In R. J. Sternberg (Ed.), *Handbook of human intelligence*. New York: Cambridge University Press. In press.

Thorndyke, P. W., & Hayes-Roth, B. The use of schemata in the acquisition and transfer of knowledge. *Cognitive Psychology*, 1979, *11*, 82–106.

Thurstone, L. L. *Primary mental abilities*. Chicago: University of Chicago Press, 1938.

Tyler, L. E. The intelligence we test—An evolving concept. In L. B. Resnick (Ed.), *The nature of intelligence*. Hillsdale, N.J.: Lawrence Erlbaum Associates, 1976.

Wechsler, D. *The measurement and appraisal of adult intelligence* (4th ed.) Baltimore: Williams & Wilkins, 1958.

RESIDENTIAL AND COMMUNITY SETTINGS

Deinstitutionalization, Environmental Normalization, and Client Normalization

Edgar W. Butler and
Arne T. Bjaanes

Varying levels of competence have long presented moral and social problems in our society. In the past, individuals who were unable to cope with demands of the larger environment were removed from it and placed in a special environment that completely isolated the individual from the demands of society, and, incidentally, "protected society from the individual." Few will disagree, however, that the historic *total institution* has not increased the competence of its residents. Some research indicates that it may even have contributed to retrogression of some individuals (Lyle, 1959; Bennet and Rudolph, 1960; Dentler and Mackler, 1961; Stedman and Eichorn, 1964; Tizard, 1964; Woloshin, Tardi, and Tobin, 1966).

Recently there has been a major change in philosophy regarding care of retarded persons. The asylum notion has been increasingly abandoned with a concomitant increase in emphasis on community care in various alternative settings (O'Connor and Justice, 1973). These alternative settings are expected to break down the social and economic walls that isolate retarded persons from meaningful experience and learning. They include board and care and home care facilities as well as special schools, special classes, sheltered employment, and recreation. The objective of community alternatives is to make available to impaired individuals all community resources that they are able to use.

ASSUMPTIONS

There are essentially three basic assumptions underlying changes in policy related to the care of mentally retarded persons: 1) historic total institutions (large state hospitals) have

The observations and data used in this chapter were made possible by NIMH Grant MH 08667 and support provided by the Department of Developmental Services, State of California, in conjunction with Operation PINpoint. This is a slightly revised version of a paper presented at the American Association on Mental Deficiency and National Association of Private Residential Facilities for the Mentally Retarded, San Francisco, California, May 14, 1980. An earlier version was presented at the NICHD conference on Mental Retardation, UCLA, 1979.

failed to increase the competence of their residents, and may, in fact, have deterred their development of social skills; 2) an environment providing "normal social contact" and the potential for "normal social interaction" has a positive "normalizing" effect on mentally retarded individuals; and 3) community care facilities provide a relatively "normal environment," and, therefore, have a "normalizing" effect on retarded people; that is, an increase in competence ensues (Butler and Bjaanes, 1978).

A number of questions arise regarding the general validity of these assumptions. There is little doubt about the validity of the first assumption, because considerable evidence indicates that total institutionalization tends to have a detrimental effect on motor skills, communication skills, learning skills, and social competence in general (Farber, 1968). On the other hand, only a limited number of studies support the second assumption. Several special programs have shown that if the environment is significantly different from that of the larger total institution, normalization can occur, and social and intellectual competence can be increased (Baller, 1936; Skeels and Dye, 1939; McKay, 1942; Kennedy, 1948; Mundy, 1957; Edgerton, 1967).

The last assumption is the most problematic. Are most current community care facilities significantly different from the total institution and do they provide a relatively normal environment and thus have a normalizing effect on their residents? Obviously, the first problem is that this assumption takes for granted uniformity or similarity among various community care facilities. In fact, our observations indicate that there is a lack of uniformity and that a great deal of dissimilarity exists (Bjaanes and Butler, 1974; Butler, Bjaanes, and Hofacre, 1975; Moore, Butler, and Bjaanes, 1976; Butler and Bjaanes, 1977; Butler and Bjaanes, 1978). The number of residents in community care facilities ranges from three or four persons up to 30 or more. There is considerable variation in the type and quality of life afforded individuals in community care facilities. Furthermore, there are significant differences in the amount of social interaction, incentives for normalization, and in caregiver knowledge, attitudes, behavior, and experience. In addition, there are geographical differences, for example, rural versus urban settings and differences in physical plants. Generally, facilities range in size from small family care units to facilities that are replicas of larger total institutions, or mini-institutions. In view of the dissimilarities and lack of uniformity, it is clear that systematic investigation of community care facilities is urgently needed.

An evaluation of the interrelationships between various factors in community care facilities affecting the success of placement is, by nature, a complex and difficult task (Butterfield, 1967). The ideal study would be an experimental one in which the investigator has both the ability and the authority to control and manipulate significant activities, as well as caregiver characteristics, placement, and specific environmental components. Although this is not feasible, and perhaps not ethical, a similar *in vivo* experiment is taking place in the social experiment of placing retarded individuals in community care facilities.

INSTITUTIONALIZATION, DEINSTITUTIONALIZATION, AND NORMALIZATION

A total institution is one in which the institution is self-maintaining and substantially isolated from interaction with the society at-large (Goffman, 1961). Deinstitutionalization, of course, is releasing individuals from the total institution into the community. Deinstitutionalization of retarded persons has been based primarily on the ideology/ philosophy of normalization.

First introduced by Bank-Mikkelsen (1969), head of the Danish Mental Retardation Service, normalization was defined as "...letting the mentally retarded obtain an existence as normal as possible." Although deceptively simple in definition, the principle becomes complex in application.

Wolfensberger (1972) proposed a redefinition of the term to allow it to apply more broadly throughout culture-specific situations. Normalization is the "utilization of means which are as culturally normative as possible, in order to establish and/or maintain personal behaviors and characteristics which are as culturally normative as possible." He proposed implementation of normalizing actions at personal, social system, and societal levels. He specifically recommended environments that maximized interaction and behavioral competence. Therefore, from this view, a large state or private institution is considered as a deindividualizing residence in which people are highly regimented and inwardly directed, and in which the social environment is aimed at a low common denominator of client needs and abilities. The normalization principle suggests that group residential services must be integrated within the community, which is an easier task for a smaller facility.

Proponents of normalization maintain that the more normalized service environments will result in client progress and that habilitation will be enhanced (Wolfensberger, 1972; Nirje, 1969; Bank-Mikkelsen, 1969). Although the need for more humane service settings is generally accepted, questions have been raised concerning the appropriateness of the normalization principle for achieving client progress (Fram, 1974; Browning, 1975; Rhoades and Browning, 1977).

Claims that normalization will result in client progress or questions concerning the appropriateness of normalization for achieving client progress, miss an important part of the overall picture: *What are the optimal conditions for enhancing client development and growth?* The problem is, in part, due to a dual usage of the term *normalization,* and a lack of distinction between environmental normalization and client normalization (Bjaanes, Butler, and Kelly, 1981).

Environmental Normalization

The process of developing culturally normative and appropriate residences and services, devoid of the dehumanizing stigma so often attached to being mentally retarded, is called environmental normalization. Included in this process is restructuring of the service systems, training service providers, and changing prevailing attitudes toward developmentally disabled persons. The process focuses primarily on altering the environment in which life experiences take place. Altering the environment is a necessary, but not sufficient condition for enhancing client development and growth.

Client Normalization

Client normalization is the acquisition of necessary skills for assuming culturally normative social roles and responsibilities. Client habilitation includes training in specific functional skills, and the amelioration or reduction of maladaptive behaviors. Environmental normalization focuses on environmental conditions, and client normalization focuses directly on the functional characteristics of the client. Client normalization, however, cannot proceed

without environmental normalization. Environmental normalization without client normalization is equally fruitless.

Achieving client normalization requires not only habilitation programs aimed at
enhancing skills, but also the provision of a culturally normative environment in which to
exercise achieved skills and thereby achieve normalization in the broader sense of the term.
If emphasis is placed solely on environmental normalization without a concomitant
emphasis on client normalization, it is unlikely that clients will develop skills necessary for
using the environment and for developing to their maximum potential. Current emphasis is
primarily on environmental normalization, with relatively little stress on the processes
required for individual or client normalization.

To achieve successful adjustment to placement in the community, or for that matter in
any setting, systematic attention must be paid to functional deficiencies in clients and the
provision of services directed at remediating those conditions. The need for a comprehensive, multidisciplinary, community-based service system, however, is clearly recognized (Grossman and Rowitz, 1973). Yet at present, little is known about either service
needs or service provision (O'Connor, 1976).

PLACEMENT VARIATION IN UTILIZATION OF SERVICES

Four categories of placement facilities are commonly used. They include state hospitals,
large care facilities, small care facilities, and in-home placement. State hospitals are major
state-operated residential facilities. Large care facilities provide services for 16 or more
residents and include large, skilled nursing facilities and small convalescent-type hospitals.
Small care facilities, or board and care facilities, provide services to an average of three to
six clients. In-home placement includes placement of the client with parents, relatives, or
guardians. In most cases, only one developmentally disabled person resides in such
settings.

Assuming that adaptive behavior failures (e.g., problems with appropriate social
behavior and independent living skills), maladaptive behavior (e.g., acting out), and
physical disabilities are the most prevalent causes for failure in community placement, it
can be argued that along with environmental normalization, client normalization must
emphasize habilitative services aimed at those factors constituting barriers to successful
placement and adjustment subject to remediation (Eyman et al., 1972; Wolf and Whitehead, 1975; Schalock and Harper, 1978).

Four generic service categories are especially important: 1) supportive counseling, 2)
independent living skills training, 3) behavior therapy, and 4) social interaction training.

Supportive counseling is regularly scheduled, goal-oriented intervention responsive to
the decision-making needs of the impaired individual or his or her family. The primary
focus of this intervention is solving interpersonal problems such as disability acceptance,
overanxiety, overprotection, and the ability to deal with daily demands resulting from the
client's disability.

Independent living skills training is defined as an individualized program designed to
enhance and develop skills required for independent living. The purpose of behavior
therapy is to reinforce desirable and adaptive behaviors and reduce or eliminate maladaptive
behaviors. Social interaction training is defined as regularly scheduled programs aimed at

developing and improving a person's interpersonal skills. It includes training in manners, communication, and appropriate social behavior.

The data used in this section to examine some of these service components were collected during the field test of a comprehensive evaluation system being implemented by the Department of Developmental Services in California (Kelly et al., 1978). The sample population (about 6% of all clients served by the department) was drawn from the caseloads of three diversely located Regional Centers. Clients represented all diagnostic categories and age ranges. Placement types range from state hospitals to independent living settings. Although strict sampling procedures were not used, the study population was relatively representative of the developmentally disabled population being served by the department (Day and Lebrato, 1978).

Client functional level for the study population was assessed using the Client Centered Evaluation Model (CCEM) (Bjaanes, 1976). The CCEM consists of three major modules: 1) tracking diagnostic and demographic data, 2) 127 performance measurement items, and 3) data on need for and delivery of 52 service types. All CCEM data, including the service element, are individualized. Thus, service delivery can be directly linked to client as well as to placement facility in which the client is served.

These programs should be differentially utilized by different client types. Table 1 illustrates a variety of client types derived empirically from a large-scale study of the developmentally disabled in a variety of living situations (see Baanes et al., 1981, for a more elaborate analysis of these types).

Those who have the greatest deficits in adaptive behavior, social skills, and self-help skills are more likely to be institutionalized (Eyman et al., 1972; Wolf and Whitehead, 1975). Our data suggest, however, that deficits in other functional areas, particularly communication, are also critical predictors of placement in an institution or large care facility. Clients in state hospitals and large care facilities function at a substantially lower level than clients in other placement types. In all behavioral dimensions, functioning is at the highest level for clients placed in-home. Generally, clients functioning at the lowest level are most likely to be placed in state hospitals and large care facilities.

It is generally assumed by normalization proponents that small, family-like residences and parental homes approximate the normalization principle to a greater degree than do state hospitals and large care facilities. If this assumption is valid, then a majority of clients, in fact, reside in more normalized environments. Environmental normalization, however, is only one part of the broader implications of normalization. Client normalization requires habilitation services aimed at enhancing clients' skills and reducing maladaptive behaviors.

In general, a smaller proportion of clients at the lowest functioning level receive independent living skills training. For example, those at the highest functioning level are those most likely to receive independent living skills training. As shown in Table 3, however, clients in the lower functioning group receive more social interaction training and behavior therapy services than do those functioning at a higher level.

In hospitals, small care facilities, and in-home placements, the proportion of clients in behavior therapy increases with the level of maladaptive behavior; that is, the more the maladaptive behavior, the greater the proportion of clients in therapy. The exception is large care facilities where the group with the most maladaptive behavior also has the least proportion of clients receiving behavior therapy. In spite of these variations, the general

Table 1. Summary characteristics of client "O" types*

Client category	O type**	Summary characteristics
C	1	Severe mental retardation complicated by physical disability. Clients characterized by low scores on all dimensions except those dealing with emotional adjustment and maladaptive behavior.
C	2	Severe mental retardation complicated by emotional disability and extreme disruptiveness. Clients have extremely low scores on all dimensions except motor skills.
C	3	Severe mental retardation complicated by limited social and independent living skills. This group can be distinguished from the most severely impaired by their relatively average motor, adjustment-to-change, and maladaptive scores.
B	4	Moderately disabled with deficient independent living skills and high social confidence. Clients are rated high in terms of their adjustment to change and the nondisruptiveness of their behavior. These clients are above average in social initiative. They are deficient in personal and community self-sufficiency.
C	5	Mental retardation complicated by emotional disability. Clients are slightly above average on all dimensions except the two emotional domain factors of adjustment to change and maladaptive behavior.
B	6	Mental retardation complicated by limited ability to cope with change. Clients are average with respect to the sample in all domains except the adjustment to change factor.
B	7	Mental retardation complicated by behavioral disruptiveness. Clients have lowered scores in community living skills but are within the average range for the sample in all other dimensions.
B	8	Mental retardation with limited social skills. Clients have below average scores in self-help skills and community living skills. Scores in adjustment to change, social initiative, and communication skills also tend to be low.
A	9	Mildly disabled individuals with limited cognitive skills. Clients are rated above average on all dimensions except cognitive skills.
A	10	Mildly disabled. All members of this cluster have above average scores on all eight dimensions.
A	11	Potentially autonomous with mild disability. These clients score above average on all dimensions and have extremely high scores in self-help skills, community living skills, social initiative, and communication.

*Adapted from Day and Lebrato (1978); data are from Operation PINpoint, State of California (Kelly et. al., 1978).
**"O" types are categories of residents with similar characteristics as determined by cluster analysis.

Table 2.   Client placement distribution by client category

| Placement type | Client category | | | | | | | |
| | A | | B | | C | | Total | |
	n	%	n	%	n	%	n	%
State hospital	27	1.9	53	6.3	103	16.9	183	6.3
Large care facility	18	1.2	37	4.4	70	11.5	125	4.3
Small care facility	389	26.9	255	30.6	133	21.8	777	27.0
In-home placement	1002	69.4	489	58.6	305	49.9	1796	62.3
Totals	1436	100.	834	100.	611	100.	2881	100.

Table 3. Perception of need for and provision of behavior therapy by client category and placement type

Client category	State hospitals				Large care facilities				Small care facilities				In-home placement				Totals			
	n	NR	P/S	%	n	NR	P/S	%	n	NR	P/S	%	n	NR	P/S	%	n	NR	P/S	%
A	27	14	13	48.1*	18	8	10	55.5*	388	353	35	9.0*	1002	895	107	10.7*	1435	1270	165	11.5*
			8	61.5†			10	100.†			23	65.7†			70	65.4†			113	68.5†
				29.6††				55.5††				5.9††				7.0††				7.9††
B	53	24	29	54.7*	37	17	20	54.1*	255	191	64	25.1*	484	365	119	24.6*	834	597	237	28.4*
			26	89.6†			18	90.0†			33	51.6†			84	70.6†			161	67.9†
				49.1††				48.6††				12.9††				17.3††				19.3††
C	103	33	70	68.0*	70	41	29	41.4*	133	73	60	45.1*	305	214	91	29.8*	611	361	250	40.9*
			65	92.9†			25	86.2†			31	51.7†			60	65.9†			181	72.4†
				63.1††				35.7††				23.3††				19.7††				29.6††

n – Population
NR – Clients who were judged as not requiring services.
P/S – P are clients deemed to require the service, S are clients actually served.
* – Percentage of clients judged as requiring the service.
† – Percentage of clients judged as requiring the service who are actually receiving the service.
†† – Percentage of facility type clients actually receiving the service.

pattern tends to be that those who are the most severely impaired, and, hence, also in most need of habilitation services, are those for whom services are least likely to be provided.

This raises the philosophical and moral dilemma of to whom services should be provided. Should services be provided to those for whom the greatest gain can be expected or to those with the greatest need for services? Without consciously addressing the issue, the "service system" primarily has opted for the former course. Thus, the potential of the most severely impaired is seriously restricted. Consequently, in line with our formulation of normalization in the broader sense, the potential for normalization of lower functioning individuals is limited. This issue warrants a much closer examination in practical as well as philosophical terms.

When service provision is compared across different placement types, the proportion of clients being provided with required services in small care facilities and in-home placements is generally lower than that in state hospitals and large care facilities. Furthermore, the perception of service need in in-home placements and small care facilities tends to be lower than in state hospitals and large care facilities, even when controlling for client functioning level.

When small care facilities and in-home placements are compared, with the exception of behavior therapy, a greater proportion of clients in small care facilities receive services in comparison to those in in-home placement.

The service provided most frequently for in-home placements is supportive counseling. Even so, the level of provision of this service is lower than that provided in large and small care facilities, but generally higher than that provided in state hospitals. The comparatively high rate of utilization of supportive counseling can be, at least in part, attributed to the fact that parent counseling is included. Parental involvement with the disabled person is higher in in-home placement, and hence, there is greater need for parent counseling.

When service patterns are viewed in conjunction with placement patterns, the greatest proportion of developmentally disabled clients (89.3%) are placed in settings in which the least amount of service is provided. It is evident that an adequate community service network has not yet been developed (Grossman and Rowitz, 1973). Supportive counseling seems to be an exception to this observation, but even here, the service level is low. What is clearly required is problem- and function-targeted specialized services. Hospitals and large care facilities are providing these services at a substantially higher level than are small care facilities and in-home placements.

As our earlier work suggested, there is a great deal of variation within different placement types (Bjaanes and Butler, 1974). These differences are not taken into account in this analysis. There are clear differences, however, between different placement types with a significantly smaller proportion of clients in in-home placement and small care facilities receiving required services than there are in state hospitals and large care facilities.

When these findings are viewed from our broader perspective of normalization, it seems that environmental normalization requirements *may* be being met in small care facilities, and in in-home placement; however, elements of client normalization are clearly lacking in these types of placement.

State hospitals and large care facilities may be less normalized in the environmental sense; however, they provide a substantially greater level of services to clients, and thus, at least in part, provide a greater potential for client normalization. Because both aspects of normalization must be achieved for client development to be fully maximized, state hospitals and large care facilities have significant deficiencies in environmental normalization. State hospitals and large care facilities in general place a greater emphasis on the service component of client normalization, while in-home placement and small care facilities may have a greater emphasis on environmental normalization, although many are lacking the necessary services for client normalization.

These observations lead to two conclusions. First, clients who are placed in state hospitals and large care facilities are being provided with a greater basis for skill development, but do not have the normalized environment in which to exercise those skills. Clients placed in small care facilities and in-home placement may have the normalized environment, but they lack the direct services focusing on competence development. Both conditions create barriers to normalization in the broad sense. Problems with social behavior and deficient independent living skills are major factors in community placement failure (Schalock and Harper, 1978). Provision of habilitation programs focused on these problem areas can enhance the ability of individuals to adjust. In general, these services are not being provided to the extent they are needed in small care facilities and in-home placement. Thus, a major factor in enhancing adjustment is presently lacking in these service settings.

UTILIZATION OF THE COMMUNITY SERVICE NETWORK

To provide a normalizing environment, community care facilities must provide an environment that is enriched both with internal programs and external contact and exchange. That is, the facility must be *therapeutic* as opposed to being a custodial or maintaining facility (Bjaanes and Butler, 1974). If normalization procedures are lacking, a deprived environment will tend to develop, which will effectively hinder the client normalization process. This is particularly critical in small care facilities which, by virtue of size, must include external and social elements to approximate a normal environment. Isolation in small care facilities results in a social setting populated only by developmentally disabled persons, thus restricting the number of role models and experiences necessary for normalization to occur. If available role models are at the same functioning level as the client *and* a deprived environment exists due to limited community contact, the potential for client normalization is negligible and the facility is not fulfilling its normalization function.

To examine the utilization of the community service network, we utilized data obtained from a sample of community care facilities located in Southern California. A variety of community sources, including the Inland Counties Regional Center, the Riverside Mental Health Association, and the San Bernardino and Riverside Welfare Agencies, provided listings of community facilities with mentally retarded residents. A list of 171 care facilities was compiled, of which 11 refused to participate. One hundred and sixty interviews were completed in three counties: San Bernardino (86 facilities), Riverside (69 facilities), and Los Angeles (5 facilities). Fifty-three were located in rural areas, 91 in suburban areas, and 13 in urban locations. Facilities ranged in population size from one to 95 residents, with the modal facility housing from three to six clients. The age range for the total population was as follows: 634 clients were under the age of 18, 445 clients were between 19 and 44 years of age, 116 clients were between 45 and 64 years of age, and 24 clients were over the age 65.

In our analysis of these community care facilities, we found that careprovider interaction with clients varies with several important factors. Education influences both interaction and client opportunities more in small than large facilities. Careprovider experience and attitudes were critical across facility size. Although experience has a negative effect on the amount of interaction, therapeutic careprovider attitudes create environmental support for normalizing activities (Butler et al., 1975).

As shown in Table 4, the general tendency is for overall low participation by clients in community activities. Part of the existing variation is associated with the clients' functioning level; however, some variation is also associated with facility size and careprovider interaction. Although it might be expected that this interaction would be greater in small facilities, this was not the case because careprovider interaction is somewhat constant across size.

Many small care facilities result in isolation of clients from external activities, and it is here that interaction by the careprovider becomes critical. It is assumed that placing a developmentally disabled client in a smaller facility is a normalizing panacea. Careful assessment of careprovider effects on client opportunities, however, becomes a factor in this situation. Apparently, in larger facilities, such interaction may be mediated by the increased availability of additional staff, or increased inter-client contacts. The larger facility provides more opportunities for the client without reference to specific careprovider

Table 4. Number of community programs utilized by facility

Total number of programs*			Total number of programs, excluding medical†		
Number of programs*	Number of facilities	Percentage of facilities	Number of programs	Number of facilities	Percentage of facilities
0	0	0.0	0	13	8.3
1	1	0.6	1	9	5.8
2	10	6.4	2	35	22.4
3	17	10.9	3	33	21.1
4	26	16.7	4	28	17.9
5	30	19.2	5	23	14.7
6	29	18.6	6	7	4.4
7	23	14.7	7	8	5.1
8	9	5.8	8	0	0.0
9	9	5.8			
10	2	1.3			
11	0	0.0			
Total	156			156	

$\bar{x} = 5.3$ $\bar{x} = 3.2$
$\sigma = 2.0$ $\sigma = 1.8$

* Total number possible = 11.
† Total number possible = 8.

characteristics. This demonstrates that for the small facility to provide an equivalent environment to the large facility, careprovider qualifications are paramount.

As a result of this study, several generalizations are clearly indicated:

1. There are substantial differences in the utilization of community agencies, services, and programs by community care facilities.

Generally, interaction and exchange with the community is limited. The size of the sample and the wide geographical dispersion indicate that this may be, in fact, a general characteristic of small care facilities as they are presently staffed and operated.

2. Variation in utilization of community agencies, services, and programs by community care facilities is associated with education and previous experience of the service providers, location of facility, size of facility, and characteristics of the surrounding neighborhood.
3. Larger facilities, by and large, are more likely to utilize agencies, services, and programs and thus seem to be closer to the objective of client normalization and developing social competence than are smaller facilities.

Because the above factors have a bearing on service utilization rates, the possibility of programmatic intervention that might substantially affect the overall function of community care facilities in terms of providing a truly normalizing environment is clearly indicated. Frequently, present zoning regulations force the location of facilities to rural and semi-industrial areas that tend to isolate residents. Frequently, little attention has been paid to the qualifications of the service providers. It has often been assumed, without carefully assessing the internal programs available and the extent of utilization of external community resources, that placing a developmentally disabled person in a community care facility is equivalent to providing a normalizing environment. Our data show otherwise. This study quite clearly demonstrates that if community care facilities are to provide normalizing environments, attention must be paid to the location, qualifications of service providers, and the nature and extent of internal programs and exchange with the community and utilization of community programs available for client normalization.

4. It cannot and should not be assumed that a community care facility is *a priori* a normalizing environment. That assumption is much too likely to result in a shift from larger total institutions to smaller, dispersed community-based total institutions.

A custodial or maintaining facility that has few or no internal and external programs to facilitate the client normalization process can be considered just as much a total institution as any large state institution. For a facility to be considered as therapeutic and enhancing client normalization, internal and external programs must be planned, implemented, and evaluated.

Our research suggests the following policy implications, which probably are generally applicable to all community care facilities:

1. Since "normalization" seems to be an exception rather than the rule, research and evaluation using specific outcome criteria measures of client normalization need to be implemented.

2. There is a need for "programmatic structuring" of community care facilities if "client normalization" is to become a reality.
3. Caregiver education and expertise evidently influence programmatic structuring in facilities; thus, training community care facility operators will have influence over time and will result in an increased utilization of community care programs and services and an associated tendency toward normalization.
4. Facilities located in more highly urbanized parts of the metropolis (e.g., the central area) offer more in the way of community contact. Currently, urban areas probably are better for enhancing the client normalization process.
5. Larger community care facilities (over seven clients) seem to have a broader range of contact with community services and programs and, thus, there may be a "size" factor impelling larger community care operators to utilize extended community resources.

CONCLUSIONS

Clients living in a community care facility must utilize community opportunities to participate in outside normalizing activities. If not, the experience of the facility environment itself probably is not great enough to support the client normalization process. Our data show that in small facilities, opportunities are not systematically utilized, and that wide interaction with external settings is critically absent. Many small facilities are not providing the client those activities considered necessary for individual development, and in effect are creating socially isolated total institutions within the community.

It can no longer be assumed that a small facility is necessarily more normalizing in and of itself. Perhaps some optimal mass population size exists between the total institution and the small, isolated community facility. The integration of such facilities into the community should take into account the additional factors of care facility population size, the effects of careprovider education, caregivers' attitudes and interaction, and previous experience with client normalizing opportunities for developmentally disabled clients.

Given the differences between different placement types and client characteristics, it can be assumed that different placement types may be appropriate for various client types. At present, however, there are few longitudinal studies exploring relationships between placement characteristics and client development. There are no studies systematically examining the differential impact of environmental versus client normalization for different client types. Nor are there any studies systematically examining client development when both criteria for normalization are used. Longitudinal studies must be conducted taking into account client characteristics, development, and adjustment, *and* the environment in which they are placed. That is, placement, services, and client attributes must be systematically studied in relationship to each other. Such studies must address both environmental normalization *and* client normalization concurrently.

REFERENCES

Baller, W. R. A study of the present social status of a group of adults who, when they were in elementary schools, were classified as mentally deficient. *Genetic Psychology*. Monograph 18, June, 1936.

Bank-Mikkelsen, N. E. A metropolitan area in Denmark: Copenhagen. In R. B. Kugel and W. Wolfensberger (Eds.), *Changing patterns in residential services for the mentally retarded.* Washington, D.C.: President's Committee on Mental Retardation, 1969.

Bennet, L., & Rudolph, L. Changes in direction of hostility related to incarceration and treatment. *Journal of Clinical Psychology,* 1960, *16(4),* 408–418.

Bjaanes, A. T., Butler, E. W., & Kelly, B. R. Placement type and client functional levels as factors in provision of services aimed at increasing adjustment. In R. H. Bruininks (Ed.), *Deinstitutionalization and community adjustment of mentally retarded people.* Washington, D.C.: American Association of Mental Deficiency, 1981.

Bjaanes, A. T. *The client centered evaluation model: Final report.* State of California, 1976.

Bjaanes, A. T. & Butler, E. W. Environmental variation in community care facilities for the mentally retarded. *American Journal of Mental Deficiency,* 1974, *78,* 429–439.

Browning, P. L. Several issues in mental retardation: A needed perspective? (Working paper No. 81). Eugene, Oregon: Rehabilitation Research and Training Center in Mental Retardation. Oregon University, 1975.

Butler, E. W. & Bjaanes, A. T. A typology of community care facilities and differential normalization outcomes. In P. Mittler (Ed.), *Research to practice in mental retardation,* (Vol. 1). Baltimore: University Park Press, 1977.

Butler, E. W., & Bjaanes, A. T. A model for the evaluation of alternative community care facilities. Unpublished paper, 1978.

Butler, E. W., Bjaanes, A. T., & Hofacre, S. The normalization process and the utilization of community agencies, services, and programs by community care facilities. Unpublished paper, 1975.

Butterfield, E. C. The role of environmental factors in the treatment of institutionalized mental retardates. In A. A. Baumeister (Ed.), *Mental retardation: Appraisal, education and rehabilitation.* Chicago: Aldine Publishing Company, 1967.

Day, D., & Lebrato, M. T. The analysis of rated competence and the classification of Operation PINpoint clients. In B. Kelly (Ed.), *Operation PINpoint; Part Two.* Sacramento: State of California, Department of Health, 1978.

Dentler, R. A., & Mackler, B. The socialization of institutional retarded children. *Journal of Health and Human Behavior,* 1961, *2,* 243–252.

Edgerton, R. B. *The cloak of competence.* Berkeley: University of California Press, 1967.

Eyman, R. K., O'Connor, G., Tarjan, G., & Justice, R. S. Factors determining residential placement of mentally retarded children. *American Journal of Mental Deficiency,* 1972, *76(6),* 692–698.

Farber, B. *Mental retardation: Its social context and social consequences.* Boston: Houghton Mifflin Company, 1968.

Fram, J. The right to be retarded — Normally. *Mental Retardation,* 1974, *12(6),* 32.

Goffman, E. *Asylums.* Garden City, N. J.: Anchor Books, 1961.

Grossman, H. J., & Rowitz, L. A community approach to services for the retarded. In R. K. Eyman, C. E. Meyers, and G. Tarjan (Eds.), *Sociobehavioral studies in mental retardation.* American Association on Mental Deficiency Monograph 1, 1973.

Kelly, B., et al., *Operation PINpoint: Part Two.* Sacramento: State of California, Department of Health, 1978.

Kennedy, R. J. R. *The social adjustment of morons in a Connecticut city.* Mansfield Sauthbury Training Schools, Social Service Dept., State Office Building, 1948.

Lyle, J. G. The effect of an institutional environment upon the verbal development of institutional children: I. Verbal intelligence. *Journal of Mental Deficiency Research,* 1959, *3,* 122–128, and *4,* 10–13, 14–23.

McKay, B. E. A study of IQ changes in a group of girls paroled from a state school for mental defectives. *American Journal of Mental Deficiency,* 1942, *46,* 496–500.

Moore, H., Butler, E. W., & Bjaanes, A. T. Careprovider characteristics and utilization of community opportunities for mentally retarded clients. Unpublished paper, 1976.

Mundy, L. Environmental influence on intellectual function as measured by intelligence tests. *British Journal of Medical Psychology,* 1957, *30,* 194–201.

Nirje, B. The normalization principle and its human management implications. In R. B. Kugel and W. Wolfensberger (Eds.), *Changing patterns in residential services for the mentally retarded*. Washington, D.C.: President's Committee on Mental Retardation, 1969.

O'Connor, G. *Home is a good place*. American Association on Mental Deficiency Monograph 11, 1976.

O'Connor, G., & Justice, R. S. National patterns in the development of community group homes for the mentally retarded. Paper presented at the 97th Annual Meeting of the American Association on Mental Deficiency, 1973.

Rhoades, C., & Browning, P. Normalization at what price? *Mental Retardation,* 1977, *15*(2), 24.

Schalock, R. L., & Harper, R. S. Placement from community-based mental retardation programs: How well do clients do? *American Journal of Mental Deficiency,* 1978, *83*(3), 240–247.

Skeels, H. M., & Dye, H. A. A study of the effects of differential stimulation on mentally retarded children. *Proceedings of the American Association of Mental Deficiency,* 1939, *44,* 114–136.

Stedman, D. J., & Eichorn, D. A comparison of the growth and development of institutionalized and homereared mongoloids during infancy and early childhood. *American Journal of Mental Deficiency,* 1964, *69,* 291–301.

Tizard, J. *Community services for the mentally retarded*. New York: Oxford University Press, 1964.

Wolf, L. C., & Whitehead, P. C. The decision to institutionalize retarded children: Comparison of individually matched groups. *Mental Retardation,* 1975, *13*(5), 3–11.

Wolfensberger, W. *Normalization: The principle of normalization in human services*. Toronto: National Institute on Mental Retardation, 1972.

Woloshin, A. A., Tardi, G., & Tobin, A. The institutionalization of mentally retarded men through the use of a halfway house. *Journal of Mental Retardation,* 1966, *4*(3), 21.

Environment, Characteristics, and Effectiveness of Community Residences for Mentally Retarded Persons

Barry Willer and
James Intagliata

Deinstitutionalization of the mentally retarded population is occurring and has been occurring at a rapid pace (Bradley, 1978). The ideology of deinstitutionalization includes reduction in admissions to public institutions, development of alternate community residential services, return to the community of residents who are capable of living in a less restrictive environment, and reform of institutions (Willer, Scheerenberger, and Intagliata, 1978). Support for deinstitutionalization has come from parents, professionals, and the courts. The underlying theme is that retarded persons will be happier and better adjusted in community settings than institutions, and that the environment of the community setting will encourage more adaptive, normalized behavior. However, research on the adjustment of retarded individuals to community residential programs and the impact of the social environment of the various types of community placement options has been scant.

One follow-up study of formerly institutionalized residents now in community residences found that residents definitely preferred community living over living in the institution (Scheerenberger and Felsenthal, 1977). The same residents indicated that what they liked most was the newfound freedom offered by the community setting. The freedom to decorate their rooms as desired, freedom to go outside when they wanted, and freedom to select their own clothes were all new to these individuals. Many residences, however, did not offer the level of freedom desired. Many residents had to be accompanied on trips, some had no personal allowance, and few had any say in selecting their jobs. Many were required to observe strict bedtime and working time schedules, and some of the facilities studied were found to be inflexible in their well-established routines.

This study was assisted under contract #50P10568/2 from HEW Region II Office.

The importance of the physical and social environment of the individual community residences has been demonstrated in other studies as well. Bjaanes and Butler (1974) studied a small sample of community residences but found major differences in time-use patterns and characteristics of behavior. In general, they found that variations in behavior were more a function of the environmental climate of the home than sex of the resident, location of facility, or type of facility. In this and several later studies, however, the authors concluded that larger community residences were more likely to encourage "normalized" behavior (Butler and Bjaanes, 1977, 1978).

Landesman-Dwyer, Berkson, and Romer (1979) also studied the behavior of mentally retarded residents in community residences, although their study focused more on friendship and affiliation. They found larger residential facilities had more social interaction but interactions were no more intense than in smaller facilities. They also found that resident characteristics were not related to social behavior, although homogeneity of resident characteristics within the home was directly related.

The above studies provide some indication of the relative importance of the environment in allowing or reinforcing certain behaviors for residents. They stop short, however, of discussing the relationship of environmental factors to adjustment of the individual to the residence. A problem in studies of this nature is determining what constitutes adjustment or for that matter, what constitutes normalized behavior. Nihira and Nihira (1975) examined variations in judged and reported normalized behavior from the perspective of board and care and foster caregivers. The findings suggested that the primary concern of caregivers was with the ability of residents to care for themselves and to help with domestic chores. Caregivers were also concerned with residents' abilities to acquire new skills and to develop approved interpersonal relations, but these were judged less critical than gains in self-care.

In a study of adaptive behavior changes of residents in community residences, Aanes and Moen (1976) found that the most prevalent changes occurred in self-care (eating, cleanliness, appearance, care of clothing, language, and kitchen duties). No change was found in most other areas either because the residents already were functioning at a high level or there was little effort expended to teach these new skills. Brown and Guard (1979) found that when autonomous behavior of retarded residents was encouraged in nursing homes, it was most evident in areas that eased the burden of caregivers and promoted smooth functioning of the organization (e.g., personal hygiene). Autonomy of residents in other areas, however (e.g., freedom to interact with members of the opposite sex, freedom to participate in community activities), was rarely encouraged. It is probably much more than a coincidence that adaptive behavior changes occurred in those areas judged to be the most critical by careproviders in the Nihira and Nihira (1975) study.

The studies of Aanes and Moen (1976) and others have suggested that adaptive behavior of residents in community residences shows a general improvement over time. The Scheerenberger and Felsenthal (1977) study cited above reported that residents were generally more satisfied with living in the community residences when compared with living in the institution. Eyman and Call (1977), however, provided one of the few comparison studies on institutions and community residences on actual changes in adaptive behavior. This study focused on maladaptive behavior in particular because of the recognized relationship between maladaptive behavior and reinstitutionalization (Windle, Stewart, and Brown, 1961; Moen, Bogen, and Aanes, 1975). Eyman and Call found a much higher prevalence of behavior problems in the institutions than in the community residences. Additionally, they found that the profoundly retarded were more likely to exhibit maladaptive behavior than were mildly or moderately retarded persons.

The few studies of behavior in community residences give cause for optimism. It seems that individuals in community residences are generally better off than their institutionalized counterparts. These studies are suggestive of the importance of the environment of the community residence for encouraging adaptive or normalized behavior although the precise characteristics of these environments that produce change in behavior are still unclear. In one of the few studies of residential characteristics and behavior change, Eyman, Demaine, and Lei (1979) compared changes in adaptive behavior of residents in community residences with resident characteristics (age, IQ, etc.) and environment ratings of the residence based on the Program Analysis of Service Systems procedures (Wolfensberger and Glenn, 1975). The results supported the assertion that certain normalization principles are related to the development of retarded individuals. In fact, five of six factors of normalization (administrative policies, environmental blending of facility with neighborhood, location and proximity of services, comfort and appearance) were found to contribute significantly to growth in adaptive behavior. The exception was ideology-related administration (public education, administrative control, manpower development), and this was assumed to be negatively related to change in behavior because it took staff away from direct contact with residents.

The PASS procedure employed by Eyman et al. (1979) tends to concentrate more on physical than social characteristics of the environment. Thus, although the finding that assimilation of the residence within the surrounding community may be important to individual adjustment, it does not consider other aspects of the environment that may serve to negate the usefulness of assimilation such as staff attitudes toward access of residents to the surrounding neighborhood or the importance placed on freedom and growth.

With respect to staff attitudes, the study by Brown and Guard (1979) is informative. In their research on the treatment environment for retarded persons in nursing homes they found that those homes that were characterized by greater resident autonomy and activity were staffed by individuals who were more likely to approve of admitting retarded residents. Thus, attitudes that staff have toward residents can clearly affect the degree to which the residential environment is oriented to enhance resident adaptive behavior.

The current study involved a comparison of the relative effectiveness of three types of community residences: community residential facilities (e.g., group homes, hostels), private proprietary homes for adults, and health-related facilities (nursing homes). Comparison of these residences is also made on factors of the social environment as measured by the Community Oriented Programs Environment Scale (COPES). This scale, developed by Moos (1974), measures such dimensions as relationships (involvement, support), treatment programs (practical orientation, personal problem orientation, anger and aggression), and system maintenance (order and organization, program clarity and staff control). The COPES was developed for community programs for the mentally ill but as reported by Pankratz (1975) it is suitable for use with community residences for the mentally retarded.

A second part of this study involved a detailed analysis of specific environmental factors associated with individual adjustment in community residences. Persons placed in private proprietary homes and health-related facilities were not included in this analysis so that discussion could focus on a single residence type: community residential facilities. The purpose of this second part of the research is to identify environmental factors that relate to effectiveness within a relatively homogeneous group of residential programs.

METHOD

The study involved a mailed questionnaire survey of all individuals institutionalized for at least 1 year and released from one of six institutions in New York State. Release had to occur during 1973 through 1976. In this particular study, only the results of follow-up of individuals released to community residential facilities from five of the six institutions are included. Individuals from the remaining institution were followed up using personal interviews of individuals, their careproviders, and their natural families. These interviews served as the basis for the questionnaire sent to careproviders in this study. Only those items found to be reliable and useful in interviews were included in the questionnaires. In addition, all questionnaire items were forced choice with response options based on interview results. Results of questionnaires sent to natural families and family care-providers are discussed in other papers and are not discussed here.

The total number of questionnaires sent to careproviders of individuals placed in community residences was 312. The total number returned was 190, or 61%. Many individuals were released to the same community residence; thus the total sample of 190 individuals represents 70 different residences. Of these, 40 were classified as community residential facilities (CRFs), 14 private proprietary homes for adults (PPHAs) and 6 health-related facilities (HRFs).

A CRF is typically a small group home operated by a not-for-profit organization receiving the majority of its funding directly from the state office of mental retardation and through disability (SSI) pensions to individuals. These facilities do vary a great deal in size and purpose. Some are short-term training homes and others are intended as permanent residences. Many have live-in house parents and a sizeable group have a shift-staff arrangement. The level of supervision varies with the characteristics of residents, but it is generally less than that of an institution but greater than that of a PPHA. Previous papers have identified the fact that these homes are generally fairly selective of new admissions and have higher functioning clients than do family care or natural family homes (Willer, Intagliata, and Wicks, 1979; Intagliata, Willer, and Wicks, 1979).

PPHAs generally have nonretarded residents and most frequently serve the formerly institutionalized mentally ill. Retarded persons, in fact, represent a very small percentage of the total population of PPHAs in New York State. Funding for PPHAs comes from disability (SSI) pensions and the homes are generally run on a profit basis. To achieve this, there is generally a very low level of supervision. As well, PPHAs cannot afford to deal with individuals with major behavior problems, physical disorders, or other handicaps.

The third type of community residence is the nursing home, or HRF. HRFs, as the name suggests, generally serve persons in need of more intensive supervision usually requiring skilled nursing care; of course the majority of residents in HRFs are not retarded. The funding is provided through residents' disability (SSI) pensions and medical/nursing services are funded through Medicaid.

The questionnaire was directed to the staff member of the residence who knew the resident best. The time of completion was generally about 2 years following the date of discharge from the institution. Questions asked were all forced choice and included descriptive information about the resident and his or her adjustment problems. A list of possible problems was presented, based on the pilot interviews, and the respondent was asked to check those that were a problem when the resident first arrived at the residence. Respondents were then asked to indicate which problems still existed for this resident. Other questions dealt with the resident's use of time, activities attended, use of community services, need for services and an assessment of travel skills. To complete the questionnaire several scales were included: 1) an institutional behavior rating form, which had been used to assess the resident prior to release from the institution, 2) selected subscales of the Devereux Adolescent Behavior Rating Scale (Spivack, Haines, and Spotts, 1967), and 3) the COPES (Moos, 1974).

Further information was gathered from individual resident records from the institutions. This included prerelease scores on the institutional behavior rating form, the resident's age, functional level and IQ.

In an effort to supplement the COPES data obtained on the questionnaires, we obtained additional COPES ratings from institutional follow-up social workers (SWs) for a subsample of 24 residential facilities (4 PPHAs, 5 HRFs and 15 CRFs).

Multiple stepwise regression analysis was used to identify specific environmental factors that contributed to success in community residential facilities. Outcome factors included development of self-care skills, control of maladaptive behavior, community living skills, and social support. Each factor was assessed using part or all of the various outcome instruments. Independent variables in the analysis were individual resident characteristics and factors of the social environment as measured by the COPES. Individual characteristics such as age, level of functioning, and pre-release behavior functioning were entered into the regression analysis first. Characteristics of the social environment were significantly related to individual adjustment only if they accounted for a significant amount of additional independent outcome variance.

RESULTS

Comparison of Community Residences

In discussing the results, in particular, the comparison of residential facilities, the reader needs to be reminded that this study focused exclusively on those residents who were released from public institutions for the mentally retarded. Comparisons and descriptions of the total population of residents in these community residences is not possible on the basis of this study. The results are limited to a presentation of results and descriptions of deinstitutionalized residents only.

Discharges to CRFs had a median age of 46.6 compared with 63.1 for PPHAs and 68.8 for HRFs. Of those placed in CRFs, 70.5% were mildly/moderately retarded, and 29.5% were severely or profoundly retarded. Of those placed in PPHAs, 74.1% were mildly/ moderately retarded and 25.9% were severely/profoundly retarded. Finally, 60.9% of placements to HRFs were mild/moderate retardation and 39.1% were severely/profoundly retarded.

Table 1.   Percentage of individuals with deficits in specific behavior categories upon arrival at the community residence

Problem area	CRF	PPHA	HRF
Travel skills	56.9	75.9	85.7*
Dealing with emergencies	83.5	96.6	90.9
Use of telephone	62.4	62.1	90.9*
Meal preparation	85.3	87.9	100.0
Shopping	77.6	81.0	85.7
Money management	86.0	89.7	90.9
Self cleaning	30.3*	20.7	9.1
Bathroom skills	11.0	5.2	9.1
Destructive behavior	9.2	12.1	22.7*
Disobedience	23.9	17.2	31.8*

* Significant at $p < 0.05$ using χ^2 comparison.

Comparison of the populations of the three types of facilities prior to release on the behavior rating scale used by the institutions indicates that HRF residents were more likely to have problems of ambulation (44%), dressing (33%), anxiety (48%), authority relations (30%), and peer relations (55%). Individuals placed in CRFs were quite similar to those placed in PPHAs in all behavior categories measured by the scale with the exception that there was a slightly greater tendency toward problems of peer relations (20%) and relations with authorities (14%).

Table 1 presents a comparison of individuals in each of the three types of facilities on the specific skill deficits noted in the individuals upon first admission to the facility. Differences support the earlier comparison on the institutional behavior scale. Individuals placed in HRFs were more likely to have deficits in travel skills and use of the telephone. Presumably this related to the fact that individuals placed in HRFs were more likely to be nonambulatory. Individuals placed in HRFs were also more likely to exhibit behavior problems: destructive behavior and disobedience. Persons released to CRFs and PPHAs presented much the same deficits although individuals in CRFs were more likely to have self-care needs such as self-cleaning. Personal interview data indicated a high reliability of definition of deficits on all deficit categories although self-cleaning was more subject to the expectations of the type of residential facility. This would suggest that individuals in CRFs may not have more deficits in self-cleaning but rather may have greater expectations for self-cleaning than individuals placed in other types of facilities, namely PPHAs.

The average total number of residents in HRFs was 18.9, which is similar to the average in PPHAs (18.5), but significantly greater than the average in CRFs (10.7). The staff in the HRF tended to be better educated and had an average age of 48. Staff in the CRF

Table 2.   Percentage of individuals attending activities within the past 3 months

Activity	CRF	PPHA	HRF
Ballgame	40.4*	15.5	4.3
Zoo	44.4*	25.9	0.0
Park	74.3*	55.2	60.9
Swimming	35.8*	6.9	0.0
Amusement park	35.8*	8.6	0.0

* Significant at $p < 0.05$ using χ^2 analysis.

Table 3.   Percentage of individuals receiving special services within the past 3 months

Services	CRF	PPHA	HRF
Physical therapy	12.0	8.8	39.1*
Counseling	74.0	73.7	95.7*
Speech therapy	18.0	14.0	8.7
Special bus service	28.0	42.1	82.6*
Recreational activities	96.0	94.7	90.9

* Significant at $p < 0.05$ using χ^2 analysis.

were more likely to be college graduates than those in the PPHA, but both staff groups had an average age of 36.

Residents placed in CRFs were more likely to take part in scheduled daytime activities outside the residence, such as sheltered workshop or school (78.9%). Individuals placed in PPHAs were more likely to have outside daytime activities than those in HRFs (62.1% vs. 26.1%). Similarly, Table 2 demonstrates that CRF placements were more likely to attend unstructured outside activities such as sporting, cultural, and recreational events.

Table 3 presents a comparison of the three types of facilities on the professional services received by the individual during the past 3 months. Individuals placed in HRFs were more likely to have received physical therapy, counseling, and special transportation services. Individuals placed in PPHAs were more likely to have received special bus services than individuals in CRFs. A surprisingly high percentage of individuals in all facilities received counseling and recreational activities; however, reliability checks on these two items indicated that there was inconsistency across staff on how these two service items were defined.

A final descriptive comparison of the three facility types was based on the Community Oriented Programs Environment Scale. Table 4 presents the standardized mean scores for each facility type and is based on staff reports. The only subscale for which there is significant difference is Practical Orientation, which measures the extent to which the social environment of the facility orients the individual toward release from the program. CRFs were higher on practical orientation and the difference can be traced to two specific items: 1) residents are expected to make detailed specific plans for the future, and 2) residents are taught specific new skills in the program.

Table 4.   COPES ratings by direct care staff by placement facility type

Subscale	CRF	PPHA	HRF
Involvement	57.3	45.3	52.4
Support	57.2	56.0	51.8
Spontaneity	62.7	60.8	59.9
Autonomy	49.8	48.3	45.1
Practical orientation	46.8*	35.6	34.9
Personal problem orientation	54.0	53.4	52.1
Anger and aggression	49.9	50.9	47.6
Order and organization	57.1	58.0	62.6
Program clarity	55.1	52.2	46.7
Staff control	47.6	47.8	40.9

* Significant at $p < 0.05$ using ANOVA procedures.

Table 5.   COPES ratings by institutional follow-up workers by placement facility type

Subscale	CRF	PPHA	HRF
Involvement	50.6	40.3	57.1*
Support	49.1	48.3	55.8
Spontaneity	55.2	55.3	62.0
Autonomy	41.4	44.7	42.5
Practical orientation	43.1*	34.7	33.5
Personal problem orientation	45.1	46.0	47.1
Anger and aggression	48.5	39.8	40.5
Order and organization	58.0	55.8	64.3
Program clarity	45.7	48.0	56.3
Staff control	54.7*	50.8	31.8

* Significant at $p < 0.05$ using ANOVA procedures.

Further comparison of the three facilities is based on the subsample of homes assessed by institutional follow-up workers (SWs) and is presented in Table 5. Ratings of SWs were, on the whole, lower than those of direct care staff; however, patterns of ratings were similar. Again, differences across most subscales were not significant, suggesting that variability within types of facilities was greater than the differences between. Significant differences were found, however, on the subscales of involvement and staff control. Involvement measures how active residents are in the day-to-day functioning of their programs, and was perceived as being higher in HRFs. Staff control assesses the extent to which staff use disciplinary measures to keep residents under necessary control, and was perceived as greater in CRFs than in PPHAs or HRFs.

The nature of funding and operating principles suggest that CRFs should be more effective at integrating residents into the community following release from the institution. Table 6 presents the level of travel skills currently enjoyed by the residents placed in each of the three facility types. Residents of CRFs seem to be trained or given the opportunity to use public transportation much more so than residents of PPHAs. In fact, the data in Table 6 suggest that residents in PPHAs are more likely to be limited to their own neighborhood, whereas in CRFs and HRFs those who are capable are more likely to be encouraged to use public transportation.

Table 6.   Percentage of individuals by level of independent transportation skills by type of placement

Level of transportation	CRF	PPHA	HRF
Public transportation anywhere	12.0	8.6	0.0
Public transportation to familiar place	50.9*	32.8	13.0
Walking within neighborhood	21.3	37.8*	4.3
Walking within restricted area	12.0	19.0	69.6
Nonambulatory	3.7	1.7	13.0

* Significant at $p < 0.05$ using χ^2 analysis.

Table 7. Percent of individuals scoring below or above the norm on selected subscales of Devereux Behavior Scale by facility type

Subscale	CRF		PPHA		HRF	
	Below	Above	Below	Above	Below	Above
Defiant-resistive	33.0	14.7	67.2*	10.3	43.5	21.7
Domineering-sadistic	27.8	22.2	56.9*	18.9	34.8	21.7
Heterosexual interest	13.9	8.3	53.5*	1.7	26.1	4.4
Hyperactive expansive	40.4	14.7	67.2*	5.2	43.5	13.0
Emotional control	22.0	24.8	37.9*	18.9	34.8	34.8
Need approval, dependency	9.2	41.3	34.5*	24.1	13.0	52.2
Inability to delay gratification	23.9	31.2	55.2*	20.7	21.7	39.1

* Significant at $p < 0.05$ using χ^2 analysis.

A second comparison of effectiveness of the three facility types is based on the Devereux Adolescent Behavior Rating Scale. For each subscale of the Devereux, individuals who scored significantly (one standard deviation) below the norm are considered to be restricted or stunted with respect to the behaviors in question. Individuals who scored significantly above the norm are judged to be unrestricted and, in fact, a behavior problem. These data are presented in Table 7.

Considerably more individuals in PPHAs were below the norm on the majority of subscales suggesting strongly that the PPHA represents a restrictive environment encouraging inhibition and stunting of behavior. Individuals in the CRF and HRF displayed fairly similar patterns of behavior despite differences between the types of individuals placed in the facility. As well, a comparison of Devereux scores by level of disability across all facilities (not presented) revealed strikingly similar patterns suggesting that the Devereux behavior scores are not a result of differences between individuals placed in the facilities as much as they are the result of the demands and social environment of the facility.

A problem with the use of the Devereux Scale to compare the effectiveness of facilities is that no prerelease data are available and the comparison is based strictly on postrelease differences. To counteract this deficiency we collected descriptions of residents' problems at admission (in a retrospective manner) and at the time the questionnaire was completed. The admission problem frequencies were presented earlier. Table 8 presents the percentage of individuals who had a problem or deficiency at admission, but no longer had the problem 2 years later. This index of effectiveness was used and validated in an earlier study of family care homes (Intagliata et al., 1979). Table 8 presents the percent of individuals by facility type who no longer had the particular deficit. Please note that some problem areas, namely, self-cleaning, bathroom skills, and destructive behavior, were infrequent at admission and were not included in this comparison because of very small sample sizes.

The results of Table 8 point directly to the fact that CRFs are much more effective at teaching social competence skills such as travel, use of telephone, and meal preparation. This is in keeping with the hypothesis that CRFs are more oriented toward teaching new skills and are more highly staffed to accomplish this task. PPHAs were more effective at eliminating disobedience, giving the impression of greater control over aberrant behavior. The data presented earlier suggest that this control may, in fact, lead to stunting of behavior and reduced emotional expression. The PPHAs should be given credit, however, for encouraging growth in some social competence areas, namely, shopping and money management.

Table 8. Percent of individuals who overcame a particular problem area by facility type

Problem area	CRF	PPHA	HRF
Travel skills	62.9*	31.8	0.0
Dealing with emergencies	18.7	10.7	10.0
Use of telephone	50.0*	16.7	30.0
Meal preparation	32.3*	3.9	0.0
Shopping	47.0	46.8	5.5*
Money management	32.6	30.8	10.0
Disobedience	70.4	100.0*	85.7

* Significant at $p < 0.05$ using χ^2 analysis.

In a previous study of family care homes (Intagliata et al., 1979) this measure of effectiveness was found to correlate highly with judged effectiveness of family care homes by follow-up social workers. In addition, high quality family care homes were found to be more effective at teaching social competence skills such as travel, use of telephone, and meal preparation, whereas low quality homes were more effective at eliminating disobedience. The consistency of these findings with those of the comparison of PPHAs and CRFs suggests that this measure of effectiveness is valid.

Placement in either the CRF or PPHA appears quite arbitrary beyond the decision to place slightly older clients in PPHAs. It seems, however, that individuals placed in CRFs are more likely to learn social competence skills and to enjoy a less restrictive environment. On the other hand, there is still high variability within CRFs indicating that placement in a CRF does not guarantee success. To determine factors of success in CRFs we used a multiple regression analysis of environmental and individual characteristics. The dependent factors were a development of self-care skills, control of maladaptive behavior, development of community living skills, and social support.

Factors of Success

Individuals placed from the institution to CRFs tended to be quite capable of handling self-care needs, although there were clearly greater deficiencies in behavioral functioning and social relations, and most were deficient in community living skills. Despite this, some individuals in CRFs showed demonstrative change in some or all areas of adaptation, and others remained the same or regressed. In general, gains made in one area of functioning correlated positively with gains made in other areas. In addition, individuals placed in certain homes progressed well regardless of individual characteristics. Some homes were less effective. All individuals placed in these homes showed little, if any, progress. The social environment of the home seems to play an important role in facilitating or inhibiting the residents' level of community adjustment.

Factors of the social setting that were examined in the study included each of the COPES subscales, size of home, and location (rural versus urban). Analysis of those factors most associated with gains in self-care skills is presented in Table 9. The major determinant of success in self-care was the skill level of the individual prior to release from the institution. Environmental factors also played a significant role, once individual characteristics were controlled for. The number of residents in the home was negatively related to self-care skills whereas practical orientation (goal orientation) was positively related. Those CRFs with fewer residents and more emphasis on setting goals and teaching practical living skills showed more success in self-care.

The analysis of factors of success in control of maladaptive behavior yielded similar results (Table 10). The major predictor of appropriate behavioral functioning was the

Table 9.   Predictors of self-care skills in CRF residents

Factor	Percent of variance explained	F	df	p
Initial skill level	30.5	33.39	(1,76)	<0.001
Number of residents	11.2	14.21	(1,76)	<0.001
Practical orientation	2.0	2.59	(1,76)	<0.11

Table 10.   Predictors of maladaptive behavior control in CRF residents

Factor	Percent of variance explained	F	df	p
Initial control level	24.0	24.0	(1,76)	<0.001
Resident age	7.0	6.4	(1,76)	<0.01
Anger expression	8.0	9.84	(1,76)	<0.002
Autonomy	2.8	3.66	(1,76)	<0.06

individual's behavior patterns prior to release. In addition, older residents were more likely to show gains in behavior control. Characteristics of the home environment also played an important role. Those CRFs that allowed and encouraged expression of disagreements and anger showed significantly greater success in controlling maladaptive behavior. Those CRFs that encouraged high levels of autonomy tended to have the most behavior problems.

The most gains made by residents of CRFs were made in the area of community living skills and access to community resources. This is probably as much a reflection of the orientation of the program as the needs of the residents. The multiple regression analysis of residents' community living skills at the time of follow-up demonstrated that both resident and environmental factors play a significant role on the development of community living proficiency (Table 11). Specifically, the major determinant of residents' proficiency in community living skills at follow-up was their skill level when first placed. Initial level of community living skills was positively correlated with community living skill level at follow-up ($F = 33.4$, $p < 0.001$). In addition, residents' level of intellectual functioning was also positively related to level of community living skills at follow-up ($F = 8.8$, $p < 0.004$). Mildly/moderately retarded residents were more likely to show positive change in community living skills than were severely/profoundly retarded residents.

Environmental characteristics of CRFs play a significant role in residents' development of community living skills, even after initial skill level and level of intellectual function are controlled for. Specifically, those CRFs that were located in urban settings ($F = 3.84$, $p < 0.05$) that put greater emphasis on teaching residents practical skills ($F = 2.5$, $p < 0.11$) and that encouraged more resident involvement in running the facility ($F = 4.2$, $p < 0.04$) showed significantly more success in facilitating community living skill learning.

A second measure of community living skills is use of community resources. An analysis of factors associated with expanded use of the community is presented in Table 12. Resident age was negatively related to use of the community indicating that younger residents are more likely to make use of the available community activities. Level of functioning of the individual was not related to use of the community. Important environmental factors included encouragement of resident involvement in the home (involvement) and an orientation toward development of practical living skills (practical orientation).

Table 11.   Predictors of community living skills in CRF residents

Factor	Percent of variance explained	F	df	p
Initial skill level	30.6	33.45	(1,76)	<0.001
Intellectual level	7.3	8.78	(1,76)	<0.004
Resident involvement	3.3	4.20	(1,76)	<0.04
Urban location	1.9	3.84	(1,76)	<0.05

Table 12.   Predictors of community resource use by CRF residents

Factor	Percent of variance explained	F	df	p
Resident age	11.4	9.78	(1,76)	<0.003
Resident involvement	5.7	5.17	(1,76)	<0.03
Practical orientation	4.8	4.61	(1,76)	<0.04

A final measure of resident adjustment is social relations, which is simply a measure of contact with family and contact with friends outside the CRF. Family and friends are generally viewed as providing a necessary social support network for the individual (Edgerton, 1967). The analysis of factors associated with development of a social network, presented in Table 13, suggests that younger residents are more likely to have social interaction, although the relationship between age and social interaction was not nearly as important as one would predict. Other individual characteristics were found to be even less important. Environmental factors were found to be generally more important than individual characteristics in predicting social interaction. Again, CRFs that emphasize practical living skills are clearly more successful at encouraging external social relations. In addition, smaller residences were more likely to encourage contact with friends and family.

Table 13.   Predictors of social interaction of CRF residents

Factor	Percent of variance explained	F	df	p
Resident age	6.4	5.13	(1,76)	<0.09
Practical orientation	9.8	8.71	(1,76)	<0.004
Number of residents	7.4	7.14	(1,76)	<0.009

DISCUSSION

The first part of this study concentrated on a comparison of health-related facilities (HRFs), private proprietary homes for adults (PPHAs) and community residential facilities (CRFs). There has been a tendency in the literature on community residential facilities to treat these facilities as homogeneous units when, in fact, they vary greatly in staffing structure and purpose (Baker, Seltzer, and Seltzer, 1974). Baker et al. provided one of the few available taxonomies of residential facilities. In the current study, PPHAs correspond roughly to the Baker et al. description of mixed group homes, which primarily serve the formerly hospitalized mentally ill and serve the mentally retarded as a minority population. These homes tend to be "boarding facilities" with emphasis placed on providing sheltered care rather than habilitation. In our study, PPHAs were all privately owned and operated.

HRFs include nursing homes and group homes for the elderly retarded and are comparable to Baker et al.'s description. Most of these facilities are protected settings where much is done for residents but they are closely bound to home with limited contact with the outside community. All HRFs in the current study served nonretarded persons, and retarded adults were again a minority population. These facilities are generally perceived as being more institution-like than other community residences for the mentally retarded.

Baker et al. divided the category of homes we call CRFs into small and larger group homes. We used a single classification because size did not seem to be a significant factor in placement decisions or type of program. The CRF, using the Baker et al. description, tends to place more emphasis on integration of the retarded within the community. These programs provide daily living experiences as similar as possible to those of nonretarded persons. They serve exclusively the mentally retarded. The homes tend to vary a great deal in purpose. Some are oriented toward providing training necessary for movement to a less restrictive setting, and others emphasize long-term placement in a normalized setting, with freedom to behave in a manner consistent with their capabilities.

These advance descriptions of the three types of community residences would suggest major differences in the type of resident to be placed in the facility, and the level of programming and behavior change for individuals placed there. These differences were noted in the present study, although perhaps not to the extent expected. Individuals placed in HRFs were more likely to have problems of ambulation, self-care, and relations with others. Individuals placed in PPHAs differed from those placed in CRFs only in average age and relations with others. There was no difference in all other behavior areas including level of functioning suggesting less than judicious use of these various placement options. An informal check of institutional placement staff supported this contention, suggesting that availability of a placement was more often the determining factor in placement choice than the specific needs of the individual.

Descriptions of the programs, staffing, and use of time within residences also varied across facilities although again, not to the extent that one would expect. CRFs tended to be smaller than PPHAs or HRFs and residents were more likely to be involved in structured daytime activities and unstructured recreational activities outside the residence. Residents of HRFs were more likely to receive specialized services, especially medically oriented services. Staff of CRFs and PPHAs tended to be younger than those of HRFs and the staff of CRFs were generally better educated than those in PPHAs.

Comparison of the three facilities on social environment using the COPES revealed small differences when ratings were made by direct care staff. These ratings indicated that CRFs were more generally oriented toward programs and behavior change (practical orientation). Differences were more demonstrable when COPES ratings were provided by institutional follow-up workers. These ratings indicated that HRFs provided residents with greater activity and participation in running the home (involvement). CRFs were seen as providing more programming (practical orientation) and discipline (staff control).

Comparison of residents on various measures of outcome indicated that residents in PPHAs were much more inhibited in behavior and were less trusting of staff. These residents were also less likely to be disobedient. Residents in CRFs were much more likely to learn new social skills especially those related to community adjustment (travel skills, use of the telephone, and meal preparation). HRF residents understandably showed the fewest advances.

A disappointing feature of the outcome comparison was that there was almost as much variation in effectiveness within CRFs as between CRFs and PPHAs. Some CRFs were found to be highly effective and tended to be effective with all residents placed there. Other CRFs were consistently ineffective at producing behavior change and many residents actually regressed. The second part of this study concentrated on factors of the social environment that were related to individual adjustment in CRFs.

Resident characteristics explained the greatest part of the variance in most adjustment indices examined. The analyses demonstrated, however, that particular characteristics of the CRF environments also played a significant role. Specifically, CRFs with fewer residents facilitated better self-care skills and more social interaction for their residents. CRFs that emphasized teaching practical living skills and moving residents to less restrictive settings facilitated better self-care skills, greater use of community resources and more social interaction for their residents. CRFs that encouraged residents to be active and to take responsibility for themselves and their CRF home (as opposed to CRFs with rigid, autocratic staff control) facilitated greater learning of community living skills and greater use of community resources. CRFs that allowed and encouraged residents to express their disagreements and anger openly facilitated significantly greater control of maladaptive behavior in their residents. Finally, CRFs located in urban rather than rural settings facilitated significantly greater progress in their residents' community living skills.

That certain factors of the social environment are important as determinants of behavior is no surprise. The absence, however, of major differences in effectiveness of programs having major differences in purpose and orientation suggests that we have not been entirely successful in developing effective environments. The range of quality in CRFs also attests to this fact. Given the results of the present study, what would the ideal community residence look like?

The ideal community residence would be small, with probably fewer than 10 residents. It would serve mentally retarded persons exclusively. The home would be clearly oriented toward teaching residents practical living skills. Each resident would have an individual habilitation plan with goals clearly spelled out. The home would probably have training opportunities in individual habilitation planning made available to staff.

The ideal home would emphasize contact with friends and family members outside the home. It would encourage autonomy of the individual only to the extent that the individual was capable of handling the freedom. Training of skills necessary to handle freedoms, such as independent travel in the community would be a must. Location in an urban setting, with easy access to community resources, is useful although not sufficient to teach appropriate use of community resources.

The ability of the staff of the residence to recognize and deal with behavior problems is extremely important. The best approach to handling behavior problems seems to be the encouragement of residents to express their feelings and frustrations openly. Programs that encourage autocratic control by staff also seem to encourage behavior disruption.

A danger in discussing features of the ideal environment is to ignore individual differences. Characteristics of the individual are clearly very important to the ultimate adjustment of the individual to the community. Much of the individual's potential can be predicted on the basis of prerelease behavior patterns. An individual who has underdeveloped self-care skills is less likely to show gains in self-care. On the other hand, individuals placed in smaller than average CRFs are more likely to show gains in self-care and social interaction. Obviously the ideal CRF would also have a good person-environment fit, such that the individual's needs would be matched to the social environment of the home.

This research on PPHAs, HRFs, and CRFs suggests that we are some distance away from achieving the ideal. Despite the major differences in staffing, funding, and intended function of these community residences there is as much environmental variation within as between these types of living arrangements. Placement into one home or another was generally random rather than well conceived and need-based. On the other hand, deinstitutionalization is a relatively recent phenomenon and research regarding the characteristics of effective community residential environments is just now being conducted. It is hoped that the results of this research will be used to guide the continued planning and modification of community-based alternatives to institutions.

REFERENCES

Aanes, D., & Moen, M. Adaptive behavior changes of group home residents. *Mental Retardation*, 1976, *14*, 36–40.

Baker, B. L., Seltzer, A. B., & Seltzer, M. M. *As close as possible. Community residences for retarded adults*. Boston: Little, Brown & Company, 1974.

Bjaanes, A. T., & Butler, E. W. Environmental variation in community care facilities for mentally retarded persons. *American Journal of Mental Deficiency*, 1974, *78*, 429–439.

Bradley, V. J. *Deinstitutionalization of developmentally disabled persons*. Baltimore: University Park Press, 1978.

Brown, J. S., & Guard, K. A. The treatment environment for retarded persons in nursing homes. *Mental Retardation*, 1979, *17*, 77–82.

Butler, E. W., & Bjaanes, A. T. A typology of community care facilities and differential normalization outcomes. In P. Mittler (Ed.), *Research to practice in mental retardation* (Vol. 1). Baltimore: University Park Press, 1977.

Butler, E. W., & Bjaanes, A. T. Activities and the use of time by retarded persons in community care facilities. In G. P. Sackett (Ed.), *Observing behavior* (Vol. 1). Baltimore: University Park Press, 1978.

Edgerton, R. B. *The cloak of competence: Stigma in the lives of the mentally retarded*. Berkeley: University of California Press, 1967.

Eyman, R. K., & Call, T. Maladaptive behavior and community placement of mentally retarded persons. *American Journal of Mental Deficiency*, 1977, *82*, 137–144.

Eyman, R. K., Demaine, G. C., & Lei, T. Relationship between community environments and resident changes in adaptive behavior: A path model. *American Journal of Mental Deficiency*, 1979, *83*, 330–338.

Intagliata, J., Willer, B., & Wicks, N. Factors related to the quality of community adjustment in family care homes. Paper presented at the Conference on Community Adjustment, Minneapolis, Minnesota, March 16, 1979. (Conference proceedings in press.)

Landesman-Dwyer, S., Berkson, G., & Romer, D. Affiliation and friendship of mentally retarded residents in group homes. *American Journal of Mental Deficiency*, 1979, *83*, 571–580.

Moen, M., Bogen, D., & Aanes, D. Follow-up of mentally retarded adults successfully and unsuccessfully placed in community group homes. *Hospital and Community Psychiatry*, 1975, *26*, 754–756.

Moos, R. H. *Evaluating treatment environments*. New York: John Wiley & Sons, 1974.

Nihira, L., & Nihira, K. Normalized behavior in community placement. *Mental Retardation*, 1975, *13*, 9–13.

Pankratz, L. Assessing the psychosocial environment of halfway houses for the retarded. *Community Mental Health*, 1975, *11*, 341–345.

Scheerenberger, R. C., & Felsenthal, D. Community settings for mentally retarded persons: Satisfaction and activities. *Mental Retardation*, 1977, *15*, 3–7.

Spivack, A., Haines, P. E., & Spotts, J. *Devereux adolescent behavior rating scale manual*. Devon, Pa.: The Devereux Foundation, 1967.

Willer, B., Intagliata, J., & Wicks, N. Return of retarded adults to natural families: Issues and results. Paper presented at the Conference on Community Adjustment, Minneapolis, Minnesota, March 16, 1979. (Conference proceedings in press.)

Willer, B. S., Scheerenberger, R. C., & Intagliata, J. Deinstitutionalization and mentally retarded persons. *Community Mental Health Review,* 1978, *3,* 1–12.

Windle, C., Stewart, E., & Brown, S. J. Reasons for community failure of released patients. *American Journal of Mental Deficiency,* 1961, *66,* 213–217.

Wolfensberger, W., & Glenn, L. *PASS 3, A method for quantitative evaluation of human services.* Toronto: National Institute on Mental Retardation, 1975.

The Residential Environment and Its Relationship to Client Behavior

Marsha Mailick Seltzer,
Gary B. Seltzer, and
Clarence C. Sherwood

During the past two decades, a substantial amount of professional interest has been focused on state institutions for retarded persons and on community residential alternatives. This interest in the residential environment has been manifested in many ways, including sociological examination of institutions (e.g., Goffman, 1961), journalistic exposés and photographic essays that document the conditions that exist in state institutions (e.g., Blatt and Kaplan, 1966; Rivera, 1972), descriptive accounts of individual community residential programs (e.g., Dungan, 1964; Woloshin, Tardi, and Tobin, 1966), and national statistical profiles of community residences for retarded adults (e.g., Baker, Seltzer, and Seltzer, 1977; Bruininks, 1979; O'Connor, 1976). Common to all of these and other related efforts has been the assumption that certain environmental characteristics have negative effects on clients—and these characteristics are typically found in state institutions—whereas other environmental features have more favorable effects—and these are typically found in community residences. A related assumption is that the longer the time spent in an institutional environment, the more pronounced the negative effects on the client, and similarly, the longer the time spent in a community environment, the more pronounced the positive effects.

It may be useful, at this point, to make a distinction between two potential benefits of deinstitutionalization that are often incorrectly assumed by professionals in retardation to be closely related if not identical. These two potential benefits are: 1) improvements in retarded persons' living conditions; and 2) improvements in retarded persons' level of functioning. On the basis of a great deal of experiential and anecdotal data, there does not seem to be much doubt that, on the whole, community residences provide better living conditions for retarded persons than do state institutions. Community residential environments tend to be cleaner, more personalized, less overcrowded, and generally more pleasant than institutional wards. With respect, however, to the second intended benefit of deinstitutionalization, client level of functioning, the situation is less clear. The assumption that has been made in the field of retardation is that the provision of better living conditions would result in improvements in client functioning. Because of this assumption, much of the available literature is concerned with the environmental features that are expected to produce better living conditions, whereas very little research is focused on the effect of these environmental features on client behavior. Most of the small body of research that is available regarding the effects of the environment concerns the institutional environment (e.g., Balla, 1976; Rago, Parker, and Cleland, 1978; Zigler and Balla, 1977), and almost no research is available on the community residential environment and its effect on client behavior. The purpose of this chapter is to present the results of an analysis of the relationship between the residential environment and client behavior. First, a brief review of past research is presented.

INSTITUTIONAL AND COMMUNITY RESIDENTIAL ENVIRONMENTS: A BRIEF REVIEW

There really is no question that environments affect the behavior of persons who experience them. Behavior psychologists have demonstrated conclusively that the systematic programming of environmental antecedents to, and consequences of, behavior has an impact on the targeted behavior. The question here is: Are differences in the characteristics of residential environments associated with differences in the behavior of residents? A few studies are relevant in this regard.

The single environmental feature most commonly assumed to have an effect on clients is residential unit size. Balla (1976) reviewed the literature on the relationship between institution size and resident functioning and concluded that "there is very little evidence to suggest that the behavioral functioning of residents is different in institutions of different sizes" (p. 122). This result is surprising in light of the widespread belief held by retardation professionals and reflected in retardation policy that smaller facilities produce more independent and more highly functional behavior in clients than do larger residences. Baker et al. (1977), in a study that investigated, among other things, the relationship between community residence size and various measures of client functioning, found that in smaller facilities residents were significantly more likely to work than in larger settings. It would be incorrect to infer from this result, however, that the smaller size of the facility caused the residents to work, because the residents may have had the characteristics that enabled them to work before they entered the community residence. Thus, it is possible that it was the prior characteristics of the individual (e.g., age, IQ, etc.) and not the smaller size of the facility that resulted in more competitive work placements. In Landesman-Dwyer, Sackett, and Kleinman's (in press) study of the relationship between group home size and resident behavior, the results indicated that in general, size was not related to client behavior except with respect to social behavior, which was found to be more frequently displayed in larger facilities. Thus, the available literature on residential unit size does not consistently support the widely held assumption that smaller size is beneficial.

Social policy in retardation has also been guided by the belief that facilities that possess certain characteristics that are considered to be "normalized" are likely to improve the functioning of residents. Eyman, Demaine, and Lei (1979) studied the relationship between community residence PASS scores—which are designed to operationalize normalization— and changes in resident behavior. They found that although several of the PASS factors were significantly related to client behavior change, the relationships between client behavior change and clients' individual characteristics (age, IQ, and pre-deinstitutionalization adaptive behavior levels) were much stronger. In interpreting these results, it is important to consider the explanation (as in the Baker et al., 1977, study) that client outcome is less a consequence of the environmental features than of the characteristics possessed by the clients before they entered the community residences.

The issue raised here is that differences in client outcome in different types of settings may exist because settings differentially select clients. That is, settings that possessed "better" characteristics (e.g., high degree of autonomy) may have selected for admission clients who possessed "better" characteristics (e.g., higher intelligence); the fact that later on these clients still possessed the favorable characteristics and functioned at a higher level says nothing about the effect of the residential environment on the client. Selection, of course, is one of the threats to internal validity enumerated by Campbell and Stanley (1963) and can be defined as the situation that occurs in causal analysis "when the members of the groups being studied are in the groups in part because they differentially possess traits or characteristics extraneous to the research problem, characteristics that possibly influence or are otherwise related to the variable of the research problem" (Kerlinger, 1973, p. 381). In this context, the issue is whether the clients are selected into the types of settings in which they are found on the basis of differences in their prior characteristics. This is an important issue because postplacement differences that are found among clients who live in different types of environments are often interpreted in the literature as an indication that the environments differentially affected the clients, when in fact these differences may have preceded client placement into the programs.

In the discussion that follows, data from a study concerning the performance of clients following deinstitutionalization are examined in order to determine whether differences in client performance are attributable to differences in the residential environment or, alternatively, to selection. This analysis treats as a hypothesis what has previously been held as an assumption by professionals in the deinstitutionalization and community residence movements. This hypothesis is that retarded persons who are placed in more favorable environments for a longer period of time will perform better than those placed in favorable environments for a shorter period, and similarly, that persons placed in less favorable environments for a longer period of time will perform more poorly than those placed in such environments for a shorter period. It is the interaction of quality of setting with time that presumably produces the outcome; neither the passage of time alone nor the environment in which a client is placed is hypothesized to produce as positive an outcome as placement in a favorable setting over time. Selection can be rejected as an explanation of client outcome in the event that this interaction hypothesis is supported (i.e., that client performance is found to be a function of the interaction between quality of setting and time). If, however, clients' differential levels of performance are unrelated to the interaction between the quality of their settings and the length of time they lived there, then the selection explanation cannot be rejected.

METHODS

Subjects

The subjects in this study ($n=110$), who were ex-residents of a state institution, were released to the community during the period between February 1, 1972, and October 1,

1975. These subjects constituted 76% of all adult residents who were released to the community from that institution during this time period. Half of the sample were male (47%) and half female (53%). Their average age was 23.91 and their average IQ was 51 (SD=18).

Measures

Background demographic data were gathered via systematic search of the clients' pre-release institutional records.[1] Data about the following variables were collected: sex, date of birth, age at admission, age at first release to the community, diagnosed level of retardation, IQ score, presence or absence of family contact while institutionalized, history of employment in the institution, and length of institutionalization.

Client performance of community living skills, the dependent variable in this analysis, was measured by the performance domain of the Community Adjustment Scale (Seltzer and Seltzer, 1976, 1978). Data were gathered during an interview with an informant who knew the subject well. The interview focused on the subject's independent and regular performance of community living skills in the areas of personal care, housekeeping, speech and language, basic academics, social behavior, community participation, economic management, and agency utilization. The alpha reliability of the Performance Scale was 0.91.

The residential environment was assessed with respect to five dimensions that were hypothesized to be important in promoting independent client performance. These dimensions were:

1. The extent to which clients were assigned the responsibility for caring for the house
2. The extent to which clients were afforded the autonomy to make certain decisions
3. The extent to which clients had easy access to community and in-house resources
4. The extent to which training was provided in areas of unmastered skills
5. The extent to which staff expected independent performance from residents

Because the residential environment was assumed to have both physical and social features, the 72 items included in the Environment Scale covered aspects of the physical and social environment. Each item was scored as either present (1) or absent (0). The alpha reliability of the Environment Scale was 0.85.

At the time of the research, subjects in this study lived in six types of residential settings. These types, or models, were defined according to administrative criteria used by the Massachusetts Department of Mental Health. In addition to being administratively distinct, the six models were found to be programmatically distinct when compared on the basis of mean environment scale scores, as shown in Table 1.

On the basis of the dimensions included in the Environment Scale, the institution's wards had the least favorable environments, followed by foster and family homes; group homes, semi-independent apartments, and independent apartments had the most favorable environments.

In the analysis that was conducted and that is presented in this chapter, it was necessary to construct a composite measure of the residential environments in which a subject lived

---

[1]It should be noted that although the collection of these data from the institution records was a relatively simple matter, the reliability and validity of these data were unknown, as is generally the case with data culled from old records.

Table 1. Mean environment scores, by model

Model	x	SD
Institution*	1.850	0.709
Foster home	2.455	1.706
Family home**	3.521	1.723
Group home	5.242	1.157
Semi-independent apartment	5.591	0.886
Independent apartment	5.813	0.983
	$F=38.043, p<0.001$	

*The category "institution" includes the environments of subjects who, though previously released to the community, were living at the state school at the time of the research. The environmental unit for these "returnees" was the ward, not the entire institution.

**The category "family home" includes the environments of subjects who lived with their biological parents or siblings at the time of the research.

since his or her release from the institution. This was difficult because the only environment that was studied was the setting in which the subject lived at the time of the research, although most subjects (55.5%) had lived in more than one residence since their release to the community. The goal of the present analysis is to relate the environmental input experienced by the client to his or her level of performance, and for this reason, all of the residences in which the client had lived since release from the institution must be included in the analysis. This is necessary because each environment had the possibility of contributing, either positively or negatively, to the client's present level of functioning. Therefore, the following steps were taken to construct a variable that would estimate the characteristics of each of the environments in which a client had lived since his or her initial release to the community:

1. Each client's social worker was interviewed, and the social work records were examined, in order to obtain a complete record of the client's residential history, including the name and address of each setting in which the client lived since release from the institution, and the length of time the client lived in each setting.
2. In order to relate the client's environmental history to his or her present level of functioning, it was necessary to assign an environment score to each setting in which the client had lived. To accomplish this, the environment scores of all facilities included in each model were averaged and the appropriate mean environment score was assigned to each of the previous settings lived in by a subject.[2]
3. Assuming that the length of time that a client lives in a setting should affect the extent to which he or she improves in that setting, the decision was made to calculate the client's environmental history score by multiplying each setting's environment score (arrived at through the procedures described in 2 above) by the number of months the client lived in that environment, and then adding up the products that were derived for each of the settings in which the client lived.

These procedures were intended to produce a variable that would provide an estimate of the cumulative environmental input experienced by each client since initial release from the

---

[2]These means were those presented in Table 1.

institution, weighted by the amount of time spent in each setting (the "time by environment" interaction variable).

Analytical Model

The primary issue under investigation in this chapter concerns the extent to which differences in postrelease performance of community living skills among sample members are a function of the differences in the residential environment, when the client's prerelease characteristics are statistically controlled. The statistical model used in this analysis is multiple regression analysis, in which prerelease client characteristic variables are entered first as a group, followed by the main independent variables of interest, namely, the length of time since the client's initial release, the average environment score of the settings in which the client had lived (unweighted by the length of time he or she lived in each), and the interaction between time and environment. This analytical model is graphically expressed below.

$$\textbf{PERFORMANCE} = \begin{array}{c} \text{Prerelease} \\ \text{individual} \\ \text{characteristics}^3 \end{array} + \begin{array}{c} \text{Time} \\ \text{since} \\ \text{release} \end{array} + \begin{array}{c} \text{Average} \\ \text{environment} \\ \text{score} \end{array} + \begin{array}{c} \text{Time by} \\ \text{environment} \\ \text{interaction} \end{array}$$

To conclude that differences in the residential environment have differential effects on client performance, the "time by environment" interaction must explain a significant proportion of the variance in the dependent variable "performance" after the effects of the other independent variables (prerelease variables, time since release, and average environment score) have been removed.[4]

Multiple regression was selected as the analytic technique to be used in the present analysis in order to statistically control the variance in these independent variables while allowing for the examination of the effects or relationships between the key independent variable, the "time by environment" interaction, and the dependent variable. In the analysis, all measured background demographic characteristics were controlled (by entering them first as a group into the equation). This was followed by an investigation, in analysis of variance terminology, of the relative magnitude of the two main effects ("time since release" and "average environmental score") and then of the interaction effect ("time by environment" interaction).[5] The statistical method for conducting this analysis is termed "commonality analysis" which is:

---

[3]The nine variables were: sex, age at admission, age at first release, length of institutionalization, level of retardation, IQ score, jobs held prior to release, contact with family, and medical problems.

[4]It should be noted that the utilization of this statistical model is necessary because the study upon which the present analysis is based was conducted primarily for descriptive purposes, and it therefore included neither the longitudinal collection of data (e.g., prerelease measures of performance) nor the establishment of equivalent groups in different types of residences by randomization or some other procedure. For this reason, the present analysis is necessarily exploratory. However, the procedures described above should allow for a preliminary understanding of the effects of the residential environment on client functioning.

[5]It should be pointed out that the utilization of multiple regression for analysis of variance-type problems is well accepted and recommended for instances in which there are multiple interval-level independent variables. (See Cohen and Cohen, 1975, and Kerlinger and Pedhauser, 1973.) With respect to the utilization of an interaction effect that is entered subsequent to the two main effects, Cohen and Cohen (1975) pointed out that the interaction effect is statistically and conceptually independent of the two main effects, and therefore a legitimate variable to include in a regression analysis.

. . . a method of analyzing the variance of a dependent variable into common and unique variances to help identify the relative influences of independent variables . . . The unique contribution of an independent variable is defined as the variance attributed to it when it is entered last in the regression equation. (Kerlinger and Pedhauser, 1973, pp. 297–298).

In the present analysis, the effect of the ''time by environment'' interaction is investigated after all other possible sources of variance in the independent variable set have been statistically controlled. The purpose of this analysis is to disentangle a common confusion in research on deinstitutionalization; as noted above, although it is widely assumed that performance differences among clients placed in different settings can be attributed to the differential effects of those settings, it is also possible that such differences in client performance may be a simple function of the selection of those clients into the different settings. By controlling for background demographic characteristics (by entering them first into the regression equation) the effects of selection can be controlled because the characteristics that would determine the differential selection of clients into settings are largely captured in the independent variables that are entered first. By bringing the ''time by environment'' interaction into the equation last, it is possible to estimate the unique contribution (relative to the remaining variables in the equation) of this variable and determine if the relatively high simple correlation between it and the dependent variable ($r=0.368$, $p<0.001$) was a function of selection or, alternatively, of the effect of the environment over time on client behavior.

To summarize, the following hypotheses were tested:

1. There is no relationship between differences in the length of time since clients' release from the institution and differences in their postrelease levels of performance, once the clients' prerelease characteristics have been statistically controlled.
2. There is no relationship between differences in the average environment scores of the settings in which clients lived since release from the institution and differences in their levels of performance, once the clients' prerelease characteristics and the length of time since their initial release from the institution have been statistically controlled.
3. There is a positive relationship between differences in clients' environmental history scores (the ''time by environment'' interaction) and differences in their levels of performance, once their prerelease characteristics, the length of time since their initial release from the institution, and the average environment scores of the settings in which they lived since release have been statistically controlled, with clients who have lived in ''better'' settings for longer periods of time performing better than those who have lived in such settings for a shorter period of time and with clients who lived in less favorable settings for longer periods of time performing worse than those who have lived in such settings for a shorter period of time.

RESULTS AND DISCUSSION

In the multiple regression analysis that was conducted, it was found that the nine prerelease client demographic variables as a set explained 55% of the variance in the dependent variable of postrelease client performance. When the variable ''time since release'' was brought into the equation after the prerelease variables had been entered, it did not account for any additional variance in the dependent variable, as was hypothesized. Next, the variable ''environment'' (not weighted by time) was brought into the equation and this

Table 2. Multiple regression on performance

Independent variable	Standardized coefficient				t-test (final equation)	R^2 at each key block
	Block A	Blocks A,B	Blocks A,B,C	Blocks A,B,C,D		
Block A. Prerelease variables						
1. Sex	0.239	0.247	0.261	0.260	3.89, $p<0.001$	
2. Age at admission	-0.161	-0.170	-0.121	-0.119	-0.51	
3. Age at first release	-0.006	0.005	-0.049	-0.055	-0.15	
4. Length of institutionalization	-0.149	-0.153	-0.064	-0.061	-0.18	0.550
5. Level of retardation	0.029	0.035	-0.010	-0.008	-0.07	
6. IQ score	0.636	0.625	0.514	0.513	4.44, $p<0.001$	
7. Jobs prerelease	0.188	0.182	0.042	0.043	0.56	
8. Contact with family	0.004	0.005	0.009	0.012	0.17	
9. Medical problems	0.057	0.058	0.048	0.049	0.77	
Block B. Main effect Variable #1						
10. Time (months since deinstitutionalization)		0.069	0.111	0.107	1.56	0.554
Block C. Main effect Variable #2						
11. Environment (average environment score)			0.315	0.308	3.70, $p<0.001$	0.621
Block D. Interaction effect Variable #3						
12. Time by environment interaction				0.014	0.18	0.622

Final Equation: Multiple correlation squared = 0.622; F = 13.28, with 12 and 97 degrees of freedom, $p<0.001$; multiple correlation = 0.788.

variable explained an additional 7% of variance of the dependent variable. Finally, when the key independent variable, the "time by environment" interaction, was brought into the equation, it failed to explain the equation any further. The final regression equation explained 62% of the variance in the dependent variable, performance. Table 2 presents the final regression equation. Table 3 presents a correlation matrix of all variables included in the regression analysis.

Before discussing the major results of this analysis, it may be useful to focus on one possibly surprising finding. As can be seen in Table 2, the one prerelease characteristic that was most strongly predictive of performance was IQ score. This finding warrants particular attention because, although the unique variance contributed by any single prerelease variable to the prediction of performance is not of central interest to this analysis, many readers may be surprised by this result because it has commonly been asserted in the literature that there is no relationship between IQ score and community adjustment (Clark, Kivitz, and Rosen, 1968; Eagle, 1967; Pearson, 1975; Windle, 1962). One explanation for the difference between results of the present study and the results obtained by other studies concerns the issue of *restriction in range in the IQ variable*. When a sample includes only a narrow range of IQ scores (e.g., mainly mildly retarded), then it is statistically unlikely for IQ to be related to (or predictive of) any measure of community adjustment. This explanation is supported by Cobb (1972) who noted:

> The probability of finding IQ or similar measures to be predictively related to criteria of adult adjustment is a function of the intelligence range of the population sampled: the narrower the range, the less likely intelligence will be found significantly discriminating (p. 146).

The present study included a more full range of IQ scores, and in fact a strong positive correlation between IQ score and performance was found ($r = 0.668$, $p < .001$). Parenthetically, the present study is not unique in finding such a relationship; several other follow-up studies that found a significant correlation between IQ score and a criterion of community adjustment include Bell (1974), Jones and Jones (1976), and Stephens and Peck (1968).

Returning to the major hypotheses of this study, there are two major findings of the analysis presented in this chapter:

1. It is possible to predict, to a considerable degree, the postrelease performance of retarded persons on the basis of their prerelease characteristics.
2. Once prerelease characteristics, the length of time since release, and the average environments score are controlled for, the residential history of the subject (the "time by environment" interaction) fails to predict any additional variance in performance.

These two points are related to each other, and together they suggest that the prerelease characteristics of the individual affect the residential placement decisions made for him or her at the time of and following deinstitutionalization. Clients who possess "better" characteristics apparently are placed in settings that possess "better" characteristics. Differences in postplacement performance among clients who live in different types of settings tend to be more a function of the characteristics possessed by the clients before they entered the settings than of the differential effects of the settings on the clients.

In considering these results, it actually is not surprising to find that community residences select clients on the basis of the characteristics possessed by these clients at the

Table 3.   Correlation matrix

Variables	1	2	3	4	5	6	7	8	9	10	11	12	13
Sex (1)	1.000												
Age at admission (2)	0.216*	1.000											
Age at first release (3)	−0.028	0.471††	1.000										
Length of institutionalization (4)	−0.151	−0.151	0.779††	1.000									
Level of MR (5)	−0.152	−0.097	0.115	0.151	1.000								
IQ (6)	0.075	0.125	0.020	−0.084	−0.774††	1.000							
Jobs prelease (7)	−0.105	−0.030	0.238*	0.246*	−0.068	0.231*	1.000						
Contact with family (8)	−0.029	0.199*	−0.110	−0.312††	−0.031	0.134	0.041	1.000					
Medical problems (9)	−0.090	−0.020	0.047	0.087	−0.031	0.008	0.002	0.047	1.000				
Time (10)	−0.074	0.052	−0.035	−0.076	−0.214*	0.237*	0.111	0.044	−0.000	1.000			
Environment (11)	−0.074	−0.036	0.017	0.001	−0.132	0.315††	0.484††	0.082	0.019	−0.020	1.000		
Time × environment interaction (12)	−0.050	0.061	0.127	0.090	−0.307††	0.366††	0.232*	−0.155	−0.012	0.260†	0.436††	1.000	
Performance (13)	0.245†	−0.019	−0.142	−0.165	−0.521††	0.668††	0.275†	0.107	0.030	0.215*	0.482††	0.368††	1.000

* = $p < 0.05$.
† = $p < 0.01$.
†† = $p < 0.001$.

time of placement. It is probable that referral agencies refer the clients whom they believe to have the most potential to the programs that they perceive to have the best environments. It is also reasonable to assume that residences accept or reject the clients that are referred to them on the basis of their staff's belief regarding the types of clients with whom they will have the most success. According to this line of reasoning, the settings that are considered to have the best environments have the "right of first refusal" of the less desirable clients (or the less desirable clients are not referred to them in the first place) and these types of clients eventually "filter down," or are referred, to the poorer environments. Thus, a possible explanation for the observed relationship between environment and performance ($r=0.482$, $p <.001$) is suggested: the possibility of a relationship between the prerelease characteristics of the clients and the characteristics of the environments in which they were placed. To test this hypothesis, the nine prerelease independent variables were entered into a regression analysis in which the dependent variable was the average environment score of the settings in which a subject had lived since initial release. This analysis was conducted in order to determine whether a client's prerelease characteristics would predict his or her postrelease placement history, thereby providing confirmation for the selection hypothesis. In fact, when this analysis was conducted, the nine prerelease client characteristics accounted for 17% of the variance in the dependent variable (average environment score).

As noted above, an unanticipated finding of the major regression analysis conducted for this chapter was that the variable "average environment score" made a significant contribution to the prediction of postrelease performance (7% of the variance) once the prerelease characteristics of the individual and the length of time since initial release from the institution were statistically controlled. Since this finding was not anticipated (see hypotheses, above), it may be valuable to attempt to understand its implications. The significant contribution made by "average environment score" suggests that, when many prerelease individual characteristics are controlled, those persons who have lived in better environments for a longer time perform no better than those who have lived in such environments for a shorter time. Similarly, those who have lived in less favorable environments for a longer time perform no worse than those who have lived in such settings for a shorter time. If we interpret this finding to mean that the environment had an effect, it would imply that an individual would be equally likely to perform a skill (such as cooking, cleaning, or making change) at a given level of competence after having lived in a setting, for example, for 1 week or 1 year. This would be very unlikely because if an environment has an effect on behavior, it tends to occur over time. Because it is unreasonable to accept that the environment had an instantaneous effect on the individual as an explanation for this finding, an alternative explanation is necessary. One such explanation is that this result is attributable to characteristics that clients possessed before they were released from the institution and that were not included in this study. Although nine such prerelease characteristics were controlled for in this analysis (by entering them first into the regression equation), selection variables other than those that were measured certainly do exist. One example of such an unmeasured but probably important selection variable is behavior problems. It is reasonable to hypothesize that persons with fewer behavior problems tend to be placed in better environments. The effects of the variable behavior problems were not statistically controlled in this analysis; therefore, any relationship between this variable and environment will be attributed incorrectly to environment. Thus, the additional 7% of variance in performance that is explained by "average environment score" may be a function of the relationship between this variable and unmeasured selection variables.

It was surprising to find that the residential history of the individual (the "time by environment" interaction) was not related to performance, once all other variables were controlled. Although the zero order correlation between this interaction variable and performance is rather high and statistically significant ($r=0.368$, $p<0.001$), nearly all of the variance in this correlation can be accounted for by the relationships of each of these two variables with the prerelease characteristics of the individual. This finding suggests that when a person lives in a "better" setting for a longer time, his or her performance is no better than it would have been had he or she lived there for a shorter time and that similarly, when a person lives in a less favorable setting for a longer time, he or she is not more likely to be associated with poorer performance than placement in such a setting for a shorter time. Differences in the environment, as defined here, do not seem to be having a differential effect on the individual.

One possible explanation for these results is that the differences among characteristics of the environment that were measured by the Environment Scale that was used in the present analysis might not be related to differences in performance. Differences among *other* environmental features, however, might indeed be related to differences in performance. The residential characteristics that were used to define the Environment Scale were selected in order to operationalize the normalization principle. As noted earlier, there were five domains included in the Environment Scale: autonomy, responsibility, access to resources, staff expectations, and training opportunities. Thus, high autonomy programs in which residents were given the responsibility for caring for the house themselves, rather than it being cared for by staff, in which community and in-house resources were readily available, in which staff had higher expectations of residents, and in which training programs were provided for them were hypothesized to be better environments than settings in which these characteristics were absent. The fact that differences among these environmental features were unrelated to differences in client performance does not necessarily imply that other environmental features would be unrelated as well. If, instead of using the normalization principle as the dimension underlying the Environment Scale, some other theory had been used, it is possible that differences among those features of the environment would have been related to differences in client performance. For example, it is possible that the use of certain reinforcement schedules by staff with clients may be a far more salient environmental feature than autonomy, with respect to client performance. Because data regarding schedules of reinforcement were not collected in the present study, however, there is no way to determine their potential effect on client performance. Thus, rather than conclude that no environmental feature in community residences has an impact on behavior, this line of reasoning suggests that the environmental features hypothesized to be important by the normalization principle and operationalized by the Environment Scale are actually not salient, while other unmeasured aspects of the environment may indeed be related to performance. It may be useful at this point to note again that Eyman et al. (1979) found another measure of the normalization principle (PASS) to be much less strongly related to client performance than prerelease client characteristics, again suggesting the possibility that the environmental features assumed by the normalization principle to be important simply may not be that salient in affecting client performance. These features, however, may indeed have major importance for providing more homelike living conditions in community residential settings.

Although, as discussed above, the reason for the poor prediction power of residential history (the "time by environment" interaction) might have been the content of the Environment Scale that was used in this study, it is also possible that the reason for this poor prediction was that differences among the environments actually had no differential effect on the clients' performance. Although it is discouraging to consider the possibility that differential residential environments of the types studied here were not associated with differences in client performance, this is the most parsimonious explanation for the results. Community residences have tended to be family-style settings in which loosely structured interventions are offered to residents by staff who often have not been professionally trained in the field of retardation or in specialized educational techniques. It is possible that the differential effects of such settings would have been greater with retarded adults who had lived at home and had attended school throughout their childhood than with this previously institutionalized sample. With those retarded persons who lived in state institutions for many years and experienced their deleterious conditions, however, it is possible that a more highly structured professionally staffed community residence would be advantageous.

An important conclusion that should be drawn from this analysis is that there is a serious need for innovation in program development in residential settings for retarded adults. It is incumbent upon leaders of the community residence movement to advocate program innovation in order to increase the diversity and improve the quality of programs offered to clients, with the hope that such innovation will generate more effective interventions. A related need that exists in the field of retardation at present is the need for research about program innovation. Without careful experimental and longitudinal investigations, the specific effects of community residential environments will be undemonstrated. The risk exists, therefore, that new types of interventions may be misconstrued as being likely to improve clients' performance when in fact they may not have such effects. Without research on the effectiveness of these new environmental interventions, it is likely that the field of retardation will continue to plan services on the basis of the assumed but undemonstrated effectiveness of interventions, and may therefore continue to provide services that are not maximally effective in improving clients' level of performance. In this era of ideological commitment to improved services, empirical approaches to the determination of maximally effective interventions provide a means of protecting the rights of retarded persons by determining the types of placements in which they are likely to make the most progress.

In conclusion, it is important to underscore the point that this analysis was not conducted for the purpose of questioning the need for deinstitutionalization. As noted above, the difference in living conditions provided to clients in state institutions as they presently exist and in community residences is sufficient reason for deinstitutionalization. That the findings of the present analysis suggest that differences among the residential settings that were studied seem to be unrelated to differences in clients' level of performance does not imply that clients should be returned to institutions. Rather it implies that community residences should be improved, particularly with respect to characteristics that can be demonstrated to have positive effects on client performance.

REFERENCES

Balla, D. A. Relationship of institution size to quality of care: A review of the literature. *American Journal of Mental Deficiency*, 1976, *81*, 2.

Baker, B. L., Seltzer, G. B., & Seltzer, M. M. *As close as possible: Community residences for retarded adults*. Boston: Little, Brown & Company, 1977.

Bell, N. IQ as a factor in a community lifestyle of previously institutionalized retardates. Paper presented at Region V AAMD Meeting, New Orleans, October, 1974.

Blatt, B., & Kaplan, F. *Christmas in Purgatory: A photographic essay on mental retardation*. Boston: Allyn & Bacon, 1966.

Bruininks, R. *Developmental disabilities project on residential services and community adjustment* (Vol. 7, No. 3). Minneapolis: University of Minnesota, March, 1979.

Campbell, D. G., & Stanley, J. *Experimental and quasi-experimental designs for research*. Chicago: Rand McNally, 1963.

Clark, G. R., Kivitz, M.S., Rosen, M. *A transitional program for institutionalized adult retarded. A five-year project*. VRA Project No. RD-1275-P. Elwyn, Pa.: Elwyn Institute, 1968.

Cobb, H. V. *The forecast of fulfillment: A review of the literature on predictive assessment of adult retarded for social and vocational adjustment*. New York: Teachers College Press, 1972.

Cohen, J., & Cohen, P. *Applied multiple regression/correlation analysis for the behavioral sciences*. Hillsdale, N. J.: Lawrence Erlbaum Associates, 1975.

Dungan, I. Community residence opens for mildly retarded in Hartford. *Connecticut Health Bulletin*, March 1964, *78*, 3.

Eagle, E. Prognosis and outcome of community placement in institutionalized retardates. *American Journal of Mental Deficiency*, 1967, *72*, 232–243.

Eyman, R. K., Demaine, G. C., & Lei, T. Relationships between community environments and resident changes in adaptive behavior: A path model. *American Journal of Mental Deficiency*, 1979, *82*, 22.

Goffman, E. *Asylums: Essays on the social situation of mental patients and other inmates*. New York: Doubleday, 1961.

Jones, P. P., & Jones, K. J. *The measurement of community placement success and its associated costs*. Waltham, Mass.: Brandeis University, 1976.

Kerlinger, F. N. *Foundations of behavioral research* (2nd ed.). New York: Holt, Rinehart & Winston, 1973.

Kerlinger, F. N., & Pedhauser, E. J. *Multiple regression in behavioral research*. New York: Holt, Rinehart & Winston, 1973.

Landesman-Dwyer, S., Sackett, G. P., & Kleinman, J. S. *Small community residences: Does size really matter?* In press.

O'Connor, G. *Home is a good place: A national perspective of community residential facilities for developmentally disabled persons*. Washington, D.C.: American Association on Mental Deficiency, 1976.

Pearson, D. M. Social class and vocational outcome of adult mentally retarded males. *Social Service Review*, 1975, *49*, 2.

Rago, W. R., Parker, R. M., & Cleland, C. C. Effect of increased space on the social behavior of institutionalized profoundly retarded male adults. *American Journal of Mental Deficiency*, 1978, *82*, 6.

Rivera, G. *Willowbrook: A report on how it is and why it doesn't have to be that way*. New York: Random House, 1972.

Seltzer, G. B., & Seltzer, M. M. *The community adjustment scale*. Cambridge, Mass.: Educational Projects, Inc., 1976.

Seltzer, M. M., & Seltzer, G. B. *Context for competence: A study of retarded adults living and working in the community*. Cambridge, Mass.: Educational Projects, Inc., 1978.

Stephens, W. B., & Peck, J. R. *Success of young adult male retardates*. Washington, D.C.: The Council for Exceptional Children, 1968.

Windle, C. Prognosis of mental sub-normals. *American Journal of Mental Deficiency, Monograph Supplement*, 1962, *66*, 5.

Woloshin, A., Tardi, G., & Tobin, A. Deinstitutionalization of mentally retarded men through the use of a halfway house. *Mental Retardation*, 1966, 21–25.

Zigler, E., & Balla, D. A. Impact of institutional experience on the behavior and development of retarded persons. *American Journal of Mental Deficiency*, 1977, *82*, 1.

Failure in Community Adaptation: The Relativity of Assessment

Robert B. Edgerton

The social policy of deinstitutionalization has generated growing moral concern and legal confrontation (Biklen, 1979), even though scientific reports of the successes and failures of deinstitutionalization in particular and community adaption in general have been contradictory. On the one hand, reports from a number of investigators in various parts of the country have concluded that conditions for mentally retarded persons in community settings are often deplorable, sometimes being characterized as more restrictive than residential living in large public institutions, but other investigators across the country have documented the positive consequences of community living (Biklen, 1979; Vitello, 1977; Butler and Bjaanes, 1977). It is fair to say that the evidence on which these contradictory reports about deinstitutionalization and community adaption are based can be interpreted in various ways. It may be less well understood that the evidence concerning *re*institutionalization, which would seem to be much more clear-cut, can also be interpreted in various ways.

In recent years, approximately 50% of all mentally ill persons released from state hospitals have been returned to those hospitals within the first year after release; in a 3-year period following deinstitutionalization, 65% have been returned (Gottesfeld, 1977; Bassuk and Gerson, 1978). Substantial numbers of mentally retarded persons have also been reinstitutionalized. Conroy (1977) reported that 34% of the mentally retarded persons released from public institutions in 1974 were reinstitutionalized, and indeed that readmissions have increased more rapidly than community placements. Other recent studies have reported lesser, but still substantial, return rates. For example, Gollay et al. (1978) reported that a national sample had a reinstitutionalization rate of 13%, a smaller sample from Minnesota had a return rate of 15% (Moen, Bogen, and Aanes, 1975), and for rural Nebraska, Schalock and Harper (1978) reported a 13% failure rate from an independent

This research was supported by NICHD Grant No. 09474-02, The Community Context of Normalization, and by NICHD Grant No. HD 04612, The Mental Retardation Research Center, UCLA.

living or competitive employment training program. Even those lower failure rates are sufficient to demonstrate that not everyone succeeds in the process of community adaptation. What reinsititutionalization actually involves, however, and why it is experienced by some persons rather than others is a good deal less clear. Given the seriousness of ''failure'' in deinstitutionalization both for national policy and the human beings involved, it is important to reexamine the phenomenon of failure in the community adaptation of mentally retarded persons.

This chapter first briefly reviews certain aspects of the literature concerning failure in community adaptation. Next, data concerning the community adaptation of two cohorts of mildly retarded persons are considered. Finally, an effort is made to place failure in community adaptation in social and cultural context. In doing so, the assessment of failure is shown to be both illusory and paradoxical because it is at all times relative to sociocultural circumstances.

ASSESSING FAILURE IN DEINSTITUTIONALIZATION

In the earliest days of research into the community adaptation of mentally retarded persons beginning around World War I, investigators such as Farrell (1915), Wallace (1918), Fernald (1919), and Fairbanks (1933)[1] expected to find a high rate of failure including widespread antisocial behavior. They were surprised when they found that the majority of the persons they located had made apparently satisfactory adaptations to community life. For example, when Fernald found that 34.4% of the men and 40.8% of the women he followed up after releases from Waverly had been rehospitalized or imprisoned (he had predicted that 85% could be expected to fail), he was so perplexed by this unexpectedly positive social adjustment that he delayed publication of his findings for 2 years (Goldstein, 1964).

Times change and recent investigators have commonly concluded not only that the majority of mildly retarded persons achieve a successful adaptation to community life, but that many ''disappear'' into the community where they are presumed to become normally ''successful'' citizens. As Cobb (1972, p. 145) wrote: ''The most consistent and outstanding finding of all follow-up studies is the high proportion of the adult retarded who achieve satisfactory adjustments, by whatever criteria are employed.'' Despite the few voices of dissent (Heber and Dever, 1970; MacMillan, 1977; Begab, 1978), this point of view has become an integral part of the conventional wisdom that informs the policy of deinstitutionalization. And yet it is widely recognized that remarkably little is known about what constitutes ''success'' and ''disappearance'' or why some persons succeed and others do not.

As virtually every reviewer of this subject has noted, the assessment of success in community adaptation is complex. Others have added that it may be arbitrary as well. For one thing, there is little agreement concerning the potentially relevant variables. Residential independence, success in competitive employment, the acquisition of social skills, marriage and reproduction, avoidance of bizarre and antisocial behavior—these and many others have been utilized by one or another investigator. Many approaches are complexly

---

[1] The research of Fairbanks, although not published until 1933, was begun in 1914.

multivariate. For example, Stephens (1964) used 141 criterion variables in her effort to evaluate adjustment. But if, as Scheerenberger (1976) commented, we must measure not just independence, but "quality of life," then would even 141 variables suffice? Even if there were agreement on criteria, there is as yet no agreement concerning how they can be applied appropriately to persons of widely varying intellectual abilities, physical handicaps, and age. Would they apply equally to men and women; to whites, blacks, and Hispanics; to Jews, Catholics, and Protestants; to persons from big cities and farm communities; to persons from rich and poor backgrounds? And in what settings— residences, places of employment, buses, and public streets? Success in community adaptation is not only multidimensional, its dimensions are seemingly inexhaustible, and the problems of comparability in measurement are monumental.

Confronted by these difficulties, investigators have often chosen to rely on a single, "objective," criterion of success and failure. Thus, success has often been operationalized not in terms of specific adaptational criteria, but simply by defining success as "remaining in the community." Failure, too, has often been defined not by specific criteria of inadequacy in community adaptation, but simply by "return from the community to an institution," be it a public institution for the mentally retarded, a hospital for the mentally ill, or a correctional institution (Windle, 1962; McCarver and Craig, 1974; Gollay, 1977). Therefore, the operational criteria of success or failure in community adaptation are remaining in the community and reinstitutionalization. It should be instructive to see what studies that utilize these criteria can tell us.

Because so many investigators have reported reinstitutionalization rates—sometimes as the only criterion of failure in community adaptation—there is a large corpus of relevant research. In reviewing a large portion of this research (44 studies), McCarver and Craig (1974) found that the mean success rate of 9,116 formerly institutionalized mentally retarded subjects was 69%, apparently confirming the conventional wisdom that the majority do indeed succeed. Yet McCarver and Craig (1974) also documented marked differences in failure rates over time. For example, the failure rate was only 10% in the period 1936–1953, but it rose to about 50% in the period 1960–1970. What is more, in any given period there were studies that reported high failure rates and others that reported low ones. In an earlier study, Eagle (1967) reviewed 36 follow-up studies involving 7,436 releases from state insititutions. The lowest failure rate reported was 10.2%, and the highest was 75.2%. Eagle also found that although the failure rate for the sample as a whole was 39.6%, it was 52% for the period 1960–1965 inclusive.

In a review of 122 studies of community adaptation, Windle (1962) also pointed to differences in reported failure rates as determined by a variety of criteria including the sole criterion of return to an institution. Indeed in his own research into the community adaptation of 356 patients on leave from Pacific State Hospital in Southern California, Windle found that 211, or nearly two-thirds, were "failures" by the criterion of return to the hospital. The failure rates varied dramatically, however, depending on the type of leave program involved (vocational leave, home leave, family care, or unauthorized absence). The ostensible reasons for failure varied as well, leading Windle to comment on the difficulties of predicting the outcome of community adaptation given the complex interaction between administrative considerations, the characteristics of mentally retarded persons and the nature of the environments to which they are adapting.

Windle (1962) also noted, as have many previous and subsequent reviewers (McCarver and Craig, 1974; Heal, Sigelman, and Switkzy, 1978), that existing research on community adaptation is badly flawed. In addition to an imposing array of generic methodological weaknesses, and the failure to produce consistent criterion variables (except for return to an institution), this research has relied on superficial and circumscribed means of data collection at the same time that it has suffered from serious sample attrition. These flaws must be kept in mind as we discuss variation in the assessed failure rates of community adaptation from place to place and from time to time. For these and other reasons to be considered later, it is not at all clear how one should interpret the apparent fact that seemingly similar cohorts of formerly institutionalized mildly retarded adults have highly variable failure rates. To illustrate some of the problems that beset efforts to interpret this variation, let us examine a cohort of former state hospital patients in more detail.

INTERPRETING COMMUNITY ADAPTATION

The description of the life circumstances of 48 mildly retarded adults published in *The Cloak of Competence* (Edgerton, 1967) has been construed by some readers as evidence of relatively successful community adaptation (Biklen, 1979). Even though 21 of these persons were judged to be "completely dependent," and only three were completely independent, Edgerton (1967) interpreted their adaptation of the cohort as a whole in generally positive terms. But others have construed the same evidence in a much less positive light (Heber and Dever, 1970). When the criteria by which successful adaptation is judged are global and imprecise, as they were in this study, it is always possible for interpretations to differ. Indeed it is altogether likely.

If one were to apply the "objective" criterion of reinstitutionalization to the adaptation of this sample one would first discover that most members of the original sample of 110 persons (all persons discharged from Pacific State Hospital to jobs in the community from 1949 through 1958) were returned to the hospital more than once before they were finally discharged. Had this research been conducted in the 1950s rather than in 1960–1961, one would have found (depending on the year chosen) a reinstitutionalization rate of anywhere from 40% to 70%. When the follow-up research was actually carried out in 1960–1961, only 98 of the 110 could be located, and of these, 12 were in institutions (seven of them prisons). This information is important because the study itself focused on 48 persons who were still in the community, and the "failure" of the 12 reinstitutionalized persons went largely unnoticed.

Even when the focus is confined to the 48 persons who were not reinstitutionalized, however, interpretations of the adequacy of their community adaptation can vary. For example, three had served jail sentences in the year prior to the research and six more had been arrested but not incarcerated. One more was psychotic, and another was an alcoholic; these eleven "failures" out of 48 persons would yield a failure rate of close to 25%. If one were to accept this figure, and there are reasons for not choosing to do so, what interpretation would one make? If one also concluded that a similar array of "failures" would have been found among the cohort members who were not followed up, would this lead to a different conclusion? Would this be a positive finding or a negative one?

In reaching a decision, one would presumably take into account the fact that these individuals had long records of preinstitutional delinquency, as well as the fact that many individuals in the sample who were delinquent before entering Pacific State Hospital exhibited little or no antisocial conduct after being released. One would also consider the experience of being institutionalized at this hospital as one that typically failed to provide these persons with the coping skills required for successful community adaptation. Although one might infer that their institutional confinement served to reduce or "cool off" their antisocial proclivities, one might also consider the fact that once these persons were released to jobs in the community they had quite marginal economic skills, low self-esteem, and lived in deteriorated neighborhoods where there were high rates of criminality and other serious deviance.

Given these and many other factors that should have put members of this cohort at a disadvantage in their efforts to cope with community living, was their failure rate positive or negative? This is certainly a lower rate than Windle found several years earlier, and it is also lower than the reported failure rate of some other samples of mentally retarded persons (Eagle, 1967; McCarver and Craig, 1974). It is also lower than the national failure rate for mentally ill or mentally retarded persons. As for "normal," noninstitutionalized populations, we cannot use reinstitutionalization as a criterion, but it may provide perspective to note that although retarded samples tend to have somewhat higher rates of reported crime than nonretarded controls (MacEachron, 1979), the probability that normal persons in the United States will be arrested for a crime is extremely high. For example, Deno (1965) found that 57% of a sample of former special class boys in Minneapolis had police records, compared to 37% of all boys in that city, but she also pointed out that normal boys from low socioeconomic status and ethnic minority backgrounds had a substantially higher arrest rate. Surveys of the arrest rates of nonretarded persons in other United States cities have also reported high arrest figures. For example, Wolfgang (1973) found that 50% of the nonwhite males and 29% of the white males in his sample in Philadelphia were arrested by age 18, and 43% of all males were arrested by age 27. Shannon (1978) reported that 70% of males and 24% of females in his Wisconsin sample had at least one recorded police contact for a nontraffic offense. Christensen (1967) estimated from *Uniform Crime Report* data that 50% of all males, 12% of all females, and 90% of all nonwhite males in the U.S. would be arrested for a nontraffic offense during their lifetimes.

These incidence and prevalence data and estimates are themselves difficult to interpret (Farrington, 1979) but they are likely to underestimate actual crime, and they may help to place the criminality of retarded persons in perspective. Crime or antisocial behavior is only one reason why retarded persons are returned to institutions, but it is a very common one (Scheerenberger, 1976; Edgerton, 1979). Compared to the arrest records of nonretarded persons, then, the members of the "Cloak of Competence" sample may not have fared so badly. Indeed, when the sample was restudied in 1972–1973 (Edgerton and Bercovici, 1976) none of the 30 persons located had been arrested, although two had been temporarily hospitalized for mental illness. This apparent evidence of a lesser failure rate must be treated cautiously, however, because 18 members of the original 48 could not be located, and 10 of the 30 who were located were judged to have achieved a lower quality of community life than was the case in 1960–1961.

ASSESSING THE COMMUNITY ADAPTATION
OF NONINSTITUTIONALIZED POPULATIONS

In addition to studies concerned with previously institutionalized populations of mentally retarded persons, there are many that have examined the community adaptation of retarded persons who have never been institutionalized. With a few exceptions these studies focus on mildly retarded persons identified in special classes or training programs. Most reviewers of these studies agree that the majority of such persons, like those who were institutionalized, achieve a satisfactory adaptation to community living (Goldstein, 1964; Cobb, 1972; MacMillan, 1977). Some questions have been raised, however, about the quality of that "satisfactory" adaptation. Goldstein (1964) pointed out that the occupational adaptation of mentally retarded samples has often been marginal at best, and others have noted that compared to nonretarded controls, they tend to live in deteriorated housing, to be socially isolated, and to commit more violations of the law (Deno, 1965; Lee, Hegge, and Voelker, 1959; Peterson and Smith, 1960; Heber and Dever, 1970; Gozali, 1972; Crawford, Aiello, and Thompson, 1979).

As with populations that were previously institutionalized, it seems to be possible to interpret the existing data on the community adaptation of noninstitutionalized populations in either a positive or negative manner depending on one's criteria and expectations. And also, as before, even if one agrees on a single criterion of failure—namely, institutional placement—the findings vary from time to time and place to place, and so do the interpretations. For example, Baller (1936) found that 10% of his sample in Nebraska had been institutionalized, and Kennedy (1966) found that only 2.4% of her sample in Connecticut had been institutionalized. These differences may reflect the different economic climates of those periods, from the depression times in Nebraska to more economically robust times in Connecticut, or they may be artifactual. Regardless, Baller and Kennedy both interpreted their findings positively.

Another example is provided by McKeon (1946) who examined the postschool adjustment of 210 special class graduates in a New England industrial city during World War II. She found that 36% of the sample were employed, 54% were on active duty in the armed services (about 19% of the entire sample had been rejected for military service), and 4% had been institutionalized. McKeon attributed the striking economic success of the sample to the wartime economic boom in this city, but she also pointed out—somewhat incidentally—that only one-fifth of the employed group had been employed 100% of the time. She also noted that 25% of the sample appeared in court to answer criminal charges and more than half of these were repeat offenders. It is possible to conclude then, that despite the needs of industry and the military, these retarded persons achieved only marginal success in community adaptation.

Reports such as McKeon's are susceptible to multiple interpretations. Without a greater sense of the social context of the times, and the specific social and cultural circumstances that sample members encountered, consensual interpretation is a will-o'-the-wisp. Indeed, without great detail about social context, even the use of a control population is likely to be illusory. Thus in her study comparing 122 mildly retarded persons first identified in school with 90 persons of normal intelligence, Fairbanks (1933) provided a highly positive interpretation of the adaptation of her retarded sample, concluding that the majority had married, held jobs, produced children, and generally done well in life. She also noted that only one of these 122 persons had a jail record—and that one was for only 4 days. This was a remarkably low rate of institutionalization. Yet she also reported that 25% of the sample had committed offenses that required a court appearance, a somewhat higher percentage than that found in the comparison population. Why the courts of those early times (1914–1930) chose not to imprison or hospitalize these persons (six were charged with assault, two with carrying a concealed weapon, two with burglary, and 16 with disorderly conduct, among other offenses) cannot be determined from the data presented. Neither can the data provided assure us about the quality of life these people—or their "controls"—had. The data are not only superficial, they lack all sense of social context. These people remained in the community, but that is all that we can say with any assurance.

There is reason to suspect, therefore, that the fact that a mentally retarded person had remained in a community setting without being placed in an institution may not be an ideal criterion of successful community adaptation. It may also be that institutional placement is a less than ideal criterion of failure in community adaptation. To consider these issues further, it may be useful to examine a new set of data that provide greater detail about the context of community adaptation. These data, collected over a 30-month period, document the community adaptation of 48 mildly retarded adults who had not previously been institutionalized.[2] During this 30-month period, none of these 48 persons were hospitalized or imprisoned for more than a brief period—an apparently impressive record of community adjustment. An examination of the behavior of these persons throughout that period, however, makes it abundantly clear that many of these persons led anything but trouble-free lives. Indeed, the antisocial or psychotic behavior of at least 20 of these people could easily have led to institutional placement, and at other times and in other places it probably would have done so. To understand the grounds for this assertion it will be necessary to explore some of these behaviors and the circumstances surrounding them in greater detail.

THE COMMUNITY CONTEXT OF NORMALIZATION STUDY

Beginning in May 1976 and continuing through 1978, 48 mildly retarded persons were studied by intensive, naturalistic methods of ethnography. The goal of this research was to understand the community adaptation of mentally retarded adults who were considered to have the potential for normalization, particularly independent living and competitive employment. The research sought to identify phenomena that facilitated or thwarted the normalization of these people. The sample was selected by soliciting the names of persons who were classified as being mentally retarded by some component of the mental retardation service delivery system (special education, regional centers, sheltered workshops, etc.) within the catchment areas of three regional centers in Los Angeles. We next asked knowledgeable personnel in the delivery system to identify persons on our lists whom they thought capable of independent living. Some 120 individuals were nominated, each of whom we interviewed to determine how well they met our criteria for inclusion in the final

---

[2] After the research was well underway, it was discovered that two male sample members had been institutionalized earlier in their lives although both had been released several years before this research began.

sample: 1) Caucasian, 2) "middle-class" family background,[3] 3) no major physical handicaps that would severely limit independence,[4] 4) willingness to participate in the study. In all, 50 persons were selected for intensive study. Early in the course of the research, two persons dropped out of the study, leaving a final sample of 48 persons who were studied for a period of 30 months. The remaining 70 persons constituted a secondary sample that was studied less intensively.

These 48 persons were chosen by means of a quota sample intended to represent the various categories thought to be theoretically relevant for a longitudinal study of community adaptation. Thus, at the inception of the research, there were 22 males and 26 females, 30 of whom were single, with the remainder married or separated; 22 were unemployed, 13 were in sheltered workshops and 13 in competitive jobs. Twenty-three lived independently, 14 lived with their parents, and another 11 lived in group homes. The age range was 18 to 52 with a bimodal distribution of young adults (ages 23–27) and older persons (ages 33–37); the mean age was 27. We did not have access to current IQ scores for all members of the sample but from available records it seemed that all members of the sample had recorded IQs between 65 and 70 when the research began.

Data Collection

The principal means of data collection used was a form of participant-observation. Our use of this procedure has been discussed in detail elsewhere (Edgerton and Langness, 1978), but in brief its essence is the prolonged and unobtrusive presence of a sensitive, disciplined observer with the person or persons being studied. When the procedure is used effectively, the persons being studied will in time learn to take the observer for granted, behaving almost as if he or she were not there, and in turn the observer will come to see the world almost as these persons do.

Each member of the 48-person sample was visited on an average of every 10 to 14 days. These visits sometimes consisted of only an hour or two of conversation but more often they involved many hours spent in such diverse forms of interaction as a shopping trip or an excursion to visit friends, family, or Disneyland. Over the period of this research, sample members were seen repeatedly in all the relevant settings of their everyday world—home, work, transportation, and leisure. Between visits, there was regular telephone contact, often on a daily basis. Fieldworkers also had frequent contact with significant persons in the lives of sample members (parents, siblings, spouses, friends, caregivers, employers, and social workers).

Our goal was a holistic description of the lives of these persons. To ensure comparable coverage of topics, fieldworkers were provided with a field guide of topics and questions to help them, when appropriate and natural, toward the collection of comparable information on each member of the sample. These topics included various aspects of work, self-maintenance in everyday activities, family relationships, leisure, behavior in public places, communicative competence, socioemotional problems, involvement with the service delivery system, and even fantasy. One of these domains focused on deviance, mental

---

[3] Our estimation of socioeconomic status was not precise, but it was adequate to eliminate persons whose family background included low-income, or low-education parents.

[4] Although we eliminated persons with disabling physical handicaps, it is likely that most members of our white, middle-class sample suffer some degree of central nervous system dysfunction.

illness, crime, and any involvements with the legal system either civil or criminal. The resulting corpus of data provides a detailed record of the lives of these 48 persons as they, we, and others observe and interpret them. In this chapter, we discuss only the negative aspects of their lives, those that could lead to hospitalization or incarceration.

Because of the intensity of our data collection procedures, it is unlikely that more than a few crimes were committed—whether detected or not—that we did not learn about either from the retarded person or someone else involved in his or her life. We also learned about most conspicuous forms of deviance, such as sexual promiscuity or wife beating, most emotional problems from anxiety and depression to psychotic episodes, and for most of the sample members we also learned about various minor forms of impropriety or inappropriate behavior, such as problems with hygiene, public decorum, or unusual fantasies. Although our data record undoubtedly contains omissions and is therefore an underestimate of deviant or criminal behavior, it is a reasonably complete record of the conduct of a sample of mildly retarded persons in community settings.

The methods we employed are subject to certain limitations. For one thing, because of the time these procedures require, as well as the expense of training and maintaining a staff of fieldworkers, our sample was small. Fortunately, sample attrition was negligible. Another limiting factor is the subjectivity inherent in the process of participant-observation. Participant-observation requires rapport, and rapport requires a give-and-take of human concern and emotion. Fieldworkers have an effect on sample members, who in turn affect fieldworkers. We have been unable, however, to discern any direct effects that relate to crime, deviance, or mental illness. Of course, there is always the undemonstrated possibility that the presence and concern of the fieldworkers may have influenced the occurrence of some of these phenomena, or at least the willingness of some sample members to discuss such behaviors. Although the possibility of such reactivity cannot be dismissed altogether, our use of multiple sources of data and other procedures seems to have minimized such bias (Edgerton and Langness, 1978).

Findings

As reported in detail elsewhere (Edgerton, 1979), 18 members of the sample led such trouble-free lives that they could justifiably be considered "model citizens." Although one woman among these 18 was briefly hospitalized for severe depression just before our research began, during the 30-month period of this research these persons led exemplary lives. This trouble-free adaptation was not a result of living in restricted or sheltered settings; for example, 10 of these persons were living independently and the majority were married. The ability of these 18 persons to avoid trouble of any kind is more remarkable when it is realized that several of them had records of delinquency in the years (usually during high school) before this research began, and two of them were to men who were frequently and sometimes seriously in trouble with the police.

More Troubled Adaptation

Another 20 of the 48 persons studied sometimes committed relatively minor acts of deviance or largely victimless crimes that might be considered evidence of inadequate adaptation; they might even warrant institutionalization. Like the model citizens, most (12) of these persons were women, and the settings in which they lived were similarly diverse (e.g., 11 lived independently and only three lived with parents). Six of these persons were married. Because their troublesome behavior was so varied, the best characterization possible is a brief summary of each person's deviance, crime, or mental illness during the 30-month period of research. Beginning with the eight men, their deviance during this period was as follows: 1) causing a major but injury-free auto accident while driving without a license; a fist-fight with a co-worker at a workshop; 2) three psychotic episodes leading to a diagnosis of schizophrenia; writing two bad checks; making several visits to prostitutes; occasional use of marijuana; frequently expressed threats of violence against a former girlfriend (none of these acts or threats was reported to the police); 3) hiring two prostitutes to visit his apartment at the same time; 4) one drunk driving arrest (there were other, undetected acts of drunk driving); accepting $500 to marry an immigrant woman from Taiwan to enable her to remain in the U.S. (the marriage was never consummated); selling farm produce at a roadside stand without a police permit; 5) frequent acts of passive homosexuality; knowingly buying stolen property for his own use; 6) occasionally brushing against or touching women on buses or other public places; instigating fights on buses; 7) regularly attending x-rated movies; attempting to use an illegal electronic device in an undetected attempt to defraud the telephone company; and 8) a psychotic episode leading to hospitalization in the course of which he committed $150 worth of property damage to parked cars; several acts of homosexuality; two fist-fights at a workshop. Some of these eight men (e.g., #3) engaged in very little that could be construed as evidence of inadequate adaptation, but others were involved in forms of deviance or crime that had the potential for more serious consequences.

The troublesome acts of the 12 women in this category were as follows: 1) some acts of homosexuality; several threats of violence against co-workers at a workshop; 2) occasional use of marijuana; frequent and flagrant promiscuity, which in one instance involved the death of a boyfriend in her bed (because the cause of death was determined to be chronic illness, there was no police charges; however, the circumstances of the death were ghastly and the neighbors were horrified); 3) several fist-fights with co-residents in her group home; flagrant promiscuity and contracting a venereal disease; 4) several brief periods of hospitalization for diagnosed schizophrenia; threats of suicide; some promiscuity; 5) repeated adultery; two physical assaults against her ex-husband (a sample member); various threats of violence; eviction from her apartment for maintaining it in such an outrageous condition that the bishop of her church threatened her with excommunication; 6) eviction for not cleaning her apartment; speeding ticket (80 mph); refusal to return overpayment on Supplementary Security Income (SSI), leading to a threat of litigation; 7) homosexual seduction of a teenager leading to her expulsion from a day-camp program; dependence on various medications including Librium and phenobarbital; frequent instances of driving without a license and under the influence of tranquilizing drugs; 8) adultery resulting in her disfellowship from the Mormon Church; 9) use of a knife to make repeated suicide threats and gestures; 10) occasional use of marijuana; suicide threats; illegal income while receiving SSI; birth of an illegitimate child who was given up for adoption; 11) outbursts of temper and obscene language while working as a babysitter, leading to the loss of these jobs; 12) frequently operating a motorcycle without a license; attempting to falsify her work records in an effort to increase her earnings (because she did not understand the differences between piece-work and an hourly salary, her falsification was counterproductive).

These brief depictions obviously tell us little about the context of these acts or of the persons involved. They are presented simply to indicate the range of behaviors involved, their approximate frequency, and their potential for untoward consequences. For the women, as the men, there was a great range of deviant acts some of which could have led to personal injury or to criminal charges. In fact, however, there were no injuries requiring more than first aid, and although church officials twice intervened, there was no police action taken, except for three motor vehicle citations, and the three persons who were hospitalized for mental illness were released within a month.

For these 20 people, the pattern of community adaptation included relatively minor deviance, often of a sexual nature, with very little actual criminality of any kind, especially of a violent sort. When acts or threatened acts occurred that violated the law, these were not reported to authorities. On the whole, the deviance of these men and women was neither very frequent nor very serious. The deviant behavior of the final 10 members of the sample, however, was a good deal more frequent and serious.

More Frequent and Serious Offenders

These 10 more serious offenders lived in a variety of circumstances: four with their parents, four in group homes, and two in independent apartments. Three were married, one was divorced, the rest were single. In contrast with the previous categories, nine of these more serious offenders were men, and only one was a woman. As before, it is impossible to do more than sketch the outlines of their deviance but because this more frequent and serious deviance raises questions about the assessment of failure in community adaptation, the sketches will necessarily be somewhat longer. First, one woman (married to, then divorced from, a sample member whom we shall next discuss) was engaged in a great array of troublesome and illegal activities. For example, in addition to almost ceaseless adulterous affairs with men, she maintained a prolonged homosexual relationship, and had two abortions. She frequently threatened suicide and several times made what seemed to be serious attempts at suicide. She often drove recklessly and received several speeding tickets. She became a dependent on Valium, cheated on her SSI payments, and was evicted from her apartment for maintaining it in a filthy condition. She stole small items from coffee shops (an activity she boastfully called a ''five-finger discount''), but was not detected. She was arrested for breaking and entering the house of her ex-husband (the charges were later dropped). Finally, she received an 18-month probation sentence for assaulting her second husband.

The first husband of this woman had an equally extensive list of offenses. For example, he often drove recklessly and drunkenly without being detected by the police; in addition he amassed five speeding tickets and was arrested and jailed for drunk driving. He also had two major accidents, at least one of which was due to his recklessness. Like his former wife, he attempted to defraud SSI by not reporting outside income. He kept a loaded gun under his pillow and often threatened to use it; once he arranged to have friends physically assault one of his wives' lovers, and later he assaulted this same man on the bus. Finally, he and a friend stole a newspaper dispensing machine for the coins it contained; they were arrested and convicted with a sentence of 12 months probation plus a fine of $150.

A second man who was convicted of manslaughter in an automobile accident some years before our research began had his license returned during the research and continued to drive well over the speed limit. He was not ticketed. He was threatened with eviction due to the unsightly and unhygienic condition of his apartment. He also had an explosive temper that led him to attack inanimate objects as well as people; he often put his fist through walls, sometimes beat his wife, and twice assaulted co-workers, although in no instance was there serious injury or police involvement.

Another man also engaged in violence, twice beating his girlfriend, but his principal deviance involved writing bad checks and incurring credit card debts that he could not pay. He acquired a credit card by falsifying the application form, and he remained out of jail in the face of repeated threats of litigation only because his mother paid his long-overdue debts. He also attempted to defraud SSI by not reporting extra income. In addition, he had two major auto accidents, one of which occurred in Mexico where he was jailed for his failure to have proper insurance, but he was released through the intervention of the parents of one of his passengers.

A fourth man had a long record of violence. He once attacked his mother, with whom he then lived, throwing her across a room. He also pushed a co-worker off a loading dock and threatened his employer with a knife. Although he was fired from various jobs for his violence, no charges were filed with the police. A fifth man, who had been institutionalized as a teenager for sexually molesting a child, also developed a pattern of violent behavior. For example, he threatened (or attempted) to attack a co-worker with a metal garbage can, he repeatedly put his fist through the bedroom wall of his group home, and he threatened a visitor to his group home with a gun that belonged to the caregiver. Again, none of these acts was reported to the police.

A sixth man, formerly married to a sample member, frequently reported violent dreams and fantasies, and several times directed verbal aggression at strangers in public places. He sometimes expressed violence openly as, for example, in three fights with co-workers and various conflicts with his ex-wife, which once included standing over her with a knife pointed at her throat while she slept. His only arrest was for loitering, although he sexually molested a 9-year-old niece (he kissed her and masturbated toward her). Most of these acts are said to have occurred during his "blackouts," which were variously diagnosed during a brief voluntary stay at a mental hospital as schizophrenia or epilepsy. He subsequently intentionally used his blackouts to excuse further sexual misconduct.

A seventh man, a sometimes heavy user of alcohol, threatened a co-resident at his group home with a knife (no police charges were filed), and several times engaged in theft or robbery. He is a "street-wise" man who stole from friends and co-residents as well as strangers. He also collaborated with an attractive girlfriend; while she led on a victim sexually, he stole the man's money. He has never been arrested.

An eighth man was convicted of a felony charge of aggravated assault when he attacked a 10-year-old neighbor boy and kicked him repeatedly with his heavy boots. The boy had apparently taunted him. This was not an isolated act of violence; he often beat his wife, sometimes savagely so, once dislocating her ankle. He once struck a retarded woman at a bowling alley and threatened a member of a social group for retarded persons with a knife. He drove recklessly on many occasions causing his license to be suspended and finally leading to a 3-day jail sentence. He also stole money, usually to spend at massage parlors, or to hire masseuses to come to his apartment (sometimes while his wife was locked in another room). On more than one occasion he boasted about his lawlessness, saying, "I never lie except to the police."

The final man in this category has had 12 known arrests, four of which occurred during the period of this study. Most were for petty theft or for breaking and entering homes or cars. In addition to the robberies for which he was arrested, he admitted to stealing from the manager's office of a movie theatre, from a parked car, and from friends. He also had several fights including one with inmates while he was in jail awaiting trial. He often carried a knife which he kept under his pillow at night, and he sometimes carried a realistic toy gun. On some occasions he carried both a switchblade knife in his pocket and a 6-inch hunting knife in a scabbard on his belt. He often drank beer excessively, sometimes smoked marijuana, and he was accused of masturbating publicly on at least one occasion. His last conviction for robbery led to a sentence of 18-months probation under the supervision of the caregiver of his group home. He freely admitted that his thefts were planned in advance and said that he has been stealing since he was 8.

To review, approximately one-third of this population of mildly retarded adults achieved an exemplary adaptation to life in various community settings during the 30 months that we recorded their behavior. The remaining two-thirds of these people, as we have seen, made various kinds of trouble for themselves or others. For example, 15 persons assaulted somebody physically and six of these assaults involved a deadly weapon. Only three of these assaults were reported to the police resulting in two convictions with probated sentences. Five persons possessed and sometimes carried knives; two possessed handguns although, to our knowledge, these were never fired. Nineteen members of the sample engaged in one or another form of sexual deviance or crime. Five persons were thieves, four of them repeatedly so. Thirteen members of the sample drove motor vehicles, at least occasionally. Three of these drove without any known trouble, but the remaining 10 drivers committed many traffic offenses. In addition to innumerable instances of unreported speeding, recklessness and driving while intoxicated, these 10 persons received 10 tickets for moving violations, two for drunk driving, and three for driving without a valid license. They also were involved in five accidents, four of which involved injuries. Four members of the sample (all women) made serious suicide attempts, and eight experienced severe episodes of mental illness, four of which resulted in brief periods of hospitalization.

ISSUES IN THE ASSESSMENT OF FAILURE

For 18 members of this sample, the assessment of success or failure in community adaptation is relatively simple. Those persons were not always happy or employed, and some were isolated from others around them, but for a 30-month period, they remained in the community and caused no discernible trouble for themselves or others. The adaptation of the remaining 30 persons is more difficult to assess because these persons had much more unhappy and troublesome lives during the period of this research. This emphasis on "the period of the research" raises the first of three important issues concerning the assessment of failure in community adaptation.

Longitudinal Perspective

The foregoing illustrative material provides little more than a hint of the complexities involved in describing and assessing community adaptation. The evidence presented here concerning crime, deviance, and mental illness must be seen against the total context of each person's life over a 30-month period. That context is so complex and changing that it cannot be depicted here beyond saying that these people's lives were largely free of the kinds of troublesome behavior that was highlighted above. That, perhaps, is self-evident, because most criminals and psychotics engage in criminal or bizarre behavior only a small percentage of the time. But the point needs emphasis because given the episodic nature of crime and deviance, it matters greatly how and when one samples such behavior.

The dangers of sampling behavior at one limited point in time rather than over an extended period should be obvious, yet investigators continue to rely on data collected in just this way (Heal, Sigelman, and Switzky, 1978). Longitudinal data collection is expensive, but without such a continuous perspective on community adaptation—on lives in process—efforts to assess "failure" or "success" will continue to be illusory at best. That is so because the lives of mildly retarded persons in community settings are characterized by frequent and often dramatic change. For example, we cannot assume that the 18 "model citizens" in our sample will continue their trouble-free adaptation indefinitely. For one thing, we know that two of these 18 people were in rather serious trouble in the years just prior to our research, and since we terminated our 30-month period of intensive data collection, three others have encountered difficulties (one became severely depressed, two others developed bizarre behavior patterns).

Had we examined the behavior of our sample at a restricted point in time—over 1 month, for example—we would have found some persons hospitalized for mental illness or suicidal behavior, others in jail, and still others in periods of violent conflict with parents, friends, or employers. A week or a month later, these same persons would be out of hospital or jail and would have resolved their interpersonal conflicts. Conversely, persons who seem to be trouble-free at one point in time would often look far more troubled only a short time later. In this perspective, problems in community adaptation should be seen as episodes in a rapidly oscillating process, not as "outcomes" that should operationally define current success or failure. Neither should they be accepted as accurate predictors of future success or failure.

Environmental Tolerance

As the existing literature indicates, community settings seem to have differential tolerance for the behavior of retarded persons. Reinstitutionalization may be caused most often by medical problems in one setting, by behavioral problems in another, and vocational difficulties in a third. One must presume, although here the evidence is more indirect, that at different times and in different places, entire communities differ in their tolerance for certain behaviors such as deviance, crime, and mental illness. The Puritans provide one such historical example (Erickson, 1966), the early history of institutional confinement of the mentally retarded of this country is another (Wolfensberger, 1975), and recent societal reaction to the use of marijuana is a third.

During the 30 months of this research, most of the persons who were in day-to-day contact with our sample members were remarkably tolerant of the behavior of almost all of them. Parents tolerated financial irresponsibility, workshop employers ignored violence, co-residents of group homes tolerated sexual promiscuity, theft, and bizarre conduct of all kinds. Infrequently, informal sanctions such as criticism or ostracism were brought to bear, but complaints to agents of social control such as regional center counselors, social workers, or the police were exceedingly uncommon. When complaints were made, they typically came from persons outside the network of relatives, friends, co-residents, caregivers, and employers, that makes up the effective community for most of these retarded persons. Persons in this network tolerated outrageous, bizarre, and even dangerous behavior. Persons outside it—neighbors, landlords, strangers in public places—were consistently less tolerant.

Intolerance can also occur. Victimization and exploitation do take place. As reported in detail elsewhere (Edgerton, 1979), members of this sample were "victims" as frequently as they were "victimizers." The literature contains many classic instances of victimization or behavioral intolerance. In the past, parents often institutionalized their adolescent children ostensibly to protect them from their awakening sexuality (de la Cruz and LaVeck, 1973), and police sometimes arrested innocent retarded persons as in the case reported by Turnbull and Turnbull (1975) in which a perfectly sober Down's syndrome person was arrested for public intoxication due to his "slurred" speech. In our research we encountered two examples of police victimization of sample members (neither resulted in arrest), and a few by parents (usually involving misuse of their child's money) and other relatives or friends, but a little more than two-thirds of all instances of exploitation or victimization were by strangers. However unpleasant this victimization or exploitation was—and it sometimes involved attempts to "frame" a sample member for a crime—it never led to institutional placement. As we have seen, neither did much of anything else, except for very brief periods. To understand this phenomenon of noninstitutionalization we must briefly consider recent legislation and policy.

Legislation, Policy and Institutionalization   States have historically justified their placement of mentally retarded persons in institutions either under the doctrine of *parens patriae* (enabling it to act in the interest of an individual to protect his or her welfare) or the police power doctrine (enabling it to act in order to protect the well-being or safety of society in general). These principles were used by various states to institutionalize many thousands of mentally retarded persons. But as the Supreme Court recognized in 1960 (Soskin, 1977), both principles are limited by the due process clause of the 14th Amendment, which provides the basis for the "least restrictive alternative" principle limiting the rights of the state to deprive an individual of personal liberty (Scheerenberger, 1976). Following the landmark decision of *Wyatt* v. *Stickney*, federal and state courts have extended the least restrictive alternative in a variety of ways (Turnbull and Turnbull, 1975).

As a result, at the time of this research in California, there were formidable constraints against the institutionalization of a mentally retarded adult, even if that person became mentally ill or committed a crime. While an individual in California may voluntarily commit himself or herself to a state mental hospital (as one member of our sample did for a brief period), involuntary commitment is strictly limited. Any peace officer may detain a person involuntarily for observation and evaluation at an authorized hospital facility for no more than 72 hours. This 72-hour period can be extended an additional 14 days if the facility certifies to the Superior Court that the individual is a danger to self or others, or is "gravely disabled" (i.e., unable to provide for basic personal needs of food, clothing, and shelter). An additional "hold" of 14 days may be initiated by the facility if the individual is considered to be suicidal. To hold a person beyond this period usually requires demonstration of "grave disability" at a conservatorship hearing. Although three members of our sample became overtly psychotic and suicidal, none was held beyond the second 14-day period.

California Penal Code 1370.1 provides that a criminal defendant who is mentally retarded be dealt with outside of the existing prison system. Unless the defendant has been charged with murder, armed robbery in which the victim suffers great bodily harm, or other serious felonies specified by the code, the court orders the regional center to submit a recommendation for outpatient "treatment" or for residential placement in a state hospital or other approved residential facility including a group home. Prison is rejected as a correctional alternative on the grounds that mentally retarded persons cannot benefit from such incarceration (that nonretarded persons *do* benefit from prison is, to say the least, arguable). From the early declarations of the "Task Force on Law" of the President's Panel on Mental Retardation (1963), the reasoned arguments for a special offenders court by Allen (1968, 1970), and the subsequent work of many writers (Browning, 1976; Turnbull and Turnbull, 1975; Biklen, 1977; March, Friel, and Eissler, 1975), a position has developed that an alternative to incarceration for mentally retarded persons should be provided although it should not serve as an excuse for criminal acts.

In the past, there was no such exemption for mentally retarded persons. As recently as the 1960s, 10% of the prison population in the United States was found to be mentally retarded by IQ criteria, and in some states, especially in the South, the percentage was much higher. Presumably, many retarded persons in many states including California still go unrecognized in court and consequently find their way into a correctional institution. In our sample of 48 persons, however, even repeat and serious criminal offenders avoided incarceration. With the exception of one man with 12 arrests, who spent 90 days in county jail for evaluation, and two others who spent 3 days in jail for reckless driving before the charges were dropped, the three members of this sample who were convicted of crimes (two for assault convictions, one for theft), were released on probation to a group home caregiver. Several members of the sample who committed repeated undetected criminal acts, including acts of violence, were aware of this practice. As one man who frequently stole put it, "What can they do to me? I'll be out in a few days because they'll send me right back where I'm living now." As if to prove his point, he did steal, was arrested and convicted, and the prophecy was fulfilled. This episode illustrates the contemporary climate that militates so strongly against the hospitalization or incarceration of mildly retarded adults.

RELATIVITY IN THE ASSESSMENT OF COMMUNITY ADAPTATION

The assessment or prediction of community adaptation is so complex that, for the most part, it must remain well beyond the scope of this discussion. This discussion is confined to the efforts of many investigators to utilize objective and comparable criteria of community adaptation. Of these the most widely used are "remaining in the community" as the criterion of successful adaptation, and "institutional placement" or "reinstitutionaliza-tion" as the criterion of failure. That these criteria are simplistic and mask a variety of disparate phenomena has been generally recognized, but that each may be anything but objective or comparable may not be fully recognized.

As the data in this chapter illustrate, persons who remain in the community without institutional placement can represent an exceptional range of adaptations from trouble-free independent living to varieties of dependency combined with serious deviance, repeated criminality, and major mental illness. As these same data indicate, "institutional placement'' is no longer a useful criterion of failure because the contemporary constraints against institutional placement are so imposing, especially for persons who were not previously institutionalized. The majority of mildly retarded persons now in community settings (and the majority likely to be in such settings in the future) have not been institutionalized.

From a national perspective, this criterion is particularly misleading because of the highly variable policies of incarceration that exist. This variation can be illustrated by the fact that when Brown and Courtless (1968) surveyed incarcerated offenders, they found that the percentage with IQs below 70 varied from 24.3% in Arkansas, Louisiana, Oklahoma, and Texas, to only 2.6% in Montana, Idaho, Wyoming, Colorado, New Mexico, Utah, and Nevada. A survey in 1969 of all offenders ages 17–21 in South Carolina found that 40% of these youthful offenders had IQs in the retarded range (Fries and LaBelle, 1969). In a survey of 1,491 male juvenile offenders in Texas, 13 percent were found to have IQs below 70; of these 58.3% were ''Black Americans,'' 32.3% were ''Latin Americans,'' and only 9.4% were ''Anglo-Americans.'' The artifactual nature of these ethnic disproportions is obvious. It is also significant that 33.8% of these retarded offenders had never attended school. A similar pattern was found for 175 female offenders for whom IQ scores were available (Kirkpatrick and Haskins, 1971).

One can hardly fail to question the objectivity and comparability of incarceration as a criterion of failure when repeated offenders in Los Angeles go undetected, or if detected, remain in community settings, while 40% of all youthful offenders in South Carolina prove to be mentally retarded. But such a disparity is hardly remarkable, because it must be obvious that judgments of success and failure are relative to a host of factors. First, there are the expectations of others: professionals, parents, peers, neighbors, counselors, courts, and many others. To emphasize the complex and potentially contradictory character of these expectations, one need only contrast the expectations of professionals as codified in instruments such as the ABS or PAC and those of peers (Edgerton and Bercovici, 1976). Before one dismisses this reference to peers as some sort of ritual acknowledgment of the worth of retarded persons, consider that peers do make judgments about success and failure, they deal with one another's behavior every day and they can promote success with their praise and respect, just as they can help to precipitate failure by complaining to agents of social control.

Similarly, judgments about success and failure are relative to the microenvironments in which retarded persons live: group homes, sheltered workshops, neighborhood markets, buses, public parks, and streets. Not only do these environments require different competencies, it is often true that success in one environment (e.g., a group home that requires dependency) may increase the probability of failure in another environment (e.g., a job that requires independence). These things are obvious even if they are not always taken into account in assessments of success or failure.

Less obvious, perhaps, are some of the pitfalls involved in judging the community adaptation of retarded persons relative to nonretarded persons. Most basic among the problems is the metamethodological assumption that group comparison research designs are more powerful than designs that monitor the process of single individuals over time. This assumption is contestable on several grounds (Hersen and Barlow, 1976) not the least of which is the single-point-in-time sampling issue raised earlier. Single-point-in-time sampling is characteristic of group comparison designs. Another issue involves the "matching" of "normals" with a retarded sample. Research on the community adaptation of mentally retarded persons has been remarkably naive in its use of selection criteria for normal controls, typically leaving the most suggestive variables concerning pre- and post-environments uncontrolled. Indeed the fundamental assumption that a "normal" control group can effectively be contrasted with a retarded population must be justified, not simply taken for granted (McCarver and Craig, 1974; Heal et al., 1978).

The dilemmas of relativism in assessing community adaptation are serious. If, as seems apparent, the simple but presumably objective criteria of remaining in the community or returning to an institution are so relative to shifting sociocultural circumstances that they yield both false negatives and false positives, then they cannot be relied upon any longer. And if we cannot utilize these criteria, then what will serve as reliable and valid criteria?

The answer cannot be attempted here, not only because it goes well beyond the scope of this chapter, but also because the answer is unknown. The solution could be further development of complex evaluation models like that offered by Moos (1974). Such approaches may prove useful for assessing certain environments, especially restricted ones like wards or group homes, but if they are to provide a measure of the adequacy of community adaptation in all its multi-environmental complexity, then more is needed. As Scheerenberger (1976) suggested, we must learn to measure "quality of life."

It is only a slight exaggeration to say that efforts to measure quality of life have resembled a search for a small needle in a large haystack. Most of these efforts have been highly positivistic, attempting to specify attributes of persons, features of environments and development goals, sometimes in complex interactional models. Spurred on by the legislated need for individual program planning and assessment of residential facilities, such efforts will undoubtedly proceed apace. But these efforts are likely to continue to provide simple solutions to complex problems, and as so many have warned, the best solution for a complex problem is not necessarily a simple one.

The history of anthropology does not provide a set of procedures for measuring the quality of life of any population but it may help us think about the problem in another way. A person's quality of life, like that of a population, is complex, integrated, and replete with meaning, yet it is also inherently changing, contradictory, and ambiguous. A population's way of life—anthropologists call it their "culture"—has long been assessed as good or bad, primitive or civilized, simple or complex, rigid or flexible, and so on. Anthropologists have generally regarded such evaluations as ethnocentric whether they are made with good intentions or bad ones and whether by colonialists, religionists, economists, humanitarians—or other anthropologists. Instead, anthropology has argued that all cultures must be understood in their own terms. This has led to the development of a discipline that attempts to describe and interpret cultures as much as possible through the eyes of the members of those cultures themselves.

By most standards, mentally retarded individuals do not create a culture when they move into a community setting, but they do adapt to a culture, the way of life of those persons with whom they live and interact. If we were to describe community adaptation through the eyes of these persons—including those of the mentally retarded persons—we would find that these cultures differed and so did the extent to which retarded persons were seen as being able to fit into them. In some they would be accepted, in others they would be rejected or their behavior would call for correction. Because each culture—each community—would differ somewhat, this form of description would be radically relativistic. But this, after all, is very much what we find today *de facto*. If a mentally retarded person encounters difficulty in one environment—one culture—he or she moves to another where adaptation may or may not be seen as better.

To adopt a radically relativistic view of adaptation need not be seen as scientific anarchism (Meyers, Nihira, and Zetlin, 1979), although some will do so. Until objective criteria of community adaptation can be established—and given the social, cultural, and individual diversity in the environments where mentally retarded persons live, this seems an unattainable goal—we might consider taking seriously the views and evaluations of the persons concerned rather than imposing our criteria on them. If we cannot measure adaptation effectively, why not leave it to the persons involved?

This approach obviously raises serious problems because it would permit exploitation, abuse, lawlessness, overprotection and the like to become normative in certain environments. But that, really, is a problem calling for effective program planning, for advocacy, for monitoring residential facilities, and so on. And it is nothing new; just such exploitation, overprotection, and lawlessness exist today.

The purpose of this chapter is not to propose a better means of measuring community adaptation. There is no ideal means of measurement, but measurement will continue because there will continue to be administrative reasons that make measurement desirable. This chapter suggests that published assertions to the effect that the majority of mentally retarded persons succeed in community adaptation, that they disappear into the community, or that a certain percentage fail to do either, are based on arbitrary and relativistic criteria. We know far too little about the processes of community adaptation to allow ourselves the illusion that we have already measured success or failure. It is far more likely that we will never know how to do so.

REFERENCES

Allen, R. C. The retarded offender: Unrecognized in court and untreated in prison. *Federal Probation*, 1968, *32*, 22–27.

Allen, R. C. The law and the mentally retarded. In F. J. Menolascino (Ed.), *Psychiatric approaches to mental retardation*. New York: Basic Books, 1970.

Baller, W. R. The study of the present social status of a group of adults who, when they were in elementary school, were classified as mentally deficient. *Genetic Psychology Monographs*, 1936, *18*, 165–244.

Bassuk, E. L., & Gerson, S. Deinstitutionalization and mental health services. *Scientific American*, 1978, *238*, No. 2.

Begab, M. J. In Wyatt v. Hardin C. A. 3195-N. V.S. District Court, Middle District of Alabama, Deposition of Dr. Michael J. Begab, August 21, 1978.

Biklen, D. Myths, mistreatment and pitfalls: Mental retardation and criminal justice. *Mental Retardation*, 1977, *15*, 51–57.

Biklen, D. The community imperative: A refutation of all arguments in support of institutionalizing anybody because of mental retardation. *Center on Human Policy*, 1979, Syracuse, N.Y.: Syracuse University.

Brown, B. S., & Courtless, T. F. The mentally retarded in penal and correctional institutions. *American Journal of Psychiatry*, 1968, *124*, 1164–1170.

Browning, P. L. *Rehabilitation and the retarded offender*. Springfield, Ill.: Charles C Thomas, 1976.

Butler, E. W., & Bjaanes, A. T. A typology of community care facilities and differential normalization outcomes. In P. Mittler (Ed.), *Research to practice in mental retardation* (Vol. 1). Baltimore: University Park Press, 1977, pp. 337–347.

Christensen, R. Projected percentage of U.S. population with criminal arrest and conviction records. In *President's Commission on Law Enforcement and Administration of Justice, Task Force Report: Science and Technology*. Washington, D.C.: U.S. Government Printing Office, 1967.

Cobb, H. *The forecast of fulfillment: A review of research on predictive assessment of the adult retarded for social and vocational adjustment*. New York: Teachers College Press, Columbia University, 1972.

Conroy, J. W. Trends in deinstitutionalization of the mentally retarded. *Mental Retardation*, 1977, *15*,44–46.

Crawford, J. L., Aiello, J. R., & Thompson, D. E. Deinstitutionalization and community placement: Clinical and environmental factors. *Mental Retardation*, 1979, *17*, 59–64.

de la Cruz, F. F., & LaVeck, G. D. *Human sexuality and mentally retarded*. New York: Brunner/ Mazel, 1973.

Deno, E. *Retarded youth: Their school rehabilitation needs*. Final Report of Project VRA-RD-681. Minneapolis: Minneapolis Public Schools, 1965.

Eagle, E. Prognosis and outcome of community placement of institutionalized retardates. *American Journal of Mental Deficiency*, 1967, *72*, 232–243.

Edgerton, R. B. *The cloak of competence: Stigma in the lives of the mentally retarded*. Berkeley: University of California Press, 1967.

Edgerton, R. B. Crime, deviance and normalization: Reconsidered. Paper presented at the 103rd Annual Meeting of the American Association on Mental Deficiency, Miami Beach, Florida, 1979.

Edgerton, R. B., & Bercovici, S. The cloak of competence: Years later. *American Journal of Mental Deficiency*, 1976, *80*, 485–497.

Edgerton, R. B., & Langness, L. L. Observing mentally retarded persons in community settings: An anthropological perspective. In G. P. Sackett (Ed.), *Observing behavior* (Vol. 1). Baltimore: University Park Press, 1978.

Erickson, K. *Wayward Puritans: A study in the sociology of deviance*. New York: John Wiley & Sons, 1966.

Fairbanks, R. F. The subnormal child—seventeen years later. *Mental Hygiene*, 1933, *17*, 177–208.

Farrell, E. E. A preliminary report on the careers of three hundred fifty children who have left ungraded classes. *Journal of Psycho-Asthenics*, 1915, *20*, 20–26.

Farrington, D. P. Longitudinal research on crime and delinquency. In N. Morris (Ed.), *Research in criminal justice* (Vol. 1). Chicago: University of Chicago Press, 1979.

Fernald, W. E. After-care study of the patients discharged from Waverly for a period of twenty-five years. *Ungraded*, 1919, *5*, 25–31.

Fries, W., & LaBelle, S. *A plan for the youthful mentally retarded offender* (File Y:35-8–3.0). Charleston: South Carolina Department of Mental Retardation, 1969.

Goldstein, H. Social and occupational adjustment. In H. A. Stevens and R. Heber (Eds.), *Mental retardation: A review of research*. Chicago: University of Chicago Press, 1964, pp. 214–258.

Gollay, E. Deinstitutionalized mentally retarded people: A closer look. *Education and Training of the Mentally Retarded*, 1977, *12*, 137–144.

Gollay, E., Friedman, R., Wyngarden, M., & Kurtz, N. *Coming back*. Cambridge: Abt Books, 1978.

Gottesfeld, H. *Alternatives to psychiatric hospitalization*. New York: Gardner Press, 1977.

Gozali, J. Perception of the EMR special class by former students. *Mental Retardation*, 1972, *10*, 34–35.

Heal, L. W., Sigelman, C. K., & Switzky, H. N. Research in community residential alternatives for the mentally retarded. In N. R. Ellis (Ed.), *International review of research in mental retardation* (Vol. 9). New York: Academic Press, 1978, pp. 209–249.

Heber, R. F., & Dever R. B. Research on education and habilitation of the mentally retarded. In H. C. Haywood (Ed.), *Social-cultural aspects of mental retardation*. New York: Appleton-Century-Crofts, 1970, pp. 395–427.

Hersen, M., & Barlow, D. H. *Single case experimental designs: Strategies for studying behavior change*. New York: Pergamon Press, 1976.

Kennedy, R. J. *A Connecticut community revisited: A study of the social adjustment of a group of mentally deficient adults in 1948 and 1960*. Hartford, Conn.: Connecticut State Department of Health, Office of Mental Retardation, 1966.

Kirkpatrick, D., & Haskins, J. *The mentally retarded offender, A preliminary statistical summary*. Austin: Texas Department of Mental Health and Mental Retardation, 1971.

Lee, J. L., Hegge, T. G., & Voelker, P. H. *A study of social adequacy and of social failure of mentally retarded youth in Wayne County, Michigan*. Detroit: Wayne State University Press, 1959.

MacEachron, A. E. Mentally retarded offenders: Prevalence and characteristics. *American Journal of Mental Deficiency*, *84*, 165–176, 1979.

MacMillan, D. L. *Mental retardation in school and society*. Boston: Little, Brown & Company, 1977.

March, R. L., Friel, C. M., and Eissler, V. The adult MR in the criminal justice system. *Mental Retardation*, 1975, *13*, 21–25.

McCarver, R. B., & Craig, E. M. Placement of the retarded in the community: Prognosis and outcome. In N. R. Ellis (Ed.), *International review of research in mental retardation*. New York: Academic Press, 1974.

McKeon, R. M. Mentally retarded boys in war time. *Mental Hygiene*, 1946, *30*, 47–55.

Meyers, C. E., Nihira, K., & Zetlin, A. The measurement of adaptive behavior. In N. Ellis (Ed.), *Handbook of mental deficiency* (2nd ed.). Hillsdale, N.J.: Lawrence Erlbaum Associates, 1979, pp. 431–481.

Moen, M., Bogen, D., & Aanes, D. Follow-up of mentally retarded adults successfully and unsuccessfully placed in community group homes. *Hospital and Community Psychiatry*, 1975, *26*, 754–756.

Moos, R. H. *Evaluating treatment environments: A social ecological approach*. New York: John Wiley & Sons, 1974.

Peterson, L., & Smith, L. L. A comparison of the post school adjustment of educable mentally retarded adults with that of adults of normal intelligence. *Exceptional Child*, 1960, *26*, 404–408.

President's Panel on Mental Retardation. *Report of the Task Force on Law*, United States Department of Health, Education and Welfare, January, 1963.

Schalock, R. L., & Harper, R. S. Placement from community-based mental retardation programs: How well do clients do? *American Journal of Mental Deficiency*, 1978, *83*, 240–247.

Scheerenberger, R. C. *Deinstitutionalization and institutional reform*. Springfield, Ill.: Charles C Thomas, 1976.

Shannon, L. W. Predicting adult criminal careers from juvenile careers. Paper presented at the 1978 Annual Meeting of the American Society of Criminology.

Soskin, R. M. The least restrictive alternative: In principle and in application. *Amicus*, 1977, *2*, 28–32.

Stephens, W. B. D. *Success of young adult male retardates*. Ann Arbor, Mich: University Microfilms, 1964.

Turnbull, H. R., & Turnbull, A. P. Deinstitutionalization and the law. *Mental Retardation*, 1975, *13*, 14–20.

Vitello, S. J. Beyond deinstitutionalization: What's happening to the people? *Amicus*, 1977, *2*, 40–44.

Wallace, G. L. Parole of the feeble-minded. *Proceedings of the American Association for the Study of the Feebleminded*, 1918–19, *23*, 60–81.

Windle, C. *Prognosis of mental subnormals*. Monograph Supplement to American Journal of Mental Deficiency, March, 1962, Vol. 66, No. 5.

Wolfensberger, W. *The origin and nature of our institutional models*. Syracuse, N.Y.: Human Policy Press, 1975.

Wolfgang, M. Crime in a birth cohort. *Proceedings of the American Philosophical Society*, 1973, *117*, 404–411.

WORK
SETTINGS

Workshop Society: Ethnographic Observations in a Work Setting for Retarded Adults

Jim L. Turner

Like most facilities that provide habilitative programs for the mentally retarded, sheltered workshops are complex social environments about which little is known and much is assumed. The available literature consists largely of programmatic assertions as to what a sheltered workshop for the retarded should be (e.g., Nelson, 1971; Zaetz, 1971); governmental surveys that periodically evaluate the organizational features of workshop finances, facilities, and programs (e.g., United States Department of Labor, 1979); and numerous demonstrations that behavior modification techniques can be used to enhance the task complexity and production level of mentally retarded workers (e.g., Crossman, 1969; Gold, 1972; Eilbracht and Thompson, 1977). In contrast, there is a conspicuous absence of studies that examine the human context of the workshop setting. The naturally occurring behaviors and concerns of retarded workers remain largely undocumented. Lacking such data, we know little about how retarded workers themselves perceive and utilize the workshop setting, or the extent to which their personal agendas and values help shape the environments they inhabit.

With the notable exception of Edgerton's seminal ethnographic research in a state institution (e.g., Edgerton, Tarjan, and Dingman, 1961; Edgerton and Sabagh, 1962; Edgerton, 1963; Edgerton and Dingman, 1964; MacAndrew and Edgerton, 1964; MacAndrew and Edgerton, 1966) there has been little recognition that collectivities of retarded persons are themselves a rich, complex, and dynamic "environment." In documenting the richness and complexity of peer subculture, an ethnographic data base may also enlighten more formal quantitative observations that, without this perspective, seem puzzling or contradictory. What is often overlooked in generalizations about "retarded behavior" is the social context in which that behavior is embedded and the consequences of that context for

Preparation of this chapter, and the research on which it is based, was made possible by the Mental Retardation Research Center, University of California at Los Angeles (USPHS Grand HD-04612-05) and by Program Project Grant (NICHD HD-11944-03), Robert B. Edgerton, Principal Investigator.

the variables of interest. Qualitative observation can also serve as an important reminder that retarded persons are individual human beings, no more or no less complex and variable than the rest of us—a fact that our methodological preferences, personal biases, and propensity for premature quantification have a tendency to obscure.

The goal of this chapter is to describe a collectivity of mentally retarded adults from an ethnographic perspective. It is assumed that the workshop setting can be viewed as a small society unto itself—in the sense that its members constitute a distinct group of people with a set of common experiences and qualities who interact with each other more than with any other group. The chapter illustrates that workshop society has its own ethos—a distinct system of values, conventions, and rules of conduct, and that viewed in terms of its own internal logic and focal concerns, this ethos has functional properties of both theoretical and applied significance.

ON METHODS

From October 1975 to date, the writer, research assistants, and students have been studying a sheltered workshop. Cumulatively, approximately 9,000 hours of naturalistic observation has been amassed on this one setting. Our methods include a variety of more formal quantitative procedures (e.g., behavior rating scales; standardized personality tests; direct observation of randomly selected groups of individuals using preselected behavioral categories and both time and event sampling procedures; questionnaires and structured interviews.) We have relied continuously and primarily, however, on participant observation techniques as a means of trying to access, record, and understand the experiential world of retarded adults in a sheltered workshop setting. At least 95% of the time was spent in the company of "clients" rather than staff. We interacted, listened, watched, and tried to understand what individuals were concerned about and how they acted upon those concerns. We participated in social activities and worked in the shop (e.g., one research assistant worked daily for 3 months as "a client," and another worked on and off for a year as a substitute supervisor). We met weekly with small groups of individuals to discuss their current concerns, or whatever topic they wished to introduce. We made every effort to be friendly and "nice" and remain nonjudgmental. We refused to be a part of any disciplinary action by staff, or to take sides in disputes between peers. Our tape recorders and notebooks were omnipresent, and we sought to document as accurately as possible what we saw and heard.

We now have a considerable body of data that include both quantitative and qualitative materials. This report is an attempt to combine a small sample of these two differing types and sources of information and to look for meaningful patterns that may enhance our understanding of the sheltered workshop as a social setting. Because our study involved a single setting, we begin by providing some background information on what might be termed an "outsider" view. After that, we provide a preliminary perspective on the "insider" view.

HISTORY

In 1953, a small group of parents began meeting in their homes to discuss mutual problems they encountered in trying to raise their mentally retarded children. These parents were unique in that they had decided, despite the professional lore of the times, not to institutionalize their children. They incorporated themselves as a local organization for the retarded and focused on the goal of providing schooling for their children. Within a year the first class of 11 children began meeting at a room in a city park. Parents paid tuition and volunteered their time both in the classroom and in private fund-raising activities. By 1958, the organization had purchased land and constructed their own school.

As the students grew older, the organization foresaw the need to develop programs and activities for retarded adults. In 1965, they established a combination workshop/activity center in the basement of a local church. This program served an average of 40–50 retarded adults and was also supported by parents who paid tuition and worked as volunteer staff. During its 3 years in the church, the workshop received only two contracts from private industry and, according to one informant, "work consisted primarily of bagging screws in the dark."

Beginning in 1971, the Los Angeles County Regional Centers assumed financial responsibility for the funding of workshop clients, and major changes ensued. The workshop population rapidly grew from 85 to its capacity of 150. Parent volunteers were replaced by a professional staff and a contract procurer was commissioned to seek out and bid on jobs suitable for workshop clients. New industrial machinery was also purchased, which facilitated expansion of workshop contracts.

Current Workshop

Concurrent with these developments, the parents' organization began a fund-raising effort to construct their own workshop facility. This facility was completed and operating by July 1975 and is the workshop that is the focus of this study. It is located in a middle-class suburban residential area, about 30 miles from downtown Los Angeles. The building is approximately 20,000 square feet in size and contains offices for administrative, counseling, production, and clerical staff, as well as a large, well-equipped work area. It is situated on 4½ acres of land that also contains the original school building built by the organization. The school was phased out as the public school system assumed increasing responsibility for education of retarded persons and the buildings are now used to house an activity center program for retarded adults as well as a cafeteria that serves lunch and provides an auxiliary training program in food preparation for workshop clients. Also on the grounds are a swimming pool, an outdoor basketball court, a large covered patio with picnic benches, two kilns for firing ceramic products, and considerable open space that is used for assorted recreational activities (e.g., volleyball, softball).

Client employees work a 5-day week and are off on weekends and major holidays. Work begins at 8:30 a.m. and ends at 3:30 p.m., with two 10-minute breaks (one in the morning and one in the afternoon) and a 40-minute lunch period. Most clients travel to and from work by bus. Approximately 65% ride what are called "workshop buses," school buses that transport clients to the workshop and back from their individual homes. About 32% ride the public bus system. The remainder either live nearby, or are driven by parents.

Depending on the nature of the job, clients are paid either "piece rate" or "shop time." Piece rate is determined by a formula that includes how much the workshop is being paid for the job and the production efficiency of a nonhandicapped worker. Shop time is an hourly wage based on periodic supervisor assessment of a client's average work efficiency and the prevailing minimum wage.

Checks are distributed every 2 weeks. Average earnings across the total client population are about $30.00 a month. This figure is somewhat misleading because there is a considerable variability, some clients averaging less than $10.00 a month and others averaging over $200.00 a month. Client earnings are also quite variable throughout the course of a year, because the amount and type of work available tend to be seasonal. Nearly all workshop clients also receive SSI benefits of approximately $300.00 a month.

The basic industrial services performed in the workshop include: plastic deburring, solvent and hot gluing, shrink packaging, skin packaging, blister packaging, impulse sealing, silver soldering, various drill press operations, ultrasonic plastic welding, wire cutting and stripping, light solder assembly, spot welding, and assorted other types of assembly, sorting, labeling, folding, collating, weighing, packaging, and painting. A representative sample of specific subcontracts include: collating a "Commercial and Private Pilot's Program Package" and sealing it in the heat tunnel; stripping wires and crimping terminals for a jumper wire assembly; putting cardboard backing on posters and shrink wrapping them in cellophane; assembling and packaging of a men's toiletry gift set; assembly of shower heads; assembly of shock absorbers for skate boards; sorting barrels of salvaged screws by size and type; cleaning, inspecting, and testing push button units, bridging adaptors, jack and plug assemblies, and assorted other salvaged equipment for the telephone company; collating "locator cards" for a greeting card company; and attaching adhesive to blood pressure cuffs.

Most jobs are only in the workshop from 1 to 2 weeks and the majority are available only once. About 20% are repetitive orders, and are available either once every year or from two to five times a year depending on subcontractor needs. Currently, the workshop processes between 250–300 subcontract bids a year. Some jobs, such as salvage work on telephone company equipment, screw sorting, and packaging of plastic tableware, are long-term contracts that are continuously available. These function primarily as "fill in" jobs and are assigned when other work is not available. Various efforts have been made to develop proprietary items that the workshop could produce and market themselves, but, to date, these efforts have neither generated much work nor have they been financially successful.

As noted above, the amount and type of work available follow a seasonal pattern. In general, December through March are the slow months of the year. April through June is generally slack with a significant increase in subcontracts beginning around the end of June. July through the first 2 weeks of November are the busiest months, with the amount of available work peaking around late October. This trend results from the fact that many subcontracts obtained by the workshop involve products directed toward the Christmas season market (e.g., novelty and gift items, cards and wrapping paper, and skateboards).

The Client/Employees

Since its opening in July of 1975, the workshop has operated at its capacity of 200–215 client/employees. Although the statistics varied over the course of the research, characteristics of the population are generally as follows: average age – 30, range – 18–55; average IQ – 50, range – 29–75; 60% male, 40% female. Ethnic composition reflects the surrounding community: 88% are Anglo, 9% are Mexican-American, and 3% are black or Oriental.

From 30% to 45% of clients have medical problems or physical handicaps in addition to their developmental disability. In the current client population, for example, eight clients have cerebral palsy, 34 have recurrent seizures due to either epilepsy or other neurological problems, and 13 have loss of mobility and/or motor coordination in one or more limbs due to muscular dystrophy, spinal meningitis, arthritis, hemiplegia, or dislocated hips. Others have chronic respiratory problems, bad backs, hernias, cardiovascular disease, perceptual/ motor handicaps, or severe loss of hearing or vision.

From 75% to 85% of workshop clients live at home with parents or close relatives. The remainder live in foster care, group home, or board and care facilities.

Client turnover rate remains relatively constant from year to year with an average of 48 individuals leaving and being replaced annually. Of 195 clients who left the workshop over a 4-year period (July 1975 to July 1979), the reasons listed in workshop termination records were as follows: 36% left to enter another workshop or program (e.g., Goodwill, independent living skills training programs, on-the-job training programs); 17% left because their families moved out of the area; 17% left because counseling staff determined that the workshop was not an appropriate program for their needs; 11% were terminated because of their erratic attendance; 7% left to enter competitive employment; 6% were terminated by workshop staff due to continuing emotional or behavioral problems; and the remaining 6% were either declared ineligible for funding by other agencies, quit for unknown reasons, or died.

A major trend in client turnover during this 4-year period concerns general functioning level. For about 1½ years after the workshop opened in July of 1975, the majority of incoming clients were recent educable mentally retarded (EMR) graduates from the local high schools. The number of these individuals in the workshop at any one time peaked at around 30% of the total workshop population in late 1976. These were the individuals who subsequently left the workshop to enter other workshops, independent living training programs, or competitive employment. In general, they were in the workshop from 1 to 3 years and as they left were replaced by trainable mentally retarded (TMR) graduates from local schools. Fewer than 10% of the current workshop population are young (i.e., 18–25 years) and classified as EMR. Most of these have accompanying medical problems or physical handicaps. Furthermore, the agency that is the primary source of client referral for the workshop now places most of their young EMR clients directly in programs geared toward more independent living and competitive employment.

Independent evaluation and accrediting agencies have given uniformly excellent ratings to the workshop and its programs. It has consistently been at the forefront of evolving social policy, and, compared to other workshops with similar client populations, is considered by both parents and delivery system personnel to be one of the best facilities of its kind. It also meets all the major criteria established in the programmatic literature as to what a sheltered workshop for mentally retarded persons should be.

In addition to its work program, the workshop offers a broad range of rehabilitative services, including compensatory education classes, speech therapy, individual and group counseling, training in use of the public bus system and regularly scheduled physical education classes, which include swimming and life-saving lessons. The workshop also sponsors numerous organized recreational activities.

Attitudes toward the Workshop Setting

The majority of individuals in workshop society describe the workshop setting as their "favorite place." They consistently affirm that it is preferable to home, school, other workshops or programs, competitive employment, and all other important settings in their lives.

A few words suffice to summarize hundreds of open-ended conversational interviews on this topic. The workshop setting is "fun," "nice," and "not boring." Attendance figures and other behavioral indices are consistent with this attitude. It is not uncommon for individuals to insist on coming to the workshop even when they are sick, or to resist going on family trips and vacations in order to remain at the shop.

Leaving the workshop is seldom a function of an individual's expressed dissatisfaction with the setting. Most who leave do so reluctantly, if not involuntarily. Those selected to leave for competitive employment, independent living training programs, or other workshops, for example, are often actively resistant. Typically, they turn down three opportunities for other jobs or programs over a period of 2 years and require major persuasive efforts by workshop staff and counselors from funding agencies involved, before being induced to leave. There have been several instances of particularly recalcitrant individuals where funding agency counselors finally terminated financial support as a means of forcing their departure. Although insecurities, fears, or general resistance to change account for part of the reluctance, our experience has been that at least 50% of the individuals leaving under these circumstances could be more accurately characterized as not *afraid* of leaving, but *wanting* to stay. Numerous individuals who have left for competitive employment return to the workshop frequently to visit and sometimes work as unpaid volunteers. One woman who has been employed in the housekeeping department of a local hospital for over 3 years regularly comes to the workshop on her days off to work on the lines. Her standard reply when asked why she does this is, "To keep busy, relax, and talk to my friends without being bossed around all the time."

Expressions of dissatisfaction with the workshop setting are rare and usually temporary. In most such cases the individual is angry with some peer or staff member and thus threatens to leave the shop. Such threats typically elicit solicitous concern from peers and the individual is comforted and persuaded to stay. The only persistent dissatisfaction observed was confined largely to a small sample of young, higher functioning males from low-income families who were unhappy about the amount of money they earned and/or maintained they were not handicapped.

For over 90% of the individuals we talked with and observed, the workshop setting has clearly provided the major positive reinforcing experience of their lives. This finding, however, should not be construed as evidence that the people of workshop society have a strong work ethic, that their work makes them feel good about themselves, or that they are highly motivated by the wages they receive.

Attitudes and Feelings about Work

Work attitudes and values are not a salient concern in the manifest consciousness of workshop people. On various occasions we made a concerted effort to obtain information on job preferences, the attributes and qualities of liked and disliked jobs, and feelings about work in general. Much of this effort was notably unsuccessful. Although most individuals would identify one or two jobs they did or did not like and all made an apparent effort to be responsive to our questions, they had very little to say about the jobs they were assigned, or work in general. Also, in both discussion groups and private conversation, we consistently found that workshop people rarely mention their current work activities, their feelings about a particular job, vocational aspirations, wages earned, or work accomplishments.

The same pattern holds true for a type of spontaneous verbalization that we have termed *blurts* (i.e., brief, noncontextualized expressions of whatever is on a person's mind at the time). As researchers walk around the workshop various individuals will blurt out such comments as: "My mom's in the hospital," "The Lakers lost," "That sure was a big fire," "Elvis died," "I'm gonna be an uncle," "I'm having a pot roast for dinner," "Pat and Anne broke up," "I won a bowling trophy," and so on. Of the hundreds of blurts we have collected, fewer than 5% relate to current work activities, job preferences, or wages earned.

Similarly, the dream reports of individuals in workshop society show little evidence of wish-engendered vocational aspiration. Of 509 dream reports that were transcribed from tape-recordings and coded, fewer than 5% involve the dreamer in some vocational role, and most of these are common fantasy aspirations such as movie star, astronaut, professional athlete, and policeman. Only two dream reports were concerned with obtaining a "regular job" in the outside world.

Other fantasy materials also show little evidence of vocational aspiration. Some individuals in the workshop are prone to a particular form of "active imagination," which we have termed normalcy fabrication. These are self-aggrandizing narratives of alleged personal adventures that apparently make the individual's life seem more eventful or normal. Such fabrications almost never concern having a different, more normal, or glamorous job; rather, they are about secret marriages, sexual liaisons in exotic places, and assorted adventurous encounters with motorcycle gangs, celebrities, police, thieves, rapists, and neighborhood acquaintances.

In general, members of workshop society seem to have little emotional energy invested in work-related accomplishment or aspiration. The only psychological benefit or value that seems salient is that work provides relief from boredom. When asked, the majority report that they like to work and that it's important to work, but have little to add beyond that. This is not attributable to verbal ineptitude or deficiency. Workshop people like to talk and many are capable of talking coherently and at length about a variety of topics, but they don't talk much about work.

Work Behavior

Direct observation employing pre-coded behavioral categories and time sampling procedures reveal that the average individual in workshop society spends less than 50% of his or her time on the lines actually working. This average is misleading because there is enormous variation both within and between individuals, and frequency of on-task behavior seems to be complexly affected by a host of interacting variables. Some individuals are consistently on-task over 75% of the time regardless of their assigned duties. Others vary from 75% on-task to virtually zero on-task, depending on the nature of assigned work. Average frequency of on-task varies systematically throughout the annual cycle, which determines availability of subcontracts to the workshop. Thus, average percentage of time on-task for large random samples of workers averages 70% during the October to November period, but the same individuals average less than 45% on-task when observed during a period from January to February.

Staff ratings of individual's work production efficiency often suggest systematic improvement in work habits as a function of time in the workshop. On the average, these gains are not large, and such judgments seem to be heavily influenced by the presence or absence of problematic off-task behavior. Our observations suggest that some workers do not learn to work harder, but rather acquire a set of skills that make their off-task behaviors and activities less disruptive and less noticeable to the staff. Some individuals, for example, seem to be busily working and actually display the relevant behavioral motions of the assigned task, without producing a completed product. In one such instance, an individual was observed filling, emptying, and refilling the same plastic bag with hardware items for over an hour while entertaining his immediate neighbors with his theories about the death of Elvis Presley. This type of "fake work" is usually successful in avoiding supervisor intervention.

There are also certain adaptations and workshop society norms that affect work production. During slow periods, when desirable work is scarce, individuals assigned to "good jobs" often slow down their production in order to make the job last longer and delay the possibility of being assigned less desirable work. Furthermore, peer pressure to increase production rate is extremely rare. If an individual on an assembly line is holding up production, other workers will simply slow down. To criticize a slow worker or to probe him or her to work faster is a serious breach of workshop society etiquette. Those who violate this norm acquire the reputation among their peers of being "mean" and "bossy." Although many individuals seem fully aware of the relative limitations and capabilities of themselves and co-workers, such matters are rarely discussed openly, or invoked with pejorative intent. A more general statement subsuming a variety of observations is that any verbalization, evaluative comparison, or other public behavior that asserts or implies diminished competency in others is strictly taboo.

SOCIAL RELATIONS

Although the members of the workshop society display little evidence of a strong work ethic, the bulk of everyday behavior and conversations in the work setting serves to dramatize the importance attached to interpersonal relationships and affiliative values. The overall frequency of peer interaction is very high. Our observations suggest that both at work and during free time, the average individual will interact with peers at least once every 5 minutes. The content of most such interactions does not involve work, or task-related matters, but rather consists of small talk, gossip, joking, advising, comforting, and the exchange of personal opinions and experiences. The majority of all conversations that researchers have overheard, or participated in, both privately with individuals and in small groups, concern human relationships. The role of participant-observer often requires researchers to disclose personal information about themselves, and it seems reasonable to assume that the kinds of questions people ask are revealing of their own interests and concerns. The people of workshop society showed little interest in our jobs, but did question us extensively about our family, friends, and romantic involvements.

Romantic relationships are an important feature of the general social climate in the workshop. At any given time, the majority of individuals are involved in a boyfriend/ girlfriend relationship with a workshop peer, and those who are not typically express a strong desire for a boyfriend or girlfriend. Most romantic relationships are largely confined to the workshop setting. Some couples, however, are able to get together at organized recreational activities for mentally retarded adults and a few go on private dates and visit one another at their homes. Affection for one another is expressed openly and couples are frequently observed kissing, hugging, and holding hands during their break and lunch periods. Heavy petting is strongly discouraged by workshop staff and is rarely observed, although it does happen occasionally. Most individuals seem content with milder displays of affection, the exchange of gifts and rings, and one another's company. Many assert that they are engaged and have plans to get married, but their marital plans are usually vague and set for the distant future. These romantic relationships are often a significant factor underlying an individual's reluctance to leave the workshop for other programs or competitive employment. Most members of workshop society are keenly aware that their romances seldom survive physical separation. The following quote is illustrative. The woman's boyfriend has recently left the workshop to enter an on-the-job training program and their relationship has become increasingly shaky.

> I watched that movie "Like Normal People" Friday night. That hurt me. It reminded me a lot of me and Ralph. We wanted to get married and we got a lot of resistance from everybody. Especially when he gave her the ring. That really hurt. Ralph gave me a ring, you know. It was a very good movie. The girl who played the lady . . . she exaggerated a little bit—the way she walked and her speech. Most mentally retarded don't walk like that. I'll bet you Ralph didn't see it. If he had seen it I'll bet you I would of got a phone call from him. The biggest mistake he made was taking that class over again. I didn't want him to take it. I knew something like this would happen. They started to pressure him to go out and get a job. They scared him. They scared him right out of the idea of getting married. Those people at (a local agency), they ruined everything for me. They ruined everything for Ralph and me. We would have been perfectly happy here. Now he doesn't want me or this place. Ralph has always been scared of pressure. Maybe he'll come to his senses one of these days and realize how much he misses me. I don't know what it'd take for that to happen. I really don't know. This is the thanks I get for being so good to him. I did anything and everything he asked. I went where he wanted. I did what he wanted. I bought him stuff. What more did he want from me? I guess it's a lost cause. I thought we could do it. I really thought we could hack it . . . the both of us together helping each other. I got hurt once. I don't want to get hurt again. It's been a month today since Ralph left me. What a turkey.

Parental attitudes and/or involvement in these romantic relationships are highly varied. Some parents (and other caregivers) encourage such relationships and provide opportunities for couples to be together outside the workshop setting. Others discourage any sign of interest in the opposite sex. The extremes range from those who knowingly permit an active sexual relationship to those who forbid their son or daughter to have a boyfriend/girlfriend at the workshop. Most are somewhere in between these two extremes.

Friendship relations also play an important role in setting the ambience and tone of everyday life in the workshop. Many individuals have relatively stable and enduring relationships with "best friends" of either the same or opposite sex. As with most people, these relationships seem to be based on common interests and concerns. Individuals who enjoy engaging in fantasy role play, for example, tend to spend most of their time together, and most "best friends" are from the same age group.

The frequency and intensity of peer interaction does, of course, sometimes result in conflict and disharmony. In the course of our observations in the workshop we sought to maintain ongoing records of all observed and reported instances of peer conflict, as well as the efforts individuals made to resolve their personal problems with peers, or to intervene in the problems of others. Our general finding has been that although the overall frequency of reported problems is relatively high, most of these derive from relatively few individuals, and the majority are successfully resolved by peer counseling and do not require the intervention of staff. The techniques used by peer counselors can be quite ingenious. The following synopsis from a group discussion is illustrative:

> John and Tim, who have been "best friends" for over 3 years, have a serious problem. John has accused Tim of "kissing boys" and no longer wants to be his friend. Various group members all agree. This is a very serious matter. Kissing boys is wrong. Boys should kiss girls, not other boys. Tim becomes increasingly distraught at this concerted attack on his behavior. His head droops to his chest, he avoids eye contact with everyone and appears on the verge of crying. Phil tries to soften the attack. "You are one of the nicest guys I know, Tim. You're one of my best friends in the whole world. But, you're not suppose to kiss boys. That's not right." Tim's hurt feelings are not relieved. He buries his head in his arms on the table. Group members remain silent. The tension level is very high. A researcher asks Tim to tell how he feels about what the others have said. Tim composes himself and begins his defense. He doesn't do it "that way." He knows it's true, a boy should not kiss boys. But he is an actor and actors sometimes have to do things that other people don't. He has pictures of actors at home in his bedroom. He writes letters to "the Fonz" and is a member of his fan club. He once won an Academy Award and has talked to Elvis Presley in person back in New York. Fred challenges the claim to an Academy Award. "I know you're a really good actor. I seen you be the Fonz and Incredible Hulk. But you didn't win no Academy Award because you weren't on TV." John comes to Tim's aid. Tim was on TV once. He was on "Bowling for Dollars." And Tim did win an award for acting. It was when he was in high school and he has a trophy at home. Joe agrees. He went to the same high school as Tim. Tim did win an acting award. He has seen the trophy himself. Various group members acknowledge Tim is a great actor. The problem about Tim "kissing boys" is forgotten. John reaches across the table and shakes Tim's hand using their "special hand shake." Both have huge grins on their faces. All is forgiven. The problem has been resolved. They are "best friends" again.

In the above example, and in most cases, the solutions that peers provide to problems seem to be permanent. There has been no reoccurrence of the "kissing boys" problem between John and Tim. Tim has learned that it's generally not a good idea to kiss boys and John has learned that when Tim does hug or kiss a male friend he is "just acting."

Perhaps the most important thing we discovered in our observations of social relations is that workshop society is meaningfully organized around the focal concerns of affiliative relationships and social harmony.

Work Pressure and Social Harmony

As noted above, the amount and type of subcontract jobs obtained by the workshop varies on an annual cycle and workers in general are more or less industrious depending on the desirability of the available work to which they are assigned. In examining our data on social relations, we discovered that frequency of peer conflict and other problematic behaviors also varied systematically on the same annual cycle, although they did not covary in a linear fashion with the availability of desired work. To further examine this relationship we combined our quantitative and qualitative data and organized them into two composite sets depending on whether they seemed to be a measure of "High/Low Work Pressure," or "Social Harmony/Disharmony." Work pressure includes such indices as: number and type of available subcontracts; propensity of supervisors to ignore or intervene for off-task behaviors; the percentage of workers on-task; frequency of peer interaction during work; general tendency of workers to "slow down on good jobs," or "fake work." Social harmony was composed of such indices as: frequency of peer conflict; whether or not group discussion sessions focused mainly on personal problems; frequency with which workers sought appointments with counseling staff to discuss personal problems; and general propensity of workers to defy or "bad mouth" supervisory staff.

Our analysis of these two composite sets of data revealed a systematic pattern of co-variation that seems strong and clear. As depicted in Figure 1, the overall relationship between work pressure and social harmony is curvilinear, with both unusually high and unusually low work pressure resulting in an increased incidence of general disharmony in the workshop setting. Furthermore, there would seem to be some optimal level of work demands that maximizes social harmony with relatively little loss of production efficiency.

We believe the major factors underlying this relationship are relatively straightforward and reflect two problems that are commonly identified as salient in the work lives of most

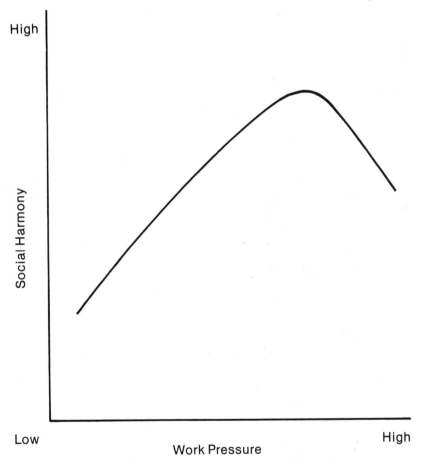

Figure 1.

people, including mentally retarded adults: boredom and stress. Thus, when workers are not provided with a satisfactory amount of desirable work they get bored and increase their interaction rates with co-workers. The combination of boredom and increased interaction creates problems, both among co-workers and for bosses. Everyone is unhappy and problems multiply. When work demands are considered excessive, workers are also being deprived of their customary interaction with co-workers. The combination of too much work, demanding bosses, and not enough affiliation generates stress, conflict, and problems for everyone.

FOUR SEGMENTS IN WORKSHOP SOCIETY

Workshop society, like any human group, can be described in terms of the uniformities of its members (e.g., they don't have a strong work ethic; their average IQ is 50; and they are a gentle and loving people), or the diversity of its members (e.g., Sara can tell you what day of the week a given calendar date fell on from 1776 to the year 2000; Fred seldom knows what day it is; Phil, Ray, and Chuck refer to themselves as mentally retarded; Bob, Lew, and Keith vigorously deny that they are retarded and claim they have no handicaps; some people interact constantly, whereas others interact rarely). To better understand the social fabric of workshop subculture, it is useful to develop mid-level generalizations that help bridge the gap between the extremes of modal uniformity and individual diversity.

Using direct observation data on work behavior and social interaction, we have identified what seem to be four differing types of people in workshop society. The initial identification of individuals was based on a factor analysis of observational frequencies, which produced two factors of high/low work, and high/low social interaction (Turner, Zetlin, and Gallimore, in press). These factors were used to identify individuals in four independent groups (i.e., high work/high social; high social/low work; low social/high work; and low work/low social.) We then used our ethnographic data and other materials to develop composite portraits of the four groups, which we have termed the Elite, the Socialites, the Loners, and the Nonconformers. Each of these groups is briefly described with respect to those qualities that characterize their adaptation to workshop society. It should be noted that members of these groups do not differ from one another with respect to age, sex, IQ, or medical diagnosis.

THE ELITE (HIGH WORK/HIGH SOCIAL)

Members of the Elite are generally acknowledged as being the best workers in the workshop and are typically assigned to the most demanding, most desirable, and best-paying jobs. Lead workers are more likely to come from this segment of workshop society than any other.

Being lead worker is a delicate position; individuals who occupy this status must balance the instrumental and socioemotional demands of the role. The job involves assisting supervisory staff in seeing that workers are supplied with the necessary materials, that completed work is properly counted and that production schedules are met. One must do this, however, while maintaining a demeanor and comportment that do not violate the egalitarian norm of peer subculture (i.e., "No one is better than anybody else.") Lead workers who behave in a curt or authoritarian manner, or who in other ways emphasize their differential status, are likely to be labeled "mean," "bossy," or "snobnob" by peers. In general, individuals from the Elite group are more successful at managing the social pressures of being a lead worker than other segments of workshop society. Certain task requirements (e.g., being able to count) are a necessary condition for appointment to lead worker status, but such competencies are not sufficient and, to be successful as a lead worker, other qualities are more important. Indeed, arithmetic ability eliminates relatively few candidates. The advent of small, inexpensive calculators, for example, provides a sort of "cognitive prosthesis" enabling many more individuals to upgrade their skills and to fulfill this aspect of the requirements for being a lead worker.

Elite individuals who are not lead workers typically aspire to this role and a few individuals sometimes assert that they are lead workers despite staff claims to the contrary. In most such cases there is a private agreement between an officially designated lead worker and a peer (usually a "best friend") in which the peer has been designated as an "assistant lead worker." Staff are usually not informed of such arrangements.

Independent observation of individuals in the Elite group confirms their reputation among staff and peers as "good workers." They are more consistently on-task and productive than any of the other groups. They rarely complain about the work they are assigned, their supervisor, or any other aspect of their daily work life. Members of this group typically describe themselves as people who "like to stay busy." Even with assigned work, which is generally viewed as boring or otherwise undesirable, they maintain high on-task behavior and are less likely than members of the other groups to complain to staff, go to sleep, malinger, or engage in disruptive horseplay with peers. Most subscribe to the belief that, "If you don't work hard when you're put on the bad jobs (e.g., sorting buckets of salvage screws by type and size), then you won't and shouldn't get the good jobs when they come along." The Elite group constitutes the most compliant and task-oriented segment of workshop society.

Many members of this group might be described as oversocialized—in the sense that what seems on the surface to be exemplary self-control and industriousness has often been achieved through a socialization history of rather extreme overregulation. One side effect of this is that their spontaneity and autonomy as individuals seem unnecessarily diminished. The general pattern that emerges from conversational interviews with the Elite is that their opinions, attitudes, values, and beliefs are somehow required to be exactly the same as their parents. Furthermore, they believe that one should always defer any decision or problem to an authority figure. Significant others (usually parents) are invoked as rightful arbiters over all aspects of their lives. Most seem genuinely content with this state of affairs, feel that they have a good life, and accept their dependency with grace and good humor.

In some cases, parental influence remains a salient and positive force in the individual's life even after parents are deceased. The following is one of a series of dream reports collected from a man in the Elite group. Both of his parents are dead and he now lives with a sister.

> Last night. It was my mother called me again. I was sound asleep. She says, "Come. Come." It was beautiful in heaven. Then my mother says, "How's your friends down there?" "Oh, they're nice. I got a lot of friends." [Dreamer goes on to list a number of friends.] All my

friends. Then she said . . . she asked me do I have a supervisor. I says, "Yes. Stan Brown." Then she says, "What are you now? What are you doing? What kind of job are you doing? So I told her, "I'm doing a assistant's job now. I'm Karl Long's assistant." "Oh, that's great son. I'm proud of you." And then my dad said, "My son is assistant. How about that! How did he get that far ahead?" I made it. Far ahead. Now I'm going out in the future. My mother says, "What are you gonna do for your life? What are you gonna do in the future? "Well, I've got a beautiful girlfriend down here that wants to marry me. And her name is Ellen Jones." "Does she love you?" I says, "Yes, mother. I love her very much." And bingo! I went . . . I open my eyes. I woke up, and that was the end of the dream. What a dream! To go to heaven! To go to heaven! Oh boy!

This man, and other individuals in the workshop population, often report recurrent dreams with this type of content. Typically, parents (or other deceased loved ones) visit them in their sleep to praise, comfort, and advise.

The majority of individuals in the Elite group are content to compare themselves to workshop peers and other comfortable standards of accomplishment and life style. When confronted by peers or social workers who promote a more independent way of life, they remain committed to the value of compliance/dependency as being in their own best interests. Underlying this is the belief that "some retarded kids" have parents who don't love them, won't let them live at home, or don't protect them from the potential dangers of the outside world. They feel fortunate that their parents are not like that and are willing to guide and help them.

Most members of the Elite are highly popular with workshop peers and enjoy rich affiliative relationships in workshop society. The majority maintain stable, long-term boyfriend/girlfriend relationships with workshop peers and nearly all have positive and enduring friendships with peers of both sexes. Their everyday relations with peers, workshop staff, and parents are rarely problematic. None of the individuals in this group has ever been suspended from the workshop as a disciplinary action, or for inappropriate behavior. They are the "model citizens" of workshop society. They conform both to the external authority structure that governs their lives and the comportment etiquette of peer subculture.

The Elite, like most members of workshop society, are cognizant of "being retarded," although they are of the opinion that it is not the sort of thing one talks about in polite company. Most describe themselves as "slow learners," but do not view themselves as significantly handicapped. They emphasize their accomplishments and seldom dwell on their limitations. Their world view is largely circumscribed by family and the workshop. They have heard about "a job outside" and "living in your own apartment," but they have been told by their parents that they "can't do that" and believe this to be true. Several individuals in this group take medication to control seizures and "my seizures" are frequently invoked as a satisfactory explanation for why they need the protection of a more sheltered life style. Most members of the Elite do not aspire to the so-called normalcy of independence and mainstream life. Nearly all are actively involved in organized recreational programs for mentally retarded adults (e.g., bowling leagues, dances, and social clubs), and their leisure time outside the workshop is rich and fulfilling. At work, at home, and at play, they are constantly in the presence of benevolent authority. They feel that it is a good life and have no plans or desire for change. Although their circumstances become increasingly uncertain as their parents get older, they know that arrangements have been made with siblings, or other relatives, and are secure and satisfied in the social ecology they inhabit. They feel good about themselves, their lives are eventful, and all important socioemotional needs are being met. Their self-esteem maintenance is based largely on the fulfillment of duty as they see it.

The Socialites (Low Work/High Social)

Few Socialites ever achieve lead worker status and in most cases their tenure in this position is temporary and short-term. Although many are considered by the staff to be capable of good work, their work attitudes and habits are highly variable depending on the nature of work assigned, the quality of their relationships with particular supervisors, and whether or not they are involved in their own or someone else's personal problems. Individuals in this group tend to be preoccupied with socioemotional concerns and are inconsistent in their work behavior and their commitment to a work ethic. Socialites are generally more talkative than members of the other groups, are prone to dominate conversations with peers, and to focus conversation mainly on themselves. Although actively involved in the problems and other concerns of peers, their style is not that of a sympathetic listener but rather one of assertive advice-giving and problem solving. They look to the counseling staff rather than the production staff for role models and prefer the informal, self-ascribed role of peer counselor to that of lead worker.

Socialites are generally popular among workshop peers. In addition to functioning as self-appointed peer counselors, this group also contains several of the more noted joke tellers, raconteurs, and gossip-mongers in workshop society. They are boisterous and extraverted and like nothing more than having an audience.

Relationships with peers are characteristically more transient for the Socialites than the Elite group. Nearly all members of this group maintain a steady boyfriend/girlfriend relationship, although relatively few sustain any particular relationship for more than a few months. The pattern is for such relationships to be intense but inconstant. Socialites are consecutive monogamists with a high turnover rate. When their romances falter they quickly find someone else. This is in direct contrast to the Elite group where boyfriend/girlfriend relationships are much more stable, enduring, and free of conflict.

The relationships between Socialites and other peers follow the same general pattern. For example, there is a high turnover rate in the people they nominate as their "best friend." They drift in and out of relationships, solving problems, telling their jokes and stories and then move on to a new friend, a new audience.

Socialites self-report a relatively high frequency of personal problems in their everyday lives. Some of the factors contributing to this include: 1) their tendency to get involved in other people's problems (which then become "their problems"); 2) the centrality of their position in the gossip/rumor network, which generates its own unique set of problems; and 3) their proclivity for fabrication. Socialites often embellish, exaggerate, and invent personal problems in an apparent attempt to combat boredom and to make their lives more exciting. Although they are often involved in minor disciplinary problems, they seldom have a history of chronic behavior disorder.

Socialites are more resistant to parental and staff authority than the other groups and are much more ambivalent regarding their dependency on others. They maintain a certain bravado that they are self-sufficient and rule their own lives. Conflict with parents and staff often involve minor restrictions on personal freedom and independence, which breach their public facade of claims and aspirations to independence.

In fact, when confronted with a realistic possibility of leaving the workshop for competitive employment, Socialites, like most members of workshop society, adopt a highly conservative stance and invoke all sorts of delaying tactics, rationalizations, and, in some cases, rather inventive counterproposals. One Socialite man, for example, had been selected by his counselor to leave the workshop and enter an on-the-job work training program. Over a period of several months he maintained: 1) he wasn't quite ready yet, but would be next year, 2) that his girlfriend was extremely upset about the possibility of his leaving and he just couldn't hurt her feelings; and 3) that he was too upset to make the change at this time because of family problems. As the pressure to leave increased he became more defensive, claiming 4) that he had enemies in the workshop that were trying to get rid of him so they could steal his girlfriend; 5) that his social worker had lied to his parents and couldn't be trusted; and 6) that his workshop counselor, whom he had considered a good friend, didn't like him anymore and was forcing him to leave out of personal animosity. After repeatedly being told how capable he was and that it was time he left for a position more congruent with his abilities, he offered what he considered an obvious and ideal solution—the workshop could hire him as a member of the staff. When told that this would not be possible, he became quite angry and for several weeks indignantly proclaimed that his counselor had implied he was retarded. Shortly thereafter, he had a "nervous breakdown" necessitating psychiatric intervention. He is currently back in the workshop, the pressure to leave has subsided, and he continues his practice of regaling peers with his repertoire of fabricated adventures (e.g., the candy striper who tried to seduce him; how he helped the police to catch some robbers; how his motorcycle was stolen from in front of his own apartment).

Socialites are extremely sensitive about "being retarded" and unlike the Elite take little comfort in such euphemisms as "slow learner." For them the workshop setting provides not only a haven from pejorative labels and comparisons, but a functional system of etiquette norms that allow considerable latitude for artifice in the presentation of self. Within workshop society, it is permissible for individuals to claim any role or identity they desire without fear of being discredited or challenged by peers. Members of the Socialite group are representative of those individuals in the workshop population who exploit this norm by engaging in extensive self-aggrandizement and public misrepresentation of their experiences, personal qualities, and accomplishments. They can thus be generally characterized as making liberal use of wish-engendered fantasy as a means of regulating self-esteem. Although this means of coping seems to be adaptive and to promote the individual's well-being within the workshop environment, it is clearly less acceptable and effective in the world outside. Social workers and other professionals, for example, typically employ such terms as "pathological liar," and "poor reality orientation," in describing such individuals. Our observations suggest that the Socialites' propensity for fabrication is not a "pathology," in the sense of some malignant trait or moral deficit, but that it does reflect a crucial problem in self-esteem maintenance. Despite all their denials, Socialites are not only aware of "being retarded," many are single-mindedly absorbed in their "spoiled" social identity and are unable to construct a sense of personal worth from other qualities. Their self-concept is ill-defined, unstable, inaccurate, and vulnerable. Their fabrications represent a complex and varied form of strategic self-presentation designed to defend a highly fragile self-image of normalcy. The extreme effects of this strategy are a form of alienation and marginality. They do not know which to prefer, the workshop or the world outside, the comforts of belonging and unchallenged semblance, or the more hazardous pursuit of trying to "pass" in a larger society.

On a different note, Socialites employ fabrication not only as a means of self-aggrandizement, but to resolve conflict and disharmony in peer relations. Consider the following synopsis from a meeting of one of the discussion groups. (Note: Ellen, Anne, and Pat are members of the Elite group. Hal is a prototypic Socialite.)

> Ellen notes that she has something very important to say. She is extremely upset. Her best friend Anne has just returned to the workshop following 2 weeks of medical tests and Anne's ex-boyfriend Pat has been very mean and rude to her. He completely ignored her and did not even say hi. Ellen goes on and on about this—encouraging other group members to agree that it was very mean of Pat to behave in this way. Anne nods her head affirmatively each time Ellen says something bad about Pat, or about how much Pat's rudeness hurt her feelings. She remains silent, however, letting Ellen speak for her. Pat also sits quietly, a sheepish, somewhat embarrassed look on his face. Ellen continues her monologue—trying to arouse other group members to her level of indignation. Finally, Anne says, "Let's hear what he (i.e., Pat) has to say about it." Pat recounts the history of their break-up, noting how upset everyone was, since they had been going together for 3 years. Things have settled down, he has a new girlfriend and he felt it was best to "just let sleeping dogs lie." The reason he didn't greet Anne was that he didn't know how she would take it. Hal enters the discussion. There is no need for everyone to be upset. He has the solution. Pat had spoken to him and had instructed *him* to greet Anne. He had done so and had even given Anne an extra kiss on the cheek "for Pat."
>
> From subsequent discussion it is clear that neither Anne nor Pat recall such an incident. Although neither in any way challenge Hal's story—Pat doesn't quite remember telling Hal to greet Anne for him and Anne doesn't recall receiving a kiss from Hal. Hal refreshes their memory, adding details about time and place. "It was just as you were coming to work in the morning. Right by the door. Just as you walked in. I gave you a kiss on one cheek from me and a kiss on the other cheek for Pat. That's the answer to the problem. He told me to do it for him. And I did." Another group member supports Hal, saying, "I think I remember seeing him do that. I just got off the bus. It was by the front. By the blue doors." Anne, Ellen, and Pat all seem a bit puzzled by this turn of events, but say nothing. Hal's story has absolved Pat of any rudeness or lack of consideration toward Anne. There is no longer any need for Ellen or Anne to be upset. The problem is resolved. Group discussion shifts to another topic.

None of Hal's story is true, of course. He made it all up on the spot. He and other Socialites do this frequently. It is one of their favorite and most successful ways of resolving peer conflict. And, if things get a little boring around the workshop, also a means of generating some stimulating problems to solve.

The Loners (High Work/Low Social)

Loners are generally described by staff as "good workers" and in most respects their work attitudes and behavior are comparable to those of the Elite. Several have been lead workers and those who have not typically aspire to that position. Several members of this group, however, have been observed faking work, suggesting that their reputation is based on nonproblematic comportment as well as production.

Loners are the least talkative and sociable members of workshop society. Their low rate of peer-interaction, however, seems to be clearly a matter of personal style and preference rather than social rejection. They are not social isolates, nor are they lacking the necessary verbal skills. They simply seem to prefer less interaction. Peers typically describe Loners as "nice," and instances of peer conflict involving individual members of this group are rare. Loners are often seen at the fringes of interaction—observing but not participating. They are quiet, passive, and introverted, although their "co-presence level" is high. Very few members of this group have maintained a boyfriend/girlfriend relationship that has lasted more than a year. Indeed, nearly half of the individuals identified as Loners have never claimed or acknowledged a steady, romantic relationship with a workshop peer. The majority, however, have stable, enduring relationships with "best friends" of the same sex. Most Loners consistently report that they are happy with the quality of their peer relationships in the shop and those who do not have a boyfriend/ girlfriend or "best friend" seem less concerned about such matters than members of the other three groups.

This dispassionate quality in the everyday demeanor of Loners also distinguishes them from the other groups in terms of emotionality and affect. The overall level of expressive behavior in workshop society is very high. Most individuals are open and demonstrative in their communication of private feeling states through posture, gesture, and facial display as well as verbally. Compared to this norm, Loners are notably less likely to display their feelings through expressive mannerisms, or to spontaneously comment on their personal well-being. They are more stolid individuals whose typical facial expression is impassive and nonrevealing of their private thoughts and feelings. In their relations with peers they are rarely observed touching, hugging, kissing, sulking, or raising their voices in anger; they are seldom active participants in the pervasive joking, teasing, bickering, comforting, and advising that typifies the social climate of workshop life. Loners consistently report that they have few personal problems either at home or in the workshop and most seem genuinely poised, serene, and at peace with themselves and others.

Of all the groups, Loners manifest the least concern about being retarded, or the pejorative connotations of the label. Unlike the Socialites, they do not deny that they are retarded. Nor do they take refuge in euphemisms or seek to redefine their disability in terms of some less stigmatizing medical condition. They speak openly of themselves as mentally retarded, and assert that those who tease or make fun of the mentally retarded have serious problems themselves. As in the other groups, Loners' attitudes toward their disability seem to be largely a function of parental influence and practices. The typical Loner was raised by parents who made a practice of speaking with their retarded son or daughter about his or her disability, communicating clearly that he or she was highly valued as a person, and integrating the child as fully as possible into a normal family life. The experience of one member of this group during the illness and subsequent death of his mother is illustrative. Throughout his mother's illness he was kept informed of her condition and prognosis. He is one of five siblings and as a sister noted, "Mom always insisted on treating him the same as all the rest of us and he is the most well-adjusted person that you will ever meet." At his mother's funeral he participated, along with his brothers and sisters, in delivering the eulogy. He spoke about how much he loved his mother and how everyone who knew her had loved her noting that, "She was great, but the greatest thing she ever did was to teach her kids to be friends." After repeating again how much he loved his mother, he said, "I'm a mentally retarded person, and I feel the same as you." He then thanked everyone for coming to the funeral and left the podium, remaining fully composed all the while.

Many Loners have special abilities or interests that serve as a means of self-expression and play an important role in their self-esteem maintenance. Phil, the man who spoke at his mother's funeral, is a poet. Although his scores on IQ tests average in the mid-40s, and he can neither read nor write, he has amassed a considerable body of work. He tape-records his poems and either researchers or family members transcribe them for him. He keeps his poems in a manila folder and usually brings them to the workshop every day. His poems cover a variety of topics including love, death, friendship, family, marriage, and his observations about other members of workshop society. The following poem is an example of his work. It is presented precisely as he spoke it. It was edited only for punctuation and arrangement of lines.

Blindness

Life is bright
If your eyes is black you cannot see.
I know this hurts, to see.
I know this life is you hurt inside.
I know you cannot see forever, true inside.
I know this life is you have to see.
You have to know you cannot see.
It hurts inside.
Can't seen nothing, including trees.
And you can't see nobody else.
Hurts, and always hurts from your heart.
I know this is hard for you,
Through your heart.
Lies is serious matter to your lives.
You better know its your life.
If your love is—cares about your dreams.
You have to care about your dreams.
I know life cannot be perfect.
It just hurts, your life.
I know blindness is deep inside.
If someone is hard of hearing, I know this,
You can hear nothing.
As I see it through your eyes,
You have to know your life always be—
Just from the heart you have to see.

The special talents and interests of other individuals in the Loner group include: playing musical instruments, building models, sports (both as fans and active participants), woodworking and carpentry, knitting, and dates (e.g., one Loner is a "calendar calculator" savant).

In general, Loners have accepted and internalized the view that they are "like everybody else." They admit their limitations but also readily assert their positive qualities. Compared to the other groups, they maintain a more balanced and accurate self-appraisal and seem considerably more secure in both their ability, and right, to construct an independent judgment of their self-worth as individuals.

The Nonconformers (Low Work/Low Social)

Members of this group are generally the least reliable and most unproductive workers in the client population. Very rarely is a Nonconformer designated by staff as a lead worker, although many claim to be lead workers. Their work behavior is often problematic for staff because they are typically not merely off-task, but wandering around, leaving their work stations, talking loudly, and disrupting other workers. As a result, they are much more likely to be embroiled in conflict with workshop supervisors than members of the other groups.

The overwhelming majority of individuals in this group have consistently reported over a period of years that they are lonely and unhappy and that their lives are fraught with personal problems. Few Nonconformers maintain long-term boyfriend/girlfriend relationships with workshop peers, and most such relationships are unstable with numerous break-ups and reconciliations. Nonconformers sometimes claim to have boyfriends/girlfriends even though these individuals have been gone from the workshop for years and have not been seen or heard from since leaving. Most desperately want boyfriends/girlfriends and often seek relationships with peers who have recently broken up with someone else. This tactic is rarely successful.

Nonconformers are the least popular group among peers. Many have the reputation of being "troublemakers" or "babies" and the frequency and intensity of conflict with peers is much higher than in the other three groups. Most seem to be so self-absorbed that they are unable to develop mutually satisfactory relationships with others. One major problem is that Nonconformers typically demand exclusivity in their relationships and become jealous and indignant when their demands for a total commitment of time and attention are not met.

Compared to other segments of workshop society, Nonconformers are notably lacking in self-control. This general characteristic is manifest in a variety of related behaviors. Several members of this group, for example, have assigned responsibility for regulating some salient aspect of their behavior to others. Thus, a woman whose "fictive boyfriend" left the workshop 3 years ago is always reminding a researcher that she had made him responsible for ensuring that she "doesn't flirt with other boys." Similarly, a male who was concerned that he might be suspended from the workshop for his bad temper appointed a peer to monitor his emotional state because, "Tom is the only person who can control me."

Related to this is the propensity of Nonconformers to rely largely on blame-attribution in coping with everyday problems. They rarely admit to any personal responsibility whatsoever and consistently maintain that all their problems are due to failures, inadequacies, or negative qualities of others.

Even within the high tolerance level of workshop society, Nonconformers violate the norms of affective expression and public display of emotion. It is not only that they sulk, cry, malinger, and throw temper tantrums more frequently than others but that they are seen by peers as strategically faking feelings and emotional displays "just to get attention." The label peers attach to such deviancy is "baby." Although such attention-soliciting displays are not uncommon throughout workshop society, it is mainly the Nonconformers who are so lacking in self-control that they abuse the norm. Compared to other groups, Nonconformers are lonely, anxious people who fret, complain, and worry, and are clearly dissatisfied with their lives. Despite all this they consistently maintain that they like themselves and steadfastly insist that they are content with their personal qualities and attributes.

Nonconformers are extremely sensitive to the slightest criticism. One behavioral indicator of this hypersensitivity has been frequently observed in the discussion groups that have been held weekly for the past 6 years. All group sessions are tape-recorded. For approximately the first 2 years, the microphone remained on the conference room table and was rarely touched by group members. Gradually individuals began holding the microphone as a means of emphasizing the importance of what they were saying and to minimize interruptions by others. Now nearly all group members request the microphone when they want to speak and it has become a concrete external means of regulating turn-taking. It has also created a situation in which individual group members are sometimes accused of "hogging the microphone." Most individuals accused of this indiscretion immediately relinquish the microphone without incident and rarely repeat the offense. Nonconformers accused of "hogging the microphone," however, invariably become angry and defensive and several have walked out of the group meeting vowing never to return. For the most part they do return, usually within 5 minutes, and most continue to "hog the microphone."

Individuals in the Nonconformer group frequently report problems involving parents and caregivers. Typically, these problems involve what the individual perceives as inappropriate and unnecessary regulation of his or her personal life (e.g., use of telephone, TV, and record players; being told when to bathe and go to bed; not being allowed to have friends over or visit at their house, and so on). Most such problems are relatively minor, but they do serve to illustrate that many Nonconformers maintain a posture of open defiance toward parental authority.

Nonconformers also tend to perseverate on what seem to be relatively trivial problems for weeks or months at a time. One individual, for example, dominated conversation in a discussion group for 3 weeks, repeating again and again how upset she was that her mother had thrown away some old clothes that she had outgrown. Another man complained bitterly for several months about his workshop supervisor although he was either unable or unwilling to discuss why he was angry. This is not to say that Nonconformers are perpetually miserable, inconsiderate people whom no one ever likes or wants to be around. They have their good moments and fun times, and some have an excellent sense of humor. A Nonconformer once told a researcher that he was forming his own rock music band that he proposed to call "Ups Syndrome and the Trisomy Eight." As best we could determine, he made it up and and it was intended to be funny. He was overheard repeating the joke several times to peers, always adding, "Get it? Ups syndrome, not Down's syndrome. Get it?"

In general, Nonconformers can be characterized as having a more restricted life experience than the other groups. They participate in fewer organized recreational programs and have less opportunity for peer contact outside the workshop setting. The older members in this group typically received little or no formal education during their childhood and adolescence and many continue to be largely restricted to their homes. Their lives outside the workshop are uneventful and lacking in social stimulation. When not at work they spend most of their time watching television.

Nonconformers show less of a modal tendency in their attitudes and feelings about being retarded than the other groups. They are a miscellany of "accepters," "deniers," "redefiners," "avoiders," and others who vacillate depending on circumstances. Members of this group who actively and consistently deny their retarded status can, in certain respects, be viewed as deviant Socialites. Although firmly committed to presenting themselves as not retarded, they can be quite insensitive to the feelings of others in this matter. They are the few members of workshop society who call other people "retards" and who make overt evaluative comparisons favorable to themselves. They are sometimes identified as "snobnobs" by peers and have the reputation of "thinking they are better than everybody else."

Nonconformers who openly admit to being mentally retarded also frankly assert that "all of us kids in the workshop are retarded." These individuals, however, never seem to make such statements with pejorative intent. Unlike Loners, those in the Nonconformer group who define themselves as "being retarded" do not manifest a positive and healthy sense of self-worth. Rather, they engage in extensive self-deprecation, emphasizing their negative qualities and failures. In both the content of everyday self-disclosure and their scores on traditional measures of self-concept, these individuals have the lowest level of self-acceptance in workshop society.

Other members of the Nonconformer group persistently avoid participating in any discussion about mental retardation. In groups where this topic was discussed they remained aloof, uninvolved, and silent. When questioned privately they either say, "I don't know," try and change the topic of conversation, or flatly state that they "don't like to talk about that." Our research with retarded adults who live independently in their own apartments, and who either work competitively or are unemployed, reveals that many of them employ the same tactic when the topic is raised by researchers. We have not yet determined, however, its role in the dynamics of self-esteem maintenance or its relationship to other indices of personal adjustment.

Some Nonconformers apparently have no consistent position regarding their retarded status and vary in what they say depending on the circumstances. One individual consistently denies that he is retarded in group discussions and other public settings. Yet in private conversations with a researcher he readily admits to being mentally retarded and has arranged for a number of private talks concerning *why* he is retarded. He is apparently attempting to arrive at some meaningful and coherent understanding of why he is mentally retarded and his brother and sister are not. Other individuals change their position within the same encounter. They either begin saying they are mentally retarded and then talk themselves into concluding that they are not, or vice versa. Such cases of vacillation are not strongly related to a lower level of functioning or deficient verbal skills as the individuals who do this are randomly distributed on those variables. In most situations researchers could not confront or directly question individuals about their inconsistencies because it would have been rude and enhanced the reactivity of our presence—we tried to respect the norms and values of workshop society as best we understood them.

In general, our data on individuals in the Nonconformer group coalesce most clearly around the dimension of boredom/eventfulness. Their experiential history has made boredom such a pervasive, noxious presence in their emotional sensibility that they are desperate for eventfulness and flounder about the workshop breaking rules and attracting negative attention from both peers and staff. Perhaps they seek to turn their everyday lives into dramaturgical scenarios, not unlike the situation comedies they watch so endlessly on TV at home.

DISCUSSION

Our purpose in describing the four segments of workshop society was to note some of the individual differences among mentally retarded adults and the relationship of these to the collective characteristics of peer subculture. To better conceptualize this relationship, we discuss what seem to be the focal concerns of workshop society at large, and suggest how each of the four segments can be characterized with respect to the relative salience of each of the focal concerns. The four focal concerns can be briefly described as follows:

1. Affiliative relationships   Mentally retarded adults, like everyone, want a sense of community. They want to have friends and romantic involvements. They need a sense of belonging to human groups that provide access to meaningful social relations.
2. Deviance disavowal   Mentally retarded adults, like everyone, want to feel good about themselves. For many, ''being retarded'' is the most salient aspect of their social identity. They need refuge from prevailing negative attitudes, pejorative labels, and unfavorable social comparisons.
3. Social harmony   Mentally retarded adults, like everyone, want harmony and order in their own lives and the lives of those they care about. When conflict and trouble breach the social fabric, they try to repair it.
4. Boredom   Mentally retarded adults, like everyone, need some optimal level of novelty and stimulation. Too little stimulation and they become bored, too much stimulation and they become stressed. For their everyday lives to be positive and fulfilling, they need a satisfying level of eventfulness.

Figure 2 provides an illustration of how each of the four groups we have identified might be ordered in terms of the general high or low salience of each focal concern for that group. This ordering is tentative and our data already suggest that finer distinctions need be made than merely ''High'' or ''Low.'' As can be seen in Figure 2, however, each group does seem to have its own unique pattern of focal concerns. Furthermore, the diagonal cells would seem to identify the primary focal concern of each group (i.e., The Elite are primarily concerned with affiliative relationships, the Socialites with deviance disavowal, the Loners with social harmony, and the Nonconformers with boredom).

From a larger perspective, it also seems clear that workshop subculture has evolved regnant values and norms which permit each of these focal concerns to be more fully satisfied. The manner in which mentally retarded adults seek to satisfy their concerns are

Focal concerns

Societal groups	Affiliative relationships	Deviance disavowal	Social harmony	Boredom
The Elite	High	Low	High	Low
The Socialites	High	High	High	High
The Loners	Low	Low	High	Low
The Nonconformers	High	High/low (mixed)	Low	High

Figure 2. Schematic illustration of the relative salience of focal concerns for four segments of workshop society.

multiple and various. They are not merely passive recipients of powerful environmental forces and/or officially designated socializing agents. They are influential determinants of the social climate they inhabit, active participants in the creation of their own social order and social reality. They interpret and evaluate their needs and experiences and assign meanings to the events and relationships of everyday life. Environments like workshop society, moreover, are the only opportunity many have to fully engage in community life; this experience has important consequences for their sense of identity and self-esteem.

The essential tensions in workshop society can also be described in terms that seem common in human affairs: instrumentality and expressiveness. From an "outsider" view, the workshop can be seen in largely instrumental terms. It has task requirements, an authority structure, rules and other demands that relate largely to work activity and the need to get things done. From an "insider" view, the emphasis is on expressive values and behaviors. The workshop provides a social support system, a sense of belonging, friends, lovers, and a sense of self-worth. Tensions between these two models of human inter-relatedness structure the rhythms of everyday life in most societies (e.g., Turner, 1969). Workshop society differs in no significant way from the larger human community.

Although we have only begun to organize and analyze our data on the workshop, some brief suggestions as to the possible conceptual, methodological, and applied implications of our findings can be offered. Embedded in the notion of focal concerns, for example, are potentially important concepts (e.g., optimal eventfulness) that may prove useful in attempts to measure and compare the social climate across differing habilitative environments. Because such concepts are clearly processes and not traits, they may also keep us sensitized to the notion that the "personalities" of environments, like those of humans, are not some hodgepodge of assorted modal qualities that just happen to fit the investigators' favorite instrument. Qualitative methods, such as participant observation, are terribly demanding of time and both personal and material resources, but they may be necessary if we are to advance knowledge and not just our individual careers.

Everything that we have learned in our research is consistent with the assertion that the workshop does provide a more normal way of life for most members of workshop society. Their focal concerns are not "mentally retarded concerns"; they are the concerns of all peoples. Due partially to their disability and limitations inherent in the larger society, many of these human concerns, which are well provided for in the workshop setting, are unlikely to be met in the world "outside." Our research group at UCLA, for instance, is currently studying a sample of mildly retarded adults who live and work independently in the community. Many of these individuals lead lonely, marginal lives, have little that could be called a social support system, and vacillate constantly between boredom and stress. This may be "normal," but it is the lousy side of normalcy and reflects the priority often assigned to self-sufficiency at the expense of other equally compelling human values. The subjective priorities and concerns of mentally retarded people should be represented both in our research and in the implementation of social policy. Too often, what passes as normalization would seem to be merely an exchange of one set of other-regulators for another (e.g., parents for social worker). This is not to say that workshop society or any sort of more sheltered environment is for everyone. Clearly, this is not the case. We should, however, make more of an investment in trying to understand the everyday lives of retarded persons from their point of view. If they like or don't like an environment, it behooves us to try to discover why. Such understandings are not likely to come easy, but it is "a path with heart."

Finally, it seems that research, like art, is a way of envisioning. It both creates new social realities and prepares us for their implications. In the course of spending thousands of hours in the company of workshop society, it was frequently found that a lot of otherwise puzzling behaviors became much more clear when the people there were thought of not as defective, but as "more than human." This phrase is recommended to other researchers, not as a sentiment, but as a source of metaphor, image, and vision. Mentally retarded persons want and need the same psychological resources as the rest of us. Our task is to better understand those qualities of environments that help meet these "all too human" concerns.

ACKNOWLEDGMENTS

I would like to acknowledge the numerous contributions of students, research associates, and colleagues who have participated in the workshop society research project. Finally, all of us are deeply indebted to the people of workshop society. They have enriched both our understanding and our personal lives, and we are deeply grateful for the many pleasures of their company.

REFERENCES

Crossman, J. E. A technique for programming sheltered workshop environments for training severely retarded workers. *American Journal of Mental Deficiency*, 1969, *73*, 814–823.

Edgerton, R. B. A patient elite: Ethnography in hospital for the mentally retarded. *American Journal of Mental Deficiency*, 1963, *68*, 372–385.

Edgerton, R. B., & Dingman, H. F. Good reasons for bad supervision: 'Dating' in a hospital for the mentally retarded. *Psychiatric Quarterly Supplement*, 1964, *38*, 221–233.

Edgerton, R. B., & Sabagh, G. From mortification to aggrandizement: Changing self-concepts in the careers of the mentally retarded. *Psychiatry*, 1962, *25*, 263–272.

Edgerton, R. B., Tarjan, G., & Dingman, H. F. Free enterprise in a captive society. *American Journal of Mental Deficiency*, 1961, *66*, 35–41.

Eilbracht, A., & Thompson, T. Behavioral intervention in a sheltered work activity setting for retarded adults. In T. Thompson & J. Grabowski (Eds.), *Behavior modification of the mentally retarded* (2nd ed.). New York: Oxford University Press, 1977.

Gold, M. W. Stimulus factors in skill training of retarded adolescents on a complex assembly task. *American Journal of Mental Deficiency*, 1972, *76*, 517–526.

MacAndrew, C., & Edgerton, R. B. The everyday life of institutionalized 'Idiots.' *Human Organization*, 1964, *23*, 312–318.

MacAndrew, D., & Edgerton, R. B. On the possibility of friendship. *American Journal of Mental Deficiency*, 1966, *70*, 612–621.

Nelson, N. *Workshops for the handicapped in the United States*. Springfield, Ill.: Charles C Thomas, 1971.

Turner, J. L., Zetlin, A., & Gallimore, R. The meaning of self-concept in a sheltered workshop. In press.

Turner, V. W. *The ritual process: Structure and anti-structure*. Chicago: Aldine-Atherton, 1969.

U.S. Department of Labor. *Sheltered workshop study: A nationwide report on sheltered workshops and their employment of handicapped individuals*. (2 vols.). Washington, D.C.: U.S. Department of Labor, 1979.

Zaetz, J. L. *Organization of sheltered workshop programs for the mentally retarded adult*. Springfield, Ill.: Charles C Thomas, 1971.

Issues Affecting the Involvement of Mildly Retarded Individuals in Competitive Employment

Paul Koegel and
Keith T. Kernan

Although it is now an issue of primary importance in this era of normalization, the involvement of mildly retarded adults in competitive employment has been of consistent interest throughout the history of mental retardation research. A vast professional literature has addressed itself to a number of important considerations. Follow-up studies of deinstitutionalized individuals, former educable mentally retarded (EMR) students, and graduates of vocational training programs have sought to discover the extent to which mildly retarded individuals have been successful in finding competitive employment positions in their communities (e.g., Baller, Charles, and Miller, 1966; Collman and Newlyn, 1955; Deno, 1965; Dinger, 1961; Edgerton, 1967; Henshel, 1972; Kennedy, 1948, 1966; McFail, 1966; Olshansky and Beach, 1974; Richardson, 1978; Skaarbrevik, 1971; Strickland and Arrell, 1974). Studies comparing the characteristics of those employed in unsheltered settings as opposed to the workshop employed or the unemployed have attempted to isolate variables that predict vocational success and failure (e.g., Abel, 1945; Appell, Williams, and Fishell, 1965; Brolin, 1972; Fulton, 1975; Kolstoe, 1961; Stephens, Peck, and Veldman 1968). (See Cobb (1972) for an extensive review of both follow-up and predictive studies.) Survey data obtained from successfully employed individuals and from employers in the community have suggested the range of employment possibilities open to the mildly retarded (Baldwin, 1966; Becker, 1976; Bernstein, 1966; DiMichael, 1967) and the manner in which employer attitudes impinge on vocational outcome (Cohen, 1963; Hartlage, 1965; Merritt, 1963; Phelps, 1965; Steward, 1977). Finally, testing procedures (e.g., Burdett, 1963; Halpern et al., 1975) and vocational program curricula (Brolin, 1976; Eskridge and Partridge, 1963; Peters and Rhode, 1964; Syden, 1963; Wehman, 1975) have been offered in recognition of the need to determine and

This research was supported by the Community Context of Normalization Study (NICHD Grant HD 09474–02), Robert B. Edgerton, Principal Investigator, and by the Mental Retardation Research Center, UCLA (USPHS Grant HD 04162–05).

173

ameliorate the deficits that prevent mildly retarded persons from attaining competitive employment. The tacit assumption in most of this literature is that all mildly retarded individuals view competitive employment as being in their best interest, that they *want* to be competitively employed, and that they thus are equally involved in seeking out either competitive employment jobs or programs designed to prepare them for such an end. The actual situation, of course, is not as simple as that. Indeed, our research suggests that it is impossible to understand the status of mildly retarded individuals in the competitive employment sphere by focusing exclusively on individual ability, employer attitude, and job availability—that is, factors that pertain only to competitive employment per se. A more complete and holistic understanding of the role that competitive employment does (and does not) play in the lives of mildly retarded adults must rest on a wider focus, one that examines related issues and settings and that attempts to understand how they contribute to whether an individual holds competitive employment to be a valued, realistic, and viable goal. In this chapter we examine in detail some of the factors that motivate and either assist or hinder the individual in seeking competitive employment in the first place. Rather than ask what effect a competitive employment setting may have on various aspects of an individual's life, we concern ourselves with the effect that aspects of an individual's life situation may have in determining whether that individual will seek to enter the competitive work world.

SAMPLE AND DATA COLLECTION

The data upon which this chapter is based come from the Community Context of Normalization study, which followed a cohort population of 48 individuals for 2 years. These individuals, ranging in age from 19 to 49 years, had all been labeled mildly mentally retarded at some point in their lives but had also been identified by professionals in the service delivery system as possessing the potential for independent community living. Most of them were from middle-class families. See Table 1 for the demographics of the sample. Our research involved constant and intensive contact with each of the sample members. They were visited, interviewed, and observed about twice a month in all the settings in which they normally interacted, including home, work, social activities, and so on. Significant others in their lives—spouses, parents, siblings, friends, employers, social workers—were also regularly visited and interviewed. Because of this intensive, open-ended, and long-term contact, field researchers were able to establish the kind of rapport with sample members that permitted intimate discussion of all aspects of their lives. (For a more in-depth discussion of our methodology, see the chapter by Edgerton in this volume.) Our resulting data base provides a first-hand understanding of employment seeking and work activities undertaken by sample members over the duration of our research period, and of the contexts in which those activities occurred.

Kernan and Koegel (1980) examined the employment status of this mildly retarded cohort. The most striking conclusions that emerged from this analysis were 1) that relatively few individuals were competitively employed full-time—only 10.4% at time of research contact (not including part-time employed and housewives) and 22.9% at the conclusion of the research, 2½ years later; and 2) that fluctuation in employment status is exceptionally high, with frequent changes in employment status being the rule. One individual, for

Table 1.   Demographics of the community context of normalization study (N = 48)

Variable	Number
Sex	
Males	22
Females	26
Marital status	
Married	15
Single	30
Separated	3
Residential arrangement	
Board and care	3
Family care	7
Independent	23
Parents	14*
Residential programs	1
Age	
18–22	3
23–27	24
28–32	8
33–37	11
38–42	1
43–47	0
48–52	1

*One subject lives with in-laws.

instance, held six different competitive employment jobs during the course of our research contact with him. Another moved from the sporadic seeking of employment to a workshop, to competitive employment, to a workshop again, to competitive employment again, and finally traveled full circle back to sporadic job seeking. The successfully versus unsuccessfully employed do not differ in intelligence, skills or other work-related abilities. There is little stability in employment status for most of the individuals in our sample. As a result, people are constantly faced with the decision of whether to seek competitive employment, and often fail when they do seek and find jobs.

The Implications of a Guaranteed Income

Perhaps the most influential factor in determining the employment activities and the attitudes toward competitive employment of the mildly retarded is the existence of a large federal and state public welfare system that is designed specifically to meet the financial needs of the disabled. The very availability of public financial support, the regulations governing the provision of this support, and the attitudes of the mildly mentally retarded toward such support are all crucial variables in determining who is and who is not active in seeking and maintaining competitive employment.

Sources of Income of Cohort Members   For most people employment is synonymous with "earning a living," so it is instructive to examine the primary sources of income for Normalization Project sample members. Table 2 summarizes these data, and indicates the extent of public financial support in the lives of this cohort. A total of 25 individuals— over half of the sample—currently receives Supplemental Security Income (SSI), an income maintenance program for aged, blind, or disabled low-income persons.

Table 2.   Primary source of support

	Number	Total	%
Supplemental Security Income (SSI)			
Living independently	14		
Board and care facility*	8	25	52.1
Residing with family	3		
Other public support			
Aid for Dependent Children (AFDC)			
Living independently	2		
Public guardian			
Living independently	1	4	8.3
Social Security survivor benefits			
Residing with family	1		
Private support			
Parental trust funds			
Living independently	2	2	4.2
Competitive employment			
Living independently	5		
Board and care facility	2	14	29.2
Residing with family	7		
Supported entirely by family			
Residing with family	3	3	6.3
		48	100

*Includes board and care, family care, and work training facilities.

As stipulated by the regulations governing eligibility for payments to the disabled, these individuals have offered the Social Security Administration sufficient proof of a long-term, medically determinable impairment and an inability, because of this impairment, to engage in ''any substantial gainful activity.'' Another four individuals receive other forms of public financial support: two mothers with small children receive Aid For Dependent Children (AFDC) benefits; one individual, a ward of the court since his youth, receives monies administered through the Office of the Public Guardian; and one individual continues to receive Social Security Survivor benefits, his disability serving to waive in his case the rule that recipients must be less than 21 years old. Thus a total of 29 individuals (60.4%) are guaranteed a basic income from the government. Thirteen of these supplement this baseline income in a number of ways: through living with their parents who provide them with room, board, and other essentials and who do not necessarily demand recompense (four individuals); through sheltered workshop employment (three of these individuals live with their parents and another four live in residential facilities); and through competitive employment in part-time positions with earnings low enough that public support is not withdrawn — although some adjustment is made (five individuals).

The remaining 19 sample members (39.6%) do not receive any direct support through government agencies. Fourteen of these individuals are competitively employed and are at least nominally self-supporting (half of those still reside with their parents, who continue to provide a certain degree of financial support by way of room and board). Three individuals are completely supported by their families. (One, however, does take care of her nieces and nephews, freeing their parents to work in the family-owned business. Another individual is recently separated from her nonretarded husband and is currently in the process of applying for SSI.) Finally, two individuals, although not receiving public assistance, do receive guaranteed monthly checks through trust funds set up by their deceased parents.

If we hold the issue of financial support by parents constant for the moment, our sample can be loosely divided into two basic groups. The first group includes individuals who receive benefits through SSI, AFDC, other governmental support programs, or parental trust funds. These, in other words, are people who are guaranteed a baseline income that can be supplemented, if the individual chooses, by workshop earnings or part-time jobs. Members of the second group are largely self-supporting through "gainful" competitive employment. Most forms of public assistance available to the members of our sample are, by definition, for those whose disability precludes the possibility of gainful employment. It is reasonable to expect, therefore, that such individuals receive a guaranteed income because they are *unable* to work, and self-supporting individuals do not receive such benefits because they *are* able to work. This does not seem to be the case in practice, however. Social Security Administration policy stipulates that the disability of mild retardation is not in and of itself sufficient to qualify an individual for SSI payments. One must also demonstrate a corresponding inability, because of that disability, to maintain competitive employment. The experience of the majority of sample members, however, indicates that the actual operating rules are very different. Some individuals (though with great difficulty) have succeeded in qualifying for SSI payments even after having held jobs for years at a time. Yet a larger number of individuals have had their applications for SSI approved solely on the basis of their being labeled mildly retarded (even in the absence of corroborating IQ scores) without ever having *attempted* to obtain competitive employment. Eight of these individuals, in fact, subsequently secured competitive jobs and held them long enough to demonstrate, by Social Security Administration standards, an ability to maintain gainful employment. In practice, then, a label of mild retardation is customarily sufficient to qualify an individual for disability payments as long as there is no record of competitive employment. Mild retardation, however, does not automatically preclude the possibility of an individual holding a competitive employment job; indeed the prevailing belief in the vocational literature is that the majority of mildly retarded individuals *are* capable of competitive employment (Baroff, 1974). Clearly something more than "disability" determines who will remain on SSI or other guaranteed income programs rather than seek competitive employment. In what follows, we explore 1) the reasons why some sample members have had no experience with guaranteed support, 2) the implications a guaranteed income holds for those who elect not to work, and 3) the factors that make guaranteed support, and in particular SSI, a more viable source of income than competitive employment for those individuals who do express interest in holding jobs.

The Role of Attitudes in Determining the Acceptance of a Guaranteed Income   Ten members of the Normalization sample have not received SSI or any other form of guaranteed income at any point in their lives. Because all mildly retarded individuals who have not held a competitive job paying more than $200 per month are eligible for SSI, it is instructive to examine why this is the case. By and large, these individuals (and their families, in most cases) are distinguished by their attitudes toward public support and their beliefs regarding their own abilities.[1] Basically, they believe either that it is demeaning to accept any form of "welfare" or believe that they are so close to being "normal" that the support available to the retarded is inappropriate for them. One woman, for instance, is currently employed part-time at a day care center but is being pressured by her father to apply for SSI because her meager monthly income is consumed by medical expenses and bus fare. She has refused to do so, however, noting that she would be ashamed to accept "welfare." Another individual, who has held a number of competitive employment jobs, expresses a similar attitude toward charity and welfare. He professes a belief in work for its own sake, which he attributes to his upbringing, pointing to his father's early demands that he work to earn his spending money and to the fact that he had a paper route by the age of 12. Yet another woman believes that those who collect SSI are doing themselves a disservice because they come to depend on it, and mentions her own boyfriend as an example of how SSI can inhibit one's motivation "to get off (one's) ass and try to find work." She feels that she has been pushed by her parents to be on her own and notes that the road toward self-reliance, although a difficult one, has been rewarding for her. Finally, another man notes that SSI is for "handicapped" people. He confesses to having had learning problems during his school days, but he has never viewed those problems as obstacles to his ability to hold a job.

Such attitudes are rare, however, as evidenced by the fact that 38 individuals (79%) have at some time collected either SSI or some other form of guaranteed support, and another four individuals (8.3%) applied for support but were turned down. Many of these 38 individuals began receiving support upon graduation from high school; some upon placement in board and care facilities; others upon the death of their parents; still others upon learning that support is available from new contacts in the service delivery system or peers in their personal network; and yet others upon the birth of their children. For all, a guaranteed income has become a significant feature in their lives, paying a room and board in residential facilities in some cases, affording them the income with which to live on their own, or permitting them to be members that contribute income to their family. This guaranteed income, however, has had an equally direct impact on the motivation to seek and obtain competitive employment. Although not a complete deterrent to such employment (as made clear by the eight individuals who have relinquished their SSI in order to work competitively), SSI and other forms of guaranteed support have often served to forestall or at least inhibit the involvement of sample members in this sphere.

Implications of a Guaranteed Income for Those Who Prefer Not to Seek Competitive Employment   Perhaps the most obvious implication of a guaranteed income is the fact that those individuals who receive SSI or other support don't *have* to work. (Presumably they are *unable* to work; however, doubt has already been raised here about the validity of this assumption.) They are assured a monthly check whether or not they seek rehabilitative services or attempt to locate employment within the realm of their capabilities. As a result, many individuals display a rather cavalier attitude toward work. Said one individual with reference to most of the people in her residential care facility, "Usually

---

[1]Four of these 10 individuals do not hold these attitudes and beliefs, however. They, in fact, applied for but were denied SSI.

the people aren't working because they're on SSI. They get their allowance. They get their three meals a day. They get their cigarettes and all that stuff and they're happy...." Another sample member, with a wife and three children, had a very spotty attendance record at the sheltered workshop at which he worked before quitting. Neither his absenteeism nor a bus strike that caused him to miss 2 weeks of work were of any concern to him. In fact, he admitted that he was quite pleased by the strike and commented, "It doesn't matter 'cause I got money no matter what," a reference to his SSI. Currently, this man is resisting the demands of his wife and mother that he get out and earn a living. His defense lies in pointing out that jobs aren't easy to find. He clinches his argument, though, with the reminder that he already brings in a respectable income through SSI and thus should be considered "employed." Another individual worked at Goodwill for 10 years until she was laid off due to unwarranted absenteeism. As a result, her SSI payments were raised. She has come to feel that she has already contributed sufficiently to the work force and is content to sit back and collect her checks. SSI, she has decided, is really the only worthwhile source of income; it frees her to do what she wants to do.

For many people, SSI is a convenience that allows them to avoid work and to live a life devoted to hobby and leisure. Thus the married man mentioned above sees work as a nuisance that distracts him from his primary passion and pursuit in life—a total absorption with aeronautical and airline operations. He spends many hours and a considerable amount of money securing all available information on airplanes and flight schedules. He not only uses his citizen's band scanner to monitor conversations between pilots and control towers but predicts, on the basis of the copious information he has accumulated in his files, the origin, destination, make, and estimated time of arrival of planes as they pass overhead. One sample member whose income derives from a trust fund doesn't consider working at all; she much prefers visiting with friends and frequenting neighborhood haunts. Likewise, a man, after working at the Post Office for 4 years and holding assorted jobs subsequent to being fired for absenteeism, openly reasons that he might as well exercise his SSI "option" in order to pursue his favorite leisure activities—painting-by-number and typing—because he never makes enough money from the jobs he is able to secure. He no longer has any interest in working and has completely rejected the idea of employment as a source of income. Each of these individuals is oriented not toward work and competitive employment but toward the support forthcoming from public and, in a limited number of cases, from private sources. This orientation is perhaps best typified in the response by one couple to their chronic money problems. Highly incensed by their financial straits, they talked about applying for welfare or food stamps to supplement their SSI because in their indignant words, "There ought to be something we can do!" When it was suggested that one option was to try to find steady jobs, they rejected that possibility, noting, "This is the only money we can get. That's why we don't do anything to destroy it. This is the only way...."

Because they receive a guaranteed income and need not work at all if they choose, work for many of these individuals loses its paramount meaning as a necessity that provides one with the means to live. Other functions of work begin to assume primary importance. Thus a good many individuals talk not of working to earn a living but to supplement the payments they automatically receive. Others talk about their desire to break up their routine, to get out of the house, to get away from family members or co-residents, to engage in some kind of useful activity, and myriad other reasons. Part-time competitive employment (rather than workshop income, for example) is certainly the most remunerative way of supplementing one's income, while satisfying the entire gamut of needs mentioned above. Of the individuals who receive support, however, relatively few—only two, in fact—are engaged in part-time competitive employment. This is largely due, it would seem, to the fact that a variety of other options can more easily satisfy the need to supplement income and/or those needs that have little to do with money. Workshop employment is one means to safely supplement one's monthly income, to socialize with peers, and so forth, and is an option currently utilized by eight of those individuals receiving guaranteed support. Volunteer work provides an opportunity for one woman to reduce her contact with annoying girlfriends in the board and care facility in which she lives; for another woman, it answers the need to be engaged in helping other people. School offers the solution to the problem of another individual, who recognizes that she is frightfully bored when not employed or taking courses. Experience has taught her that it is far easier to get into school that it is to find a job, and thus she takes classes as a meaningful way of spending her time.

Because these activities are undertaken primarily to satisfy personal rather than financial goals, their tenure is often short-lived. For example, one woman became a client at a workshop with the stated intention of earning extra money for herself and her boyfriend with whom she was living. But her covert intention was to reactivate a past relationship with a man who was currently working at the shop. She accomplished her goal, and soon left the man with whom she was living in order to marry the man at the shop. After her new husband left the shop, however, she stopped working regularly and finally quit. Likewise, the individual who volunteered in order to avoid her girlfriends stopped working when her peer problems were resolved. Because the glue that holds supported individuals to their ''job'' is personal satisfaction rather than financial necessity, individuals in this category think nothing of ending their work or work-substitute activities if they become even mildly dissatisfying.

The Dilemma of Those Who Do Express an Interest in Competitive Employment   Thus far we have dealt only with those individuals who have not expressed any real desire to become self-supporting. There are many ''supported'' sample members, though, who *are* at least nominally committed to the idea of a job and who, in some cases, evince a real commitment to the concept of full-time employment. These individuals, however, are often caught in a bind brought on by 1) the nature of their employment experiences, and 2) the structure of disability support.

We have already discussed the flux that characterizes the employment careers of mildly retarded individuals. Jobs, for them, are neither easily obtained nor maintained and it is not unusual for an individual to experience many failures before achieving some modicum of job stability. Often, it is a question of finding the ''right'' job—one that is tailored to the competencies of the individual or one in which the employer is especially patient and understanding. Even these jobs, however, carry with them an ever-present measure of insecurity and uncertainty in that mildly retarded workers, usually the most expendable, are especially vulnerable to layoff.

Recognizing the difficulties faced by disabled individuals in finding jobs, the Social Security Administration has incorporated into the SSI program a ''trial work period'' for individuals who do want to try to become self-supporting. This ''trial work period'' is designed to allow such individuals to attempt to become gainfully employed without fear of losing their eligibility in the meantime. Should an individual secure a job, he or she continues to receive adjusted SSI payments for a 9-month period. At the end of 9 months of consecutive competitive employment with a monthly salary of more than $200, the individual is then considered to be capable of self-sufficiency and no longer receives disability payments. Should the individual subsequently lose the job, he or she is directed to the Department of Employment and is henceforth considered to be an ordinary unemployed member of the work force.

Although Social Security Administration (SSA) policy holds that the trial work period is enough incentive and sufficiently protective to motivate individuals to seek competitive employment should they wish to work, sample members remain concerned about the possibility of eventually not having a guaranteed income. For most, involvement in employment has taught them that stable jobs are elusive, requiring an arduous search with many short-lived attempts. Faced with the choice between the trauma and tenuousness of competitive employment and the security of guaranteed monthly payments, it is not surprising that so many opt for the payments and forego a job search. It is possible that a certain degree of laziness inhibits the search for a job in a few cases, despite protestations of a desire to work. Protecting one's SSI at all costs, however, stands as a typical (and viable) response to the bind in which mildly retarded individuals find themselves.

Thus one individual, for example, when told by her counselor that she was capable of more than volunteer work, pointed to the fact that a regular job would endanger her SSI. She insisted that she couldn't accept a job unless her prospective employer were willing either to pay her ''off the books'' or pay her a nominal salary such as $2 a day, a sum for which she would be willing to work in order to protect her SSI. Another individual, who in the past held numerous short-lived jobs, talked about a job opportunity of which he was aware, that would pay $5 an hour. He noted that should he take advantage of such an opportunity, his SSI would eventually be cut off. Clearly wary of his job security, he commented, ''So what do I do? No matter what I do it's no good.''

Interestingly, this individual's mother, like many other parents of sample members, shares his concern over protecting his disability payments, and communicates this concern to her son both explicitly and implicity. When he mentioned having seen a notice at the employment office for a delivery job that paid $3.50 an hour, she reminded him that he had unsuccessfully tried working before and that if he did find a job he would lose his SSI. When he finally did secure a job paying minimum wage at the loading dock of a local Goodwill, his mother was worried rather than excited and pleased. She immediately went down to the Social Security office to determine the effect his new job would have on his check. She learned that because he would be working in a ''handicapped shop,'' his SSI would not be cut off but adjusted. She then busied herself plugging figures into the formula, and seemed worried by the sum at which she arrived. Thus she implicitly suggested to her son that his move may not have been a wise one. She and parents who share her concern are not necessarily interfering with their children's progress or expressing a financial stake in their children's SSI. Their concern arises rather from an awareness of the struggle involved in maintaining employment and a fear for the financial future of their children. One mother with a strong commitment to ''normalization'' and to seeing that her son lives in the ''least restrictive environment'' possible, remains apprehensive about the work aspect of her son's independent living program. She openly acknowledges her fears that he will lose his SSI and eventually face the loss of a job with no income to fall back on. As she is approaching old age, she has become yet more concerned, knowing that she will not always be around to support him. Reflecting on this, she admits that she would be quite content to see him living independently and only supplementing his SSI, rather than depending solely on his own vocational skills for a living. For many parents and mildly retarded individuals alike, the future is threatening. They are often more willing to place their trust in the government's sense of responsibility to the disabled than in their children's ability to persevere in a competitive job market. Indeed their concern over their children's employment security is not unwarranted—six individuals no longer receive SSI since losing their jobs after the 9-month grace period, and not all attempts at getting payments reinstated have been successful.

Other problems in the structure and practice of SSI also act as a deterrent for those individuals who might otherwise work, or remain a harsh reality for those who have been willing to face the risks they present. The SSA holds relatively fast to its criteria for "gainful employment," failing to take into account the special circumstances under which that money is often earned.

The following example of a 22-year-old woman illustrates the harsh realities for a mentally retarded person willing to face the risks of competitive employment. This individual secured a job as a kitchen aide in a senior citizen's nutrition program, her salary paid through a local Continuing Education Training Act (CETA) program. About a year later, she received word that due to a cutback in CETA funding, she would be losing her job at the end of 6 months. At the same time, she was informed by the SSA that her payments were being cut off because of her successful completion of 9 months of employment. This woman's parents approached her employer in the hope that the grant that funded the nutrition program would be able to pick up her salary. It was then that they learned that their daughter's success at the job had been mixed at best, and that she had only been retained because her salary was paid through CETA. Upset by this new development, they wrote to the SSA to apprise them of the situation and to suggest that their daughter's "trial" had not been valid due to the nature of her funding. A letter from the SSA stated that because their daughter had demonstrated the ability to earn a substantial monthly salary, her SSI was being discontinued. Although this individual is currently looking for alternative employment, primarily because of the strong support and aid forthcoming from her family, other individuals have allowed such experiences to turn them away from any activity that would endanger their SSI. This is true in the case of another individual who lost her SSI after having been involved in a job training program that paid her full-time salary at a clerical job. As was known from the start, at the end of a year, funding for the program lapsed, and the woman lost her job. After a period of accepting unemployment compensation and a few unsuccessful job ventures, she was finally placed on SSI again after showing serious symptoms of psychological stress. She has learned her "lesson," however, and currently refuses to look for work for fear that she will hold a job, federally subsidized or not, just long enough to lose her SSI. Thus the inability of the SSA to recognize the special employment circumstances of the mildly retarded serves to discourage some individuals from working at all.

One final and striking deterrent built into the structure of SSI is the fact that under certain circumstances, individuals can make more money by remaining unemployed than they can by working. At the urging of her mother, one individual applied for SSI despite the fact that she held a part-time job as a day-care aide. The mother did not feel that her daughter should get the full amount allotted to single individuals—she only wanted the SSA to make up the difference between the salary her daughter was earning and the amount she would receive had she opted for SSI. The SSA turned her down, claiming that her job constituted evidence of the ability to work. Both mother and daughter were upset by the SSA's insensitivity to the difficulty of finding full-time, secure work, and were dismayed that she was to be penalized for working. Indeed, when this woman married some 2 years later, her husband, who was not working but collected SSI, contributed more to their household income than she.

We see, then, that the existence of a guaranteed source of income often serves to forestall or at least inhibit the efforts of mildly retarded individuals to seek competitive employment. Contrary to popular belief, not all of the individuals in this predominantly middle-class cohort view work as being fundamental to their self-esteem. Many have found alternative arenas of self-expression—a myriad of hobbies and leisure activities—to be more satisfying than work. (See Edgerton and Bercovici, 1976, for a discussion of similar attitudes in an older, deinstitutionalized cohort.) These individuals are quite content to reject work in favor of the meager income provided by SSI despite the fact that many of them, given the right situation, might be capable of engaging in competitive employment. For those individuals, on the other hand, who do view employment as a valued activity and who do voice a desire to work competitively, SSI often stands as a more viable choice, again because of job instability in the competitive work world and the rigid regulations guiding the provision of federal support.

THE AVAILABILITY OF SHELTERED WORKSHOP EMPLOYMENT

SSI is only one aspect of a vast network of services designed to meet the needs of mentally retarded individuals. The sheltered workshop is also important in considering the issue of the mentally retarded and competitive employment. As in the case of SSI, the sheltered workshop has offered many retarded individuals experiences to which they may not otherwise have been exposed, such as the opportunity for vocational self-expression in an environment tailored to their needs and abilities. Like SSI, however, the sheltered workshop exists as an "easier" option for more competent individuals who might otherwise attempt to find that "right" competitive employment job. The experiences of many sample members suggest that the workshop is seductive both in its ability to meet a wider range of needs than can competitive employment (see Turner, 1979) and its very presence as an alternative to the difficulties of the competitive employment process.

Because the workshop environment is by definition sheltered, the demands imposed upon and the features offered to its clients differ dramatically from those that mentally retarded individuals encounter in the competitive sphere.[2] The workshop offers a non-pressured work situation (an especially enticing feature to those who have attempted to hold competitive employment jobs but have failed), an accepting peer group with which to

---

[2]Indeed, the very term *client* as opposed to *worker* implies a service relationship, which contrasts markedly with the more contractual relationship found in the everyday work world.

socialize, a pool of potential boyfriends or girlfriends, extravocational activities such as classes, physical education, and trips to ballgames, and the opportunity, in the case of many mildly retarded individuals, to be the ''big fish in a little pond.'' Furthermore, the workshop provides a setting that tolerates a much greater degree of absenteeism (a characteristic of many sample members). It is a setting in which the consequences of absenteeism are far less severe.[3] Finally, the workshop represents *guaranteed* employment, much in the same way that SSI offers guaranteed income. A few sample members, in fact, have worked in a total of three different workshops on as many as seven separate occasions. Not surprisingly, they have come to view workshop employment as an option that they can activate, deactivate, and reactivate depending on their circumstances at the time.

The experience of one sample member in particular indicates that workshops can, as a comfortable alternative, inhibit the motivation of individuals capable of competitive employment. This individual left the sheltered workshop at which he had worked for 3 years to accept a regular job in a linen company. He quit shortly thereafter, complaining of the distance he had to travel and of interpersonal problems with fellow employees. To fill his time, he began volunteering at the workshop, where his girlfriend and many of his friends continued to work. Seven months later, he left the shop once more to fill a job secured through his brother, doing welding on a production line. He was laid off 6 months later, however, for being too slow. Hardly nonplussed by this development, he said that he would eventually look for another job, and returned to volunteering at the shop once more. He reacted evasively to efforts by the staff to impel him toward a renewed job search and did not respond to their suggestion that he was using the shop as a refuge when indeed he was really capable of doing competitive work. It was not until they severely restricted the amount of time he was allowed to work at the shop and until a counselor approached him with news of an assembly job opening, that he took serious steps toward securing a job again. He did become successfully employed, and has currently held his job for over a year. Had he been allowed to remain at the shop, however, as many people are, he might never have obtained that job for which he is so well-suited.

This is not to say that the sheltered shop is a regrettable institution. For every one individual who might find a competitive job were it not for the workshop alternative, there may be four or five individuals who might sit at home alone in front of a television set, denied the opportunity to be active and productive. Nor is it to say that the workshop is viewed by all individuals as a preferable alternative to competitive employment. Many individuals find the workshop experience to be exceptionally stigmatizing and choose to work either competitively or not at all. Others are, to varying degree, happy at the workshop but profess the desire for competitive, well-paying, ''outside'' jobs. It is to say, however, that the workshop is a significant feature in the seeking of competitive employment by the

---

[3]Witness, for example, the case of one individual who became bored by shop routine and began coming in to work only when there was nothing to do at home, or when she was sure that there would be work to her liking at the shop. For months her attendance was erratic, including 2-week lapses. Her absenteeism was tolerated, however, in part due to her ability to construct reasonable, even if untruthful, excuses. She was finally taken to task by her counselor for her slipshod attitude toward work in a meeting to which she reacted with righteous indignation, angered by his nerve in telling her what to do. A threat of termination produced a temporary change in behavior, but some 2 weeks later she slipped into her former pattern. Even so, it was another month or so before she was terminated. Furthermore, she was immediately referred to a ''higher level'' shop, allowing her to construe her move as a positive transfer, rather than a serious reprimand.

mentally retarded, one which must be considered in trying to understand who is and who is not competitively employed, and why.

THE EFFECT OF FAMILY SUPPORT

SSI and sheltered workshops, we have seen, are alternatives that sample members may choose should they decide not to seek and maintain competitive employment. As mentioned earlier, such alternatives may be explored from the start or after a series of unsuccessful efforts at holding a competitive job. Indeed, given the psychologically taxing and often traumatic experiences of failure, the temptation is very real to retreat to the security of workshop employment and/or public assistance, meager though it is. The experiences of our sample members suggest that the extent to which this happens (or, to put it positively, the extent to which sample members succeed in achieving competitive employment) is to a large degree a function of the support, encouragement, and help available to them. As such, both an individual's family support system, consisting of parents and/or siblings, and his or her service delivery support system, consisting of social workers and rehabilitation counselors, become highly relevant variables in determining who is and who is not seeking competitive employment.

The effect of family and delivery system support on the competitive employment status of sample members has been explored by Kernan and Koegel (1980). Essentially, this analysis revealed that where there is an active and involved family or service delivery support system impelling sample members toward the competitive employment world, individuals are likely to be competitively employed, or at least making their way up the employment ranks. Where there is some encouragement from either family or service delivery systems but little active involvement, individuals are less likely to be successful in attaining employment, or take longer to do so. Last, where family support systems are not intact, where the support potentially forthcoming from the delivery system fails to emerge, and where negative influences are in operation, individuals are likely to remain in workshops or not to seek any kind of employment at all. It should be noted that all but one of our 48 sample members are either on the active case roster of a social worker or counselor or have at some point during the period of research contact sought the special services of a rehabilitative agency. For the most part, these delivery system liaisons have not been effective in either pushing sample members toward competitive employment or in actually helping them find jobs *unless* strong family or caregiver presences have pressured them to do so. Independent living work training programs are an exception to this tendency. The two individuals who entered independent living programs during the course of research contact both left the ranks of the unemployed, one obtaining a part-time competitive job with the help of his counselors, the other placement in a workshop.

The dynamic impact that strong and active advocates can have on the paths traveled by the member of their family who is mentally retarded may be best exemplified by the experiences of one cohort member. When it came time for Pat to find a job, her involved family, including two siblings, played a crucial role. In Pat's mind, a job in the kitchen of a place such as Goodwill was enticing—she had worked at a transitional workshop for a year and welcomed the absence of pressure. But her family felt she was capable of competitive employment in her chosen field of food service, and their judgment prevailed. A campaign in which all family members were involved was initiated with the aim of obtaining Pat a job. With the aid of her family, Pat prepared a résumé, complete with references, and a self-composed letter advising prospective employers of her desire to work, her assets, and the nature of her handicap. The Yellow Pages were combed for potential employment sites. An organized looseleaf contained the dates résumés were sent out, the date of a follow-up phone call, the status of the job at hand, and possible leads worth exploring. To add strength to her campaign, Pat also enlisted the aid of the Department of Rehabilitation, bringing her counselor classified ads that she and her mother found in the paper, and having the counselor make initial phone calls so that offers of on-the-job training funds could be made. Through her counselor, she also learned of various community agencies that could provide help in finding jobs as well.

This strategy proved successful in finding jobs for Pat, but it took a while before the "right" job was found. Pat's first three attempts at competitive employment were unsuccessful. These failures were devastating to her, and had she been given the opportunity, she would have gladly washed her hands of the competitive employment world. Her family consistently urged her on, however, even in the face of their shaken confidence in her ability to succeed. Pat finally found a satisfying job in a senior citizens' nutrition program, where she has worked for 1½ years. Sadly, her CETA funding for this job has been cut off, and she once again finds herself in the position of having to find a job. Undaunted, however, she and her family are readying themselves for the struggle once again. Knowing Pat as we do, there is no doubt in our minds that without the aid of her active family she would have long since retreated to a sheltered workshop. She no longer thinks in terms of workshop employment despite her intense anxiety over new employment situations. Her orientation is toward competitive employment, a direct result of her family's attitudes and willingness to offer a great amount of time and energy.

Like Pat's experiences, those of other sample members demonstrate how strong family support provides a framework for individual growth and development. The absence of support and, in some cases, negative input, can impede involvement in competitive employment. One individual, for instance, who currently lives in a large board and care facility and collects SSI, has a history of marginal kitchen employment but is neither working now nor interested in doing so. Dissatisfied with his current living situation, he is aware that a well-paying job is the first step toward a more independent existence but is unwilling to make an effort in that direction. He has relatively little contact with his family and is only occasionally visited by his social worker, who expends little energy on urging him to work and absolutely none on helping him find a job. Actually, this individual is content with his social worker's noninvolvement. He is convinced that delivery system personnel do nothing but place clients in sheltered workshops, and he will have nothing to do with such "dollar-a-day" jobs. Another individual remains in a workshop despite the impression of the staff there that he is capable of competitive employment. His caregiver in the family care home in which he lives has a limited view of his abilities, and his social worker, who meets with the residents of his home as a group every 6 months, has far more contact with his caregiver than she does with the individual himself. Yet another individual's caregiver feels that competitive employment would place too great a strain on her charge's mental stability. The caregiver thus firmly suggests that her resident's intention to work competitively, while commendable, is far too ambitious. It is enough, she assures her, that she work at the sheltered workshop where she has been employed for the last 3 years. As this sample member's social worker offers little input, the decision of the caregiver stands. Thus we see the critical role played by the degree of support available to individuals. Had these individuals the same degree of support that Pat has enjoyed, they more likely would be involved either in competitive employment or at least the search for a job.

The examples above illustrate that those individuals who are not exposed to a family support system that stresses the value of competitive employment and who are thus more dependent on less personally involved advocates are far less active and successful in finding jobs. Social workers and counselors, beleaguered as they are by huge case loads, simply cannot provide the same degree of commitment and involvement displayed by a highly motivated family. With rare exceptions, they tend to follow established and easy paths, placing clients in workshops "as a first step" even when the clients express an interest in competitive employment. Thus one individual, upon leaving a state hospital where she had been housed for 4 months following a nervous breakdown, professed a desire to work in a nursery school or day care center — something she had done in the past. Her social worker, however, made no effort to help her accomplish her goal, placing her instead in a sheltered shop. Another individual, currently employed for 4 years as a day care aide, was initially placed in a workshop by her Department of Rehabilitation counselor, whose attitude was distressing to both this woman and her mother. As her mother commented about the counselor, "He just stood with his foot on the chair and chewed gum, and kind of look down on both of us." "What can *she* do? Just send her down to the workshop and be glad they have them." Neither mother nor daughter were content with that rudely offered suggestion and finally, after a prolonged struggle, they found her the job she presently holds. (Interestingly, evaluations of her performance on this competitive job have been strikingly positive, and her workshop evaluations had been negative. In fact, workshop personnel believed that she could not be competitively employed.) Not all social workers and counselors are as condescending and as unresponsive to the abilities of retarded individuals as was this counselor. Workers in the service delivery system, however, given its resources and pressures, do not customarily offer the time, patience, and commitment that is often necessary for success in competitive employment placement unless there is unusual pressure on them to do so. Given this fact, the presence or absence of family support with regard to employment becomes all the more critical.

Actual aid and encouragement in the job-seeking process is only one aspect of the family's effect on a retarded individual's involvement in competitive employment. Without doubt, the early and continuing socialization process that individuals undergo contributes heavily to their competence, values, and attitudes (Koegel, 1978). The family affects, either negatively or positively, a number of job-related areas, for example: individual basic orientation toward work in general, self-image, willingness to jump into a risky situation to try to make it work, beliefs concerning what the world (and the government in particular) owes one, and job aspirations. Most of these issues have been highlighted in any number of examples throughout this chapter. But the relationship between one's family environment and job aspirations is a particularly thorny one and deserves further attention.

A problem for many sample members is the incongruence between their job aspirations and career goals and their abilities and resources. One individual, for instance, dreams of being a musician. Another has expressed interest in becoming a doctor. Others have considered being policemen, teachers, aviators, nurses, actors, or social workers. For people such as these who emerge from middle-class backgrounds, these are not surprising aspirations, especially given the fact that their siblings, their parents, and others to whom they were exposed in their formative years held such jobs. The general environment in which they have lived their lives has engendered in them a certain image of employment that is closed to them due to limitations imposed by their handicap. For some, though certainly not all, their distaste or scorn for low-level occupations stands in the way of obtaining jobs that may be available and suitable for them.

Most parents have accepted the likelihood that their children will occupy low-level employment positions and, as a consequence, will find it difficult to maintain a middle-class life if left to their own resources. A few, however, have not. Their difficulties in reconciling their aspirations with their children's ability result in the same kind of dissonance faced by mildly retarded individuals themselves. Thus one individual's parents want nothing less than for their daughter to be married to a doctor (she is in actuality married to a rather shiftless man who hasn't held a serious job since they were wed). She herself, discouraged by a number of failure experiences in competitive employment, has largely depended on workshops to supplement her SSI payments. Her parents, however, abhor workshops, believing them to be a waste of time. They make their feelings clear to their daughter, challenging her to broaden her education with math and reading classes so that she will be qualified for better jobs. She, on the other hand, is not sure how reading and math will improve the quality of jobs open to her. "What do they want me to be?" she asks, "A mathematician?!" Again, very few parents are uncomfortable with the nature of the jobs their children will hold. The majority are thankful for any secure employment. But where this is a problem, the conflict it raises can serve to inhibit involvement in jobs that are indeed available.

PEER AND SPOUSE INFLUENCE

Much in the same manner as family environment, peer contact and peer influence in a variety of settings play an important role in determining who is and isn't involved in seeking competitive employment. Leaving the workshop, for instance, might result in restricted access to one's friends, or perhaps to a girlfriend or boyfriend whom one has little opportunity to see outside the shop. This was certainly one factor in the situation of the individual mentioned earlier who found it difficult to stop volunteering at his workshop. It is also apparent in the experiences of other cohort members. In one case, the importance a woman placed on being together with her boyfriend outweighed his own desire to leave the shop for a good paying job. For another individual, the fact that he left his girlfriend behind when he took a competitive job was distressing to him. The realization that she was eating lunch and socializing with other men was a major source of anxiety. When his job, for a variety of reasons, proved transitory, he returned to the shop and remained, in fact, until his girlfriend took the initiative of finding herself competitive work. Shamed by the fact that she was competitively employed while he remained at the shop, and goaded by workshop personnel, he urged his caregiver to initiate contact with the Department of Rehabilitation and was soon successfully placed in a warehouse job. Thus in the experience of one individual we see how peer contact can either negatively or positively affect an individual's involvement in competitive employment.

The workshop is only one of many settings in which peer contact can heavily influence the employment status of any given person. A number of mildly retarded individuals, for instance, live in large board and care facilities or attend organized social meetings of the mildly retarded in which the vast number of people are either not working or are workshop employed. Such an environment provides little impetus toward competitive employment. Lack of involvement in competitive employment, after all, is the norm. Other individuals, because they live independently on meager resources, live and "hang out" in lower socioeconomic neighborhoods. Given the marginal groups with which such individuals tend to interact, a high rate of unemployment or at best unstable employment is not at all unusual. Witness the case of one woman whose husband, brother-in-law, sister-in-law, boyfriend, and friends are all out of work the majority of the time. Stable employment, in her circle, is the exception, not the rule.

In addition to peer influence, spousal influence is often primary in affecting job-seeking and job-holding behavior. Even where an individual is interested in pursuing competitive employment, interference and/or pressure from a spouse can sabotage the best intentions. Thus there is evidence to suggest that the absenteeism that led one individual to be fired for his late night janitorial job was due to his wife's apprehensions over staying in their apartment alone until 2:00 a.m. and her repeated requests that he call in sick. There is clear-cut evidence in another case that a wife's dissatisfaction with her husband's job resulted in her taking direct action that eventually cost him his job; refusing to eat so that he would not leave the house, harping on the idea of other and (in her mind) better jobs, and finally revealing to his employer that he was actually considering another job. In yet another case, the process of undermining a job search was far more subtle and insidious. When one individual spoke of finding a job, his wife reminded him that employment would result in his losing his SSI. "But if I could find a job I could stick to and they like my work..." he replied. "That's just the problem," said his wife, turning to the researcher. "If they like his work...If he loses the job, we're out of luck." Thus we see how, through the influence of peers and spouses, one's immediate social environment can have a very real impact on motivation to seek and maintain employment.

CONCLUSION

We hope to have demonstrated that the decision of mildly mentally retarded individuals to seek and find competitive employment, and their ability to do so, is influenced by factors above and beyond the availability of jobs and the individual's capacity to perform them adequately. SSI policy, the availability of a guaranteed income, sheltered workshop environments, support by the family, the influence of peers, and certainly other factors as well interact in many ways in the lives of individuals to make it likely or unlikely that they will obtain and maintain competitive employment. If the goal of our society is that those who are able should contribute to their own support, and if our belief is that competitive employment benefits not only society but the individual as well, then prevocational and vocational training programs, the creation of jobs, and the education of prospective employers, although crucial, are not enough. Adjustments must also be made in these other areas of life that directly influence the process of seeking and finding work.

It is clear, for example, that the SSI system requires restructuring. Given that the average length of time jobs were held by our sample members over the course of their working careers to date is 10 months and given, at the same time, the fact that they are unemployed more often than they are employed, it seems to us that 9 months of continuous employment is hardly a realistic measure of some underlying and permanent ability to support oneself in competitive employment. The individuals in our study know this. On the other hand, neither should individuals receive public support who are able to work but who for some reason, perhaps one of those we discussed, choose not to. One possible solution would be to require, from those who are able, some sort of satisfying public service in return for their public support. Whatever the details of SSI restructuring, however, the results should be the removal of concerns that prevent recipients from seeking employment and the presentation of work as an attractive alternative or supplement. Furthermore the family support that is so crucial in the job-seeking process of many individuals should be encouraged and effectively directed. Overworked employment counselors and social workers could perhaps more easily and efficiently accomplish their ends if programs were devised that stress the very real role that an actively supportive family can play in the job seeking process. Last, workshops could more effectively and systematically evaluate client potential, and urge competent individuals toward competitive employment. (We realize that this is constantly recommended and sporadically attempted.) Social workers and rehabilitation counselors might consider job aspirations more than has been done. One cohort member who wants to teach deaf children might be found a job as a teacher's aide, another who wanted to be a doctor or a nurse might be found some meaningful job suited to her abilities in a medical setting, and surely the individual who thinks of nothing but airplanes could perform some useful tasks in an airport or aircraft factory.

Not all mentally retarded individuals are capable of securing and maintaining competitive employment. But for those who are and for those who wish to be employed, a consideration of all these factors is crucial to their ability to become self-supporting citizens.

REFERENCES

Abel, T. M. A study of a group of mentally retarded girls successfully adjusted in industry and community. *American Journal of Mental Deficiency,* 1945, *40,* 66–72.

Appell, M. J., Williams, C. M., and Fishell, K. N. Factors in the job holding ability of the mentally retarded. *Vocational Guidance Quarterly,* 1965, *13*(2), 127–130.

Baller, W. R., Charles, D. C., and Miller, E. L. *Mid-life attainment of the mentally retarded: A longitudinal study.* Lincoln, Neb.: The University of Nebraska Press, 1966.

Baldwin, W. K. Employment possibilities for the educable mentally retarded. *Digest of the Mentally Retarded,* 1966, *2,* 124–125.

Baroff, G. S. *Mental retardation: Nature, cause, and management.* New York: John Wiley & Sons, 1974.

Becker, R. L. Job training placement for retarded youth: A survey. *Mental Retardation,* 1976, *14*(3), 7–11.

Bernstein, J. Mental retardation: New prospects for employment. *Journal of Rehabilitation,* 1966, *32*(3), 16–17, 35, 37.

Brolin, D. Value of rehabilitation services and correlates of vocational success with the mentally retarded. *American Journal of Mental Deficiency,* 1972, *76,* 644–651.

Brolin, D. *Vocational preparation of retarded citizens.* Columbus, Ohio: Charles E. Merrill, 1976.

Burdett, A. D. An examination of selected pre-vocational techniques utilized in programs for the mentally retarded. *Mental Retardation,* 1963, *1,* 230:237.

Cobb, H. V. *The forecast of fulfillment.* New York: Teachers College Press, 1972.

Cohen, J. S. Employer attitudes toward hiring mentally retarded individuals. *American Journal of Mental Deficiency,* 1963, *67,* 705–713.

Collman, R. D., and Newlyn, D. Employment success of educationally subnormal ex-pupils in England. *American Journal of Mental Deficiency,* 1955. *60,* 733–743.

Deno, E. *Retarded young: Their school-rehabilitation needs.* Final Report of Project VRA-RD-681. Minneapolis: Minneapolis Public Schools, 1965.

DiMichael, S. Are jobs for the retarded increasing? *Mental Retardation,* 1967, *5*(4), 40–41.

Dinger, J. C. Post school adjustment of former educable retarded adults. *Exceptional Children,* 1961, *27,* 353–356.

Edgerton, R. B. *The cloak of competence.* Berkeley: University of California Press, 1967.

Edgerton, R. B., & Bercovici, S. M. The cloak of competence: Years later. *American Journal of Mental Deficiency,* 1976, *80,* 485–497.

Eskridge, C. C., & Partridge, D. L. Vocational rehabilitation for exceptional children through special education. *Exceptional Children,* 1963, *29,* 452–458.

Fulton, R. W. Job retention of the mentally retarded. *Mental Retardation,* 1975, *13*(2), 26.

Halpern, A. S., Raffeld, P., Irvin, L., & Link, R. Measuring social and pre-vocational awareness in mildly retarded adolescents. *American Journal of Mental Deficiency,* 1975, *80,* 81–89.

Hartlage, L. C. Factors affecting employer receptivity toward the mentally retarded. *American Journal of Mental Deficiency,* 1965, *70,* 108–113.

Henshel, A. *The forgotten ones.* Austin: University of Texas Press, 1972.

Kennedy, R. J. *The social adjustment of morons in a Connecticut city.* Hartford: Mansfield-Southbury Training Schools, 1948.

Kennedy, R. J. *A Connecticut community revisited: A study of the social adjustment of a group of mentally deficient adults in 1948 and 1960.* Hartford: Connecticut State Department of Health, Office of Mental Retardation, 1966.

Kernan, K. T., & Koegel, P. Employment experiences of community-based mildly retarded adults. Working Paper No. 14. Socio-Behavioral Group, Mental Retardation Research Center, School of Medicine, University of California, Los Angeles, 1980.

Koegel, P. The creation of incompetence: Socialization and mildly retarded persons. Working Paper No. 6. Socio-Behavioral Group, Mental Retardation Research Center, School of Medicine, University of California, Los Angeles. Los Angeles, 1978.

Kolstoe, O. P. An examination of some characteristics which discriminate between employed and not employed mentally retarded males. *American Journal of Mental Deficiency,* 1961, *66,* 472–482.

McFail, T. M. Postschool adjustment: A survey of 50 former students of classes for the educable mentally retarded. *Exceptional Children,* 1966, *32,* 633–634.

Merritt, T. E. Influencing the employer to hire. *Journal of Rehabilitation,* 1963, *29*(4), 12–14.

Olshansky, S., & Beach, D. A five-year follow-up of mentally retarded clients. *Rehabilitation Literature,* 1974, *35*(2), 48–49.

Peters, J. S. II, & Rhode, H. J. Successful work-study program for the mentally retarded. *Rehabilitation Record,* 1964, *5*(3), 11–15.

Phelps, W. R. Attitudes related to the employment of the mentally retarded. *American Journal of Mental Deficiency,* 1965, *69,* 575–585.

Richardson, S. A. Careers of mentally retarded young persons: Services, jobs, and interpersonal relations. *American Journal of Mental Deficiency,* 1978, *82,* 349–358.

Skaarbrevik, K. J. A follow-up study of educable mentally retarded in Norway. *American Journal of Mental Deficiency,* 1971, *75,* 560–565.

Stephens, W. B., Peck, J. R., & Veldman, D. J. Personality and success profiles characteristic of young adult male retardates. *American Journal of Mental Deficiency,* 1968, *73,* 405–413.

Steward, D. M. Survey of community employer attitudes. *Mental Retardation,* 1977, *15*(1), 30–32.

Strickland, C. G., & Arrell, V. M. Employment of the mentally retarded. In L. K. Daniels (Ed.), *Vocational rehabilitation of the mentally retarded.* Springfield, Ill.: Charles C Thomas, 1974.

Syden, M. Guidelines for a cooperatively conducted work-study program for educable mentally retarded youth. *Mental Retardation,* 1963, *1,* 91–94, 120–124.

Turner, J. L. Workshop society: An ethnographic study of a work setting for retarded adults. Paper presented at NICHD/UCLA Conference on the Impact of Specific Settings on the Development and Behavior of Retarded Persons. Los Angeles, 1979.

Wehman, P. H. Toward a social skills curriculum for developmentally disabled clients in vocational settings. *Rehabilitation Literature,* 1975, *36*(11), 342–347.

EDUCATIONAL
SETTINGS

Mainstreaming

Jay Gottlieb,
Terry L. Rose, and
Elliott Lessen

In terms of its educational history, the concept of mild mental retardation is slightly more than 80 years old; the first special classes for this population were established in this country in 1896 (Esten, 1900). For approximately 70 of these 80 years, the predominant method of educating educable mentally retarded (EMR) children was to place them in self-contained classes. During the last 10 years, however, self-contained classes for EMR children have lost favor in the eyes of the professional community and have been replaced by a variety of alternative educational models, including resource rooms, itinerant teachers, and tutors. The social and political forces that propelled the changes in the structure of special education were so overwhelming that at times the literature gave the impression that any change was better than no change at all. The rapidity with which the change occurred, however, while it may have solved old problems, also created many new ones. One purpose of this chapter is to raise some of the new issues vis-à-vis mainstreaming that require attention. A second purpose is to review research on the effects on handicapped children of variations in mainstreaming programs. We begin by highlighting some of the methodological difficulties and limitations inherent in research on mainstreaming.

MAINSTREAMING: WHAT ARE THE VARIABLES?

In educational research, as in all experimental research, the investigator attempts to manipulate the independent variable and examine its systematic effects on the outcome variables of interest. The greater the precision with which the independent variables are defined and measured, the more likely it is that the investigator is able to understand and explain their effects. Although it may seem trite to suggest to the reader of this volume the importance of knowing precise definitions and characteristics of independent and dependent variables, research on mainstreaming has suffered greatly on this point. To date, there has not been advanced a single definition of mainstreaming that could serve as a basis for program development, generation of relevant variables, or evaluation. Although one definition of mainstreaming (Kaufman et al., 1975) has received relatively wide currency in the special education literature, it has been criticized as encompassing so many components that it precludes virtually all existing programs from being considered as mainstream programs (MacMillan and Semmel, 1977). The lack of an acceptable definition has resulted in a situation where any program that places a handicapped child in contact with non-handicapped children is referred to as a mainstreaming program. In fact, the reality is that contact between handicapped and nonhandicapped children is the sole defining feature of mainstream programs. The contact may range from only a few minutes per day to almost the entire day. It may occur only in nonacademic classes or it may occur in core academic subjects, such as reading. The contact may be in the regular classroom or it may be in a study hall, resource room, gym, and/or playground. If the contact occurs in the regular grade classroom, the handicapped child may receive special education support in that classroom, or he or she may leave the room to receive specialized education.

The picture becomes even more complicated when we consider specific instructional variations that occur in each of the physical settings under the mainstreaming heading. As an example, the handicapped child in the regular class may receive the bulk of instruction in class-size groups, small groups, or individually. The child may be taught by an experienced teacher, a paraprofessional, or a peer tutor, each of whom presumably has a different degree of competence in instructional delivery. It is immediately apparent that the range of alternative mainstreaming features makes it impossible to attribute cause/effect statements to a specific variable. Any one or combination of programmatic features may be responsible for outcomes.

The lack of an adequate definition of mainstream programs is only one of the problems confronting research on the effects of mainstreaming. Another problem is a lack of well-conceptualized anticipated goals. Public Law 94-142 has mandated that handicapped children are to be placed in the least restrictive environment that is appropriate. The law itself does not define an appropriate environment, nor does it specify how environments are to be measured. Undoubtedly, Congress assumed that professional educators would be in a better position than legislators to identify appropriate environments. When we view the assumption in historical perspective, there was indeed reason to expect that educators would be able to define the purpose that an educational program was intended to serve.

It will be recalled that, historically, there was thought to be a two-fold benefit from the creation of special classes for mentally retarded children. On the one hand, the removal of slow learning children from the regular classes was supposed to enable the normally progressing children to advance more quickly, partly by ridding the classroom teacher of the tensions and difficulties that retarded children caused (Wallin, 1924). On the other hand, it was argued that if retarded children were placed in special classes, they would no longer be ridiculed by their regular class peers and could be provided with an educational curriculum tailored to their needs and abilities (Lazerson, 1975; Wallin, 1924). At that time, the curriculum offered to slow learning children in segregated classes emphasized vocational preparation and nonacademic skills (Wallin, 1924). The purposes and goals for special classes were thus clearly articulated. Unfortunately, this is not presently the case with mainstreaming.

We are now in a period in history when we believe that separation of retarded learners from their nonretarded peers is wrong and harmful. We now believe that it is to the retarded child's advantage to be placed in a mainstream program. But what do we mean by the word *advantage*? What indices should we employ to determine that it is to the retarded child's advantage to be placed in a regular class program, even for part of the school day? Should we employ as criteria the claims that were made to justify the initial creation of the special education system? If we do, there is little hope that mainstreaming will prove beneficial to retarded children. A considerable amount of research has already indicated that merely placing retarded children in regular classes does not improve the social acceptance of them by nonretarded peers (Goodman, Gottlieb, and Harrison, 1972; Gottlieb and Budoff, 1973; Shotel, Iano, and McGettigan, 1972). The data indicate that the behavior exhibited by the retarded child is the main determiner of acceptance by peers. Retarded children in regular classes who misbehave or cannot conform to the standards of the classroom are apt to be socially rejected, regardless of whether they are labeled as mentally retarded (Leyser and Gottlieb, 1981). In short, placement of a retarded child in a regular class could result in the child being ridiculed or ignored by peers.

If we decide to employ the second of the two reasons for the creation of special classes, that is, the availability of an appropriate curriculum, as a potential criterion for judging the adequacy of mainstreaming, we are also not likely to emerge with optimistic findings. Special classes were initially established because the regular classes could not successfully accommodate the handicapped learner. The prevailing thought was that an academic curriculum was too rigorous for the retarded learner, and that a vocationally oriented curriculum would better serve his or her needs. Why should an academic curriculum be appropriate now when it wasn't then? If retarded children require direct instruction in social and vocational skills, where will they receive it? Certainly not in the regular classroom where the main emphasis is on academic instruction. If retarded children receive social and vocational instruction from special education teachers in resource rooms, how will that curriculum interface with the regular education curriculum to form a coherent, continuous educational program, given that regular and special educators have only the vaguest notions of each other's daily programming? Furthermore, most resource room programs view their mission as offering supplemental academic instruction and not social/vocational instruction. It seems that social, vocational, and general survival skills have been relegated to lesser importance now that the thrust of special education is on normalized environments.

One concrete example will suffice. A defining feature of mental retardation is poor adaptive behavior, often manifest in expressions of frustration. Special classes usually include instruction or counseling in social adjustment as part of the curriculum. The inclusion of instructional time devoted to social adjustment skills, probably at the cost of time spent on academic instruction, was one of the explanations offered for the failure of special class EMR children to achieve as well as EMR children in the regular grades (Fine, 1967). Attention to social adjustment concerns was not in vain, however, because the empirical literature suggested that segregated retarded children had better social and personal adjustment than retarded children in the regular classes (Kirk, 1964).

It is likely that the mainstreamed retarded child will experience at least the same level of frustration that he or she did in the self-contained class. The child will be in a setting where he or she simply cannot compete academically with the other children. Who will help the child deal with the frustration? The regular class teacher who has 30 other children with whom to contend? This is not very likely at all. To the extent that this question cannot be answered, we are shortchanging retarded children.

The point is not that mainstreamed programs are inherently wrong or bad. Our purpose is simply to alert special educators so that they begin to consider the purposes that mainstreaming serves. We must identify the child's needs, develop goals accordingly, and attempt to achieve them. In the following section, we briefly review some of the major findings of the mainstreaming research, especially the results of one study that attempted to relate variations in mainstreamed environments to learner outcomes (Kaufman, Agard, and Semmel, in press).

MAINSTREAMING RETARDED CHILDREN: A REVIEW OF THE DATA

Although there are a number of ways to organize a review of mainstreaming research, a simple way is to group the students by academic achievement, social acceptance, and adult status.

Academic Achievement of Mainstreamed Learners

Since as early as 1932, researchers have been concerned with the academic achievement and social adjustment gains of EMR children in varying placements (Bennett, 1932). These studies are usually known as the "efficacy" studies. In many ways, the early efficacy studies are identical to the more contemporary research on mainstreaming. Both efficacy studies and mainstreaming research have been concerned with differences between retarded children who attended segregated classes and retarded children whose primary affiliation is the regular class. The major difference between the efficacy research and the mainstreaming research is that in the former studies, EMR children in regular classes did not receive any support beyond the regular education curriculum. Mainstreamed EMR children, on the other hand, do receive special education support in addition to the regular education program.

Between 1932 and 1965, 10 so-called efficacy studies were conducted. Of these, five indicated that retarded children in the regular classes posted higher achievement scores than children in segregated classes, and the remaining five studies failed to detect any significant differences in reading performance. Although these studies have been harshly criticized for a variety of methodological inadequacies (Guskin and Spicker, 1968; Kirk, 1964), which precludes definitive comparisons of special and regular classes, one glaring point must be acknowledged. The average reading performance of each subject sample in all 10 studies never exceeded a grade level of 3.8. This finding should have compelled special educators to focus on instructional inadequacies that existed in both class placements rather than on the physical properties of the placement itself. Regardless of placement, EMR children were consistently failing to read, both at their mental age expectancy and at a functional literacy level.

The argument could be made that the results of these early efficacy studies are not generalizable to mainstreaming. As previously stated, the efficacy studies examined the performance of retarded learners who remained in the regular classroom and did not indulge in any of the benefits of special education. Presumably, had the EMR children remained in the regular class and shared in the specialized educational instruction to which they should have been entitled, their performance might have improved.

This presumption can be explored by directly reviewing a recent body of research that is more appropriately entitled "mainstreaming research," because it concerned the performance of EMR children who remained in regular grades but who also had available the support of special education. In an early study on the effects of mainstreaming on the academic achievement of EMR children, Rodee (1971) identified three samples: 1) 36 children who attended regular classes and received additional academic instruction in a resource program; 2) 16 children who attended regular classes without supplemental resource instruction; and 3) a special class contrast group of 40 children. The author found one significant effect: children who attended resource programs scored higher on the reading subtest of the Metropolitan Achievement Test than children who attended a special class. The achievement scores, however, of EMR children who attended regular classes with resource room supplemental instruction did not differ from those of EMR children who did not receive resource room instruction. In other words, resource room instruction failed to produce achievement gains in EMR pupils beyond those resulting from regular class placement alone. This is the only investigation of which we are aware that directly compared two groups of EMR children whose primary assignment was the regular classroom. The failure of resource room supplemental instruction to produce mean reading scores in EMR children beyond what the regular class alone produced calls into question the appropriateness of supplementary instruction as a necessary addition to the mainstreamed EMR child's instructional program. The appropriateness of resource room instruction is called into further question when we note that the mean reading score of this group was only 3.2. The Rodee data clearly suggest the urgent need for alternative instructional systems for EMR children; emphasis on the location of the instruction is less warranted.

Another investigation of the effectiveness of resource rooms was conducted by Walker (1972), who compared the academic achievement gains of EMR children who attended a resource program for 2 years with the gains posted by EMR children who remained in segregated classes. Walker (1972) observed that the children who attended the resource room program made significantly greater gains in reading than the control group, but no significant differences in arithmetic achievement occurred. Because Walker lacked a control group that attended regular classes without resource room support, we have no way of knowing whether the achievement gains made by the mainstreamed children were attributable to the special education in the resource room or to the regular education program.

The studies by Rodee and Walker both indicate that mainstreamed children who attended resource rooms achieved significantly higher than EMR children who remained segregated. Although it is conceivable that the differences were the result of the differences in education offered in the two settings, another explanation for the results is possible. Because neither Rodee nor Walker was able to assign their subjects randomly to treatments, there is a distinct likelihood that achievement differences were the result of pre-experimental differences between the experimental and control subjects. When a school system implements a new program—and in 1970 mainstreaming was far more novel than it is now—it often selects the most capable children in order to increase the probability of the program's success. If this were the case, differences favoring the resource program may be due to the superior ability of the experimental group children, as was true in a study conducted in California by Meyers, MacMillan, and Yoshida (1975).

Meyers et al. (1975) conducted a large-scale, nonexperimental evaluation of mainstreaming in which they had no control over the subject selection bias. Several years ago when California was under court mandate to depopulate the special classes, school systems throughout the state decertified many EMR children who had attended special classes and returned them to the regular grades. Not surprisingly, the children who were returned to regular classes were considerably better students than those whom school administrators opted to retain in their segregated classes. As a result, the decertified pupils scored higher than the segregated children on tests of reading and arithmetic. These differences were probably totally attributable to the subject selection bias, not the mainstreamed placement. In fairness, the California school authorities were less concerned with experimental elegance than they were with an imminent need to relocate large numbers of children. By purposely identifying the most capable children for regular class placement, they undoubtedly averted a host of problems.

Criticism of previous research for confounding subject selection biases and the experimental treatment was considered by Budoff and Gottlieb (1976) who were able to assign children randomly to mainstreamed and segregated settings. These investigators established a resource room program in a new school building. Seventeen children attended the resource program for approximately 45 minutes per day. The remainder of the school day was devoted to instruction in the regular grades. The control group consisted of 14 EMR children who attended a self-contained classroom in that school. Results indicated no significant differences in academic achievement between the mainstreamed and self-contained classroom EMR children. These data indicate that when subject selection bias is ruled out, children who attend a resource room program do not achieve more than children who attend a segregated class program.

The lack of progress in achievement scores made by EMR children in special and mainstreamed settings was also illustrated in Project PRIME, a large-scale study of mainstreaming conducted in the early 1970s throughout the state of Texas (Kaufman et al., in press). EMR children, regardless of whether they were mainstreamed ($N = 345$) or segregated ($N = 265$), scored in the lowest 1 percentile on reading and arithmetic achievement scores as measured by the Metropolitan Achievement Tests. Few differences between mainstreamed and nonmainstreamed children were found in any area of norm-referenced academic achievement.

The chief contribution of Project PRIME to our understanding of academic achievement among mainstreamed learners was not its demonstration of a lack of difference in achievement, however. Its main contribution was in its study of the relationship of specific facets of mainstreamed environments to academic performance. Before presenting some of these data, a digression is necessary in order to recount very briefly the model of mainstream environments that was advanced in Project PRIME.

Project PRIME viewed a child's educational competence to be influenced by two main factors: the characteristics of the learner who is of interest; and the nature of the classroom into which he or she enters. The learner variables were straightforward, and included sex, socioeconomic status, IQ score, chronological age, and so forth. Classroom environment was conceptualized far more elaborately. It was seen as including the participant composition of the children in the mainstreamed class, the prevailing instructional conditions, and the socioemotional climate of the class. These three factors, participant composition, socioemotional climate, and instructional conditions, combined to define classroom environment. Although the conceptualization of the three-factor representation of classroom environments was the result of a variety of theoretical orientations, the actual construction of each factor was the end-product of a complex set of statistical manipulations of direct observation and questionnaire data. Because the scope of this volume focuses on the effects of environment, we emphasize this aspect of the Project PRIME data.

The first component of a classroom environment in Project PRIME was participant composition. It was included for examination mainly because previous research on school effects in the area of racial desegregation found that the composition of the classroom related to academic achievement of pupils (Coleman et al., 1966). Although participant composition was defined quite elaborately in Project PRIME, three variables are of major interest: 1) the size of the class into which EMR children were mainstreamed; 2) the racial composition of the classrooms; and 3) the number of handicapped learners who were mainstreamed into a single classroom.

Briefly, analyses of the approximately 250 classrooms upon which the PRIME data were based revealed that EMR children were mainstreamed into classes averaging 29 children (S.D. = 4.5), including the handicapped learners. Also, mainstreamed classes were comprised of approximately 46% Spanish-surnamed children, 37% Anglo pupils, and 16% Black children. The percentage of Black children was approximately half of the corresponding figure for self-contained classes. The percentage of Spanish-surnamed children in mainstreamed classes, however, was about 9% greater than in segregated classes. Thus, whereas Black children seem to benefit from mainstreaming insofar as they are in classrooms that are less racially segregated than self-contained classrooms, Spanish-surnamed children are likely to be placed in classes that are more racially segregated.

The final variable defining participant composition with which we are concerned is the number of handicapped children who are mainstreamed into a single classroom. The Project PRIME data indicated that 45% of mainstreamed classes accommodated two or fewer handicapped learners, and 55% accommodated three or more handicapped children. Furthermore, almost 20% of the mainstreamed classes sampled enrolled six or more handicapped learners.

Teacher leadership abilities and peer cohesiveness were the main constructs comprising the second component of environment, socioemotional climate. Teacher leadership, a construct developed from factor analysis of 13 discrete variables, was informative both for its demonstration that regular classroom teachers employed a range of behaviors in order to influence their children's performance, and for its demonstration of few differences in leadership behaviors engaged in by regular and special education teachers. To illustrate, few regular or special class teachers attempted to influence children when they were off-task. Also, both regular and special class teachers tended to employ "legitimate influence" (i.e., direct verbal commands or elaborations on class rules), rather than coercion or rewards in order to manage children's behavior.

The second defining feature of socioemotional climate was peer cohesiveness, a construct resulting from an amalgam of seven sociometric and direct observation variables. Here, too, the data suggested considerable variation within mainstreamed classes and relatively few differences between mainstreamed and self-contained classes. An example of the within mainstreamed class variability is the distribution of social acceptance choices. Children in 256 mainstreamed classes accepted anywhere between 20% and 61+% of the other children in their classes, with the mode being between 41% and 60%. Overall, the majority of mainstreamed classes were marked by children's statements that they were happy, by few instances of observed disruptive behavior, and by sociometric data revealing that children accepted their classmates about 2½ times as often as they rejected them.

The third and final factor comprising the PRIME model of classroom environment was instructional conditions. PRIME's instructional conditions factor is an empirical composite of nearly 50 variables. The instructional conditions component of the environment was conceptualized as reflecting two major subconstructs: instructional contexts and instructional behaviors. Instructional context describes the relatively stable, externally controlled aspects of the classroom environment and establishes the conditions within which instructional behaviors occur. Instructional behavior is characterized by observable activities that reflect instruction.

Without delving in detail into the conceptualization and construction of this complex component, suffice it to indicate that among the more interesting findings to emerge from a description of this factor was the substantial range in the percentage of time that teachers of mainstreamed classes spent on reading instruction. Regular class teachers reported that on the average, they devoted about 16% of the school day to reading instruction, with the standard deviation surrounding these data being 12%. As a point of interest, these data may be compared with those reported by special class teachers who spent an average of 27% of the time on reading instruction. The corresponding standard deviation for these data was 19%.

To summarize, this cursory review of the descriptive statistics of mainstreamed classes suggests that relatively few major differences were detected between the daily routines in regular and special classes. When differences did exist, the authors usually interpreted them as favoring the self-contained classes.

Project PRIME also investigated the effects of classroom environments on child performance. To facilitate this analysis, a hierarchical taxonomy (from global to increasingly finer indices) of the various environments present in mainstreamed classes was developed concurrently with a catalogue of performance measures, which were then related to the environmental taxonomy. The resultant data were analyzed through the use of commonality analysis, which allows the identification of the shared and unique variance of each predictor variable.

Several academic competence variables were identified empirically, including academic status, academic behavior, and academic attitudes. This discussion is limited to academic status, that is, a composite of standardized achievement test data. Because of the similarity of academic status to dependent variables reported in previous mainstreaming research, any resulting conclusions regarding the impact of environmental variables on academic achievement can be more appropriately generalized.

Although the breadth of Project PRIME's data base cannot be discussed in detail here, an illustrative example should serve as a reasonable foundation for our subsequent conclusions. The results of the analysis of the relative contribution of learner-background characteristics and of environment to normative academic status in mainstreamed classes indicated that 7% of the unique variance in academic status was explained by learner-background variables and 21% was explained by environmental variations. These environmental variables were further partitioned into participant composition, instructional conditions, and socioemotional climate, and the unique contributions of these variables were analyzed. Low coefficients generally emerged. For example, with regard to normative academic status, participant composition contributed 9% to the variance, instructional conditions contributed 8%, and socioemotional climate only 4%. Even though each of these coefficients attained statistical significance, they are only marginally useful for predictive purposes. The corresponding data for self-contained classes were: participant composition, 10%; instructional conditions, 16%; and socioemotional climate, 2%.

As can be seen from our examination, albeit superficial, of Project PRIME's data, any particular set of environmental descriptors individually accounted for only small amounts of the variance found in the dependent measures. More specifically, the entire universe of environmental variables generated by Project PRIME was only able to explain 21% of the unique variance in standardized academic achievement in mainstreamed settings and 32% of the unique variance in segregated classes. The inescapable conclusion is that the explanation of academic achievement is still beyond our grasp.

Social Acceptance of Mainstreamed Learners

In spite of apparent early evidence that EMR children were better adjusted in special classes than in regular classes (Kirk, 1964), special educators continued to insist that children were stigmatized by special class placement and, further, that placement in mainstreamed classes would alleviate this problem (Christoplos and Renz, 1969). As a result, numerous studies were initiated to determine whether differential class placement had an effect on the social acceptance of EMR pupils. Goodman et al., (1972) compared the sociometric status of 10 EMR children who attended regular classes in a nongraded elementary school and 8 EMR children who remained in a special class in the same school. It was hypothesized that non-EMR children would rate the mainstreamed EMR children more favorably than they would rate the segregated children because of their increased contact with the mainstreamed children. A forced-choice sociometric scale was administered to 40 non-EMR children who rated three groups of their peers: 1) integrated EMR, 2) segregated EMR, and 3) randomly selected non-EMR pupils. The non-EMR raters were asked whether they liked, tolerated, didn't like, or didn't know each child listed. Results indicated that nonretarded children occupied a more favored social status in the peer hierarchy than either integrated or segregated retarded children. Furthermore, male raters rejected integrated EMR children whom they knew significantly more frequently than they rejected segregated EMR children whom they also knew. Females did not rate the integrated and segregated EMR children differentially. The authors concluded that these results failed to support the popular hypothesis that mainstreamed placement promotes social acceptance of retarded children by providing greater interaction between retarded and nonretarded children.

In a subsequent study, Gottlieb and Budoff (1973) continued the above line of research by investigating whether increased exposure of nonretarded to retarded children is accompanied by lower perceived social status of the retarded group. One hundred thirty-six nonretarded elementary school pupils provided sociometric ratings of a randomly selected group of nonretarded peers, 12 partially integrated EMR children, and 12 segregated EMR children who attended the same school as the raters. Two architecturally different schools served as the settings for this study: The first school building was traditional in that it contained discrete classrooms accommodating approximately 25 to 30 children; the second school building did not contain any interior walls. As may be expected, the segregated EMR students in the former school were the least visible, while all children, including the retarded children, were at least somewhat visible to all other peers in the "open" school. The segregated EMR children in the "open" school occupied a corner of the building and were the least visible children in that school.

The authors advanced two specific hypotheses regarding the effects of the EMR pupils' visibility and the degree to which they were integrated. One, because of their increased visibility, it was thought that the EMR students in the no-interior-wall school would have lower social status, regardless of placement, than would the EMR children in the traditional school. Two, partially integrated EMR students, regardless of school setting, would receive lower social status ratings than their segregated peers, again due to increased visibility. The reported results uniformly confirmed these predictions and lent further credence to the previous findings of Goodman et al. (1972) that, as a group, non-EMR children enjoy a more favorable social status than do EMR pupils, whether integrated or not.

Results of studies employing nonsociometric measures support the above findings. For example, Gottlieb, Cohen, and Goldstein (1974), using an adjective rating scale, assessed attitudes of 399 nonretarded elementary school pupils toward their retarded peers. The study consisted of two independent replications employing children of different SES levels who were drawn from three different types of elementary schools: a no-interior-wall school where visibility of EMR children was maximized, a traditional school with both integrated and segregated EMR pupils, and a third school in which there were no special education pupils. Attitudes toward EMR children were found to be most favorable in schools with no special education pupils for the lower and upper SES samples.

In a behaviorally based social-choice experiment by Gottlieb and David (1973), nonretarded children in the intermediate grades were asked to select either a nonretarded or an EMR child to be their partner in a ring-toss game. Results indicated that, given the above choice, non-EMR children almost invariably selected another non-EMR child, that is, 27 out of 28 possible times during the first two treatment conditions. In the third treatment condition, when the non-EMR subject was asked to choose either a segregated or an integrated EMR child, there was no statistically significant difference in the choice distribution; integrated EMR children were selected by 8 of 14 non-EMR subjects. These results argue against the notion that greater contact between retarded and nonretarded children is accompanied by an increase in the social acceptance of retarded children.

Only one reviewed investigation seems to be inconsistent with the findings of the previous studies. Sheare (1974) administered a questionnaire measuring attitudes toward special class pupils to 400 nonretarded junior high school pupils, half of whom were randomly assigned to classrooms with no EMR pupils and half of whom were assigned to classrooms with partially integrated EMR pupils. Results indicated that following interaction opportunities, non-EMR adolescents expressed significantly more favorable attitudes toward EMR pupils than did non-EMR pupils who were not exposed to EMR pupils in their classes. This finding, however, contradicts the findings of an earlier study of adolescents' attitudes toward EMR children (Rucker, Howe, and Snider, 1969).

With the exception of Sheare's (1974) study, research has failed to support the proposition that increasing contact between retarded and nonretarded children through integration into regular classrooms improves the social status of EMR children. Although effects of integrated placement may reflect factors other than contact (e.g., an absence of the mentally retarded label), the greater opportunities for non-EMR children to observe the behavior of retarded children following integrated placement cannot be minimized. The increased exposure factor is also present in studies that examined the effects of no-interior-school-walls on acceptance of retarded pupils (e.g., Gottlieb and Budoff, 1973; Gottlieb et al., 1974). Assuming that schools without interior walls increase visibility, results of studies of integration in the presence of this architectural variable are remarkably consistent: Retarded children whose behavior is more visible to their nonretarded peers occupy a social position that is lower than that of their less visible retarded peers.

Class placement and architectural structure affect the availability of observational opportunities, that is, visibility. Another critical variable, the amount of time that retarded children are actually exposed to nonretarded children during the school day, also affects visibility but was not directly examined in any of the previous studies. Given the findings of studies of placement along an architectural dimension, as well as the findings of earlier studies that indicated that rejection may be a function of perceived misbehavior (Baldwin, 1958; Johnson, 1950), one could speculate on the presence of an inverse relationship between the amount of time available for observation of EMR students by their non-handicapped peers and the social position occupied by the EMR student. In other words, one could hypothesize that a negative linear relationship exists between a retarded child's social status and the amount of time during which he or she is integrated into regular classes.

This hypothesis was tested by Gottlieb, Semmel, and Veldman (1978), who assessed the relative contribution of perceptions of classroom behavior, of academic ability, and of the amount of time integrated, to the acceptance and rejection of retarded children. Three hundred elementary school EMR children who were integrated with nonhandicapped peers for varying amounts of time during the school day served as subjects. Sociometric status was measured by the forced choice sociometric instrument discussed previously in this chapter. Rejection and acceptance were the dependent variables in two commonality analyses in which the predictor variables were peers' and teachers' perceptions of EMR pupils' academic ability and aggressive behavior, and number of hours of weekly academic integration. Results indicated a significant relation between teachers' and peers' per-ceptions of EMR children's misbehavior and scores indicative of social rejection. More-over, teachers' and peers' perceptions of EMR children's academic competence correlated significantly with social acceptance scores and indicated that children who were perceived as competent were better accepted. Amount of time did not contribute a significant percent of unique variance in social acceptance or rejection scores. The authors concluded, then, that increased amounts of time for which a retarded child is integrated have little effect on social status. These results concurred with pervious findings that mere contact between normal and retarded children does little to improve attitudes toward retarded children. Rather, this study suggests that the retarded child's perceived behaviors are more influential than simple exposure on others' attitudes toward him or her.

The implication of the reviewed research, then, is that contact between retarded and normal children will not produce positive attitude change unless the retarded children can be instructed to exhibit behavior that conforms to the standards expected by their nonretarded peers. In other words, placement of retarded children with nonretarded children must be accompanied by efforts to modify the retarded children's inappropriate behavior patterns.

This speculation has received empirical support in a controlled laboratory study by Strichart and Gottlieb (1975), who investigated the extent to which normal children will imitate a retarded child as a function of the latter's competence on a task "rigged" in his or her favor. As predicted, a direct relationship was found between the competence displayed by the retarded pupil and the instances of imitation by the normal students. Furthermore, competence on the experimental tasks led to the child being selected more frequently as a play companion on subsequent game tasks. This study demonstrated that more competent behavior displayed by retarded children may lead to improved or increased social acceptance by nonretarded peers.

EMR children's sociometric status also was investigated in Project PRIME, with particular reference to contributions to social acceptance and rejection made by children's background characteristics and by classroom environmental variations. The most global level analyses of the data, in which learner background and environment were treated as two variables, indicated that learner background accounted for 6% of the variance in social rejection and that environmental characteristics accounted for 37% of the variance. More specifically, mainstreamed EMR children in classrooms with low levels of dislike among children in general, tended to be less rejected than EMR children who were enrolled in classes where peer dislike was greater. Also, EMR children tended to enjoy a more favorable social status in classes where the teacher engaged in large group instruction rather than small group or individual instruction. Conceivably, large group instruction enables EMR children to mask their poor achievement to a greater extent than do other instructional arrangements.

The instructional conditions operating in the classroom affected children's sociometric status, but only for social rejection, accounting for 14% of the variance. Instructional conditions did not explain a significant amount of variance in acceptance. One instructional conditions variable, the use of teacher-made material, was related to rejection more strongly than other variables in this domain. Children in classes in which extensive use was made of teacher-made materials were rejected more than children in classes where there was less reliance on teacher-made material.

It is of interest to note that the participant composition of the classroom did not explain a significant amount of variance in either social acceptance or social rejection. The complex array of variables representing participant composition, including peer and teacher attitude, the ethnicity of the children in class, as well as their reading ability, did not affect the extent to which EMR children were socially accepted or rejected.

Overall, the data on mainstreaming suggest that classroom environment affects the social acceptance of EMR children, and that EMR children are most likely to occupy a favorable sociometric status in classes having a cohesive social structure, that is, in which the social acceptance choices are spread out across many children in the class rather than being directed toward only a few of the children.

Follow-up Studies

Because mainstreaming programs were propelled by the philosophy of normalization, a compelling argument could be made that the most valid test of the efficacy of mainstreaming is the extent to which it prepares handicapped youngsters to lead normal, independent lives when they become adults. The use of adult status as a measure of school effects is especially important for retarded people whose vocational adjustment does not relate highly to their school performance (Cobb, 1972).

Unfortunately, mainstreaming as an educational treatment is too new a development for long-term follow-up studies to have been conducted. There are, however, a number of studies that compared the comparative adult adjustment of retarded people who attended either segregated or regular classes during their school careers (Bobroff, 1956; Carriker, 1957; Porter and Milazzo, 1958; Skodak, 1970). Of these studies, the one conducted by Skodak (1970) most closely approximates a test of the long-term effectiveness of mainstreaming.

Skodak (1970) identified two groups of young adults who earlier had been enrolled in special education programs. One group of 42 attended a totally segregated program for 3 years. A second group of 174 also attended special classes but in addition were integrated into regular class programs for varying amounts of time. Both the segregated and "mainstreamed" special education programs were designed to prepare retarded adolescents for vocational employment upon completion of the respective programs.

Of the original sample of 216, 196 (91%) were available for follow-up study. Data were collected on a number of dimensions including, but not limited to, school attendance records, nature of full-time employment, occupational levels of the sample, income, post-high school education, amount of savings, marriage and divorce rates, number of illnesses reported, and so forth. Skodak (1970) summarized her report by indicating that:

> Graduates of the integrated program had a better school attendance record, more frequently held full-time jobs and at a higher occupational level, were more likely to seek further education, manage their money with greater prudence, marry later or remain single more often, have better homes and take part in more community activities than their peers in a segregated program (p. 36).

Of the various follow-up studies referenced earlier, the investigation conducted by Skodak was the most supportive of "mainstreamed" education for retarded adolescents. Scrutiny of Skodak's (1970) sample selection procedure, however, limits the confidence we may place on her conclusions. In the study, all adults attended the segregated program in a rural school system, whereas all "mainstreamed" subjects attended school in an urban center (Dearborn). Consequently, differences that arose between segregated and mainstreamed programs could just as easily have been attributed to the different general educational systems or to different economic opportunities that existed in the two locations and not to differences in the special education programs. Conclusions that special education programs were responsible for the differences are unfounded.

Review of other follow-up studies provides equally inconclusive results regarding the relative effectiveness of segregated or "mainstreamed" programs. For example, Bobroff (1956) reported that the hourly wage of his segregated sample was $2.09, compared to an hourly rate of $2.08 for the "mainstreamed" group. Porter and Milazzo's (1958) data further complicate the picture. They reported that 75% of the special class follow-up sample was self-supporting as adults, compared to only 17% for the regular class sample. Overall, the follow-up literature offers no conclusive support for the superiority of mainstreaming or segregated education for mildly retarded children.

ALTERING EDUCATIONAL ENVIRONMENTS

As we indicated earlier, few studies have examined the effects of different educational variations on the academic and social behavior of mentally retarded children. The only study to examine the effects of in-class variability was Project PRIME. At this point, we wish to indicate two features of the educational environment that are easily modifiable, and that could be implemented in mainstreaming programs in order to increase the likelihood of academic behavior change among mainstreamed EMR pupils: 1) transfer of training, and 2) curriculum interfacing.

Transfer of Training: A Missing Element in Mainstreaming Programs

We have indicated earlier that mainstreaming is defined differently by different educators, and that the only commonality among mainstream programs is that the handicapped children spend at least some time together with nonhandicapped peers. A second feature that is common to a great many mainstreaming programs is that handicapped children receive supplemental academic support in a resource room. School administrators realize that handicapped learners cannot have all of their academic needs fulfilled in the regular class so they often establish a resource room to fill the void in the child's education. Previous research has been concerned with the effectiveness of resource room support (the data suggest they are not effective in improving academic performance). An almost totally ignored topic of research, however, is the nature of the interfacing between the child's academic program in the resource room and his or her program in the regular classroom. More technically, the question of the extent of stimulus generalization between resource rooms and regular classes must be addressed.

Kazdin (1977) described two types of stimulus generalization. One, *resistance to extinction*, refers to the maintenance of a given behavior within a particular setting subsequent to the termination of any intervention program. Two, *transfer of training*, is the relocation of behavior(s) from the situation or setting wherein training was provided to another situation or setting in which no training or dissimilar training occurred. Although the former type of stimulus generalization is certainly important and worthy of more detailed discussion, the focus of the following discussion is on the latter type, transfer of training, because of its apparent relationship to the maintenance of adaptive behaviors in less restrictive educational placements.

Implicit in many mainstreaming activities is the notion that transfer of training will occur, perhaps spontaneously. Thus, little attention is paid to programmatic variables that may ensure that transfer actually occurs. Evidence has accrued recently, however, that this assumption is fallacious and that, in fact, transfer of training rarely occurs unless it has been specifically programmed (e.g., Kazdin, 1977; Kazdin and Bootzin, 1972; O'Leary and Drabman, 1971; Rincover and Koegel, 1975; Stokes, Baer, and Jackson, 1974; Tracey, Briddell, and Wilson, 1974).

Because behavior is a function of its consequences, we may assume that when an intervention program is withdrawn, the level of performance of the target behavior will decline. Hence, to ensure generalizations, specific (perhaps intrusive) contingencies would have to be programmed across different classroom settings (e.g., Lovaas and Simmons, 1969; Redd, 1969; Redd and Birnbrauer, 1969). Recent research efforts, however, have indicated that, although this may occasionally be the case, quite often other less intrusive techniques may also be valuable when transferring training across settings (e.g., O'Leary and Drabman, 1971; Stokes and Baer, 1977; Sulzer-Azaroff and Mayer, 1977; Wildman and Wildman, 1975). One technique that may prove useful in this regard involves including the number of discrimination stimuli in the resource room that also appear in the regular classroom.

Attention to Discriminative Stimuli

Because handicapped individuals have demonstrated the ability to make very fine discriminations among stimuli and respond differently in the presence of those stimuli, for example, in the presence of different adults within the same setting (Redd, 1969; Redd and Birnbrauer, 1969), and to such extraneous stimuli as nonrelated gestures by the trainer (Rincover and Koegel, 1975), it may be inferred that stimuli that are characteristic of any generalized setting may also be employed in the training procedure. For example, Stokes et al. (1974) investigated the effects of staff presence during training on the transfer of a greeting response, that is, handwaving, across a variety of settings. They found that the response was under the stimulus control of the individual staff member who conducted the training and did not generalize to settings where other staff were present. When these other staff's presence was systematically introduced to the training sessions, the response transferred to new settings. Various stimuli have been successfully manipulated, including 1) elements of a classroom into a training setting (e.g., Jackson and Wallace, 1974; Koegel and Rincover, 1974), 2) peers as contingency "managers" (e.g., Kazdin, 1971; Stokes and Baer, 1976), and 3) training in the presence of a variety of conditions, e.g., time of day or activities that occur consistently throughout a school day (Emshoff, Redd, and Davidson, 1976).

The above studies, as well as others (e.g., Allen, 1973; Garcia, 1974; Horner, 1971; Lovaas and Simmons, 1969), indicate that transfer of training can be established by systematically introducing various stimuli that are present in the generalized setting. Consequently, the general technique may be of great significance for those who are to provide the training necessary for a handicapped student to function in an adaptive manner in a less restrictive environment. As an example, if most special classes employ one-to-one or small group instructional groupings, it may be most beneficial to gradually increase the group size for those individuals who will soon be placed in a regular class setting. And, as Jackson and Wallace (1974) indicated, if the extra members of the group came from the regular class, transfer may actually be enhanced.

The point that we wish to emphasize is that EMR children are educated in several different environments during the course of the day. If mainstreaming programs are to be effective, we must not only attend to improving performance in each of the environments, but we must also learn how to interface environments and their accompanying programs so that one complements the other. In the absence of efforts in this direction, EMR children may be subjected to different programs, each working at cross purposes to the other.

Curriculum Interfacing

Historically, curriculum for the mentally retarded has been based on one of three approaches: arts and crafts, the unit-based approach, and a diluted regular class curriculum. The arts and crafts approach has not been used now for a number of years. The unit-based approach in which a series of lessons are developed on a single topic subsuming different academic areas has been used mainly in self-contained special classes. The watered down regular class curriculum introduced by Inskeep (1926) met with considerable professional scorn during the 1950s and 1960s by critics who complained that there were few "special" educational strategies in the curriculum.

Today, as increasingly EMR children are being retained in regular classes, attention must be given to the curriculum material that they will experience in the regular classes. Unlike past curriculum practices that had to concentrate exclusively on one class placement or another, however, present-day practices require that curriculum interventions be designed for both regular class and resource room placement. Moreover, curriculum material covered in regular classes should interface with the material covered by the special education teacher. Although in theory the individual education program (IEP) provision of the Public Law 94–142 specifies the educational program that the child will receive during the entire school day—in both special and regular education programs—in practice special and regular education personnel have only a slight knowledge of each other's programming for a particular handicapped child.

What we are suggesting is that there must be a smooth transition between the different environments in which handicapped children are educated. Rather than thinking of mainstreamed versus segregated environments—a stance that lends itself to educational differences—we must begin to think of educational continuities and transitions, a perspective in which similarities in educational programming are considered. Unfortunately, given the long history in the United States of special education being a separate delivery system, it may take quite a while for educators to re-orient their thinking away from educational differences and toward educational similarities.

CONCLUSIONS

Our review of the literature on mainstreaming revealed several findings. First and foremost, the concept of mainstreaming has not been thoroughly conceptualized. Mainstreaming is presently operationalized as the placement of handicapped children in the same classrooms as nonhandicapped children for part of the day. No attention has been paid to the type of educational intervention the child receives when he or she is in the regular class. In other words, mainstreaming is equated with the physical integration of handicapped children; it is not concerned with social or instructional integration (Kaufman et al., 1975).

As a consequence of the inability of educators to include instructional integration as a component of mainstreaming, few differences exist between the kind of instruction offered in special and regular classes (Agard, 1975). When differences do exist, they are usually confined to grouping practices rather than to substantive instructional practices, such as type of questioning by teacher, kind of classroom management strategies employed, and so forth. In short, as presently conceived, mainstreaming does not connote an instructional environment, only a physical environment.

A second finding of our review of the mainstreaming literature is that the goals and objectives of mainstreaming have remained elusive and, for the most part, unstated. Although the legislatively mandated goal of mainstreaming is to educate handicapped children together with nonhandicapped children, from an educational vantage point, attention to this goal alone shortchanges handicapped children. A substantial body of literature suggests that amount of time spent in mainstreamed classes is not predictive of either academic or social outcomes (Gottlieb, Semmel, and Veldman, 1978; Gottlieb and Baker, 1975). Moreover, the literature also indicates that merely placing an EMR child in a regular class without providing the teacher adequate training to involve the child in the social structure of the classroom is apt to result in the child being more socially ostracized than when he or she was in a segregated class (Goodman et al., 1972; Gottlieb and Budoff, 1973).

Our third finding is that there is no evidence to date that the class placement in which an EMR child is educated differentially affects his or her adult status. The follow-up literature suggests that young adults who as children were classified by the schools as EMR tend to disappear into the larger society, although at somewhat marginal levels of adjustment. These data must be viewed cautiously, however, because research on this topic is extremely sparse.

Finally, we suggest that in order to improve the education that special education children currently receive, at least two critical elements must be considered. First, attempts must be made to identify meaningful, measurable, and manipulable aspects of the special education environment and relate them to the general education environment. Second, and related to the first, we must start to develop curriculum units that are geared specifically for mainstreamed instruction. At present, it is not known whether simple adaptations of already available curricula will suffice.

REFERENCES

Agard, J. A. The classroom ecological structure: An approach to the specification of the treatment problem. Paper presented at the American Educational Research Association. Washington, D.C., March 31, 1975.

Allen, G. J. Case study: Implementation of behavior modification techniques in summer camp studies. *Behavior Therapy,* 1973, *4,* 570–575.

Baldwin, W. K. The educable mentally retarded child in the regular grades. *Exceptional Children,* 1958, *25,* 106–108.

Bennett, A. *A comparative study of subnormal children in the elementary grades.* New York: Teachers College, Columbia University, 1932.

Bobroff, A. Economic adjustment of 121 adults formerly students in classes for mental defectives. *American Journal of Mental Deficiency,* 1956, *60,* 525–535.

Budoff, M., & Gottlieb, J. A comparison of segregated EMR pupils with EMR pupils who were reintegrated into regular classes. Unpublished manuscript, 1976.

Carriker, W. R. *A comparison of post-school adjustment of regular and special class retarded individuals served in Lincoln and Omaha, Nebraska, public schools.* Omaha, Neb.: Nebraska State Department of Education, 1957.

Christoplos, F., & Renz, P. A critical evaluation of special education programs. *Journal of Special Education,* 1969, *3,* 371–379.

Cobb, H. V. *The forecast of fulfillment.* New York: Teachers College Press, 1972.

Coleman, J. S., Campbell, E. Q., Hobson, C. J., McPartland, J., Mood, A. M., Weinfeld, F. D., & York, R. L. *Equality of educational opportunity.* Washington, D.C.: Office of Education, U. S. Department of Health, Education, and Welfare, U. S. Government Printing Office, 1966.

Emshoff, J. G., Redd, W. H., & Davidson, W. S. Generalization training and the transfer of treatment effects with delinquent adolescents. *Journal of Behavior Therapy and Experimental Psychiatry, 1976, 7,* 141–144.

Esten, R. A. Backward children in the public schools. *Journal of Psychoaesthenics,* 1900, *5,* 10–16.

Fine, M. J. Attitudes of regular and special class teachers toward the educable mentally retarded child. *Exceptional Children,* 1967, *33,* 429–430.

Garcia, E. The training and generalization of a conversational speech form in non-verbal retardates. *Journal of Applied Behavior Analysis,* 1974, *7,* 137–149.

Goodman, H., Gottlieb, J., & Harrison, R. H. Social acceptance of EMR's integrated into a nongraded elementary school. *American Journal of Mental Deficiency, 1972, 76,* 412–417.

Gottlieb, J., & Baker, J. L. The relationship between amount of integration and the sociometric status of retarded children. Paper presented at annual meeting of the American Educational Research Association, 1975.

Gottlieb, J., & Budoff, M. Social acceptability of retarded children in nongraded schools differing in architecture. *American Journal of Mental Deficiency, 1973, 78,* 15–19.

Gottlieb, J., & David, J. E. Social acceptance of EMRs during overt behavioral interaction. *American Journal of Mental Deficiency, 1973, 78,* 141–143.

Gottlieb, J., Cohen, L., & Goldstein, L. Social contact and personal adjustment as variables relating to attitudes toward EMR children. *Training School Bulletin, 1974, 71,* 9–16.

Gottlieb, J., Semmel, M. I., & Veldman, D. J. Correlates of social status among mainstreamed mentally retarded children. *Journal of Educational Psychology, 1978, 70,* 396–405.

Guskin, S., & Spicker, H. H. Educational research in mental retardation. In N. E. Ellis (Ed.), *International review of research in mental retardation* (Vol. 3). New York: Academic Press, 1968.

Horner, R. D. Establishing use of crutches by a mentally retarded spina bifida child. *Journal of Applied Behavior Analysis, 1971, 4, 183–189.*

Inskeep, A. L. *Teaching dull and retarded children.* New York: MacMillan, 1926.

Jackson, D. A., & Wallace, R. F. The modification and generalization of voice loudness in a 15-year-old retarded girl. *Journal of Applied Behavior Analysis, 1974, 7,* 461–471.

Johnson, G. O. A study of social position of mentally handicapped children in the regular grades. *American Journal of Mental Deficiency, 1950, 55,* 60–89.

Kaufman, M. J., Agard, J. A., & Semmel, M. I. *Mainstreaming: Learners and their environments.* Baltimore: University Park Press. In press.

Kaufman, M., Gottlieb, J., Agard, J., & Kukic, M. Mainstreaming: Toward an explication of the construct. In E. L. Meyen, G. A. Vergason & R. J. Whelan (Eds.), *Alternatives for teaching exceptional children.* Denver: Love Publishing Co., 1975.

Kazdin, A. E. Toward a client administered token reinforcement program. *Education and Training of the Mentally Retarded, 1971, 6,* 52–55.

Kazdin, A. E. Artifact, bias, and complexity of assessment: The ABC's of reliability. *Journal of Applied Behavior Analysis, 1977, 10,* 141–150.

Kazdin, A. E., & Bootzin, R. R. The token economy: An evaluative review. *Journal of Applied Behavior Analysis, 1972, 5,* 343–372.

Kirk, S. A. Research in education. In H. A. Stevens & R. Heber (Eds.), *Mental retardation.* Chicago: University of Chicago Press, 1964.

Koegel, R. L., & Rincover, A. Treatment of psychotic children in a classroom environment: I. Learning in a large group. *Journal of Applied Behavior Analysis, 1974, 7,* 45–59.

Lazerson, M. Educational institutions and mental subnormality: Notes on writing a history. In M. J. Begab & S. A. Richardson (Eds.), *The mentally retarded and society.* Baltimore: University Park Press, 1975.

Leyser, Y., & Gottlieb, J. Improving the social status of rejected pupils. *Exceptional Children, 1981, 46,* 459–461.

Lovaas, O. I., & Simmons, J. Q. Manipulation of self-destruction in three retarded children. *Journal of Applied Behavior Analysis, 1969, 2,* 143–157.

MacMillan, D. L., & Semmel, M. I. Evaluation of mainstreaming programs. *Focus on Exceptional Children, 1977, 9,* Number 4.

Meyers, C. E., MacMillan, D. L., & Yoshida, R. K. Correlates of success in transition of MR to regular class. Final report. Grant OEG-O-73-5263. The Psychiatric Institute. Pacific State Research Group, November, 1975.

O'Leary, K. D., & Drabman, R. Token reinforcement programs in the classroom: A review. *Psychological Bulletin, 1971, 75,* 379–398.

Porter, R. B., & Milazzo, T. A comparison of mentally retarded adults who attended regular school classes. *Exceptional Children, 1958, 24,* 410.

Redd, W. H. Effects of mixed reinforcement contingencies on adult's control of children's behavior. *Journal of Applied Behavior Analysis*, 1969, *2*, 249–254.

Redd, W. H., & Birnbrauer, J. S. Adults as discriminative stimuli for different reinforcement contingencies with retarded children. *Journal of Experimental Child Psychology*, 1969, *7*, 440–447.

Rincover, A., & Koegel, R. L. Setting generality and stimulus control in autistic children. *Journal of Applied Behavior Analysis*, 1975, *8*, 235–246.

Rodee, M. A study to evaluate the resource teacher concept when used with high level educable retardates at a primary level. Unpublished doctoral dissertation, University of Iowa, 1971.

Rucker, C. N., Howe, C. E., & Snider, B. The participation of retarded children in junior high academic and nonacademic regular classes. *Exceptional Children*, 1969, *35*, 617–623.

Sheare, J. B. Social acceptance of EMR adolescents in integrated programs. *American Journal of Mental Deficiency*, 1974, *78*, 678–682.

Shotel, J. R., Iano, R. P., & McGettigan, J. F. Teacher attitudes associated with the integration of handicapped children. *Exceptional Children*, 1972, *38*, 677–683.

Skodak, M. A follow-up and comparison of graduates from two types of high school programs for the mentally handicapped. Final Report. U.S. Department of Health, Education, and Welfare, Project No. 6–8680, 1970.

Stokes, T. F., & Baer, D. M. Preschool peers as mutual generalization-facilitating agents. *Behavior Therapy*, 1976, *7*, 549–556.

Stokes, T. F., & Baer, D. M. An implicit technology of generalization. *Journal of Applied Behavior Analysis*, 1977, *10*, 349–367.

Stokes, T. F., Baer, D. M., & Jackson, R. L. Programming the generalization of a greeting response in four retarded children. *Journal of Applied Behavior Analysis*, 1974, *7*, 599–610.

Strichart, S. S., & Gottlieb, J. Imitation of retarded children by their nonretarded peers. *American Journal of Mental Deficiency*, 1975, *79*, 506–512.

Sulzer-Azaroff, B., & Mayer, G. R. *Applying behavior-analysis procedures with children in youth.* New York: Holt, Rinehart, & Winston, 1977.

Tracey, D. A., Briddell, D. W., & Wilson, G. T. Generalization of verbal conditioning to verbal and nonverbal behavior: Group therapy with chronic psychiatric patients. *Journal of Applied Behavior Analysis*, 1974, *7*, 391–402.

Walker, V. The resource room model for educating educable mentally retarded children. Unpublished doctoral dissertation. Temple University, 1972.

Wallin, J. E. W. *The education of handicapped children.* Boston: Houghton Mifflin, 1924.

Wildman, R. W., II, & Wildman, R. W. The generalization of behavior modification procedures: A review with special emphasis on classroom applications. *Psychology in the Schools*, 1975, *12*, 432–448.

Effects of Integrated versus Segregated Education for the Mildly Impaired Student

C. Edward Meyers,
D. L. MacMillan,
and Gale M. Morrison

Integrated education for the mildly impaired student refers to an arrangement in which the student attends a regular school class or program for half or more of the school week, instruction being provided by the regular teachers, who are ultimately responsible for the student's entire educational program. The student otherwise receives specialized assistance, in the regular class or elsewhere, and the regular class teacher may also be provided expert help on how to cope with the handicapped student's special needs. Segregated education refers to the model of instruction in which all or nearly all instruction is provided by a special teacher in a self-contained class of limited enrollment, and in which the other students are similarly handicapped. Mildly impaired students are otherwise referred to as educable mentally retarded (EMR) or mildly handicapped students—those who are not severely mentally retarded and who tend to have normal qualities except for very poor academic promise.

The title of this chapter implies a simple empirical research issue that should lead to straightforward conclusions about the comparative merits of educational methods. The fact that this question is raised after more than 30 years of investigation of the education of the mildly retarded student should suggest that the expectation is not easily satisfied. The school as an ongoing system cannot easily be made to surrender its operations to research needs. Rarely can they permit the investigator to make random assignments of students to planned programs of sufficient length to provide usable data. Furthermore, there are great

This study was supported in part by the National Institute of Child Health and Human Development Research Grants No. HD-04612, HD-05540, HD-72847, and DHEW/OHD Grant No. 54-P-71117/9.

215

variations in what are called segregated and integrated programs, curriculum and instructional variations, teacher variables, resource allocations, etc.

As a topic of research, therefore, the issue posed by the title can be met only
piecemeal. Furthermore, time brings changes into the nature of research. An earlier era of
investigation had the limited task of determining whether the segregated special class was
sufficiently superior to regular class enrollment for the mildly retarded student to justify its
extra cost. In these earlier, so-called efficacy studies, the retarded student in the regular
class as a rule received none of the specialized help provided today under the integration
banner. Competent reviews of this earlier research may be found in Kirk (1964) and Guskin
and Spicker (1968).

Another change came with litigation due to excess identification of minority and low
SES students in the EMR program. The consequence was to restrict the EMR definition,
resulting in a current EMR population with a much lower general average learning ability.
Results secured 10 years ago may not be valid today.

The most profound change affecting the meaning and significance of research in the
education of the mildly impaired was the developing thrust, since about 1970, toward the
normalization of education for the handicapped. Schools are mandated to place the special
learner in the least restrictive educational environment compatible with the student's special
needs. These and other changes mandated by federal and state law mean that empiricism
must give way to principle. Research now can have little influence on fundamental
decisions, and it is to a large extent relegated to pointing out the consequences of what has
otherwise been decreed.

In spite of the problems and limitations in conducting research with the mentally
handicapped learners, their educational programming continues to fascinate investigators.
The EMR and other marginal learners are so close to full normalcy that they proceed, for the
most part, unlabeled and little distinguished in adult life, even if they prove to be only
marginally successful. Hence educational provisions have the potential of leading to
increased self-respect, greater social acceptability and job skills, and the avoidance of
adjustment and legal differences that can easily be the consequences of their limited abstract
abilities.

Reviews of the more recent investigations, leading to the present, may be found in
Corman and Gottlieb (1979) and Meyers, MacMillan, and Yoshida (1980). Inasmuch as a
comprehensive review of the nature and determinations of the various investigations is
otherwise provided in this volume, no summary is attempted here. This chapter consists of
reports of two large-scale investigations conducted by the authors that are related to the
topic of segregated and integrated education.

THE CALIFORNIA DECERTIFICATION STUDY

Some of the data of a recently completed study, for which we continue to analyze data and
publish findings, are presented here. The study began before our current NICHD-supported
study of EMR and educationally handicapped (EH) learners. Most of the data reported here
had not been previously published except for the report to the funding agency. Other data
reports may be found in MacMillan, Meyers, and Yoshida, 1978; Meyers, MacMillan, and
Yoshida, 1975; Meyers et al., 1978; and Yoshida, MacMillan, and Meyers, 1976. This
study was sponsored by the Bureau of Education for the Handicapped, to permit us to

examine the consequences of the massive decertification of 11,000 or more EMR students in California and their return to regular class. The decertification provided a natural experiment in the regular or mainstreamed education of EMR students. The study secured data in 12 school districts in the state, north and south, rural, inner city, and suburban. The study unintentionally became the largest of all ''mainstreaming'' studies in terms of number of cases.

The study had several purposes. For this chapter, the most relevant purpose was to determine how well the decertified EMR students fared in their regular class experience, and this report is essentially restricted to data on that success.

Procedures

To facilitate the study of the success of the decertified students, we composed two contrast groups. One consisted of regular class students, never referred for possible special class placement, to be matched on sex and ethnicity. Each student was to be selected from the same class (with the same teacher) in which a decertified student was enrolled at the time we would secure data. The school officials were to select some student, within the limitations of matched sex and ethnicity, who would be in the lower half of the class on some criterion of academic ability or achievement, preferably an objective test. For the secondary school, in which each student would be enrolled in several classes, the class chosen was the English or reading class. This selection resulted in a tight control within each pair over such factors as the teacher, peers, subject matter, and neighborhood.

A second contrast group was drawn according to the same criterion of matched sex and ethnicity. Here the matched student was a nondecertified EMR student who had been enrolled in the same EMR class from which the decertified student had been decertified some 2 to 6 years before. This match was retrospective; the match with the regular class students was current. This second contrast group, the EMR group, was not intended as a control group, for there could have been no random assignment of the then EMR students to the decertified and the EMR groups. The purpose was to investigate later success of the nondecertified as well as the decertified students under controlled comparison. The students who were decertified were identified by the school district in the process of court-mandated annual reassessments. The state, in responding to civil rights litigation, had lowered the effective IQ level to qualify for EMR placement. It had been IQ 79, plus or minus the error of measurement, which meant that many borderline students had been placed in EMR programs. The new guideline conformed to the change provided by the AAMD, IQ 70. Furthermore, the school could no longer dare to exercise judgment about whether the student was better served in EMR than in regular placement. Any IQ above 70, verbal or performance, secured on any scale, was sufficient to remove the student for return to regular class. The proportion removed from EMR placement in 3 years' time (1969 to 1972) was nearly 40 percent (see Table 1), with further reduction in subsequent years.

Results of the Decertification Study

The immediate results of the massive decertification varied with the school district. Those districts that had already introduced integration showed lower reductions. Ethnic minority overrepresentation was corrected only moderately (Table 1), but subsequent placement into EMR programs of ethnic minority students was greatly reduced. Our examination of the

Table 1. California statewide enrollments, October 1969 and June 1973

	White %	Black %	Hispanic %	Total
Total California public school pupils (1969)	72.4	8.9	15.2	
Percent of own ethnic group in EMR (1969)	0.7	3.3	2.1	
Percent which ethnic group is in total EMR (1969)	43.1	27.1	28.2	55,519
Percent which ethnic group is in total EMR (1973)	50.0	25.0	23.0	35,110

Source: Simmons, Allan, and Bringegar, Leslie. *Ethnic survey of EMR classes, 1973.* Sacramento, California: California State Department of Education, 1973.

records of the decertified and of the nondecertified EMR students in our 12-district samples indicated that only a minor difference in mean IQ obtained at the time of the initial EMR placement, from 2 or 3 points up to 7 points. Because IQs vary somewhat upon retesting, however, and because the decertification was a matter of receiving an IQ that happened to be above 70, the mean IQ differences at decertification time were greater than at EMR placement, 10 points or more. An examination of the records before placement indicated no systematic difference in teacher-assigned marks in regular class between the decertified and EMR groups, no difference in entries indicating deportment or emotional adjustment problems, no differences in mean age of EMR placement, and no difference in mean duration of regular class enrollment before placement (Meyers et al., 1978).

We secured any information by which a judgment could be made about the educational success of the decertified students, including continued enrollment in school, teacher marks in academic subjects and citizenship, measured achievement, and teacher reactions on questionnaires.

Attendance   Attendance is a measure of the extent to which a student accepts school and hence is an indicator of at least minimal adjustment. Table 2 provides data on mean absences per school year for the three groups; decertified, regular class, and EMR. Regardless of group, it was noted that the Hispanic students were most frequently absent, confirming a common local observation. The data show that contrary to some expectations, more EMRs tended to be absent than members of the other two groups.

Staying in School   On the logic that staying in school during the ages of compulsory attendance is a superior adjustment to dropping out, the continued enrollment of the EMR and decertified matched pairs was investigated. The decertification had occurred from 2 to 6 years before the study of current status, and the decertified students were found, at the time

Table 2. Mean days absent in school year for three combined school districts according to group, ethnicity, and sex

Group	White		Black		Hispanic	
	Male	Female	Male	Female	Male	Female
Decertified	9.92	8.17	12.15	10.04	15.44	12.92
EMR	12.42	7.54	8.73	13.35	16.56	22.56
Regular class	16.00	18.67	10.10	12.58	15.65	8.86

of our study of current status, to be in grades 5 through 12, the majority in the junior high school grades 7 through 9, traditionally a time of heavy truancy and dropping out. There had been many "scare" stories of what was happening to the decertified students when they had to return to the severe competition and ridicule of the regular class from which they had been removed some years before, whereas in contrast, the nondecertified EMR student was supposed to feel protected in the segregated condition. We sought to determine the then present whereabouts of the decertified students and their EMR matches for a study of comparative proportions of those still in school. If a student was found not to be enrolled in the same district, a phone call or letter attempted to ascertain if the student was still in school somewhere.

Our data showed that, in spite of the anxieties and the anecdotes of actual distress, the decertified students had not disappeared in any greater proportions than the EMR students. In fact, in two inner city areas, EMR disappearance was greater. On this criterion, as on the criterion of absence rate, the decertified students were as well adjusted as the EMR students.

Grade Placement   This is an indirect criterion of school success in that it would normally be considered better to compete with one's age peers than to fall behind. The typical child starts kindergarten at age 5 and is socially promoted each year. The normal age-grade placement is hence given by age minus 5; one expects a typical 12-year-old child to be in grade 7. We calculated the normal age-grade expectancy for both the decertified and the regular class students and also the differences between that and the actual grade placement. Generally, the EMR student had lost 1 year in early school history; schools tend to have the very slow learner repeat 1st grade in order to avoid having to make an EMR placement. The decertified students in our study, having already lost that year, were typically placed even further below their age peers when returned to regular class. A decertified student of 13 years, for example, might have a reading level of 3rd or 4th grade, but the school could not set him or her back that far for fear the student might leave school. The school would compromise, placing the student 2 or so years under the expected grade placement. In those districts in which we had sufficient information, we found placement of the decertified students to be about 1½ to 2½ years behind unselected age peers. The classes in which the decertified students were put were generally below average in achievement. For example, if an elementary school had two 6th grades, the decertified student would have been put in the slower one; if the secondary school had five English classes, the student would be placed in the slowest one. This meant that our matching regular class students, who were, when possible, taken from the bottom half of that regular class, were also below average students. Table 3 shows that they tended to be about ½ year younger than the decertified match cases of the same placement, while being about 1 year or more below normal expectancy themselves. The age-grade placement is relevant in interpreting the next data, measured school achievement.

Measured School Achievement   In those school districts that permitted it, we administered the reading and math sections of the Metropolitan Achievement test to all subjects of the three groups. Although the grade placements of the decertified and the regular class students ranged from grade 5 through 12, with few at the extremes and most in junior high, the median placement was 8th grade. The measured achievement of none of our subgroups came as close as 3 grade levels to the actual placement. For example, the best

Table 3.   Expected versus actual age-grade placements of decertified students and age differences between decertified and regular class matched students

School district	Program level	N	Mean difference in grade placement[a]	Average difference older than regular class[b]
3	All	60	−1.86**	0.61**
	Elementary school	13	−2.15**	0.93**
	Junior high school	37	−1.89**	0.57**
	Senior high school	10	−1.40**	0.30 NS
4	All	33	−1.58**	0.63**
	Elementary school	2	c	0.50
	Junior high school	12	−1.83*	0.55*
	Senior high school	19	−1.47*	0.68**
6	All	19	−1.22**	0.08 NS
	Elementary school	2	c	−1.00
	Junior high school	10	−1.3 **	0.0 NS
	Senior high school	7	−1.00*	0.10 NS
12	All	38	−2.13**	0.66**
	Elementary school	6	−2.67**	0.33*
	Junior high school	19	−2.16**	0.13 NS
	Senior high school	13	−1.85**	1.10**

[a]The null hypothesis tested is that the mean difference between actual and expected grade placement is zero.
[b]The null hypothesis tested is that the mean age of the decertified students is not greater than that of the regular class matches.
[c]Too few cases.
* $p < 0.05$
**$p < 0.02$

subgroup mean in reading was the Spanish females of the regular class, but it was only 4.17 in grade level equivalent. The lowest was for Black male students in EMR, 2.07. For reading there was a sex by ethnicity interaction in which male Black students tend to be below female Black students without a similar sex difference in Whites and Hispanics. Comparing the three groups, the results of the reading and the arithmetic tests showed the regular class students to be the highest followed by the decertified, the EMR being the lowest. The sex by ethnicity interaction found for reading was not present in arithmetic scores.

The superiority of the regular class to the decertified students in measured achievement is more impressive if their younger age is kept in consideration. The measured achievement of the decertified students was about 4 grade levels below placement. Considering that the actual placement was about 2 years below expected age-grade placement, then we conclude that these students, 2 to 6 years after decertification, had nearly a 6-year deficit in measured academic achievement.

Teacher Marks of Achievement and Citizenship   Table 4 presents average teacher marks for reading, math, and citizenship for the decertified and the regular class groups. The marks for each pair were awarded by the same teacher. Because EMR students had different teachers, we did not analyze the data for that group. All marks were converted, if necessary, to the standard 4-point basis with 4 being high. As is usual, and with the common

Table 4.   Mean teacher marks for achievement and citizenship for the decertified and regular class groups[a]

	White		Black		Hispanic	
	Male	Female	Male	Female	Male	Female
Reading						
Decertified	3.09	3.31	2.50	3.02	2.55	3.07
Regular class	2.81	3.00	2.54	2.93	2.43	2.86
Math						
Decertified	2.75	2.64	2.46	2.48	2.45	2.67
Regular class	2.84	2.40	2.31	2.47	2.65	2.64
Citizenship						
Decertified	3.19	3.50	2.73	3.50	3.24	3.12
Regular class	3.06	3.14	3.03	3.28	2.91	3.50

[a]Based on a 4-point marking system with 4 being high.

exception of math, the girls received better marks than the boys; this sex difference was more pronounced than in the data on achievement measured by standardized tests. The contrast of decertified with regular class student marks reveals little systematic difference. This finding was in contrast with the difference in test-measured achievement in which regular class students were higher than the decertified.

Teacher Response to Questionnaires   These regular class teachers were sent separate questionnaires for the two students. We were fortunate to receive over 90% response from the teachers, 250 responding. Some teachers, of course, had more than one pair of students. The data (given in full in MacMillan et al., 1978) indicate how the given pupil was perceived in relation to the class as a whole in achievement and in social acceptance (Table 5). Two-thirds of the decertified students were judged to be very low or below average in the class in academic achievement quality, compared with a little over half of the regular class individuals. There was less difference in perceived social acceptance, but again, that difference favored the regular class students. Perhaps most striking about the data of Table 5

Table 5.   Decertified and regular class match teacher judgment of subjects' achievement and social acceptance relative to subjects' classmates

	Decertified subjects		Regular class match subjects	
	Frequency	%	Frequency	%
Achievement level				
No response	4	1.6	9	3.6
Very low	76	30.2	42	16.8
Below average	96	38.1	94	37.6
Average	47	18.7	80	32.0
Above average	25	9.9	23	9.2
Highest	4	1.6	2	0.8
Social acceptance				
No response	4	1.6	9	3.6
Very low	27	10.7	12	4.8
Below average	54	21.4	39	15.6
Average	124	49.2	121	48.4
Above average	40	15.9	63	25.2
Highest	3	1.2	6	2.4

is that different decertified students were rated by their teachers across the whole range of possibilities, from very low through highest categories, as were the regular class students.

The information on teacher acceptance would have been considerably different had the information been secured within a short time after the regular class teacher had received this once-segregated student. We know from other data, including the large Texas PRIME project (Kaufman, Agard, and Semmel, in press), that regular class teachers show varying degrees of resignation, resentment, challenge, and insecurity. In our data both the student and the teacher had had sufficient time to stabilize their adjustment to the situation of regular class enrollment. One of our questions asked whether the presence of the decertified student affected the class and how the instruction was affected. Only 29% answered that the student had provided some impact; put another way, seven of ten teachers found no unusual impact.

Decertification altered the nature of the EMR population as well as the regular class into which they were placed. Teachers of remaining EMR classes were asked if any of the remaining EMR could succeed in a regular program. Although 64.2% responded "no," 23.7% indicated that success could be achieved only if assistance were provided to the child in the regular class. EMR teachers also indicated that the removal of the decertified children reduced the average learning level in the EMR class (59.9%). Moreover, they noted that the homogeneity of EMR became greater after decertification because virtually all of the remaining children required individual attention. It is apparent that the removal of the decertified children resulted in an EMR population that was more debilitated and required intensive individual assistance.

Conclusion   The data of our large study were more or less confirmed in completely separate, smaller investigations. Most of the decertified EMR students were found to "survive" their enrollment in the regular class. They apparently adjusted well enough to stay in school and to seem to their teachers to be not greatly inferior to the selected regular class match students. After 2 to 6 years of education in the regular program, however, their state of academic underachievement continued to be a real concern. If one defines literacy as the attainment of a 5th grade level of reading and mathematical ability, few seemed to have achieved it at the time of our careful small group administration of achievement tests. This fact is a late confirmation of the need for the school to have intervened, as it did, when failure in early grades caused the steps of assessment and eventual placement into the EMR program. The return of the decertified students to regular class could not automatically have made them normal learners, and did not.

Given today's knowledge it is possible to say that the initial EMR placement for the decertified students might not have been the most appropriate, but at the time (the 1960s and early 1970s) when most of the decertified students had first been placed, there did not exist the presently available alternatives for a less radical and less stigmatizing placement.

CURRENT NICHD STUDY

Our current NICHD program-project was designed to study home and educational environments as they affect the performance of EMR and educationally handicapped (EH) subjects. The reason for including EH subjects derives from the drastic reduction in EMR enrollments accompanying the shift in the EMR definition, which has resulted in serving children with learning problems whose IQs fall between 70 and 85 under the rubric of EH.

We have delimited ourselves to those EH students with IQs under 85, to be consistent with earlier definitions of mental retardation, which had used an IQ of one standard deviation below the mean as the upper cut-off.

EH students have been, like EMR students, the subject of failure in the regular educational program for 1 or more years and have been referred, evaluated, and finally placed into the partly segregated and labeled program, all with due process including parental involvement. The California EH category includes the so-called learning disabled or LD student as well as a miscellany of others having severe underachievement, but in all cases regarded as *not* mentally retarded in the more recent, stricter definition.

A more compelling reason to include the EH in California is that the EMR enrollment in this state has shrunk to less than 40 percent of what it was in 1970 as a consequence of court litigation, as well as the test ban for EMR placement. Consequently, the State of California has the second lowest proportion of its public school enrollment in special programs for the mentally retarded as shown in Table 6. The data have been abstracted from information supplied by the Bureau of Education for the Handicapped, based on the child count of December 1, 1978, required of state education offices. Most data in Table 6 are based on the 50 states and the District of Columbia. The data for the entire United States include information from the Virgin Islands, Puerto Rico, trust territories, etc., as well. California is seen to be next lowest among the 51 jurisdictions in proportion of enrollment in special programs for the mentally retarded. The great bulk of this would be EMR. Additionally, California is below the states' median in the proportion of LD and also in the percent for all special education taken together. The scene, then, from which we have drawn our current EMR and EH subjects, is a state that has become conservative in the identification of its special education students.

Sample

Descriptive information regarding our two samples (EMR and EH) are displayed in Table 7. The major distinguishing feature of EH from EMR is the discrepancy in IQ; however, both samples exhibit serious achievement deficits, as shown by achievement scores secured on a random subsample of each group. The EH sample also contains a high proportion of males. In the initial year of study the range of chronological age was 7 to 14, leading one to project that the median grade placement in reading and arithmetic expected is approximately 5th or 6th grade, if there were not a serious achievement lag.

Design

Initially, we were interested in making comparisons, when possible, of integrated versus segregated educational settings on selected outcomes; however, the overarching concern was to study within-setting variables and the relationships between these setting variables and the dependent measures. The rationale for this derives from Kirk's (1964) critique of the efficacy studies along with the belief that it is what goes on within the classroom that determines the benefits or detriments to child outcomes, not the settings in which these variations exist. Stated differently, the variables most likely affecting self-concept, social status, etc., are those factors within a class (teacher handling of failure, reinforcement patterns, classroom climate) that will explain the most variance; administrative arrangement is expected to account for very little variance.

Table 6. Range of percentages of total public school enrollments in mental retardation, learning disability, and all special education among 51 states with District of Columbia, and in California. Source: Bureau of Education for the Handicapped, U.S. Office of Education, Child Count of 1 December 1978.

	Percent in mental retardation		Percent in learning disability		Percent in all special education	
Lowest	(So. D.)	0.85	(N.Y.)	0.49	(D.C.)	5.14
Next low	(Cal.)	0.86	(Miss.)	0.98	(Haw.)	5.36
Median	(Mass.)	2.07	(Neb.)	2.66	(Ariz.)	8.52
Highest	(S.C.)	3.95	(Wyo.)	4.68	(Tenn.)	11.30
Next high	(Ark.)	3.65	(Tenn.)	4.55	(Utah)	11.05
United States[a]		1.83		2.30		7.86
California		0.86		1.95		7.05

[a]Total includes Puerto Rico, Trust Territories, etc.

Table 7.   Some descriptive information on the EMR and the EH subjects in the current NICHD study

	EMR	EH
Initial year subjects	246	76
Initial age range	7–14 years	7–14 years
Sex		
Males	52%	80%
Females	48%	20%
Ethnicity		
White	71%	62%
Black	9%	21%
Hispanic	13%	9%
Other	7%	8%
IQ on sample[a]		
Mean	66.4	79.3
S.D.	10.0	8.9
Grade placement on		
Wide Range Achievement Test		
Reading		
Mean	2.50	3.07
S.D.	1.52	1.56
Arithmetic		
Mean	2.36	3.05
S.D.	1.20	0.85

[a]IQs and achievement scores based on a random sample of EMRs ($N=145$) and most of the first year ($N=61$) EH subjects.

Description of Integration

In our first data year very little integration was attempted in California schools, as the then new Public Law 94–142, mandating enrollment in the least restrictive environment, was not yet fully in force. Some integration had frequently been tried, but no serious attempts, except for experiments, were made to exploit the possibilities of the regular class enrollment with some form of special assistance to mainstreamed students. Thus, most of our efforts to investigate effects of integration were in the second and third project years. The school districts were sincerely trying, but as we will show, they had not successfully implemented much integrated instruction in the academic subjects.

Tables 8 and 9 summarize the pattern of integration found for our two samples. Data in Table 8 show the number of minutes that the EMR and EH students were integrated into regular classes during the second and third years of study. Forty-one percent (62 children) were educated exclusively in special classes, and 73% were integrated for 6 minutes or less in the average school day. If one accepts a definition of mainstreaming that requires 50% or more of the school day to be under the instruction of a regular class teacher, the picture in our districts indicates that mainstreaming is rare with either EMR or EH children. For example, if the school day has 4 hours of available instructional time, then 50% would be 120 minutes, which very few of our subjects have received. In the second year, 92% of EMR subjects and 93% of EH subjects received fewer than 120 minutes of integrated instruction. Although there was some improvement in the third year for EMR, the changes were not dramatic.

Table 8. Minutes of school day spent in integrated instruction reported for EMR and EH students (EMR, $N=151$; EH, $N=49$)

Minutes integrated	EMR, second year		EMR, third year		EH, second year		EH, third year	
	Cum. freq.	Cum. pct.	Cum. freq.	Cum. pct.	Cum. freq.	Cum. pct.	Cum. freq.	Cum. pct.
0	62	41	42	28	24	49	22	45
0–50	110	73	83	55	37	76	33	67
0–120	139	92	122	81	46	93	44	90
0–200	146	97	143	95	48	98	48	98

Table 9. Integration of EMR students over 2 years by subject matter areas

	Integrated both years		Integrated only year one		Integrated only year two		Integrated neither year	
	Number	Percent	Number	Percent	Number	Percent	Number	Percent
Reading	4	2.6	9	6.0	13	8.6	125	82.8
Language arts	2	1.3	5	3.3	9	6.0	135	89.4
Arithmetic	1	0.7	4	2.6	13	8.6	133	88.1
Science	0	0.0	4	2.6	12	7.9	135	89.4
Social sciences	2	1.3	7	4.6	9	6.0	133	88.1
Art	7	4.6	19	12.6	25	16.6	100	66.2
Music	11	7.3	24	15.9	18	11.9	90	59.6
Vocational studies	12	7.9	11	7.3	27	17.9	101	66.9

The relative lack of integration of our EH sample can, in part, be explained by the sampling procedures used in our study. In California EH children have been served in large numbers in learning disability groups (LDG), and if a child is placed in segregated EH classes it is because of more generalized learning problems and/or behavior problems. In fact, our reasoning in selecting EH with IQ below 85 was to establish a sample reasonably like the higher functioning EMR prior to the onslaught of litigation that led to redefining EMR in most states.

Table 9 summarizes the integration of EMR subjects by subject matter area for the second and third year of study. Clearly, EMR children were seldom integrated for instruction in academic subject matter areas (e.g., reading, language arts, arithmetic, science, and social studies) in either the second or third project year. There was more integration in subject matter areas where mental limitations would not be as crucial a liability (e.g., music, art, and vocational studies); however, even in these areas, over half the EMR subjects were not integrated either year. We concluded that the lack of integration noted in Table 9 is supportive of what school personnel have expressed to us: that the EMR child of today is far more debilitated than was the EMR child before the litigation. EMR classes today have a lower IQ limit for placement (roughly 70 versus 85+ prior to 1970) and include more children with moderate degree of retardation and accompanying physical stigmata. We are convinced that school personnel have conformed to the mandate for least restriction and integration of mildly handicapped children for instruction. This has had to be tempered by regular class teacher tolerance, however, and the abilities of the children to be integrated. It seems reasonable to conclude that self-contained special class placement with very limited integration (primarily for nonacademic subjects) is the least restrictive placement possible for the current EMR population.

Consider what has happened to the 151 students between years two and three in terms of the kind of labeling/placement changes made, if any. Table 10 shows that 123 (81%) remained in labeled EMR status for basic instruction. Another 12 (8%) were placed into either EH or a combined EH-EMR program. Two were placed into other special education. A total of 14 were placed into the regular class. Of these, seven were regarded as mainstreamed and were pulled out to go to a resource room for assistance in academic learning. The other seven were reclassified as regular class and lost their EMR identification, this almost assuredly through parental request. Only one of these seven children was integrated during the preceding year (while still EMR labeled) for more than 4 minutes a day, and that child was integrated for 48 minutes per day. A parent can always question a placement and may be able to force a change. Some of these seven are known to be receiving special help for their learning problems as though they had continued in EMR

Table 10. Movement among 151 EMR students from second to third year

	Number	Percent
Remained EMR	123	81
To EH or combined EMR-EH	12	8
To other special education	2	1
To regular class without EMR identification	7	5
To regular class, pulled for resource room	7	5

status. The difference is that the school district cannot charge the state for the extra costs when the special status is not designated.

Variability in Integration Practices

Thus far the data indicate that integration is still a goal to be strived for but that it has not been reached to any great extent, either in terms of total time or, at the ideal level, for instruction in basic subjects with nonhandicapped students. For those integrated, the integration seems to have taken place primarily for nonacademic activity and for small percentages of the school day or week. The common pattern is for EMR or EH students to attend a special classroom for the majority of the time, going to regular classrooms for brief interludes for either nonacademic or quasi-academic activity such as group music or physical education. But as indicated above, there is a slow transfer away from the more segregated toward the more integrated models. Nearly always, when we have found EMR students to become registered in the regular class, they go either to the special teacher or to a resource room for instruction in the basic academic subjects.

Morrison (1979), as part of the NICHD project, differentiated two groups of combined EMR-EH (mildly learning handicapped) children according to the type of integration in which they were involved. One group, learning handicapped-special class children, was enrolled in special classrooms for the majority of their school day and attended regular classrooms primarily for nonacademic subjects such as music or physical education. This "integration" averaged 3 to 5 hours per *week*. Informal observation indicated that there was little systematic effort to provide instruction for the combined handicapped and non-handicapped students. As one regular class teacher aptly described the situation, "They (the children) come into my room 3 days a week for music but do nothing more than sit at the back of the classroom and clap hands to the beat of the music."

The other group, learning handicapped-resource room children, on the other hand, spent the majority of their school hours (5 to 6 hours a *day*) in a regular classroom, attending a special or resource setting only for remedial instruction. These handicapped children most probably had the opportunity for more intensive interactions with their nonhandicapped classmates than the learning handicapped-special class group, reflecting the differing programmatic or administrative arrangements. Both these groups are "integrated" in a sense but there are clear differences in the amount of integration interaction time, the extent of interpersonal contact during that time, and the extent to which the contact occurs with instruction. These two groups represent only two of the several possible administrative models in current use to effect a less restrictive educational environment.

Results of the Morrison study indicated that the distinction in integration practices for mildly learning handicapped children may be an important one when studying the outcome variable of social status. The above investigation found that the learning handicapped-special class group was significantly less well known to the nonhandicapped raters than were the learning handicapped-resource room children (results are displayed in Table 11). There was clearly less interaction of handicapped with nonhandicapped in the former arrangement. The difference in the extent of acquaintance was associated with a greater number of nominations as social isolates in the less integrated group (Table 12). These children were neither accepted nor rejected in significant proportions. Note, however, that in contrast to the social isolation of the learning handicapped-special class group, the more

Table 11.   Means and standard deviations of question mark responses for males and females in the LHSC, LHRS, and regular class groups

Group	n	Percentage of social status nonacquaintance	
		M	S.D.
LHSC*			
Females	22	0.15	0.12
Males	15	0.27	0.21
LHRS**			
Females	7	0.02	0.03
Males	16	0.03	0.06
Regular			
Females	260	0.08	0.15
Males	227	0.08	0.15

*LHSC = Learning handicapped-special class.
**LHRS = Learning handicapped-resource room.

integrated learning handicapped-resource room group exhibited higher rejection rates. These results were interpreted to indicate that the more thorough integration experienced by the resource room group makes them better known to the nonhandicapped students, this greater exposure leading to more rejection. This finding confirms the results of Goodman, Gottlieb, and Harrison (1972) who concluded that the more the handicapped are exposed to the nonhandicapped, the greater are the chances for negative evaluations and rejection.

Additional measures were taken in the Morrison (1979) study of the social status, the self-perception of social status (socioempathy), and the ideal social status (socioideal) of mildly learning handicapped (EMR and EH) and nonhandicapped children. Pertinent to the current discussion are the findings that the learning handicapped-special class children significantly overestimated their social status; those in the resource classes did not. One interpretation is that the increased time and interaction with nonhandicapped children received by learning handicapped-resource room children results in more accurate (real-istic) social status self-perceptions. Handicapped learners in special classes have less opportunity to receive feedback on how others react to them and thereby retain unrealistic

Table 12.   Group percentages for sociometric classifications

Sociometric classification	Percentage of group members		
	LHSC*	LHRS**	Regular
Social acceptance			
Star	3	4	19
Middle	19	43	55
Isolate (s)	78	52	26
Social rejection			
Rejectee	8	26	15
Middle	24	65	59
Isolate (r)	68	9	26

*LHSC = Learning handicapped-special class.
**LHRS = Learning handicapped-resource room.

perceptions. Another way of viewing these results is that the protectiveness of the special class achieves its intended goal of shielding enrolled children from undue social failure, which might otherwise result in depreciation in feelings of self-worth.

In summary, the Morrison investigation suggests that variation in type and degree of integration of mildly handicapped children is associated with differences in important outcome variables (e.g., social status).

Other Integration Variables

Other variables to be considered as part of the "integration" environment are the type of curriculum and instruction received, setting variables such as the type of classroom administrative arrangement, class size, characteristics of peers and teachers, and classroom climate.

Classroom Climate   Some of our early analyses on the NICHD project have revealed some prediction of second year student cognitive variables from school environmental variables. In these analyses, the student status and school environment variables are entered into a partial correlation, with initial year student status held constant.

Cognitive measures were obtained from EH and EMR students; these included achievement in basic subjects (reading and arithmetic scores from the WRAT, Stanford-Binet IQ and mental age, and scores on the Goldschmid-Bentler conservation scales). Classroom environment was measured by the Teacher Attitude and Classroom Climate Questionnaire (Veldman, 1973). The results indicated that the teacher's individualization of instruction had some value in predicting reading scores on the WRAT, but not arithmetic scores. Similarly, the absence of rigid classroom control was predictive of better conservation scores on the Goldschmid-Bentler scale. Although these are preliminary findings, they reinforce the notion that the setting or environment could be useful in explaining child outcomes in the context of the integration question.

The results of another investigation predicting the self-concepts of EMR and EH children from classroom climate may serve as a caution for integration practices. Morrison, MacMillan, and Borthwick (1980) found that high academic, social, and behavioral self-concepts of EH and EMR children are predicted by different classroom environments. In particular, high academic self-concepts of EMR children are associated with emphases on cognitive activities and high individualization whereas high academic self-concepts of EH children are associated with a highly structured, *non*individualized, competitive environment. Although the dynamics of these patterns are in need of further investigation, they may serve as a warning to educators who think "wholesale" integration of exceptional children into regular classrooms will be effective. Variations in child characteristics and the interaction of these characteristics with variations in classroom climate may be crucial in their effects on self-concept and other child outcomes.

Self-Concept   In addition to curricular and programmatic variables, characteristics of the students are likely determinants of the extent and kind of integration to which they will be exposed. To explore the characteristics of self-concept and its possible correlates, we examined the extent to which social and academic self-concept could be predicted by teacher ratings. Social and academic self-concept was measured by About You and Your Friends (Veldman, 1973a). Teacher ratings of child traits (academic competence, misbehavior, anxious-depressed, outgoing-expressive) were entered as independent variables (these were measured by the Teacher Rating Scale; Agard and Kaufman, undated).

Different predictors emerged for the two samples, indicating the potential importance of variations in child characteristics. For EMR subjects, the anxious-depressed variable (e.g., "Becomes upset when makes a mistake," "Expresses feelings of inadequacy about self") entered first in a stepwise regression for both self-concept measures (i.e., social and academic), suggesting that self-concepts for EMR children are related to a pervasive anxiety about themselves and their abilities. For EH subjects, academic competence and misbehavior variables entered for social self-concept, indicating more focused determinants of self-concept related to specific school-related abilities and behavior, as opposed to the generalized anxiety associated with the self-concepts of EMR subjects. The academic self-concept measure for EH subjects was related to the outgoing-expressive variable, to a willingness to contribute in class, and to an assuredness that these contributions would be well received.

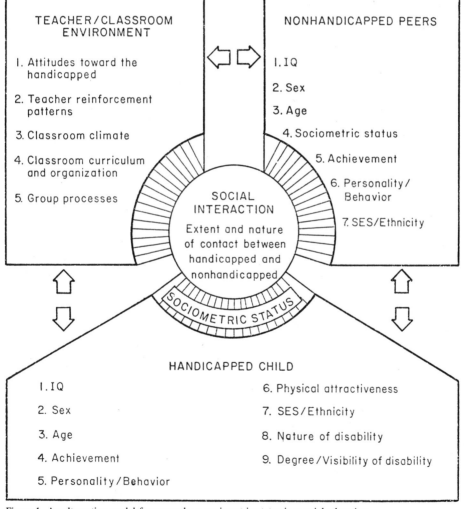

Figure 1. An alternative model for research on sociometric status in special education.

In summary, we have indicated some potential variables and areas in need of further investigation as they possibly affect or influence the integration problem. These various factors may be represented in a multicomponent model that would assist in conceptualizing integration. MacMillan and Morrison (in press) have proposed such a model (shown in Figure 1). Note that teachers, peers, and classroom variables are seen as potential determinants in the interaction possibilities of handicapped and nonhandicapped children.

Social Status   One effort to clarify the role of setting variables entailed a comparison of the correlates of social status of mildly handicapped learners in self-contained special classes with the same correlates in integrated classrooms (Gottlieb, Semmel, and Veldman, 1978). Gottlieb et al. had investigated the correlates of social status of mildly retarded children in mainstreamed settings and concluded that perceived cognitive factors contributed to the acceptance of these children, whereas perceived misbehavior predicted rejection scores, suggesting that social status has two separate continua, each with its own determinants. We investigated the same variables in self-contained EMR and EH classes as a part of our present study. The results (displayed in Table 13) indicated that the same patterns of cognition and misbehavior were related to both acceptance and rejection. That is, perceived cognition and behavior predicted both acceptance and rejection for EMR subjects, while cognition alone predicted both acceptance and rejection for EH subjects.

The variation in results from Gottlieb et al., (1978) in patterns of perceived traits predicting social status was attributed to differences in the settings in which the ratings took place and to the characteristics of the raters. Whereas Gottlieb et al. used nonhandicapped children as raters, our study secured ratings from other handicapped learners. The data reflect the possibility that EMR raters are less perceptive in discerning cognition and behavior variations (although their teachers made such distinctions). The frame of reference of the setting in which perceptions were measured seemed to be crucial for the EH sample. The strong association of cognition with both acceptance and rejection in this group reflects the fact that the sample of EH children serving as subjects were those with the lowest IQs in their EH classes. Thus, in comparison with classmates, the cognitive variable may have been the most obvious or potent difference. We may conclude that because of the contribution of setting, frame of reference, and raters to the patterns of results, educators should exercise caution predicting social status in learning handicapped students in mainstreamed settings from social status measures taken in self-contained special classes.

SUMMARY AND CONCLUSIONS

The question of the efficacy of integrated education as opposed to segregated education for mildly retarded children has been a popular one. As we have suggested, however, this question as stated has become increasingly harder to answer. Indeed, the nature of the particular question may have lost its relevance in the context of today's educational practices.

In recent years we have seen educational treatment of mildly retarded children increasingly come under control of policy, litigation, and legislation; this treatment has been relatively uninfluenced by research evidence or theoretical models. As a result, one does not find "real life" school situations to match research comparisons such as integrated versus segregated education; and random assignment to such treatments is ethically and

Table 13.   Commonality analysis for unique and shared variances among peer and teacher nominations and social acceptance and social rejection

	Social acceptance			Social rejection		
	Gottlieb et al. (n=324)	EMR–SC (n=222)	EH–SC (n=65)	Gottlieb et al. (n=234)	EMR–SC (n=222)	EH–SC (n=65)
Unique variance						
Dull (A)	2.2	0.4	9.1	0.3	0.4	9.6
Disruptive (B)	0.1	1.2	2.6	1.4	1.3	3.0
Academic conc. (C)	4.6	1.8*	1.9	1.6	2.7	3.3
Misbehavior (D)	0.3	3.7*	2.0	2.2	0.9	1.1
Shared variance						
A B	3.6	0.3	1.0	0.6	0.3	1.2
A C	-0.2	1.1	3.2	0.9	0.2	4.2
A D	0.2	-0.2	-1.2	-0.2	-0.1	1.7
B C		-0.2	-0.1	-0.3	-0.3	-0.2
B D	2.2	3.0	5.4	4.3	1.5	4.6
C D	-0.3	4.9	2.3	2.6	2.9	2.4
A B C	0.2	0.3	0.07	0.3	0.4	0.2
A B D	-0.2	0.04	-1.0	0.3	0.04	-3.6
A C D		0.8	0.06	0.2	0.06	-2.8
B C D		2.4	3.5	1.8	2.0	4.0
A B C D	1.5	1.7	1.2		1.2	3.8
Highest combined predicted variance	10.4 A+C+AC	10.4 C+D+CD	14.2 A+C+AC	7.9 B+D+BD	6.5 C+D+CD	17.1 A+C+AC

organizationally opposed to school system operations. Thus, researchers have been forced to modify and broaden their questions and research methodologies to accommodate variations in educational treatment.

In this chapter, we present data to describe the integration taking place in southern California and the effects on mildly retarded children. Data from the BEH study were used to describe the status of decertified EMR students in the regular classroom. It was suggested that although no obvious ill effects were found, these decertified students were still extremely behind their regular class peers in academic subjects. Data from a current NICHD study were presented to describe the amount of integration of EMR students now taking place in schools. Integration was found to be minimal and to be concentrated in nonacademic rather than academic subject areas. Preliminary substantive data from the NICHD study suggest that in actuality, a wide variety of integration practices are in effect; and in order to study this variation, *within* setting variation of child characteristics, outcome correlates, and classroom climate need to be recognized and incorporated into research designs. Data presented confirm the link between settings or environmental variables and child outcomes such as self-concept or social status.

In conclusion, as a result of policy decisions and school system variability in treatment implementation, questions concerning simple integration versus segregation comparisons have become difficult to answer and ultimately irrelevant even to pose. A more accurate picture of the integration of mildly handicapped children can be achieved by broadening both the questions asked and the research models used to answer these questions. We are convinced that the critical variables affecting success of an integrated educational program are not the formal aspects of the program but rather the characteristics of the handicapped students and their normal peers together with the attitudes of their teachers.

REFERENCES

Agard, A. J., & Kaufman, M. J. *Teacher Rating Scale.* Washington, D.C.: United States Office of Education, Bureau for the Education of the Handicapped, Intramural Research Program, undated.

Corman, L., & Gottlieb, J. Mainstreaming mentally retarded children: A review of research. In N. R. Ellis (Ed.), *International review of research in mental retardation* (Vol. 9). New York: Academic Press, 1979, 251–275.

Goodman, H., Gottlieb, J., & Harrison, R. H. Social acceptance of EMRs integrated into a nongraded elementary school. *American Journal of Mental Deficiency,* 1972, *76,* 412–417.

Gottlieb, J., Semmel, M. I., & Veldman, D. J. Correlates of social status among mainstreamed mentally retarded children. *Journal of Educational Psychology,* 1978, *70,* 396–405.

Guskin, S. L., & Spicker, H. H. Educational research in mental retardation. In N. R. Ellis (Ed.), *International review of research in mental retardation* (Vol. 3). New York: Academic Press, 1968, 217–278.

Kaufman, M. J., Agard, J. A., & Semmel, M. L. *Mainstreaming: Learners and their environments.* Baltimore: University Park Press. In press.

Kirk, S. A. Research in education. In H. A. Stevens & R. Heber (Eds.), *Mental retardation: A review of research.* Chicago: The University of Chicago Press, 1964, 57–99.

MacMillan, D. L., Meyers, C. E., & Yoshida, R. K. Regular class teachers' perceptions of transition programs for EMR students and their impact on the students. *Psychology in the Schools,* 1978, *15,* 99–103.

MacMillan, D. L., & Morrison, G. M. Sociometric studies. In R. L. Jones (Ed.), *Attitudes and attitude change in special education.* Minneapolis: University of Minnesota, in press.

Meyers, C. E., MacMillan, D. L., & Yoshida, R. K. Correlates of success in transition of MR to regular class. Volume I and II (Appendix). *Final Report*. Pomona, Calif.: University of California at Los Angeles, Neuropsychiatric Institute, Pacific State Hospital, 1975. (ERIC Document Reproduction Services Nos. EC 081 038 and EC 081 039.)

Meyers, C. E., MacMillan, D. L., & Yoshida, R. K. Regular class education of EMR students, from efficacy to mainstreaming: A review of issues and research. In J. Gottlieb (Ed.), Educating mentally retarded persons in the mainstream. Baltimore: University Park Press, 1980.

Meyers, C. E., MacMillan, D. L., & Yoshida, R. K. Validity of school psychologists' work in the light of the California decertification experience. *Journal of School Psychology*, 1978, *16*, 3–16.

Morrison, G. M. A methodological study of the social status of learning handicapped children in mainstreamed settings. Unpublished doctoral dissertation, University of California at Riverside, 1979.

Morrison, G. M., MacMillan, D. L., & Borthwick, S. Self-concept and social acceptance in EMR-LD students as a function of school variables. Presented at the annual meeting of the American Association on Mental Deficiency, San Francisco, May 11–16, 1980.

Veldman, D. J. *About you and your friends*. Washington, D.C.: United States Office of Education, Bureau for the Education of the Handicapped, Intramural Research Program, 1973.

Veldman, D.J. *Teacher attitude and classroom climate questionnaire*. Washington, D.C.: United States Office of Education, Bureau for the Education of the Handicapped, Intramural Research Program, 1973.

Yoshida, R. K., MacMillan, D. L., & Meyers, C. E. The decertification of minority group EMR children in California: Its historical background and an assessment of student achievement and adjustment. In R.L. Jones (Ed.), *Mainstreaming and the minority child*. Reston, Va.: Council for Exceptional Children, 1976, 215–233.

LANGUAGE
AND SETTING

Interactional Basis
of Language Learning

Ann K. Rogers-Warren,
Steven F. Warren,
and **Donald M. Baer**

Language is an essential human behavior. To a great extent, it shapes the quality of the social and intellectual activities that comprise our daily lives. Because it is such a critical skill, it is frequently the target of intervention efforts with populations who exhibit developmental delays. In many ways, remediation of the effects of developmental disabilities relies on the successful teaching of adequate language skills for normal, day-to-day interactions.

This chapter discusses the relationship between person and environment necessary for learning language. In the course of this discussion, a model of language learning is offered, prescriptions for ideal language-learning environments are considered, and possibilities for comprehensive intervention programs and research are reviewed. Although there is an implicit consideration of the environment as a whole, the specific focus of the chapter is on language skills and the critical components of environments related to language. The goal of the chapter is to offer directions for language interventions that occur within natural ecobehavioral systems and utilize their support.

This chapter is divided into six sections, each focusing on a single issue related to environmental influences on language acquisition and interventions to teach language to developmentally delayed populations. In the first section, current strategies for language intervention are reviewed and the outcomes produced by these strategies are discussed. The purpose of this section is to summarize current technology for teaching language and to evaluate the degree to which current strategies achieve their implicit goal of teaching a comprehensive communication repertoire. The second section takes up the topic of environmental influences in normal acquisition and focuses on the role of caregivers in teaching language to young children. The accumulating evidence for specific adaptation of adult speech to accommodate and facilitate children's language learning is reviewed. Particular emphasis is given to recent arguments by Moerk (1977) and Schachter (1979)

Preparation of this manuscript was supported in part by USOE Grant #300–77–0308 from the Bureau for the Education of the Handicapped.

regarding strategies mothers may employ to support their children's language learning. The third section reports on studies describing the interactions of mothers with atypical children; it emphasizes the similarities and differences in interactions when the child is developmentally delayed and when the child is normal. Because the literature in this area is limited and there are methodological factors that may have inadvertently had an impact on the results, alternative interpretations of the findings of these studies are offered. In sum, sections one and two characterize interventive and naturally occurring language-teaching processes with the intent of emphasizing the differences between the two, and sections two and three contrast the behavior of caregivers during interactions with normal and atypical children.

The second half of the chapter is divided into three sections outlining a language intervention strategy based on the findings from current intervention programs and knowledge of normal and atypical caregiver-child interactions. The fourth section outlines a model of language learning that is consistent with descriptions of facilitative mother-child interactions. The fifth section characterizes an ideal language-learning environment for developmentally delayed populations. This environment based on components of the normal child environment but incorporates some selected contingencies of structured intervention programs. The fifth section also offers specific recommendations to caregivers of developmentally delayed children based on the research findings discussed in the first half of the chapter. The final section discusses directions for future research to document the effectiveness of the proposed intervention strategy. Together, the final three sections attempt to identify teachable skills that contribute to communicative competence and that facilitate continued language learning, and to suggest environmental arrangements to support acquisition of such skills.

The overall purpose of the chapter is to offer a model of language intervention that utilizes the existing strengths of typical child environments by teaching language-deficient children to interact with the environment, particularly with their caregivers, in ways that ensure support for acquisition of new language skills. The proposed model emphasizes teaching skills that maximize language learning by facilitating child participation in everyday interactions rather than by teaching specific aspects of the language code. This model is consistent with both current psycholinguistic models of language competency and behavioral theories of reinforcement.

LANGUAGE INTERVENTION: CURRENT STRATEGIES

There is a long history of attempts to teach language to atypical children who fail to devleop language normally (Schiefelbusch and Lloyd, 1974). These attempts generally represent two types of intervention strategies: individualized training of the structural aspects of language, and interventions to increase language display in natural settings.

Individualized Training

Most language intervention has been in the form of individualized training in specific structures of the linguistic system, including vocabulary, syntax, semantics, and to a very limited extent, pragmatic use. During the late 1960s, many studies were conducted to demonstrate that language could be taught to the retarded, especially the severely retarded (e.g., Guess, 1969; Guess and Baer, 1973). By the early 1970s, comprehensive language-training programs were emerging to train arrays of communication skills considered functional by various theoretical approaches (Bricker and Bricker, 1974; Gray and Ryan, 1973; Guess, Sailor, and Baer, 1978; MacDonald et al., 1974; Miller and Yoder, 1974). Fristoe (1976), in a review of language-training programs, noted the existence of 176 "language training curricula"; perhaps a score of these were used widely.

Most training programs have tried to be comprehensive. But in fact, most teach only a few specific language skills. One reason is that they assume that the student possesses or can be taught the basic prelinguistic skills necessary to learn a rudimentary linguistic repertoire. These skills include simple instruction following, generalized imitation, and the ability to form functional response classes, derived from more basic cognitive abilities such as mnemonic capacity and intermodal association. If these prelinguistic skills are lacking, they must be trained first, and in some programs, they are.

A further assumption is that the child will generalize from the trained language exemplars to a full repertoire of descriptive language. Thus, for training to be worthwhile, the student must utilize recombinant generalization[1] and also learn new vocabulary from the natural environment. After all, it is impractical to teach more than a few exemplars of each linguistic response class. Therefore, training programs must select the salient exemplars, teach them, and assume that the student will generalize the underlying rule.

The linguistic rules chosen vary somewhat according to the theoretical bases of the programs. For example, a semantically based program (e.g., MacDonald et al., 1974) trains exemplars of agent-action-object. A syntactically based program (e.g., Stremel and Waryas, 1974) teaches noun-verb-noun constructions, and a function-based program (e.g., Guess, Sailor, and Baer, 1978) teaches specific uses of language such as requesting ("want ball") or questioning. Because there is overlap among semantic, syntactic, and functional systems, similar examples are trained in all three types of programs. Table 1 contains several syntactic, semantic, and pragmatic training examples.

Current programs represent various theoretical approaches and incorporate a range of training strategies for a range of populations. Two theoretical models are represented in language-training programs: a function-based model closely related to the operant experiments, and a developmental model influenced by psycholinguistic studies of normal language acquisition. Despite these theoretical orientations, a surprising number of similarities exist. All programs maintain that language can be taught. Most curricula begin with rudimentary verbal and nonverbal skills and progress to more sophisticated verbal skills. Most use operant procedures (although not all that do are aware of doing so), and all rely on regular assessment of student performance and on data collection within the training. Quite similar surface structures (grammatical examples) are taught across programs despite their different theoretical orientations. Students receiving language training range from mildly delayed preschool children capable of achieving normal development with extra stimulation, to severely retarded adolescents for whom the training goal is a functional but limited productive repertoire.

Most programs are tailored to specific language-deficient populations. Some teach a specific set of skills applicable for the severely retarded; others train general language skills as part of a broader academic curriculum. Programs vary according to their relative

---

[1] "Recombinant generalization" is the ability to combine forms trained in examples to make novel combinations. For example, if "boy run" and "girl eat" are trained as examples of the noun-verb structure, the student should be able to produce the structures "girl run" and "boy eat." Recombinant generalization is an example of response generalization.

Table 1.   Training examples

Trained example	Characterization in syntactic training model	Characterization in semantic training model	Characterization in pragmatic[a] training model
Boy hit it	Noun-verb-pronoun	Agent action	Request or description
He hit ball	Pronoun-verb-noun	Agent action	Description
Cat sits chair	Noun-verb-noun	Agent action location	Description
Cat chases dog	Noun-verb-noun	Agent action object	Description
Cat likes me	Noun-verb-noun	Experiencer state complement	Description
Mommy sock	Noun-noun	Possessor-possessed or agent object	Request/command or description
Hit it	Verb-pronoun	Action object	Request/command

[a]Pragmatic function is usually determined by the context of the utterance. The designations here are arbitrary because context was not considered.

emphasis on stimulation or remediation, use of operant or nonoperant procedures, degree of structure, recommended format (i.e., one-to-one, group), required criterion levels, prerequisite skills, grammatical content, skills needed by trainer, assessment strategies, and emphasis on data collection.

Direct Interventions

In addition to individual training programs, some strategies rely on direct intervention with the target subject in natural environments. Experimental studies range from simple interventions to increase children's talking in social settings (e.g., Blake and Moss, 1967; Wolf, Risley, and Mees, 1964) to complex incidental teaching strategies designed to increase the use of specific grammatical forms (Hart and Risley, 1975; Rogers-Warren and Warren, 1980). In general, direct interventions have been highly successful in increasing verbalization rate, and in some instances the verbalization complexity, of moderately language-delayed populations. Use of direct intervention with severely delayed retarded populations is not documented extensively. Recent studies, however, have used environmental rearrangement to facilitate verbalizations by institutionalized mentally retarded adolescents. Halle, Marshall, and Spradlin (1979) used delays and prompts to teach residents to request trays during lunch and breakfast. Strong generalization to other settings and persons was demonstrated. VanBiervliet, Spangler, and Marshall (1979) reorganized a residential dining hall from cafeteria to family-style service and thereby increased conversation among residents and between residents and staff.

With few exceptions (e.g., Hart and Risley, 1975; Rogers-Warren and Warren, 1980), the primary data in direct intervention studies have been talking rates or use of specific utterances. Thus, the success of direct intervention strategies in teaching new linguistic repertoires is unknown. The limited data available on complexity do, however, suggest that rate increases are correlated with complexity (Hart, 1980). For example, Rogers-Warren and Warren (1980), using incidental teaching, increased grammatical complexity and its generalization far beyond the proportion that talking rate increased.

Generalized Effects of Training

Individualized training and direct interventions to increase rate have been effective in terms of acquisition of new responses and increasing verbalization rate. The generalized or secondary effects of these procedures, however, are virtually unknown. Successful remediation of language deficiency requires that the student use language in all day-to-day social settings. Thus, *generalized* increases in language skill should be the measure of success. If results from other behavioral intervention programs (Stokes and Baer, 1977) and from our recent work are indicative, much more effective training strategies are needed to change students' actual language use.

Thus, it is the study of generalization that is critical to the evaluation of language remediation. The goal is to teach or improve communication. Then the new skills must be used outside the training setting, with persons who are not trainers, to describe objects and events that usually are physically different from, but conceptually similar to, those described during training sessions.

Our recent work in analyzing the generalization resulting from one-to-one language training (Warren and Rogers-Warren, 1980; Warren, Rogers-Warren, Baer, and Guess, 1980) with language-delayed and mentally retarded children suggests that current language-training procedures typically do not yet produce sufficiently comprehensive communication skills. Thirty students, ranging from severely mentally retarded adolescents to mildly language-delayed preschoolers, were observed regularly in nontraining settings for at least 1 year. Records of students' speech were made in academic classrooms, special vocational classrooms, and homes or other living settings. Most students were observed in at least two settings for a total of four to six observations each week. Using a computer program (Owen and Rogers-Warren, 1977), verbatim samples were analyzed for evidence of generalization, by comparing the students' daily natural language samples with the examples trained in language teaching sessions.

Nearly all students were successfully trained to criterion (correct responses on at least 80% of all training trials during two or more consecutive sessions) on all training steps, and probes conducted across stimuli, trainers, and settings suggested that students generalized newly trained vocabulary and syntactic forms to circumstances similar to training sessions. Analyses of data collected in everyday unstructured settings revealed relatively high levels of generalization for trained nouns and verbs, suggesting that language training was effective in teaching new vocabulary. Simple syntactic forms (e.g., noun-verb) also generalized when multiple exemplars of them were trained across increasingly complex steps (e.g., noun-verb, noun-verb-noun, noun-verb-adjective-noun). More complex syntactic forms (e.g., pronoun-verb-noun, noun-verb, noun-verb-adjective-noun), however, did not generalize quickly or thoroughly. Yet when syntactic categories were combined to represent structures of similar complexity, and a broader class of forms was considered, the evaluation of training was more positive. For example, few subjects showed high levels of generalized usage of specific four-word utterances (examples: noun-verb-article-noun; noun-verb-adjective-noun; pronoun-verb-article-noun). When similar utterances were grouped and considered as a broader class (i.e., nominal verb (modifier) nominal), generalization from training was evident.

The number and diversity of examples required before generalization of the simplest form occurred varied greatly depending on the skills of the student. Profoundly retarded children required many exemplars (sometimes 30 or more) even at the earliest levels of training. In general, there were some positive effects of training but the effects were variable and often limited. Most students' use of specific, more complex language did not increase rapidly or extensively as a result of individual training. Few changes were noted in subjects' rate or topography of social verbal interaction.

An examination of the critical assumptions underlying current individualized programs suggests at least one reason for their failure to effect large-scale positive changes in students' communication skills. An implicit assumption shared by almost all programs is that language deficiency can be remediated by teaching students to produce the grammatical or semantic structures absent from their productive repertoires. Language is viewed as a formal structural system, and so the surface manifestations of the system are taught. But language is both a formal structural system and a social response mode. The social behaviors that typically co-occur with language may be critical to developing a communicative repertoire. Generalized use of newly trained examples of the code (syntax or semantics) may be dependent on sufficient skill in social interaction.

Traditionally, behaviorists have looked on failure to generalize from training to nontraining settings as incomplete transfer of skills across settings. Although this argument is essentially correct, the reasons for limited across-setting generalization merit further examination. Use of newly trained language structures may require more than simple generalization across stimuli; it may require particular social interaction skills as a basis or context for employing the linguistic code.

Communication involves the use of a rule system to order words (syntax) that have specific representational meanings alone and in combination (semantics) to express particular intentions of the speaker (pragmatics). Each aspect of communication is comprised of requisite skills that may require training with developmentally delayed populations. For example, the complex semantic system begins with acquisition of sufficient vocabulary to map the environment and the speaker's intentions, and progresses to the knowledge of relational concepts expressed by two or more words. Expressing intention may require a number of social interaction skills (turntaking, verbal and nonverbal responsiveness, knowledge of cultural social distance and interaction rules) as well as the ability to recognize and code specific intents (request, description, protests, etc.).

Establishing a comprehensive communication repertoire may require teaching both linguistic and social aspects of communication; however, few training programs specify training for anything except the structural aspects of language. Some training programs have attempted to teach relational concepts (agent-action, action-object, etc.) as precursors to training grammar (cf. Miller and Yoder, 1974); and a few interventionists have considered the social communication function of language in recommending training content and procedures (e.g., McLean and Snyder-McLean, 1978). Translation of these concerns into replicable and data-based teaching procedures, however, has not occurred as yet. At least in part, such translations have been limited by the current understanding of the interface among components of the social-communication system.

The study of child language has been marked by sequential acceptance of three models of language: syntax, semantics, and pragmatics. Potentially, integration of these models into a cohesive theory of language that describes the concurrent operations of the coding system (syntax), relational representation (semantics), and the social, communicative, and interactional aspects of language (pragmatics) is possible. While attempts at understanding the complexities of language continue, remediation efforts must proceed, based on whatever data or theories are currently available.

Direct interventions to increase rate have not required linguistic theories; they have relied strictly on reinforcement principles. The positive results evidenced in experimental studies to increase rate are encouraging. These procedures, however, have been applied to populations that displayed some linguistic competency, and for whom language use was possibly an issue of performance of known skills rather than acquisition of basic linguistic competencies. Thus, increased opportunities, use of salient models of appropriate language, and reinforcement for language use are effective for rate increases, but much more comprehensive research documenting their effects on complexity and generalized use of language outside the intervention setting are needed. Further analyses of interventions to increase rate should be particularly sensitive to changes in the verbal behavior of the intervention agent in addition to the changes in rates of prompts, models, and reinforcement that are prescribed by the intervention strategy. It is possible that such interventions alter the linguistic and social environment in ways that are not targeted by the intervention but that are critical to the acquisition and display of increasingly complex language by the student.

In summary, there are two current models of language intervention: individual training in linguistic structures, and interventions to increase rate of language display. They represent somewhat dichotomous approaches to the problem of teaching language. Individualized instruction teaches language structures; direct intervention increases the performance of linguistic responses. Individualized instruction may also encompass concept learning, but it frequently does not prepare the child for everyday social interactions in which language is required. Direct intervention utilizes the communicative context by intervening in the settings in which interactions occur, but may alter the context by offering high levels of prompts and reinforcement so that the child experiences an environment similar but not identical to day-to-day conversational contexts. Some research has shown that individualized training does not readily produce a generalized, comprehensive communication repertoire, but there is insufficient documentation of the effects of direct intervention to compare the effectiveness of the two techniques.

ENVIRONMENTS AND NORMAL ACQUISITION: A CHANGING FOCUS

Since the early 1960s, theories of child language have focused on nonenvironmental variables. Language acquisition was viewed as a result of cognition (Slobin, 1973; Wells, 1974), and external variables such as reinforcement, modeling, and the topography of language heard by the child were considered only minimally important (e.g., Brown and Bellugi, 1964). Recently, that perspective of language development has changed. Although operant variables such as reinforcement still are not recognized as viable forces in the processes of acquisition, other environmental variables related to caregivers' language and responsivity are viewed as important.[2] There has been a critical shift from studying child language in isolation to studying it in the context of dynamic interactions with caregivers and peers. Thus, the role of the environment has become a specific concern of those

---

[2]From a behaviorist's point of view, *reinforcement, responsivity,* and *environmental support* may be interchangeable terms because they represent a common positive consequence for language use that may serve to increase its frequency and complexity.

interested in natural acquisition. Two classes of environmental variables have been examined: characteristics of the language directed to language-learning children, and patterns of interaction among children and their caregivers.

Structural characteristics of child-directed language were studied first. Researchers (cf. Broen, 1972; Drach, 1969; Phillips, 1973; Remick, 1976; Sachs, Brown, and Salerno, 1976; Snow, 1972) began by describing the characteristics of mothers' speech when they were talking to young children. For the most part, these studies utilized grammatical analyses and measures of complexity similar to those employed in preceding studies, and did not focus on specific interactions between child and adult in the context of conversations. Mothers' speech was considered as input, child speech as output. Children between 8 months and 12 years were observed, and the speech of mothers, nonmothers, fathers, and peers was analyzed. Cumulatively, the results of these studies documented that speech to children was simple and redundant, filled with brief utterances that are repeated, apparently for clarity and emphasis. Child-directed speech contained many questions, many imperatives, few tense markers, and few complex grammatical constructions. Mothers' speech was about the "here and now" and mapped the current environment and actions of the child. In addition, the pitch of child-directed speech was higher and had an exaggerated intonation pattern that perhaps served to engage the child's attention.

Consistently, it was found that adult and older child speakers adjusted their input according to the age and linguistic abilities of the child listener (cf. Phillips, 1973; Sachs and Devin, 1976; Shatz and Gelman, 1973). Importantly, this adjustment does not take place until the child begins to respond to the mothers' speech, usually about the time the child begins to communicate vocally (around 8-12 months of age). Mothers' speech varies systematically with increases in the child's linguistic abilities. The level of mothers' expansions and repetitions corresponds with small changes in children's linguistic skills (Cross, 1975; Newport, 1976). Mother speech is not perfectly tuned to any single aspect of the child's abilities (Cross, 1977), however, and factors such as activity and intent of mothers' speech influence the structural characteristics of mothers' language in a given communication episode.

A small number of studies document the specific effects of mothers' adjustment of the structural characteristics of their language on the subsequent language acquisition by their children. For example, recent studies in which expansions of child utterances were systematically manipulated (Nelson, Carskaddon, and Bonvillian, 1973; Nelson, 1978) have reported predicted effects on the acquisition of specific forms. Convincing naturalistic evidence showing correlations between aspects of motherese (adjusted mother speech) and aspects of child language development has been offered by Nelson (1973), Newport, Gleitman, and Gleitman (1975), and Furrow, Nelson, and Benedict (1979); however, these data are not comprehensive enough to offer a definitive test of the natural function of motherese. It is apparent that mothers adjust their speech in ways that are facilitative to child language acquisition; but the specific child behaviors that prompt these adjustments and their influence on children's language learning have not been delineated.

In part, this evidence of adjustment of mothers' speech led to the second type of investigations of mothers' language. Studies describing the structural characteristics of mothers' speech to their language-learning children had grown out of the syntactic-semantic models of language acquisition popular during the late 1960s and early 1970s. The second area of study reflected studies of mother-infant interaction (cf. Bell, 1968; Lewis and Freedle, 1973; Lewis and Rosenblum, 1974) that described interactions as dynamic and bidirectional: mother and child each influencing the other's actions. Although the significance of vocal behavior in mother-infant interactions had been emphasized (cf. Bowlby, 1969; Bateson, 1975; Brazleton, Koslowski, and Main, 1974), until recently few linguists had examined the interaction patterns between mothers and children for their potential contribution to language acquisition. Mothers' language had been considered as a somewhat preadjusted input, rather than as immediately responsive to the specific behavior of the child. Moerk (1972, 1977) proposed an interactional structure encompassing feedback cycles and calibration processes. He sought to document this model from naturalistic data on mothers' adjustment of their language within conversational episodes, and demonstrated facilitation of children's learning of specific information. Moerk (1977) concluded that mothers systematically provide linguistic information, attend to the child's response, and acknowledge, correct, or elaborate that response. Questions are used to test linguistic skills. Mothers model utterances that accurately translate the immediate environment for the child, and then test the child's understanding. Moerk's data showed several types of common teaching interactions in mother-child exchanges, and a large number of related but idiosyncratic strategies.

Schachter's (1979) study of black and white advantaged and disadvantaged mother-child dyads concurs with Moerk's supposition that mothers actively teach language as they interact with their children. Schachter's view of the interaction is slightly broader than Moerk's; it focuses on language but concludes that the mothers are supportive of the ''whole child,'' and integrate language learning with other social and conceptual learning. Her conclusion that skilled mothers support and facilitate learning is based on analyses of patterns of interaction. Frequency of many specific types of utterances did not vary widely among the three groups of mother-child dyads studied, but the specific patterns of interactions did: skilled mothers used sequences of questions and expansions to aid their children in communicating, and sequentially requested increasingly more complex utterances as the child's skills increased. These mothers were less directive and more inclined to offer the child substitutions or gentle corrections.

Both Schachter (1979) and Moerk (1977) guessed about useful environments for language learning. Schachter concluded that language is best taught and learned when the child is already engaged in communication and is focused on the interaction. Playful settings, those in which specific tasks such as feeding and dressing do not need to be accomplished, are more likely to engender facilitative interaction, because both mother and child may focus on the linguistic or conceptual task at hand. Talking and pleasant interactions occur more frequently in such settings. Moerk and Schachter concur about the usefulness of games, rhymes, and ritualized role-playing in language learning. Tasks for which the child already knows the routine allow the child to participate without specific attention to the task, and thus permit full attention to linguistic information being presented and offer opportunities to learn about the turn-taking structure of conversations.

Data on the interactional aspects of mother-child conversation and their effects on language development are much sparser than those on the structural aspects of mother and child speech. Thus, the conclusions about this area of research must be even more tentative. It seems that in addition to the adjustment of the structural aspects of language, mothers accommodate their children's language-learning attempts, responding to attempts to communicate by structuring interactions to support and facilitate transmission of information and control of the environment. The pattern of interaction, perhaps more than the frequency of any particular type of linguistic response, gives the child information that is immediately useful, allows the child to test hypotheses about language or practice using new information, and provides feedback about language. Except for Schachter's comparisons between advantaged and disadvantaged families, there are no data to document the outcomes of differences in interaction style and patterns of interaction. Schachter's data seem to indicate that there are differences, but her data are too limited to allow extensive or strong conclusions.

These studies of mother-child linguistic interactions support the conclusion that responsivity of the mother to her child's communication attempts and level of linguistic competence is a force in language acquisition. Responsive adjustment of their speech complexity apparently is a natural process that mothers, adults, and older children perform (Snow, 1977) without conscious intention, although some mothers are more adept at accommodation and facilitation of the child's attempts to convey intentions than others (Schachter, 1979). Mothers' adjustments of their linguistic and conceptual complexity are made unobtrusively, and teaching is imbedded in the flow of conversation, closely bound to the child's interest, and guided by the child's communication attempts.

Interestingly, the current view of environmental variables in language acquisition offers a potential intersect between previously divergent psycholinguistic and operant models of language learning. Although the current psycholinguistic model does not describe mother-child interactions with terms such as *reinforcers*, *stimulus control*, and *shaping*, it does in fact identify these processes. For example, when mothers facilitate their children's attempts to communicate by offering alternative interpretations of the utterance, and allow them to indicate their intentions by imitating part or all of the model, they are probably shaping new, more complex child utterances. The use of modeling is documented in many naturalistic studies of child language (cf. Bloom, Hood, and Lightbown, 1974; Shipley, Smith, and Gleitman, 1969). Moerk's data on feedback cycles suggest that parents provide consistent information about the function of children's utterances, if not about the specific form. Psycholinguistic data purport to describe the focus of language teaching, and in doing so, in fact describe the probably central contingencies of reinforcement. Apparently, the primary concern of both mother and child in these interactions is successful communication and continuance of the interaction. Early research concluding that reinforcement was not a critical variable in natural language acquisition (e.g., Brown and Bellugi, 1964) was based on an absence of contingencies related to syntactic correctness rather than to functional use. The current functional or pragmatic analysis of language (Bates, 1976; Dore, 1975; Halliday, 1975; Searle, 1969) seems to be entirely consistent with operant (Skinner, 1957) principles regarding the language functions of requesting and describing. These and other issues relating to the convergence of some aspects of behavioral and psycholinguistic models are discussed more fully by Moerk (1977) and Hart (1980). This convergence is mentioned in the current context to point out that two separate paradigms have arrived, on the basis of different data, almost 20 years apart, at a very similar conclusion about environmental interactions and their role in language acquisition.

ENVIRONMENTS AND LANGUAGE ACQUISITION BY ATYPICAL CHILDREN

In contrast to the rich literature describing variables affecting language acquisition by normal children, few studies are directed at atypical children, and only a minority of these studies focus on the characteristics of mother-child interactions that might influence language learning. Early studies of retarded language development focused on the behavior of normal adults with retarded children of different competencies (cf. Siegel, 1963a; Siegel and Harkins, 1963; Siegel, 1963b; Spradlin and Rosenberg, 1964). These studies concluded that adult speech directed to retarded children used briefer utterances, more repetitions, and less complex structures than speech directed to normal children. Language directed to high-level retarded individuals was systematically more complex than language directed to lower-level retarded individuals. In general, the studies reported findings quite similar to more recent studies of normal children (cf. Broen, 1972; Lord, 1975; Nelson, 1973; Snow, 1972): adults adjust their linguistic input according to the perceived competencies of the listener they are addressing.

Some recent studies (Buium, Rynders, and Turnure, 1974; Kogan, Wimberger, and Bobbitt, 1969; Marshall, Hegrenes, and Goldstein, 1973; Rondal, 1978) have compared the maternal linguistic environments of normal and mentally retarded children. Unfortunately, normal and handicapped subjects in most of these studies were matched on the basis of chronological age rather than linguistic skills (a single exception is Rondal, 1978). Hence, the results indicating differences in verbal environments of retarded and normal children of the same age are confounded by mothers' adaptation of their responses to children of different abilities. For example, Rondal (1978) pointed out that in a frequently cited study by Buium et al. (1974), comparing mothers' speech to normal and Down's syndrome 2-year-olds, many of the Down's syndrome children would have been nonverbal; the normal children of the same age typically would have been combining two words. Mothers' language to children at these two levels of acquisition would be different.

Measures of the child's language are rare in studies comparing interactions of typical and atypical children, and it is difficult to specify the exact differences in language skills between groups. This aspect in design is an important consideration in evaluating the results of comparisons based on complexity measures of mothers' speech. Because relatively less research has been done on variation in interaction patterns across age and linguistic skill levels, the effects of the linguistic ability mismatch cannot be estimated. Yet the paucity of research with mothers and handicapped children makes consideration of these studies necessary in spite of their methodological flaws.

The most detailed examinations of the structural characteristics of mothers' speech to handicapped children have been offered by Buium et al. (1974) and Rondal (1978). The results of these studies are contrastive, apparently because of the method of matching handicapped and nonhandicapped children. In the Buium et al. study, children were matched for chronological age rather than language abilities, and it was concluded that the verbal environment of Down's syndrome children differed from that of normal children along several dimensions. Down's syndrome children were exposed to more utterances, yet the utterances were shorter and less complex than those directed to normal children of the same age. There was also a higher frequency of grammatically incomplete sentences, imperatives, and single-word responses. In the Rondal (1978) study, typical and Down's syndrome children were matched by mean length of utterance (MLU) rather than age, and it was found that maternal speech to normal and Down's children did *not* differ in terms of mothers' MLU, type-token ratio, or a variety of syntactic, semantic, and pragmatic aspects of language. That is, maternal speech was significantly influenced by children's language level regardless of their normal or handicapped status. Rondal's findings confirmed the reports of mothers' adjustment of their language's structural variables according to the linguistic skills of their children, found in studies of normal children. Rondal argued convincingly that previous studies with handicapped populations, including the Buium et al. study, have failed to consider differences in mother speech that occur as a result of specific child behavior (i.e., linguistic performance) rather than developmental status (retarded or normal) of the subjects.

Although none of the studies of handicapped children has examined interactions for teaching patterns, such as those described by Schachter (1979) and Moerk (1977) with normal children, several studies have measured variables in mothers' language that might affect language-learning interactions. Marshall, Hegrenes, and Goldstein (1973) analyzed the verbalizations of mothers to normal and handicapped children, using Skinner's classification of verbal operants: mands, tacts, and intraverbal and echoic responses (Skinner, 1957). Mothers of retarded children used more mands (requests for behavior) than normal mothers; mothers of normal children used more tacts (descriptive statements) and made greater use of verbal operants. Kogan et al. (1969) also reported that giving specific orders occurred much more frequently in mothers of retarded children, and that the most frequent verbal interactions in mothers of normal children were statements of agreement or acknowledgement of their children's activities, and statements of their own thoughts and ideas. These interactions were ranked sixth and seventh for mothers of retarded children, but first and second for normal mothers. The findings of Buium et al. also support the characterization of mothers of retarded children as more demanding and less descriptive.

Terdal, Jackson, and Garner (1976) and Rondal (1978) offer plausible explanations of stylistic differences between mothers with normal children and those with handicapped children. Lowered responsiveness has been observed in several studies comparing normal and retarded children (Terdal et al., 1976; Kogan et al., 1969; Vietze et al., 1978). Possibly, lowered responsiveness prompts mothers to increase directiveness and structure in interactions with their children. This seems particularly plausible because Terdal et al. found that responsiveness increased in mental age and correlated with a decrease in mother-directiveness. Mothers of retarded children might reasonably need to issue more controlling statements to their children, if the children were not under instructional control; or they might need to assist children with tasks that are difficult for them, but easily accomplished by normal children of the same age.

The dyadic interactions observed between language-learning children and their mothers probably are the result of patterns established in infancy. Many patterns of interaction between infant and caregiver (vocalizations, eye contact, fine body movements, and gross body movements) are reciprocally coordinated (Ainsworth, 1967; Bateson, 1975; Bowlby, 1969; Lewis and Freedle, 1973). Vocalization between infants and mothers seems to establish and maintain dyadic contact (Mahoney and Seely, 1976). Early interaction patterns gradually increase in complexity and possibly lead to linguistic communication patterns (cf. Bruner, 1975; Bullowa, 1979).

Vietze et al. (1978) offered evidence that at least some part of the typical reciprocal vocal patterns of mothers and infants may be disrupted in the case of developmentally delayed infants. Although normal and delayed infants behaved quite similarly until about 12 months of age, thereafter, lower-functioning developmentally delayed children showed less differentiation between their mothers' vocalizing and not vocalizing than the higher-functioning children. Because the mothers in the two groups did not seem to differ, the children's patterns were assumed to be responsible for the increasingly atypical pattern of interaction between mothers and children.

Almost no research analyzes the contingencies existing in mothers' interactions with their atypical children. Because there is no empirical basis (other than that implied from the studies discussed above) from which to draw conclusions about the disruptions that may occur in mother-child interactions, the following descriptions of interactions with atypical children are offered with some caution.

First, it must be remembered that mothers accommodate their speech to fit the skills of their retarded children to a similar extent that mothers of normal children do. The differences in style (increased control, decreased descriptions) may result from the limited motor and cognitive skills of the atypical child. More instruction is required to control the child's behavior and to assist in task completion. Schachter (1979) observed that skillful mothers follow the lead of their child, responding to initiations with related comments. The delayed child initiates less (Kogan et al., 1969), and thus, offers the mother fewer opportunities to elaborate or comment on topics of apparent interest to the child. The increased number of instructions may result because the child is less likely to respond verbally and the mother uses instruction-compliance episodes as a means of maintaining the child's engagement in a task and in the interaction. Schachter (1979), Bruner, Roy, and Ratner (1980), and others have argued for the importance of shared contexts as a basis for linguistic interactions. The less responsive and possibly less active developmentally delayed child is likely to participate in fewer interactions with the environment that would provide the joint focus necessary for mothers' language teaching. If language is most easily taught in the context of ongoing communication, as Schachter suggests, delayed infants may simply offer fewer opportunities for their mothers to teach them, and thus delay language even further.

A SOCIAL INTERACTION-BASED MODEL OF LANGUAGE LEARNING

The literature on language intervention and on normal and atypical mother-child inter-actions suggests several conclusions about the processes involved in language learning and what is necessary for successful intervention to facilitate learning. Training grammatical or semantic structures as a means of increasing overall communicative competency does not necessarily result in immediate or extensive increases in students' actual language use. The accumulating evidence from analyses of generalization resulting from individualized language training indicates that such intervention strategies may not be sufficient to remediate serious language delays. Training on specific structures does not generalize readily across settings and persons, and students typically do not increase either their rates of language use or overall responsiveness to verbal initiations from others in their environment (Rogers-Warren and Warren, 1980). Interventions designed to produce increases in rates of language display offer a possibly promising technique for facilitating the development of communication. There are few data on changes in linguistic complexity and generality or maintenance of rate-intervention effects, however, and any conclusions must be tentative ones.

There are consistent data documenting mothers' adjustment of the structural characteristics of their language to accommodate to their children's language skills. The small number of studies analyzing mother-child interactions in terms of possible teaching strategies further suggest that the child's language acquisition is facilitated by an environment that adjusts to the child's interests and skills. Naturalistic analyses of mother-child interactions that demonstrate cause-effect relationships between specific mother strategies and child acquisition are lacking. A considerable number of experimental studies, however, suggest that systematic changes in mothers' use of specific teaching techniques (modeling, expansions, expatiations) accelerate children's acquisition of specific forms (Schumaker and Sherman, 1978). In addition, recent analyses of mother-child interaction have identified sequences of mother behavior that might serve teaching functions; these studies show the active use of at least some strategies that have been examined in experimental studies. Data from parent-based intervention programs corroborate the premise that systematic alteration of parent behavior can facilitate language acquisition by handicapped children (MacDonald et al., 1974; Seitz and Stewart, 1975). Possibly, the naturalistic analyses of interactions between mothers and their handicapped children offer additional evidence about the importance of specific teaching strategies, as well as adjustment of structural aspects of language to support acquisition. These analyses verify that mothers with atypical children adjust the complexity of their language to fit the skills exhibited by their children in the same way that mothers of normal children do. The most significant difference between mothers with normal children and those with handicapped children is the degree of directedness and conversely the lower rate of nondirective and descriptive language posited by Moerk (1977) and Schachter (1979) to be important aspects of facilitative interactions.

Language learning occurs in the course of dyadic interactions between caregiver and child (possibly, any number of adults may fulfill the basic teaching functions because the literature on fathers and nonmothers indicates that at least adjustment of the structural input to children is done by all sophisticated speakers when addressing less competent children). The roots of language-learning interactions seem to lie in the pattern of interaction established during infancy (Bruner, 1975). That pattern involves mutual attention, joint action, turn-taking, and accommodation between the two participants. From these early interactions, the child learns to behave responsively (vocally or nonverbally) in the presence of adults, and to cease behaving periodically in order to give the other member of the dyad opportunities to behave (Vietze et al., 1978). Implicitly, the child learns the cues for participation, and, in coming under the stimulus control of these cues (which may be facial, vocal, or gestural), learns the turn-taking structure of conversational interactions. One possible explanation for the lowered responsiveness observed in handicapped children is that they have failed to take turns in mother-infant interactions, and their behavior is not controlled by the verbal and nonverbal cues that affect the behavior of normal children.

They do not respond because events that signal to normal children that a response is appropriate do not function in the same way for them. The more obvious the cue is (such as a question or a direct instruction), the more likely the handicapped child is to respond. Mothers may use explicit cues because these cues are more efficient in eliciting a response than descriptive or nondirective statements. Intervention studies demonstrating the effectiveness of prompts and modeling plus contingencies for appropriate verbal responses seem to support this premise: if the cues for vocal responses and the contingencies for reinforcement are apparent, even severely language-deficient children respond at much higher rates (Hart and Risley, 1975; Hart and Rogers-Warren, 1978; Rogers-Warren and Warren, 1980).

To learn language through dyadic interactions, the child must be an active participant. Several types of participation are needed. First, the child must interact with the ecological environment in order to establish a context for teaching and for his or her own talking. Nelson (1973) observed that children talk about what they are doing as they do it. The child who actively explores the environment and uses available toys and materials will have much to talk about. Interacting with the environment informs the caregiver of the child's focus and interest at a particular moment, and thus provides a context in which the caregiver can provide salient linguistic information. Schachter's (1979) observations that mothers tend to follow the child's lead and speak about the events and objects of his or her immediate interest suggest that the child's activities are the basis for much teaching.

Second, the child must interact with the caregiver. These interactions can take a variety of forms. The most basic is visual attention to the caregiver, signaling the child's availability as a listener. The common patterns of mother-infant interaction seem to lead directly to the type of signaling required in verbal communication: mutual or sequential gaze, orientation toward the speaker, or participation in joint activities. Kaye (1976) pointed out that mothers are quite adept at presenting information or requests during a teaching task at moments when the child's attention is focused on the mother or the task. The child's attention not only indicates to the mother that a particular moment is suitable for teaching,[3] but also may increase the likelihood that the information the mother presents will be salient to the child. Attention to the caregiver during and immediately following child vocalizations, while the child's attention is still focused, also seems to be important for feedback from the caregiver to be effective—to be informative and reinforcing.

Child interaction must include attempts to communicate with the caregiver, but these attempts need not always be verbal. If the child signals interest or communicative intention by gesture or vocalization, the caregiver has an opportunity to support the child's attempt with feedback and to offer new, related information while the child is interested. Bates (1976), Rees (1975), and others working in pragmatics have suggested that vocal and nonverbal communications allow the mother an opportunity to offer an interpretation of the child's communicative intent, as well as to model appropriate verbal responses. For example, when a child points to a toy placed on a high shelf, the mother may indicate the name of the toy (''doll'') and interpret the intent of the child's gesture as a request (''Oh, you want the doll'') or a description (''Yes, that's a doll'').

---

[3]Throughout this section, ''teaching'' is used to mean simply the presentation of linguistic information, rather than the use of elaborated routines with specific child response requirements such as those reported by Moerk (1977).

Vocal initiations and responses need to occur at a moderate rate to allow the mother sufficient opportunities to provide feedback and additional information. Although mothers seldom negate children's utterances for being poorly formed (Brown and Hanlon, 1970), they do offer models of correct utterances and expansions of the child's verbalization (cf. Nelson, 1973). A great deal of mother speech is a direct response to child initiations, particularly questions (Baldwin and Baldwin, 1973). If children do not speak frequently, as both initiators and responders, opportunities to provide feedback about the content and form of their utterances will be much fewer, and the match between mother input and child linguistic competence, thought to be critical in facilitating language learning (Schiefelbusch, in press; Hunt, 1961), will be difficult to obtain.

Nonverbal responses also can indicate the child's understanding of mother verbalizations. Potentially, low rates of nonverbal responses impede the adjustment of mother speech to fit the child's skills, in the same way that low rates of verbal initiations and responses do. Nonverbal responses allow children to maintain participation in the interaction when they are unable to formulate a verbal reply. The nonverbal response is a way of taking one's turn by utilizing the maximum support of the context. Mothers of very young children typically give many instructions (Baldwin and Baldwin, 1973), apparently structuring the interaction to allow the child to participate with a minimum of productive language. Two-year-olds often interpret anomalous mother utterances as instructions, when it is unclear what type of verbal reply is expected (Shatz, 1975). For example, a 2-year-old might respond to the rhetorical question "Can 2-year-olds close the door?" by closing the door, rather than answering the question. A shift to non-instructional speech (questions, comments, etc.) occurs as the child's productive repertoire increases (Rogers-Warren et al., 1979).

Nonverbal responses accompanied by imitative responses may be opportunities for children to talk about what they are doing, with maximal support from the environment; and they may provide particularly salient opportunities to learn a new word or structure while performing a related action. Instructions are imitated only a little less frequently than descriptive forms of mother speech (Nelson, 1973). Because high levels of mother instruction and of child imitation tend to occur at about the same age, the pairing of imitation and requested action may be an important aspect of early language learning.

Imitations offer children means of participating in conversations and fulfilling their turns even with a minimum of linguistic knowledge. If the mother has addressed a topic of current focus to the child (as is likely), the child can imitate within a specific linguistic context, with attention focused on some aspect of the activity described by the imitative utterance. This natural pairing, resulting from the mother's provision of linguistic information relevant to the child's activity, may account, in part, for the particular function of imitation in early learning.

The role of imitation in language learning has long been a topic of discussion among language theorists. The current explanation of the importance of imitation has not been tested in any published reports. An examination of this premise would require noting the context in which imitation occurred and determining if subjects who imitated in the context describing their own actions while performing them acquired those particular imitated forms more rapidly than other subjects who did not map their actions during imitation or after. It is especially interesting that many of the experimental studies of elicited imitations have examined imitation with no nonverbal communicative context.

In summary, the child has a number of options that may be used to participate in interactions with the caregiver: signaling attention, nonverbal responses and initiations, imitations, and spontaneous verbal initiations and responses. Whatever response mode is selected, it is important that children fulfill their turns and indicate their interest in the ongoing interaction. With acquisition of new skills, the child's participation should become increasingly verbal and more sophisticated in terms of form and content.

The process that occurs in natural mother-child interactions seems to be very close to the shaping account of language acquisition offered by behaviorists (Moerk, 1977; Sherman, 1971). The child's attempts to communicate are met with reinforcement—with encouragement and support in the form of additional information (expansions), confirmations, and prompts for elaboration. Gradually, the mothers' demands shift so that increasingly complex utterances are expected and reinforced (Schachter, 1979). In order for this process to occur, the child must respond to the caregiver at a reasonable rate. The rules and skills (always respond, signal attention, etc.) learned in early nonverbal exchanges between mother and child may be important bases for the later language learning.

Several typical characteristics of developmentally delayed children may impede or disrupt the natural process that supports language learning. First, if developmentally delayed children are less responsive, their lower rates of verbal and nonverbal initiations and responses reduce their caregivers' opportunities for teaching. To maintain a level of responding, mothers may use more directive speech, and thus less nondirected or descriptive language. Lower levels of responsiveness may also make matching linguistic input to child output more difficult, so that the fine tuning present in normal mother-child interactions is less accurate with delayed children. (There is no evidence yet to verify this premise, however.)

Second, children who are not under instructional control (i.e., do not usually follow their mothers' instructions) may simply require more instructions. The relative difficulty of everyday tasks for the developmentally delayed child, and their typically shorter attention span, might both contribute to the need for additional mother instructions. If Schachter's (1979) assumption that language teaching occurs most effectively and most frequently when there are no tasks to be accomplished and at the lead of the child, there may be fewer opportunities for teaching developmentally delayed children, who have greater difficulty and require more time to complete simple tasks and who interact less freely with the environment and their caregivers.

Third, the same deficiencies that define developmental delay (difficulty in acquiring and generalizing new information, short-term memory constraints, and difficulty making small discriminations between similar stimuli) make the learning of languages in interactions more difficult than it is for the normal child. If children do not easily discriminate fine cues for behavior, they must rely on more obvious cues. In the case of child responsiveness, the child may rely only on direct cues, such as questions or instructions, rather than responding to finer cues, such as pauses in the mothers' speech, content of language other than instructions, facial expressions, and gestures that indicate to the normal child an opportunity to speak. Attention to fine cues in mother behavior seems necessary, if the descriptions of mother feedback and support for verbal behavior are correct. Mothers seldom praise or punish verbalizations, but typically provide corrective feedback in the form of models or restatements of the child's utterance, usually in a warm, supportive tone of voice. Unless the child is able to discriminate the content of the mother's feedback, it may not function as reinforcement or feedback.

Along these same lines, behaviors that support or serve a reinforcing function in normal interactions (continued conversation, eye contact, adult proximity) may not serve the same function with delayed children. No evidence suggests directly and clearly that adult attention is less reinforcing for developmentally delayed children; however, a wealth of literature (see *Journal of Applied Behavior Analysis*, 1968–1980) attests to improved responding by retarded children when tangible reinforcers are provided contingent on target behaviors. Furthermore, the majority of direct-training studies teaching the structural components of language, and interventions to increase rates, have used highly discriminable reinforcement as a part of the intervention procedures (Hubbell, 1977). Although the evidence is indirect, at least a part of the developmentally delayed child's difficulties in learning language in natural interactions may be due simply to a lack of functional reinforcers.

A model for language learning based on child-caregiver interactions must take into account the characteristics of mothers' behavior with their children, and the differences in responding by normal and atypical children. Although mother-child interactions are dynamic, and the behavior of each participant affects the behavior of the other, the accumulating evidence describing mother-child interactions suggests that mothers are fairly adept at adapting their styles to fit the output provided by their children. For example, Jones (1977) pointed out that Down's syndrome children participate in prelinguistic communication with their mothers, because their mothers are adept at providing easy opportunities. Schachter (1979) concurs with this view and offers a description of mothers' "scaffolding": surrounding their children's attempts to communicate with support and additional information to make the intent of the children's utterances clear. Increased directiveness reported for mothers with delayed children may also be considered as evidence of mothers' accommodation to their children's responses. Reports of parents' modifications of their behavior to their children (Cheseldine and McConkey, 1979; MacDonald et al., 1974; Schumaker and Sherman, 1978) verify that adults can alter their interactions to encourage verbalizations by their children.

On the other hand, developmentally delayed children may be notably less adept in conversational interactions, because they lack some skills that enable participation in interactions and that potentially facilitate rapid learning of new conceptual and linguistic information.

Figure 1 presents a model of the child's behavior in dyadic linguistic interactions. Only the child's behavior is shown, because it is assumed that most adults will respond competently to the child's behaviors. Three assumptions underlie our conception of the ability to learn in dyadic interactions: 1) Children must actively engage in interactions, by approaching potential conversants, by signaling attention, by listening, and by attempting to respond whenever it is appropriate. 2) The turn-taking structure of conversations is essential. Thus, children should fulfill their turns with whatever appropriate response is possible. Responsiveness and discrimination of subtle cues for turns underlie this structure and must be learned before the children can engage effectively in conversation. 3) Within

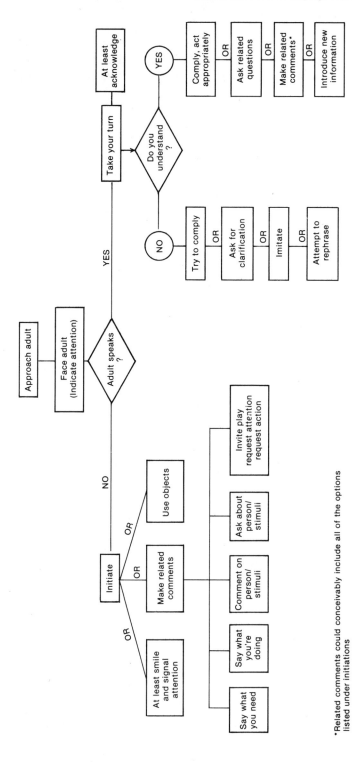

*Related comments could conceivably include all of the options
listed under initiations

Figure 1.   Conversation-based language learning model.

the guidelines of conversational interactions, children use particular strategies to practice language as well as to convey communicative intent. For example, initiations may take several forms: requests, description of own action, description of other action, invitations to joint activity, and information seeking. These forms represent major pragmatic functions of language (Dore, 1975) used by adult and normal child speakers. Responses may be either verbal or nonverbal. Nonverbal responses are primarily related to compliance to specific or implied instructions as a means of indicating understanding of the previous adult utterance. This strategy has been observed in very young children (Shatz, 1975) and seems to be viable both in testing comprehension of utterances and in indicating attention and engagement to the conversational partner. Verbal response options include those pragmatic responses available for initiations and some specific language-learning strategies: imitation, request for clarifications, and requests for related information (Mahoney and Seeley, 1976).

Attentional processes are implied but not specified within the model. Attention is essential for all of the interactive behaviors suggested, but it is difficult to characterize it separately from the interactive behaviors.

In addition to the model, ten rules for conversation-based language learning are proposed. The rules are listed below.

1. Find a listener, approach, and indicate your attention.
2. Initiate to the listener by using language or nonverbal cue.
3. Express your needs or comment on ongoing events.
4. Respond. Take your turn however you can (verbally, imitatively, nonverbally).
5. Check your information using whatever strategy is appropriate and possible and solicit additional information.
6. Use the most complex form you can when speaking.
7. Look for the referent, the contextual cues, the relationship, etc., mentioned by the speaker.
8. Listen for new things and repeat them and/or query your listener about them.
9. Let your listener know when you understand or fail to understand anything that is said.
10. Exhibit all the above at an appropriate rate.

The first four rules require the display of particular observable behaviors. The remaining six rules are less explicit, primarily because they involve attentional, discriminative, and linguistic comprehension skills that may not prove to be immediately observable. Components of the last six rules could be described behaviorally, however, and, if so, procedures to teach them could be devised. These components might be trained within the context of individualized instruction typically used in teaching the syntactic and semantic aspects of the language system, and generalization to less structured conversational formats could be carefully programmed using already available technology (Stokes and Baer, 1977).

Logically, if children are able to participate in conversations following these rules, making decisions in the manner suggested by the model, they should be in sufficient contact with a supportive teaching environment to learn language. The model does not include underlying cognitive functions often posited to be an important aspect of language acquisition, and so may seem less then completely explanatory. Perhaps some level of cognitive skill is necessary for language learning, but there is no empirical research to document specifically what level is necessary or how these skills can be taught. In the absence of such information, the current model is offered as a description of the socially based aspects of language learning, recognizing that it may not be a comprehensive statement about the conditions necessary and sufficient for learning—but that it may work, nonetheless.

IDEAL ENVIRONMENTS FOR
LANGUAGE LEARNING BY DEFICIENT POPULATIONS

The normal interactions of mothers and children represent an apparently adequate environment for most children to acquire language. In the case of children who are not acquiring language normally, adjustments in the environment or specific intervention with the child may be necessary to make the normal child-rearing environment function as a language-learning setting. Although large-scale topography and rate changes in parent support for language (increased questions, increased prompts, use of material reinforcement) have been effective in increasing children's levels of verbalization (Harris, 1975), it is suggested that interventions to teach specific child behaviors are a more acceptable long-term strategy for effecting language learning. The literature on generalization by severely deficient populations suggests that generalization across persons, settings, and events is sometimes difficult to obtain and is not a certain outcome of intervention efforts (Stokes and Baer, 1977; Warren et al., 1980). Although increased rates of language may change child behavior, there is no evidence to suggest that parents effectively maintain their increased prompting across settings and events. Thus, the procedures may work while they are being actively employed, but the generality of their employment, and consequently of their effect, is unknown. More importantly, intervention strategies that rely on major systematic changes in the environment do not necessarily prepare the child to respond in other more typical settings where the intervention is not in effect. Parent-based or therapist-based techniques typically place the child in the role of only the respondent, and do not teach social interaction or pragmatic skills that would further future interactions. Thus, there may be immediate and impressive increases in child verbalizations, but the maintenance of these effects, and the usefulness of the intervention to future language learning, is unknown. These assumptions are clearly untested with parents, although the conclusions are consistent with findings about the impact of individualized training on the structural aspects of language (Rogers-Warren and Warren, 1980).

The ideal environment for the language-deficient child is one in which learning to learn is stressed, rather than learning answers. The environment supports the child's active exploration and description of the setting in much the same way that mothers support and accommodate their children's attempts to learn about the environment. The singular difference in environments for developmentally delayed children may be the amount of effort required to ensure that the adult continues to support approximations of communication without rigidly placing the child in the role of the respondent. The ideal teaching environment contains persons who do not respond naturally to the child's lowered responsiveness, but who seek to increase responsiveness without becoming unusually directive of the child's behavior.

An ideal environment incorporates the characteristics of normal language-learning environments: appropriate language models presented when the child's attention is focused on relevant aspects of the setting or interaction that the linguistic model describes; frequent opportunities to respond and appropriate cues for responding; and a supportive, responsive caregiver who follows the child's lead and consistently provides feedback about the child's attempts to communicate. The environment may need to be counterbalanced against the characteristics of developmentally delayed children that typically disrupt the normal teaching processes. Because the child is typically less responsive, the environment should evoke and support verbalizations in more obvious ways. The caregiver works harder at doing the things that work with normal children, but should not preclude the types of interaction that support learning. For example, the environment needs to solicit the child's attention to make a context for comment. It must contain things the child wants so there will be a need to request. The same objects or events that are of interest to the normal child may not attract a developmentally delayed child, so materials should be provided and the child's interest observed. The caregiver ought to notice what the child finds attractive and use instances of focused attention to support language. Because the child is less active, the instances may be fewer, and because the child's attention may be of short duration, teaching opportunities will be brief.

It is important that environments for developmentally delayed children are consistent in providing information about the function and structure of the child's language. In order to accomplish this, the caregiver must be precisely aware of the child's skills. Although caregivers typically adjust the structural aspects of their input to the child's level, there is no information to indicate how precisely they tailor their requests for information and feedback. Logically, caregivers of less responsive children have a more difficult time being appropriate, and because delayed children progress more slowly, changes in child skill may not be noted immediately. Cheseldine and McConkey (1979) reported that parents alter their language to include more appropriate models for specific forms once they are instructed about their child's linguistic skills and set goals to teach needed skills. Awareness of the child's skills may require specific sampling of the child's behavior or consultation with the child's language trainer or teachers.

It is critical that caregivers offer not only consistent information about the structure of the child's language, but also assist the child in learning about how language functions to control the environment. Bates (1976) and others pointed out that one of the most important aspects of parent-child communication is the assumption of intentionality by the parents. The parents treat the children's utterances as having meaning, discriminate different meanings among utterances marked by different intonation and the use of constant sounds, and assist children in communicating their intentions. Parental provision of consistent responses to different topographies of communication attempts seems to shape those attempts into recognized forms. Bruner's analyses of mother-child interactions (Bruner, 1975; Bruner et al., 1980) and their impact on the development of language posits such a process, even though Bruner does not describe it in behavioral terms.

Finally, it is important that at least some settings for language learning are ones that do not have other tasks to be accomplished. Settings that are pleasant and playful for both the child and the caregiver allow both persons to focus their attention on language and social interaction. Although much language may be learned incidentally by normal children, delayed children may require relatively less complex contexts to notice and acquire new linguistic information. It is important, however, that a context and purpose for communication and interaction be established and maintained. The games and activities that engage the child's attention and serve as a context for conversation are important aspects of the setting. Teaching and learning must be integrated in the context of social interaction prompted by the stimuli available in the setting.

The behaviors of caregivers have been described only implicitly; they are summarized below.

1. Follow the child's lead. Focus attention on the objects and events the child finds of interest. Comments should map linguistically the environment the child is preceiving visually and tactilely.
2. Assume the child is trying to communicate and accommodate attempts by asking questions, offering choices, or attempting to comply. Make a reciprocal comment or incorporate the child's words into an expanded utterance. Assist the child in achieving the child's own interactional, task, and communication goals.
3. Consequate every child utterance with attention and support. Eye contact and touching, as well as verbal indications of approval, signal attention and interest in the child's attempted communication. Approval need not be obvious praise—simply acknowledgment that you are listening.
4. When providing corrective feedback about the child's utterances, do so in a gentle, positive way, emphasizing what is correct or appropriate and minimizing negative statements.
5. Talk *with* the child. Limit instructions and directives. Offer alternatives that maintain child activity and responsiveness rather than discourage exploration of the environment.

The adult caregiver is the most critical element of the language-learning child's environment. The adult not only provides models of language, but offers interpretations of the child's communication attempts, and assists the child in controlling the environment through language. Thus, the ideal environment for the delayed child will be the one that has caregivers who are especially sensitive to the child's attempts to communicate, who are supportive of the child's activity and communication to an even greater extent than normal environments, but who operate in basically the same interactional structure.

Some of the extent to which an environment functions as a language-learning setting can be measured by assessing child engagement and rate of spontaneous talking. If the child is engaged frequently in interactions with the caregiver and objects available in the setting, the environment is functioning. If the rate of spontaneous verbalization (that is, verbalization not resulting from direct questions or mands for verbalization) is moderate, and there are regular interchanges between caregiver and child, opportunities to learn language are occurring and the child is probably is responding to these opportunities. Longitudinally, the rate of acquiring or displaying new forms in a particular setting should indicate the effectiveness of that setting as a language-learning environment.

DIRECTIONS FOR FUTURE RESEARCH AND INTERVENTION STRATEGIES

A literature suggesting a pattern of naturalistic teaching is just beginning to emerge. Much more data representing a greater range of normal and atypical children are needed to verify the validity and generality of such interactions. Particularly, the interactions of developmentally delayed children and their caregivers should be examined for differences and similarities with the interaction of normal children and their parents. Indication of differences might suggest useful directions for developing intervention strategies.

Until new directions for intervention are clearly indicated, current language intervention strategies, especially those relying on parents as therapists, should be evaluated for evidence of generalization, maintenance, and impact on the child's subsequent learning of new language. Measures of spontaneous speech when the intervention strategy is not in effect, and rates of acquisition before, during, and after the intervention, provide a clearer analysis of the impact of interventions. Particular attention should be given to parent-based techniques, because parents typically play the largest role in their children's language acquisition and thus might be most likely to facilitate it when remediation is needed.

Finally, experimental attempts to teach language-deficient children specific interaction strategies should be made, and the impact of these interventions should be measured in much the same way that the effects of direct language teaching have been measured: increases in vocabulary and syntax, analysis of rate and directedness of spontaneous speech, generality, and maintanence. The behaviors and rules outlined in Figure 1 are potential targets for intervention. In combinations with well-analyzed experimental interventions, naturalistic studies of children's interaction and language-learning strategies should be carried out to verify the suggested rules and model for interaction.

REFERENCES

Ainsworth, M. *Infancy in Uganda: Infant care and the growth of love.* Baltimore: Johns Hopkins University Press, 1967.
Bates, E. *Language and context: The acquisition of pragmatics.* New York: Academic Press, 1976.
Bateson, M. C. Mother-infant exchanges: The epigenesis of conversational interaction. In D. Aaronson & R. W. Rieber (Eds.), *Developmental psycholinguistics and communication disorders.* Annals of the New York Academy of Science, 1975, *263*, 101–113.
Baldwin, A. L., & Baldwin, C. P. The study of mother child interaction. *American Scientist*, 1973, *61*, 714–721.
Bell, R. Q. A reinterpretation of the direction of effects in studies of socialization. *Psychological Review*, 1968, *75*, 81–95.
Blake, P., & Moss, T. The development of socialization sills in an electively mute child. *Behavior Research and Therapy*, 1967, *5*, 348–356.
Bloom, L., Hood, L., & Lightbown, P. Imitation in language development: If, when and why. *Cognitive Psychology*, 1974, *6*, 380–420.
Bowlby, J. *Attachment and loss*: Part I. London: Hogarth Press, 1969.
Brazleton, T. B., Koslowski, B., & Main, M. The origins of reciprocity: The early mother-infant interaction. In M. Lewis & L. A. Rosenblum (Eds.), *The origins of behavior* (Vol. 1) New York: John Wiley & Sons, 1974.
Bricker, W. A., & Bricker, D. D. An early language training strategy. In R. L. Schiefelbusch & L. L. Lloyd (Eds.), *Language perspectives: Acquisition, retardation, and intervention.* Baltimore: University Park Press, 1974.

Broen, P. The verbal environment of the language-learning child. *American Speech and Hearing Association Monographs*, December 1972 (Whole No. 17).

Brown, R., & Bellugi, U. Three processes in the child's acquisition of syntax. *Harvard Educational Review*, 1964, *34*, 133–151.

Brown, R., & Hanlon, C. Derivational complexity and order of acquisition in child speech. In J. R. Hayes (Ed.) *Cognition and the development of language*. New York: John Wiley & Sons, 1970.

Bruner, J. S. The ontogenesis of speech acts. *Journal of Child Language*, 1975, *2*, 1–19.

Bruner, J., Roy, C., & Ratner, N. The beginnings of requests. In K. E. Nelson (Ed.), *Children's language* (Vol. 3). New York: Gardner Press, 1980.

Buium, N., Rynders, J., & Turnure, J. Early maternal linguistic environment of normal and Down's syndrome language-learning children. *American Journal of Mental Deficiency*, 1974, *79*, 52–58.

Bullowa, M. *Before speech: The beginnings of interpersonal communication*. London: Cambridge University Press, 1979.

Cheseldine, S., & McConkey, R. Parental speech to young Down's syndrome children: An intervention study. *American Journal of Mental Deficiency*, 1979, *83*, 612–620.

Cross, T. G. Some relationships between motherese and linguistic level in accelerated children. *Papers and Reports on Child Language Development*, No. 10, Stanford University, Stanford, Calif., 1975.

Cross, T. G. Mothers' speech adjustments: The contributions of selected child listener variables. In C. Ferguson & C. Snow (Eds.), *Talking to children: Language input and acquisition*. Cambridge: Cambridge University Press, 1977.

Dore, J. Holophrases, speech acts, and language universals. *Journal of Child Language*, 1975, *2*, 21–40.

Drach, K. M. The language of the parent: A pilot study. Working paper No. 14 of the Language Behavior Research Laboratory, Berkeley: University of California, 1969.

Fristoe, M. Appendix D / Language intervention systems: Published programs in kit form. In L. L. Lloyd (Ed.), *Communication assessment and intervention strategies*. Baltimore: University Park Press, 1976.

Furrow, D., Nelson, K., & Benedict, H. Mothers' speech to children and syntactic development: Some simple relationships. *Journal of Child Language*, 1979, *6*, 423–442.

Gray, B., & Ryan, B. *A language program for the nonlanguage child*. Champaign, Ill.: Research Press, 1973.

Guess, D. A functional analysis of receptive language and productive speech: Acquisition of the plural morpheme. *Journal of Applied Behavior Analysis*, 1969, *2*, 55–64.

Guess, D., & Baer, D. M. An analysis of individual differences in generalization between receptive and productive language in retarded children. *Journal of Applied Behavior Analysis*, 1973, *6*, 311–329.

Guess, D., Sailor, W., & Baer, D. M. *Functional speech and language training for the severely handicapped*. Lawrence, Kan.: H & H Enterprises, Inc., 1978.

Halle, J. W., Marshall, A. M., & Spradlin, J. E. Time delay: A technique to increase language use and facilitate generalization in retarded children. *Journal of Applied Behavior Analysis*, 1979, *12*, 431–439.

Halliday, M. A. K. *Learning how to mean: Explorations in the development of language*. London: Edward Arnold, 1975.

Harris, S. L. Teaching language to nonverbal children—with emphasis on problems of generalization. *Psychological Record*, 1975, *82*, 565–580.

Hart, B. Pragmatics and language development. In B. B. Lahey & A. Kazdin (Eds.), *Advances in clinical child psychology* (Vol. 3). New York: Plenum Press, 1980.

Hart, B., & Risley, T. R. Incidental teaching of language in the preschool. *Journal of Applied Behavior Analysis*, 1975, *8*, 411–420.

Hart, B. M., & Rogers-Warren, A. Milieu teaching approaches. In R. L. Schiefelbusch (Ed.), *Bases of language intervention*. Baltimore: University Park Press, 1978.

Hubbell, R. D. On facilitating spontaneous talking in young children. *Journal of Speech and Hearing Disorders*, 1977, *42*, 216–231.

Hunt, J. McV. *Intelligence and experience*. New York; Ronald Press, 1961.

Jones, O. H. M. Mother-child communication with prelinguistic Down's syndrome and normal infants. In H. R. Schaffer (Ed.), *Studies in mother-infant interaction*. New York: Academic Press, 1977.

Kaye, K. Infants' effects upon their mothers' teaching strategies. In J. C. Glidewell (Ed.), *The social context of learning and development*. New York: Gardner Press, 1976.

Kogan, K. L., Wimberger, H. C., & Bobbitt, R. A. Analysis of mother-child interaction in young mental retardates. *Child Development*, 1969, *40*, 799–812.

Lewis, M., & Freedle, R. Mother-infant dyad: The cradle of meaning. In P. Pliner, L. Krames, & T. Alloway (Eds.), *Communication and effect: Language and thought*. New York: Academic Press, 1973.

Lewis, M., & Rosenblum, L. (Eds.). *The origin of behavior* (Vol. 1): *The effect of the infant on its caregiver*. New York: John Wiley & Sons, 1974.

Lord, C. Is talking to baby more than baby talk? A longitudinal study of linguistic input to young children. Paper presented at the biennial conference of the Society for Research in Child Development, Denver, 1975.

MacDonald, J. D., Blott, J. P., Gordon, K., Spiegel, B., & Hartman, M. An experimental parent-assisted treatment program for preschool language-delayed children. *Journal of Speech and Hearing Disorders*, 1974, *39*, 395–415.

Mahoney, G., & Seeley, P. The role of the social agent in language acquisition: Implications for language intervention. In N. Ellis (Ed.), *International review of research in mental retardation* (Vol. 8). New York: Academic Press, 1976.

Marshall, N. R., Hegrenes, J. R., & Goldstein, S. Verbal interactions: Mothers and their retarded children vs. mothers and their nonretarded children. *American Journal of Mental Deficiency*, 1973, *77*, 415–419.

McLean, J. E., & Snyder-McLean, L. K. *A transactional approach to early language training*. Columbus, Ohio: Charles E. Merrill, 1978.

Miller, J. R., & Yoder, D. E. An ontogenetic language teaching strategy for retarded children. In R. Schiefelbusch & L. L. Lloyd (Eds.), *Language perspectives: Acquisition, retardation, and intervention*. Baltimore: University Park Press, 1974.

Moerk, E. L. Principles of dyadic interaction in language learning. *Merrill Palmer Quarterly*, 1972, *18*, 229–257.

Moerk, E. L. *Pragmatic and semantic aspects of early language development*. Baltimore: University Park Press, 1977.

Nelson, K. Structure and strategy in learning to talk. *Monographs of the Society for Research in Child Development*, 1973, *38*,(1–2, Serial No. 149).

Nelson, K. E. Early speech in its communicative context. In F. D. Minifie & L. L. Lloyd (Eds.), *Communicative and cognitive abilities—Early behavioral assessment*. Baltimore: University Park Press, 1978.

Nelson, K. E., Carskaddon, G., & Bonvillian, J. Syntax acquisition: Impact of experimental variation in adult verbal interaction with the child. *Child Development*, 1973, *44*, 497–504.

Newport, E. L. Motherese: The speech of mothers to young children. In N. J. Castellan, D. B. Pisoni, & G. R. Potts (Eds.), *Cognitive theory* (Vol. 2). Hillsdale, N.J.: Lawrence Erlbaum Associates, 1976.

Newport, E., Gleitman, L., & Gleitman, H. A study of mothers' speech and child language acquisition. *Papers and Reports on Child Language Development* No. 10, Stanford University, Stanford, Calif., 1975.

Owen, M. M., & Rogers-Warren, A. A software system for monitoring language generalization in behavioral science research. Paper presented at the annual meeting of Digital Equipment Users Society, San Diego, Calif., 1977.

Phillips, J. Syntax and vocabulary of mothers' speech to young children: Age and sex comparisons. *Child Development*, 1973, *44*, 182–185.

Rees, N. S. Imitation and language development: Issues and clinical implications. *Journal of Speech and Hearing Disorders*, 1975, *40*, 339–350.

Remick, H. Maternal speech to children during language acquisition. In W. von Raffler-Engle & Y. Lebrun (Eds.), *Baby talk and infant speech*. Lisse, Netherlands: Swets and Zeitlinger, 1976.

Rogers-Warren, A., Gendreau, S., McQuarter, R., & Warren, S. F. *Teaching talking: Analysis of mother-child verbal interactions.* Paper presented at the annual meeting of the American Psychological Association, New York, September, 1979.

Rogers-Warren, A., & Warren, S. Mands for verbalization: Facilitating the display of newly-taught language. *Behavior Modification*, 1980, *4*, 361–382.

Rondal, J. A. Maternal speech to normal and Down's syndrome children matched for mean length of utterance. In C. E. Meyers (Eds.), *Monographs of the American Association on Mental Deficiency,* 1978.

Sachs, J., Brown, R., & Salerno, R. Adults speech to children. In W. von Raffler-Engle & Y. Lebrun (Eds.), *Baby talk and infant speech.* Lisse, Netherlands: Swets and Zeitlinger, 1976.

Sachs, J., & Devin, J. Young children's use of age-appropriate speech styles in social interaction and role-playing. *Journal of Child Language*, 1976, *2*, 81–98.

Schachter, F. F. *Everyday mother talk to toddlers: Early intervention.* New York: Academic Press, 1979.

Schiefelbusch, R. L. The development of social competence and incompetence. In M. J. Begab, H. Garber, & H. C. Haywood (Eds.), *Psychosocial influences in retarded performance.* Baltimore: University Park Press, 1981.

Schiefelbusch, R. L., & Lloyd, L. L. (Eds.). *Language perspectives: Acquisition, retardation and intervention.* Baltimore: University Park Press, 1974.

Schumaker, J. B., & Sherman, J. A. Parent as intervention agent. In R. L. Schiefelbusch (Ed.), *Language intervention strategies.* Baltimore: University Park Press, 1978.

Searle, J. R. *Speech acts: An essay in the philosophy of language.* New York: Cambridge University press, 1969.

Seitz, S., & Stewart, C. Expanding on expansions and related aspects of mother-child communication. *Developmental Psychology*, 1975, *11*, 763–769.

Shatz, M. How young children respond to language: Procedures for answering. *PRCLD*, 1975, *10*, 97–110.

Shatz, M., & Gelman, R. The development of communication skills: Modifications in the speech of young children as a function of listener. *Monographs of the Society for Research in Child Development*, 1973, *38*, (5, Serial No, 152).

Sherman, J. A. Imitation and language development. In H. W. Reese & L. P. Lippsitt (Eds.), *Advances in child development and behavior.* New York: Academic Press, 1971.

Shipley, E. F., Smith, C. S., & Gleitman, L. R. A study in the acquisition of language: Free responses to commands. *Language*, 1969, *45*, 322–342.

Siegel, G. Adult verbal behavior in "play therapy" sessions with retarded children. *Journal of Speech and Hearing Disorders Monograph*, 1963a, *10*, 34–38.

Siegel, G. Verbal behavior of retarded children assembled with preinstructed adults. *Journal of Speech and Hearing Disorders Monograph*, 1963b, *10*, 47–53.

Siegel, G., & Harkins, J. Verbal behavior of adults in two conditions with institutionalized retarded children. *Journal of Speech and Hearing Disorders Monograph*, 1963, *10*, 39–46.

Skinner, B. *Verbal behavior.* New York: Appleton-Century-Crofts, 1957.

Slobin, D. I. Cognitive prerequisites for the development of grammar. In C. A. Ferguson & D. I. Slobin (Eds.), *Studies of child language development.* New York: Holt, Rinehart & Winston, 1973.

Snow, C. Mothers' speech to children learning language. *Child Development*, 1972, *43*, 549–565.

Snow, C. Mothers' speech research: An overview. In C. Ferguson & C. Snow (Eds.), *Talking to children: Language input and acquisition.* New York: Cambridge University Press, 1977.

Spradlin, J., & Rosenberg, S. Complexity of adult verbal behavior in a dyadic situation with retarded children. *Journal of Abnormal and Social Psychology*, 1964, *68*, 694–698.

Stokes, T. F., & Baer, D. M. An implicit technology of generalization. *Journal of Applied Behavior Analysis*, 1977, *10*, 349–367.

Stremel, K., & Waryas, C. A behavioral-psycholinguistic approach to language training. *American Speech and Hearing Association Monographs*, 1974, *18*, 96–130.

Terdal, L., Jackson, R., & Garner, A. Mother-child interactions: A comparison between normal and developmentally delayed groups. In E. Mash, L. Hamerlynch, & L. Handy (Eds.), *Behavior modification and families.* New York: Brunner / Mazel, 1976.

VanBiervliet, A., Spangler, P. F., & Marshall, A. M. An ecological approach for increasing language during mealtime. Paper presented at the fifth annual convention of the Association for Behavior Analysis, Dearborn, Michigan, 1979.

Vietze, P. M., Abernathy, S. R., Ashe, M. L., & Faulstich, G. Contingent interaction between mothers and their developmentally delayed infants. In G. P. Sackett (Ed.), *Observing behavior* (Vol. 1): *Theory and applications in mental retardation*. Baltimore: University Park Press, 1978.

Warren, S. F., & Rogers-Warren, A. Current perspectives in language remediation. *Education and Treatment of Children*, 1980, *3*, 133–153.

Warren, S. F., Rogers-Warren, A., Baer, D. M., & Guess, D. The assessment and facilitation of language generalization. In W. Sailor, B. Wilcox, & L. Brown (Eds.), *Methods of instruction for severely handicapped students*. Baltimore: Paul H. Brooks Publishers, 1980.

Wells, G. Learning to code experience through language. *Journal of Child Language*, 1974, *1*, 243–269.

Wolf, M. M., Risley, T. R., & Mees, H. Application of operant conditioning procedures to the behavior problems of an autistic child. *Behavior Research and Therapy*, 1964, *1*, 305–312.

Because No One Asked . . . Setting Variables Affecting the Generalization of Trained Vocabulary within a Residential Institution

Steven F. Warren and
Ann K. Rogers-Warren

During the past 15 years a technology for teaching language to retarded individuals has been developed and disseminated nationally (Schiefelbusch, 1978; Schiefelbusch and Lloyd, 1974). Language training programs are now widely used by parents, and in clinics, schools, and state residential institutions. Efforts to remediate the language of institutionalized retarded children are the focus of this chapter.

THE STATE OF RESIDENTIAL INSTITUTIONS

Research reported in the 1960s revealed residential institutions to be anything but therapeutically oriented (e.g., Klaber, 1969; Lyle, 1960; McCarthy, 1964; Zigler, 1966). Several studies reported that institutionalized children were significantly poorer than comparable non-institutionalized children in terms of language skills (e.g., McNutt and Leri, 1979; Montague, Hutchinson, and Matson, 1975; Newfield and Schlanger, 1968). During the past 10 years, improvements in attitudes, financial support, and therapy in institutions have been noted (Graham, 1976; Miller and Yoder, 1974; Schiefelbusch, 1972;

Our colleagues in this research include Steven Anderson, Donald M. Baer, Barry Buchanan, C. Robert Campbell, Doug Guess, Thomas Longhurst, Ann M. Marshall, Kathleen Stremel-Campbell, and R. L. Schiefelbusch. This research was funded by grants from the National Institute of Child Health and Human Development (NICH HD #00870-13) and the Bureau for the Education of the Handicapped (USOE #G0076-05086).

Tarjan et al., 1973). Institutions seem to be changing in fundamental ways as a result of the rights for the retarded movement. Historically, institutions provided a minimal level of physical care and little academic or vocational training; now they are required to offer 6 hours of training daily to each resident under age 21 (Blee and Sheldon, 1979).

Although the size of institutional populations has declined, it is likely that institutions will continue to exist in one form or another, at least for the care and treatment of the severely and profoundly retarded (Throne, 1979). Fortunately, there will also be continuing pressure to further improve their facilities and treatment programs (Repp, 1978; Sailor and Haring, 1977).

Institutional Setting Analysis: A Model

Residential institutions should not be conceptualized as a single environment but as several environments each having a specific purpose (i.e., classroom, dining hall, living unit). Some settings may be effective treatment environments. Others may have little therapeutic value and even militate against the development of functional skills by residents. In order to develop effective treatment programs, the therapeutic and nontherapeutic components of institutions must be identified and the nontherapeutic components modified. One strategy for characterizing the therapeutic impact of settings is to study the generalization of trained target behaviors across different settings where the behaviors should be functional (assuming that the target skill has been well-trained). If trained behaviors generalize to one environment better than another, the second environment may be a less functional setting. Steps should be taken to make this environment more supportive of the trained behavior. The success of this modification could be determined by further generalization analyses.

This approach to interpreting the meaning of generalization failures is atypical. Usually, when generalization does not occur it is assumed that the trained behavior is not functional. The current logic, however, assumes that it is the environment that is not supportive of potentially functional behavior. Such an approach may be justified in residential institutions because these environments have been designed to minimize the need for functional behavior by the residents (and to maximize economy). For example, institutions typically contain large dining halls instead of family-sized dining rooms, televisions that remain on permanently, and technicians who anticipate residents' needs while rigidly following predetermined schedules.

VOCABULARY GENERALIZATION: A SETTING ANALYSIS

In this study, the therapeutic characteristics of three settings within a state residential institution for the severely and profoundly retarded were studied. The purpose of the study was to teach a basic set of noun referents to six severely retarded children and to investigate the generalization of these terms in the subjects' classroom, dining hall, and living unit. The relative functionality and therapeutic effectiveness of these settings were evaluated in terms of the amounts and patterns of generalization found.

Noun referents were studied because the acquisition and use of such terms represents an important conceptual breakthrough for a severely retarded child. The first words acquired and displayed by normal children are almost invariably noun referents (Nelson, 1973). These terms become the building blocks of productive language acquisition (Anglin, 1977). Thus, for the language-deficient child, therapy often begins with the training of labels for common objects in the environment (e.g., Guess, Sailor, and Baer, 1978).

The authors and several colleagues conducted a systematic study of language general-ization to nontraining settings resulting from comprehensive language training programs (Warren et al., 1980). This research has resulted in the development of reliable ways to measure and quantify generalization under the conditions imposed by the normal environ-ment on language-delayed children. Within this research program, an analysis of noun referent generalization[1] was conducted.

Several clinical studies (e.g., Acker et al., 1973; Blake, 1969; Drash and Leibowitz, 1973; Marshall and Hegrenes, 1970) reported success in teaching noun referents to language-deficient children through the systematic use of imitation, differential re-inforcement, and other training procedures; however, analyses of generalization of trained labels to either probe situations or the natural environment have been absent from the literature. This study provides an analysis of generalized use and an examination of the impact of different institutional settings on the display of the trained referents. Based on this analysis, a model for facilitating language use by institutionalized residents is proposed, and methods for modifying institutional environments to make them more functional for language remediation are discussed.

METHODS

Six severely retarded institutionalized children served as subjects. The two females and four males ranged in age from 10.5 to 16.0 years at the conclusion of the longitudinal observations. Their receptive and expressive language abilities were assessed on the Houston Test for Language Development (Crabtree, 1963) at the conclusion of the analysis period. The language ages of the children, as determined from the Houston scores, ranged from 17 to 35 months. The children also were tested on the Peabody Picture Vocabulary Test (Dunn, 1965), which provides an estimate of a subject's verbal intelligence by measuring receptive vocabulary. Mental age estimates derived from this test ranged from 21 to 43 months for the subjects. The mean length of utterance (MLU) for each child was determined on the basis of verbatim language samples taken during the last 3 months of the observations. MLUs ranged from 1.3 to 2.4 words. The size of each child's vocabulary, derived from the verbatim samples of each subject's language during the entire longitudinal observation period, was calculated at the conclusion of the study. Vocabulary sizes ranged from 34 to 593 words. Subject characteristics are shown in Table 1.

All six children had resided in a state residential institution for several years. Observations were taken in three institutional settings: the classroom, the dining hall, and the living unit. Each environment is described below.

Classroom

All the children attended the same classroom located on the institution grounds. The class met for 6 hours each day, 5 days each week, approximately 11 months of the year. It was

---

[1]In this research, the display of trained noun referents was measured in the subjects' natural environ-ments. It is debatable whether the display of these terms should be called generalization and/or mainte-nance from training because observations were conducted some time after the completion of training, and bacause no guarantee can be given that the subjects did not learn some or all of the terms from the natural environment. Severely retarded subjects rarely learned language from the natural environment, however, and usually required massed training trials to learn even a single term. In any case, the question of whether the display of trained referents by the subjects should be called generalization is tangential to the purpose of this analysis.

Table 1.   Subject characteristics

Subject	Sex	Chronological age	Houston Language Age	Peabody Picture Vocabulary Test	Vocabulary size		MLU
T.F.	F	10–5	35 mo.	38 mo.	593	wd.	2.2
S.B.	M	13–11	33 mo.	43 mo.	512	wd.	1.5
B.Q.	F	14–9	27 mo.	23 mo.	450	wd.	2.0
J.L.	M	13–5	20 mo.	21 mo.	422	wd.	2.4
D.M.	M	16–0	18 mo.	24 mo.	80	wd.	1.3
B.F.	M	11–10	17 mo.	21 mo.	34	wd.	1.7
Means		13–4	25 mo.	28.3 mo.	348.5	wd.	1.85

staffed by one certified special education teacher, and three college-educated assistants. The class consisted of 16 severely retarded children. Individual academic programs and one-to-one language training were provided for each child. Four children generally worked with each staff member during the majority of the day, although some large group activity occurred each day also (e.g., show and tell, group singing).

Dining Hall

The subjects ate in a large communal dining hall where meals were served cafeteria style. They sat at tables (six at each table) with their classmates and one of their teachers or a staff member. The typical dining period lasted about 30 minutes. After completing their meal, the children waited for their peers and teachers to finish before leaving the setting.

Living Unit

The children spent the late afternoons, evenings, early mornings, and weekends in their living unit. Each unit consisted of 16 children, four bedrooms each housing four children, a large dayroom where some toys were occasionally available, a TV room, and a large communal bathroom. Two staff members were usually present. Most of the children's time was unstructured, however, and they typically roamed the halls, watched TV, or engaged in stereotypic and self-stimulatory behavior.

Training

Each subject received training on the Guess et al. (1978) language training program. This 66-step training program was developed to teach severely retarded children basic productive and receptive communication skills. The first step of the program is intended to provide the student with a productive vocabulary of functional labels. These labels are used in sentence forms trained later in the program.

Subjects received training on an average of 15 labels. The labels chosen for each child were the result of an initial skill test given by the language trainer. During the test, children were asked to name a large number of objects or body parts. The trainer held up the object or pointed to the body part, and asked "What's this?" Labels to be trained were selected on the basis of the child's incorrect answers. All six subjects were unable to label most objects or body parts presented during the skill test. The objects were chosen because they represented functional items commonly present in the institutional environment. Once the training terms were selected, staff members were asked whether they had ever heard a given subject

Table 2.   Labels trained for each subject

T.F.	S.B.	B.Q.	J.L.	D.M.	B.F.
Apple	Apple	Apple	Apple	Apple	Bubble
Ball	Ball	Ball	Ball	Ball	Candy
Cookie	Balloon	Car	Car	Car	Cereal
Cup	Candy	Chair	Chair	Chair	Cheese
Dish	Car	Coke	Cookie	Cookie	Cookie
Hat	Cookie	Cookie	Ear	Cup	Doll
Pop	Cup	Cup	Hat	Ear	Ear
Spoon	Hat	Daddy	Milk	Ear	Eye
Token	Lamb	Dress	Nose	Hat	Leg
	Milk	Ear	Pants	Milk	Hat
	Peanut	Hat	Shoe	Nose	Nose
	Pop	Milk	Spoon	Pants	Shape Box
	Shoe	Mommy	Table	Pop	Shoe
	Spoon	Nose	Truck	Shoe	Sock
		Shoe	Tummy	Spoon	Wig
		Spoon		Table	Yogurt
		Table		Tummy	
		Tummy			

use these terms. Words that subjects already used were replaced with other labels. The labels trained for each child are presented in Table 2.

Training was conducted by the children's language trainers who were members of the institutional teaching staff. Labels were trained in sets of two. The trainer held up an object and asked the child "What's that?" If the child answered correctly, the teacher praised the child ("That's right, good"). If the child answered incorrectly, the trainer repeated the question. If the child failed to respond, the trainer modeled the correct label ("ball"), then praised the child for the correct imitation. These procedures were followed in training all the labels. In addition, the children received tokens for correct responses; later tokens were exchanged for candy or toys. Production training continued until subjects had achieved a criterion performance level of 80% or more correct responses in one session (32 trials), or 12 correct responses in a row in one session.

When children reached criterion, they proceeded to the second step of the program. In this step, the items trained in the first step were presented in groups of four. The child was instructed to point to the item that corresponded to the label the trainer said. If the trainer said "Point to the ball," a correct response was pointing to the ball. If the child made an incorrect response, the trainer said "No, that's a (label), this is the (label)," and pointed to the correct choice. The trial was then repeated. Correct responses were consequated the same way they had been in the first step and criterion for completing the step was also the same. All six subjects were successfully trained to criterion on both steps.

Observation System

Generalization was measured during longitudinal observations of subjects. These observations commenced an average of 16 months after the labels were trained initially and continued for an average of 16 months. Subjects were observed an average of 148 times. Observations were conducted across the three settings described. The point at which observations were implemented and ended, and the number of observations per setting varied from child to child depending on the child's availability for observation.

Each observation lasted 15 minutes. The subject being observed wore an apron containing a small, wireless microphone that transmitted utterances to an FM receiver connected to a high-quality tape recorder. An observer concurrently watched the subject and made a written record of the child's utterances, noting the context and utterances that were echoic or imitative. After the observation, the observer, aided by the tape recording and the written notes, made a complete written transcript of the subject's verbalizations.

Verbatim records of all observations were entered into a computer that analyzed word generalization by comparing each child's list of trained labels with the spontaneous (nonimitated) words in the child's verbatim samples. Each occurrence of a trained word was counted, a dictionary of the child's entire vocabulary was compiled, and the mean length of the child's utterances was determined for each sample.

In addition to the verbatim observations, an interval observational system was used to measure rates of different verbal behaviors displayed by the subjects and directed to the subjects by adults and peers. Overall rates of adult speech to the subjects, rates of obligatory adult speech to the subjects (statements that required a verbal response from the subjects including non-yes/no questions, mands, and indirect models), subject initiations (verbalizations not immediately preceded by an adult statement to the child), and total child verbalizations were recorded. These data were used to compile quantitative descriptions of the demand and support for verbalizations provided in each setting.

Observational reliability was carefully assessed throughout the entire study. A total of 145 reliability observations were taken for the verbatim observation system. Reliability was assessed morpheme by morpheme for the entire transcription. Overall reliability was 86% across the entire study and ranged from 63% to 100%. For the rate code observations, reliability was calculated for the exact recording and coding of the defined verbal events, in the exact order in which they occurred. A total of 38 reliability assessments were made across the three settings. Overall reliability ranged from 75% to 85% agreement.

RESULTS

Only noun referents that the subjects could display in structured generalization probes were tested for functional use. A word was not considered to have been trained adequately unless the child produced it in a structured probe situation. If this less difficult form of generalization was demonstrated, the question of generalization to the natural environment was considered. This criterion was intended to ensure that the noun usage patterns observed in the institutional settings were not the result of poor training but instead reflected the demand requirements of those settings. Structured generalization probes were presented to each child at the same time that the longitudinal generalization observations began.

Table 3 indicates the percent of trained words observed at least once (nonimitatively) in the natural environment.

The data shown on Table 3 suggest that subjects may generalize a noun to a structured probe situation, but not use this word in the natural environment. This was true for five of the six subjects. Only S.B. used all words in the natural settings that he had generalized to the structured probe. Conversely, B.F. generalized only five of the eleven nouns displayed

Table 3.   Generalization ratios per child

Subject	Ratio
S.B.	14:14 = 100%
B.Q.	17:18 = 94%
J.L.	11:13 = 85%
T.F.	7:9 = 78%
D.M.	9:15 = 60%
B.F.	5:11 = 45%
Mean	63:80 = 79%

in the structured probe situation. Overall, the group displayed an average of 79% of the trained nouns in the natural environment.

When these data are examined by specific setting, a partial analysis of setting variables affecting noun referent display is possible. Table 4 shows the percentage of the generalized labels (one occasion criterion) observed in each setting. For example, seven of nine trained labels were generalized by T.F. Of these seven, two were observed at least once in the dining hall, two in the living unit, and all seven were observed in the classroom.

The classroom was the most likely setting in which to observe a trained noun, although nearly half the trained nouns were also observed in the dining hall and living unit. Thirty-four percent more of the generalized words were used in the classroom than in either the dining hall or the living unit. More observations were taken in the classroom than in either the dining hall or living unit, but no significant correlation was found between the number of observations in each setting and the number of different trained nouns observed per child in each setting.

There are two reasonable explanations of the differential generalization patterns observed. One is that the verbal interaction found in the classroom was sufficiently different from that found in the other environments to account for the differential noun usage. It is also possible that specific words represented objects found and used at differential rates across the settings.

Differences in Probability of Usage

The trained words that generalized are shown for each child in Table 5. The words in Table 5 can be categorized into general object classes representing foods, clothes, toys, eating utensils, furniture, body parts, and miscellaneous items. Different probabilities of occurrence are possible for these classes across different settings. For example, in the dining hall,

Table 4.   Percent of generalized labels observed on at least one occasion by setting

Subject	Classroom	Living unit	Dining hall
T.F.	7/7 = 100%	2/7 = 28%	2/7 = 28%
S.B.	13/14 = 93%	5/14 = 36%	5/14 = 36%
B.Q.	11/17 = 65%	8/17 = 44%	13/17 = 76%
J.L.	7/11 = 64%	6/11 = 55%	3/11 = 27%
D.M.	6/9 = 67%	5/9 = 56%	4/9 = 44%
B.F.	5/5 = 100%	2/5 = 40%	1/5 = 20%
Means	49/63 = 78%	28/63 = 44%	28/63 = 44%

Table 5.   Labels generalized for each subject·

T.F.	S.B.	B.Q.	J.L.	D.M.	B.F.
Ball	Apple	Apple	Apple	Apple	Candy
Cookie	Ball	Ball	Ball	Ball	Cheese
Cup	Balloon	Car	Car	Car	Shoe
Dish	Candy	Chair	Cookie	Coke	Sock
Hat	Car	Coke	Cup	Cookie	Yogurt
Pop	Cookie	Cookie	Hat	Ear	
Token	Cup	Cup	Milk	Milk	
	Hat	Daddy	Nose	Shoe	
	Lamb	Dress	Shoe	Spoon	
	Milk	Ear	Spoon		
	Peanut	Hat	Table		
	Pop	Milk			
	Shoe	Mommy			
	Spoon	Nose			
		Shoe			
		Spoon			
		Table			

all classes of words were used but only four terms (apple, milk, spoon, and cookie) were repeatedly used by the subjects. These terms reference the primary function of this setting—eating. Only in the dining hall, however, was any particular propensity for using certain trained words found. Furthermore, no patterns or correlations were found between types of words that generalized (one occurrence criterion) and any setting. The contention that the differential generalization observed between the classroom and the other settings was caused by the nature of the words trained is weak. Even in the dining hall all word classes were used.

Differences in Adult Verbal Behavior

The other reasonable explanation of the differential generalization is that the verbal interactions in the classroom were fundamentally different from those that occurred in the other settings. As noted above, an observational code was used to measure overall rates of adult speech to the subjects, rates of obligatory adult speech to the subjects (statements that required a verbal response from the subjects including non-yes/no questions, mands, and direct models), subject initiations (verbalizations not immediately preceded by an adult statement to the child), and total child verbalizations. The mean rates of these behaviors per child per 15-minute observation period are shown in Table 6.

The data in Table 6 suggest some fundamental differences between the classroom and the other settings. First, the rate of adult verbalizations to subjects was much greater in the

Table 6.   Mean rate per child per 15 minutes

Setting	Total adult verbalizations	Obligatory verbal response occasions	Total child initiations	Total child verbalizations	Mean observations per child
Classroom	28.9	12.2	14.7	33.4	14.0
Dining hall	6.6	1.1	14.7	17.3	12.0
Living unit	11.9	1.2	15.7	16.3	12.0

classroom. Second, the number of occasions when the subjects were obligated to respond verbally to a question or mand was approximately 10 times greater than in the other settings combined. The implications of these data are strengthened by the results of a correlational analysis. A strong (0.69) positive correlation was found between percent of generalization observed in each setting and the rate of adult verbalizations to the subjects ($p > 0.001$). Furthermore, a 0.74 positive correlation was found between the rate of obligatory speech situations in each setting and percent of generalization observed ($p > 0.001$). Table 6 also indicates that subjects verbalized more frequently in the classroom than in the other settings, although only a weak (0.32) correlation was found between rate of subject verbalization and percent of generalization per setting ($p > 0.1$). In summary, the data strongly suggest that the single greatest factor effecting noun usage in each setting was the verbal behavior of the adults present.

DISCUSSION

Given the strict training criteria applied in this study, the basic nature of the vocabulary trained, and the large number of observations taken, the conclusion that the living unit and dining hall settings were not very functional environments in terms of demand and support for language usage is quite tenable. The current results support the observations of other investigators (Paton and Stirling, 1974; Pratt, Bumstead, and Raynes, 1976; Prior et al., 1979) that verbal responses are seldom required or elicited from retarded residents in unstructured (i.e., nonclassroom) institutional settings. Based on these findings, it is not surprising that the language of institutionalized retarded residents deteriorates over time (Phillips and Balthazar, 1979), or that language generalization is difficult to obtain (Warren et al., 1980).

Assessment of generalization across settings indicated the residents' classroom was a relatively functional setting for the use of basic vocabulary. The uniquely "residential" components of the institution, the dining hall and living unit, were considerably less functional. This finding supports those of Prior et al. (1979) that structured, organized, purposeful situations optimal for encouraging language usage rarely occur in institutional settings. Yet, institutions for the severely retarded are likely to survive despite their inadequacies. Because institutions are a continuing reality, a general model for facilitating language use by retarded individuals and some procedures that exemplify the model's application in a residential institution are proposed.

A Functional Model

There are at least two prerequisites for productive generalized language usage by severely retarded individuals. First, a functional communication repertoire must be sufficiently trained. Language training procedures are not of primary concern here; nevertheless it is important to note that retarded individuals may fail to generalize linguistic responses because they were not well trained. Sufficient training could be ensured by requiring a student to demonstrate generalization under probe conditions as the criteria for completing a given training step.[2] Unless the student can generalize to structured probes across settings,

---

[2] A complete discussion of this and related training issues can be found in Warren and Rogers-Warren (1980).

persons, and objects, training is not sufficient to support generalization to unstructured interactions in daily living settings.

The second prerequisite for productive language usage is that newly-learned responses are functional for the speaker. The speaker must *need* to use language in general and the specific trained forms in particular. The results of this study suggest it was not necessary to speak or to use trained noun referents in the living unit or dining hall. The classroom, however, supported both general and specific language display.

The institution's dining hall was designed to require a minimum of behavior from those using it. For example, food was provided virtually automatically. Residents were handed filled trays as they entered the room or when they were seated at a table. There were no choices to be made or options to request, and thus, little basis for interaction with staff or peers. The setting was almost the opposite of dining in a typical home. In most homes, a child may control (to some extent) what kind of food he or she gets, how much, and when it is served by expressing preferences. Food frequently is delivered contingent on specific polite forms of requests (e.g., "please"). Parents become powerful generalized reinforcers for the child, in part because they provide food and are paired with this primary reinforcer. On the other hand, cafeteria attendants typically do not become generalized reinforcement agents for institutional residents because the pairing between agent and primary reinforcement is minimal and interactions between resident and staff are limited. As a result, the institutional dining hall typically is not a good language-learning environment because it does not require or facilitate language display. Potentially, it could be one of the best settings for learning or practicing the basic social functions of language because there are objects and services to be requested and provided, and peers and staff available for interaction.

The institutional living unit required minimal behavior from residents and was not responsive to their preferences. Access to toys and entertainment was based on the staff's schedule rather than the interests or desires of the residents. The television and lights were left on most of the time. Dressing, toileting, and other basic needs were anticipated in advance and met efficiently, but noncontingently.

The dining hall and living unit were designed to operate efficiently, safely, and economically. Little verbal or nonverbal behavior (other than compliance with simple instructions) was required of the residents. Low staff-resident interaction rates reflected the success of these environments in anticipating the basic needs of the residents. The unit area ran smoothly if not responsively. The behaviors that are critical to new learning (resident autonomy, initiations, and exploration) are counter to the basic nature of these settings and can even impede staff completion of caregiving procedures (Stone and Church, 1957).

The classroom design provided a total contrast to the dining hall and living unit. It facilitated a high rate of adult-resident interaction, the feature that correlated most strongly with the level of noun generalization observed in this setting. Teachers did two things adults in the dining hall and living unit did not do: they talked to the children and they required the children to talk to them. To a considerable extent, the differences between the classroom and living areas were a result of the purposes of the settings and the adults who staffed them. Dining halls and living units are primary care settings and classrooms are instructional settings. Instruction requires frequent interaction between resident and teacher. Because much of the instruction requires linguistic responses, the interactions were typically verbal.

Teachers in the classroom, unlike dining hall and unit staff, regarded interaction as an integral part of their job.

The key to achieving productive language usage from institutionalized retarded persons across all settings is to ensure that the staff frequently talks to them in ways that require verbal responses from them. Conversational comments (Prior et al., 1979) and obligatory speech acts such as non-yes/no questions, and mands are especially likely to prompt verbal responses. Instructions and rhetorical statements usually do not. Interesting stimuli (objects and actions) are important but it may be necessary to draw the residents' attention to the stimuli and to provide atypical objects to engage residents. It has been posited that the motivation of normal, young children in labeling objects is not to inform the listener of the object's name but to gain (Halliday, 1975) or direct (Bruner, 1975) the attention of the listener. Young children's single-word utterances usually label the aspect of the situation undergoing the greatest amount of change (Greenfield and Smith, 1976). Severely retarded children may have similar motivations and attend to change, but unless attentive listeners are available in an active, stimulus-rich environment expressions of notice and interest will be infrequent. The classroom contained both stimuli and listeners. The living unit and dining hall were limited in these dimensions; however, these settings could be redesigned to include both interesting stimuli and attentive listeners.

Setting Modifications

Some modifications of institutional environments may require extensive staff training. Other modifications easily can be built into the existing system. Two procedures implemented in an institutional dining hall are presented as examples of easily implemented modifications.

Halle, Marshall, and Spradlin (1979) altered the standard cafeteria line procedure to increase residents' use of requests. They instructed the staff member who gave the food trays to the residents at breakfast to delay briefly before giving trays to six residents. Instead of handing children their food trays immediately, the staff member held the tray for 15 seconds, and then handed it over. Following a short training period during which the response "Tray please" was modeled for the children, subjects began verbally requesting their trays whenever the delay was encountered. All six subjects generalized requesting when the time-delay procedure was introduced at lunchtime.

A second example was provided by VanBiervliet, Spangler, and Marshall (1979) who instituted a family-style dining arrangement for two groups of institutionalized children. Instead of going through the cafeteria line, children went directly to their tables and obtained food by passing serving bowls to each other in the manner typical of the family dining table.

VanBiervliet et al. reported a large increase in verbal interactions among the children and found that the children ate more slowly (which was considered a positive effect by observers) than they had under cafeteria conditions. The results of this experiment prompted a number of staff members to request a family-style arrangement for their tables. There was some resistance to these requests from the institution administration because it meant the highly efficient cafeteria line would be poorly utilized!

The two examples demonstrate some simple ways by which institutional settings can be made into functional environments for language usage. Many other common situations can be restructured to make language functional. These modifications are desirable because they are simple, require very little staff training or motivation, and should not be seriously affected by such chronic institution problems as staff turnover and absenteeism. There are limitations on their remedial effects, however, and resultant gains will reflect these limitations. Interested, motivated adults play a critical role in language acquisition (Furrow, Nelson, and Benedict, 1979; Moerk, 1977) and remediation efforts (Schiefelbusch, in press). Ultimately the direct-care staff are the most valuable resource for training residents (Zaharia and Baumeister, 1979). The potential of truly effective remediation efforts depends on trained, motivated, reliable staff members.

Staff Utilization

Some highly effective procedures for supporting language display and teaching new language have been developed, but can only be utilized by trained staff who see themselves as more than custodians or supervisors. This necessitates reconceptualizing the function of the "caregiving" settings within the institution so that settings like the living unit and dining hall are viewed as important learning environments, just as the classroom is. Routine, common activities such as washing, toileting, dressing, sleeping, and playtime provide frequent, highly functional situations for language learning in these settings. These same day-to-day events are utilized constantly for incidental teaching by mothers of normal children (White, 1971). In a typical example of these events offered by Hart and Risley (1977), a child comes into the kitchen and says "Gimme another cookie." The parent asks, "What's the magic word?" If the child does not answer, the parent suggests "Can you say, 'Please give me another cookie?' " Not until the child says 'please' is the cookie jar opened.

The process of incidental teaching has been systematized (Hart and Rogers-Warren, 1978) and applied to the problem of teaching language to developmentally delayed children utilizing naturally occurring situations throughout the day (e.g., Hart and Risley, 1968; Rogers-Warren and Warren, 1980). The incidental teaching approach specifies a sequence of language eliciting and modeling behaviors for the adult and requires that the physical environment be structured to make it necessary for, and to encourage the child to request both objects and actions. When the child attempts (verbally or nonverbally) to make a request, the adult may institute incidental teaching. A number of decisions must be made by the adult at this point and the interested reader is directed to Hart and Rogers-Warren (1978) for a detailed description. An outline of the procedural sequence is presented below.

1. Give the child your undivided attention immediately following the request attempt.
2. Say the word or phrase you want from the child (if necessary).
3. Ask a question aimed at the language response you want.
4. Give a hint if the child fails to respond appropriately.
5. Tell the child the answer if he or she fails to respond appropriately.
6. Let the child know he or she has given the right answer and repeat it once more.

When employed frequently, incidental teaching strategies have the advantage of allowing the adult to adjust his or her input to the level of the individual child. The adult can continually require the child to operate at the edge of his or her current ability level while shaping the child's language toward the next more proficient level. This matching between the level of the child's abilities and the communication demands placed on him or her mimics the critical communicative matching that goes on between language-learning children and their parents (Cross, 1977; Moerk, 1977; Newport, 1976; Snow, 1977).

A number of systems designed to encourage incidental teaching in day-to-day interactions between severely retarded individuals and adults have been offered recently (Guess et al., 1978; Hart and Risley, 1975, 1976; Hursh et al., 1978; Sosne, Handleman, and Harris, 1979). Each of these describe routine activities that naturally provide opportunities to prompt child language, reinforce its use, and to teach the child to control his or her environment. The use of these strategies in residential settings minimizes the need for specific language generalization training, increases the likelihood that staff will notice and reinforce new learning by residents, and ensures at least a minimal level of staff-resident interaction.

CONCLUSION

It has been posited that the functionality of an institutional setting can be assessed on the basis of the generalization that occurs in the setting. This assumes that the behaviors for which generalization is desired are well-trained and that they would typically be functional in a less restrictive setting. If these conditions are met, then restricted generalization indicates the environment is dysfunctional. The research reported here identified one functional and two relatively dysfunctional settings based on the diversity of generalized noun usage observed in these settings. Observations of the classroom setting suggested the critical variable was the rate of adult-resident interaction, especially those that required residents to respond verbally.

Functional staff-resident interactions can be increased by restructuring the environment in ways that change basic interaction patterns, or by requiring staff to utilize interaction techniques such as incidental teaching strategies. Both approaches can make institutional settings more therapeutic environments. But individual residents' differences are most effectively treated using the latter approach. Ultimately, institutional settings that lack responsive adults will remain dysfunctional and their residents will continue to be denied their basic right to effective treatment.

REFERENCES

Acker, L. E., Kelley, W. R., Mason, C. R., & McAmmond, D. M. Short-term team implemented behavior modification of speech in a young boy. *Canadian Journal of Behavioral Science,* 1973, *5,* 174–182.

Anglin, J. M. *Word, object and conceptual development.* New York: W. W. Norton, 1977.

Blake, J. N. The therapeutic construct for two seven-year-old nonverbal boys. *Journal of Speech and Hearing Disorders,* 1969, *34,* 363–369.

Blee, B., & Sheldon, J. *Legal rights: A Kansas guide to developmental disabilities law.* Lawrence, Kan.: University of Kansas, 1979.

Bruner, J. S. The ontogenesis of speech acts. *Journal of Child Language,* 1975, *2,* 1–19.

Crabtree, M., *Houston test for language development.* Chicago: Stoelting Co., 1963.

Cross, T. Mother's speech adjustments: The contributions of selected child listener variables. In C. Ferguson & C. E. Snow (Eds.), *Talking to children: Language input and acquisition.* Cambridge: Cambridge University Press, 1977.

Drash, P. W., & Leibowitz, J. M. Operant conditioning of speech and language in the nonverbal retarded child—recent advances. *Pediatrics Clinics of North America,* 1973, *20,* 233–243.

Dunn, L. M. *Peabody picture vocabulary test.* Circle Pines, Minn.: American Guidance Service, Inc., 1965.

Furrow, D., Nelson, K., & Benedict, H. Mother's speech to children and syntactic development: Some simple relationships. *Journal of Child Language,* 1979, *6,* 423–442.

Graham, L. W. Language programming and intervention. In L. L. Lloyd (Ed.), *Communication assessment and intervention strategies.* Baltimore: University Park Press, 1976.

Greenfield, P. M., & Smith, J. H. *The structure of communication in early language development.* New York: Academic Press, 1976.

Guess, D., Horner, R., Utley, B., Holvoet, J., Maxon, D., Tucker, D., & Warren, S. A functional curriculum sequencing model for teaching the severely handicapped. *AAESPH Review,* 1978, *3,* 202–215.

Guess, D., Sailor, W., & Baer, D. *Functional speech and language training for the severely handicapped.* Lawrence, Kan.: H & H Enterprises, Inc., 1978.

Halle, J. W., Marshall, A. M., & Spradlin, J. E. Time delay: A technique to increase language use and facilitate generalization in retarded children. *Journal of Applied Behavior Analysis,* 1979, *12,* 431–440.

Halliday, M. A. K. *Learning how to mean.* New York: Elsevier North-Holland, 1975.

Hart, B. M., & Risley, T. R. Establishing the use of descriptive adjectives in the spontaneous speech of disadvantaged preschool children. *Journal of Applied Behavior Analysis,* 1968, *1,* 109–120.

Hart, B., & Risley, T. R. Incidental teaching of language in the preschool. *Journal of Applied Behavior Analysis,* 1975, *8,* 411–420.

Hart, B. M., & Risley, T. R. Environmental programming: Implications for the severely handicapped. In H. J. Prehm & S. J. Deitz (Eds.), *Early intervention for the severely handicapped: Programming and accountability.* University of Oregon: Severely Handicapped Learner Program Monograph No. 2, 1976.

Hart, B. M., & Risley, T. R. Incidental teaching: Making language work. Unpublished manuscript. University of Kansas Living Environments Group, 1977.

Hart, B., & Rogers-Warren, A. A milieu approach to teaching language. In R. L. Schiefelbusch (Ed.), *Language intervention strategies.* Baltimore: University Park Press, 1978.

Hursh, D. E., Latimore, J., Reid, D., Mayhew, G., & Harris, F. Designing an environment that maintains toy play. Paper presented to the Association for the Advancement of Behavior Therapy, Chicago, 1978.

Klaber, M. M. *Retardates in residence: A study of institutions.* West Hartford: University of Hartford Press, 1969.

Lyle, J. G. The effect of an institution environment upon the verbal development of imbecile children: II. Speech and language. *Journal of Mental Deficiency Research,* 1960, *4,* 1–13.

Marshall, N. R., & Hegrenes, J. R. Programmed communication therapy for autistic mentally retarded children. *Journal of Speech and Hearing Disorders,* 1970, *35,* 70–83.

McCarthy, J. J. Linguistic problems of the retarded. *Mental Retardation Abstracts,* 1964, *1,* 3–27.

McNutt, J., & Leri, S. Language differences between institutionalized and noninstitutionalized retarded children. *American Journal of Mental Deficiency,* 1979, *83,* 339–345.

Miller, J., & Yoder, D. An ontogenetic language teaching strategy for retarded children. In R. Schiefelbusch & L. Lloyd (Eds.), *Language perspectives: Acquisition, retardation and intervention.* Baltimore: University Park Press, 1974.

Moerk, E. L. *Pragmatic and semantic aspects of early language development.* Baltimore: University Park Press, 1977.

Montague, J. C., Hutchinson, E. C., & Matson, E. A comparative computer content analysis of the verbal behavior of institutionalized and non-institutionalized retarded children. *Journal of Speech and Hearing Research,* 1975, *18,* 43–57.

Nelson, K. Structure and strategy in learning to talk. *Society for Research in Child Development Monographs,* 1973, 38.

Newfield, M. U., & Schlanger, B. B. The acquisition of English morphology by normals and educable mentally retarded children. *Journal of Speech and Hearing Research*, 1968, *11*, 693–706.

Newport, E. L. Motherese: The speech of mothers to young children. In N. J. Castellan, D. B. Pisoni, & G. R. Potts (Eds.), *Cognitive theory* (Vol. 2). Hillsdale, N.J.: Lawrence Erlbaum Associates, 1976.

Paton, X., & Stirling, M. A. Frequency and type of dyadic nurse-patient verbal interactions in a mental sub-normality hospital. *International Journal of Nursing Studies*, 1974, *11*, 135–145.

Phillips, J. L., & Balthazar, E. E. Some correlates of language deterioration in severely and profoundly retarded long-term institutionalized residents. *American Journal of Mental Deficiency*, 1979, *83*, 402–408.

Pratt, M. W., Bumstead, D. C., & Raynes, N. V. Attendant staff speech to the institutionalized retarded: Language use as a measure of the quality of care. *Journal of Child Psychology & Psychiatry*, 1976, *17*, 133–143.

Prior, M., Minnes, P., Coyne, T., Golding, B., Hendy, J., & McGillivray, J. Verbal interactions between staff and residents in an institution for the young mentally retarded. *Mental Retardation*, 1979, *17*, 65–71.

Repp, A. C. On the ethical responsibilities of institutions providing services for mentally retarded people. *Mental Retardation*, 1978, *16*, 153–156.

Rogers-Warren, A., & Warren, S. F. Mands for verbalization: Facilitating the display of newly-taught language. *Behavior Modification*, 1980, *4*, 361–382.

Sailor, W., & Haring, N. G. Some current directions in education of the severely/multiply handicapped. *AAESPH Review*, 1977, *2*, 3–24.

Schiefelbusch, R. L. The development of social competence and incompetence. In M. J. Begab, H. Garber, & H. C. Haywood (Eds.), *Psychosocial influences in retarded performance*. Baltimore: University Park Press, 1981.

Schiefelbusch, R. (Ed.). *Language and the mentally retarded*. Baltimore: University Park Press, 1972.

Schiefelbusch, R. L. *Language intervention strategies*. Baltimore: University Park Press, 1978.

Schiefelbusch, R. L., & Lloyd, L. *Language perspectives: Acquisition, retardation and intervention*. Baltimore: University Park Press, 1974.

Snow, C. E. The development of conversation between mothers and babies. *Journal of Child Language*, 1977, *4*, 1–22.

Sosne, J. B., Handleman, J. S., & Harris, S. L. Teaching spontaneous functional speech to autistic type children. *Mental Retardation*, 1979, *17*, 241–247.

Stone, L. J., & Church, J. *Childhood and adolescence*. New York: Random House, 1957.

Tarjan, G., Wright, S. W., Eyman, R. K., & Keeran, C. V. Natural history of mental retardation: Some aspects of epidemiology. *American Journal of Mental Deficiency*, 1973, *77*, 369–379.

Throne, J.M. Deinstitutionalization: Too wide a swath. *Mental Retardation*, 1979, *17*, 171–176.

VanBiervliet, A., Spangler, P., & Marshall, A. M. An ecological approach for increasing language during mealtime. Paper presented to the Association for Behavior Analysis, Dearborn, Michigan, June 1979.

Warren, S. F., & Rogers-Warren, A. Current perspectives in language remediation. *Education and Treatment of Children*, 1980, *3*, 133–152.

Warren, S. F., Rogers-Warren, A., Baer, D. M., & Guess, D. The assessment and facilitation of language generalization. In W. Sailor, B. Wilcox, & L. Brown (Eds.), *Methods of instruction for severely handicapped students*. Baltimore: Paul H. Brookes Publishers, 1980.

White, B. An analysis of excellent early educational practices: Preliminary report. *Interchange*, 1971, *2*, 71–88.

Zaharia, E. S., & Baumeister, A. A. Technician losses in public residential facilities. *American Journal of Mental Deficiency*, 1979, *84*, 36–40.

Zigler, E. Personality structure in the retardate. In N. R. Ellis (Ed.), *International review of research in mental retardation* (Vol. 1). New York: Academic Press, 1966.

Communicative Design in the Speech of Mildly Retarded Adults

Sharon L. Sabsay and
Keith T. Kernan

Language use is a behavioral phenomenon that is especially sensitive to the settings in which it occurs. This is so not only in terms of the social interactional functions of language—which involve considerations of politeness, appropriateness of topic and style, and the like—but also in terms of the central function of language: the conveyance of meaning from speaker to hearer. Meaning is conveyed by more than just words and their arrangement. It depends upon consideration of such things as the social relationships between the participants of the conversation, the cultural definition of the situation in which the speech occurs, the personal knowledge the participants have of one another and the background knowledge they share, what has been said before and what follows, and much more. If speakers are to be understood in the way they intend to be understood by their interlocutors, they must take various aspects of the total speech situation into account in constructing their utterances. By total speech situation we mean not only physically or culturally defined settings such as sheltered workshops, board and care facilities, super-markets, and so forth, but also the linguistic setting, the social setting, and the interpersonal setting. [See, for example, Hymes (1967) and Gumperz (1972).]

Thus the communicative competence of any speaker depends not only on grammatical and phonological abilities, but also on the ability to recognize and take into account the relevant aspects of a given speech situation and then to utilize the rules of speaking that apply to that situation. For this reason, speakers may be said to be required to design their utterances to fit the communicative situation. This chapter examines the failures of mildly mentally retarded speakers to construct utterances that exhibit adequate communicative design.

Work on this chapter was supported in part by NICHD Grant No. HD 09474-02 and NICHD Grant No. HD04612. In writing this chapter, we benefited from discussions with Ron Gallimore, Andrea Zetlin, and Jim Turner.

283

In the speech of more severely retarded individuals grammatical and lexical deficits are usually so pronounced and problems with the physical production of speech so extensive that difficulties in other areas of communicative competence go unnoticed. Articulation problems, syntactic and morphological errors, and vocabulary limitations are much less pronounced for mildly mentally retarded speakers and, on the whole, pose much less of an obstacle to successful communication. Yet despite the relative grammaticality of their speech, interlocutors find much of what mildly retarded speakers say difficult to understand. Some of the difficulty, we will argue, lies not in the more narrowly defined linguistic abilities but in the speaker's use of otherwise grammatical utterances that in other ways do not exhibit adequate communicative design. The utterance, "He died, didn't he?" for example, is perfectly grammatical. The speaker's use of the pronoun "he," however, is interpretable only if the person to whom the utterance is addressed can identify to whom it is the speaker is referring with that pronoun. Such identification is dependent upon the context—linguistic and extra-linguistic—in which the utterance occurs. When, as actually happened, this question is asked by someone who has just walked up to a stranger, the speaker's meaning is inaccessible to the addressee.

In our research with a sample of 48 mildly mentally retarded adults over the last few years, we and our research associates have observed a high incidence of such failures in communicative design. Our task here is not to measure the incidence, but to identify and analyze the types of problems that do occur and to speculate about their underlying causes.[1] Unless such preliminary descriptive work is done, it will be impossible to accurately measure incidence in any retarded population.

THE DATA

The data on which this chapter is based were collected as part of a 3-year study that investigated the normalization experiences of mildly mentally retarded adults living in the community.[2] One of the domains covered by the study was the use of language in naturally occurring conversations and interview speech situations. Because the research was conducted over a period of 2 to 3 years with each subject, and because they were visited about once every 2 weeks, usually by the same researcher, great rapport was established between researchers and subjects. As a result, the data considered here should be viewed as being produced not in interview situations in the usual sense but in information-seeking conversations between familiar acquaintances or, in many cases, friends. They are not unlike many conversations and speech situations in which the mildly retarded naturally find themselves in the course of their everyday lives. We take the difficulties in communicative design discussed below to be ordinary and common in the speech of mildly mentally retarded speakers. They are certainly common in the speech of the members of our sample.

The examples used here were taken from transcripts of tape-recorded conversations

---

[1]In fact, little attention has been paid to either positive or negative aspects of communicative design in the speech of nonretarded populations and there are, therefore, no incidence figures available for comparison. It is our judgment, however, that incidence of poor communicative design is far higher in this retarded population than in normal populations and that it accounts for much of the impression that "something is wrong" with the way these people speak.

[2]For fuller descriptions of this study, see Kernan et al. (1981).

between sample members and researchers. Comments made by researchers in the field notes based on those conversations are taken as representative of the problems interlocutors in general have understanding these individuals. Frequent characterizations include: unclear or ambiguous identification of referents; starting stories in the middle; leaving out information relevant to stories; making comments "out of the blue"; starting too far back in a story (giving information already known); and giving irrelevant information. The researchers' descriptions, as it turned out, did not always accurately characterize the underlying communicative difficulties, similar descriptions being used for what were analytically different problems, for example. Their descriptions did, however, provide a starting point for analysis and indicated some pervasive problems.

The difficulties sample members have in adequately conveying their intended meaning can be subsumed under two very broad categories. These are, in the order discussed below, a failure to adequately identify referents or to provide other types of information necessary for a hearer's understanding of the speaker's communicative intent, and providing more information than required for the communicative goal at hand.

INSUFFICIENT INFORMATION: REFERENTS

Perhaps the most obvious manifestation of the failure of mildly retarded speakers to design the content and form of their utterances in accordance with the informational needs of interlocutors is the inadequate or inappropriate identification of referents. A speaker usually has a number of alternative ways of characterizing or referring to any given person, object, event, and so on. (In fact, a speaker usually has a number of choices for encoding anything he or she says, but for the moment we are concerned only with reference.) For example, the same person may be referred to as "Dr. Jones," "Sam," "the guy with red hair that you met at the party last night," "my next door neighbor," or "he." The speaker's choice among these alternatives is determined primarily by his or her perception of what information the hearer needs to be able to identify the referent in the context of a particular conversation. In making the choice, then, the speaker takes into consideration such things as what the hearer already knows about the person being referred to, the topic of the conversation and how the referent figures in it, whether the referent is physically present, whether he or she has been previously mentioned in the conversation and how long ago, and, if relevant to what is to be said later, the speaker's own attitude toward the referent. When the speaker fails to take such considerations into account, communicative difficulties ensue.

In Example 1, for instance, one of the cohort members referred to someone mentioned for the first time as "he." This constitutes a misuse of the definite pronoun, which is appropriately used only to refer back to someone already mentioned in prior discourse or to someone physically present at the time he is mentioned; that is, to someone the hearer can identify by means other than the information contained in the utterance itself. A pronoun gives no information about the identity of the referent, but simply indicates to the hearer that he already has the information needed to locate or identify him. In this case, because there was no likely antecedent for the pronoun in the entire hour and a half of conversation preceding this exchange, the researcher could only guess, incorrectly, to whom the speaker was referring. The first time someone is mentioned, the hearer needs more information than that.

(1)   The researcher was talking with Jeff and Rhoda Hope about the newly acquired camel bell hanging on their front door. Rhoda just remarked that the door was a good place for it because they could hear when someone came in.

      Jeff: *Well one night he was here, he could–and he can't stand horses.*

                              ((pause))³

      Researcher: *He what?*
      Jeff: *He can't stand horses.*
      Researcher: *Oh really?*
      Jeff: *And uh he uh ((pause)) came at one up here one day, he (' s scared of) horses. Rhoda came in and he says, and he started to say "Oh no." He thought it was horses coming.*
      Rhoda: *Uh hm.*
      Researcher: *This was, was um Donald? No?*
      Jeff: *No. Frank.*

There are also, of course, occasions when the identity of the referent is actually irrelevant to the point the speaker is making. In such cases, however, an indefinite pronoun such as "someone" or "this guy" is used. The use of pronouns such as "he" or "his" in such instances, as in Example 2 and in many such utterances of cohort members, implies a more definite reference than is actually required, leading the hearer to search for some previously identified referent which in fact is not present in the discourse.

(2)   Bill: *. . .it was raining. I went to the bar and got two drinks to take to his room. One for him and one for his wife.*

In this particular example, because the pronouns "his" and "him" refer to whomever it was that ordered the drinks, the speaker's statement could be phrased more appropriately as "I went to the bar and got two drinks to take to this guy's room." Although the identity of the man involved is irrelevant to the story, he still plays an important part in it. In Example 3, the speaker not only introduced a referent with a pronoun, without identifying him, she did not need to refer to anyone at all. It is the fact that the door was open, not that someone left it open, which was important, a fact that the researcher recognized when he ignored the question of the referent's identity and asked instead where the incident took place.

(3)   Researcher: *Have– Like– When a job comes up does–or like in–when Louise finds a job or your mom finds a job in the paper do they then discuss it with you and ask you if you've, y'know, if that's a place where you'd like to work or stuff like that? How does it work?*
      Pat: *Well, I would really like a tour of the place, if they allow it. Now MAKE gave a tour. An' I was lucky enough to get one, y'know, ta–cuz, y'know, how would you know what kind of work is going on, and you hear these machines going on, you don't know what's going on. So, y'know, it's better idea ta take a tour than– and ta find find out what's really going on.*
      Researcher: *Right.*
      Pat: *Y'know?*
      Researcher: *That makes sense.*
      Pat: *It does. Definitely.*
      Researcher: *Yeah. They don't always do that though, y'know?*

---

³The following symbols are used in transcription: – indicates a cut-off word; ( ) indicate that hearing is unclear or unintelligible; (( )) indicate situational information; and // indicate overlap by another speaker.

Pat: *Yeah. But you're not– But he had the door open so I could hear all these machines going.*

Researcher: *This was at MAKE?*

Pat: *No. Over today, today at this place.*

Researcher: *Oh. I see. . . .*

A number of cohort members introduced referents inappropriately in these two ways; that is, failing to identify them at all on first mention or using definite pronouns to refer to indefinite individuals. They also identified referents inadequately or inappropriately in other ways. In Example (4), the speaker introduced a referent only as ''he.'' When questioned, she additionally identified the referent by name and position, but still left out the important information that he was the boss of the hospital, just mentioned, where the speaker had applied for work. The researcher could not understand who or even what the speaker was talking about until he had confirmed this final piece of information. (What made the speaker's comment even more confusing was the fact that the researcher had just asked her a question and was expecting an answer to it when she made this unrelated comment.)

(4)   Pat: *Okay that was Pleasantville Community.*

Researcher: *Pleasantville Community. That's a hospital?*

Pat   *Uh huh.*

Researcher: *What did they say?*

Pat: *They says they don't have any openings right now.*

Researcher: *No in– openings right now. But they'll keep you in mind?*

Pat: *I didn't go to Glendale–*

Paul: *Did your counselor get you that one?*

Pat: *U: : :m He– He's at– He takes care of the kids over at Pleasantville High.*

Paul: *Who? Who's he?*

Pat: *The boss over there. Mr. Harper.*

Paul: *The boss over at Pleasantville Community Hospital?*

Pat: *Yeah.*

In this example, as in many others in our data, it is not simply a question of the speaker's failing to identify someone the first time he is mentioned. It is also a question of failing to identify him in the most appropriate or relevant way. Even proper names, as we can see here, are not sufficient identification if the hearer does not already know the relevant facts about the person named.

Problems also arose with the identification of referents on subsequent mention. In extended discourses involving several referents of the same sex, for example, speakers need to make sure that the hearer can distinguish who is being referred to at any given point in the discourse. In some cases the identity of the referent is clear from the context—what the speaker has already said—and a pronoun is sufficient. In others either a proper name or some identifying phrase is necessary. In Example (5) we see the consequences of the speaker's failure to so identify a referent.

(5)   Pat has been talking about two boyfriends, Luke and John.

Pat: *So we went out there. Outside. Y'know, he says, ''Wanna go outside?'' He says, ''Come on, go outside, it's too stuffy in here.''*

Researcher: *Who's this? You and John?*

Pat: *Luke.*

Researcher: *Luke. Okay.*

The consistent failure of many mildly retarded speakers to identify referents on first mention, or to identify them appropriately on first or subsequent mention suggests that they have difficulty determining—or do not pay attention to—the informational needs of their interlocutors. This conclusion is further supported by communicative difficulties that involve informational gaps other than referential ones.

Insufficient Information: Narrative Components

Failure to provide sufficient information of other kinds is especially clear in the case of narratives of personal experience: that is, when the speaker is relating the story of something that has happened to him or her in the past. In Labov and Waletzky's (1967) framework, a well-formed, extended narrative consists of six segments. These are, in their usual order of occurrence: abstract, orientation, complicating action, evaluation, result or resolution, and code. Not all six segments are necessary for a narrative to be well-formed and understandable; the complicating action segment alone may constitute a narrative (Umiker-Sebeok, 1979). The point is, however, that *some* narratives do require one or more of the five remaining segments. Moreover, if these segments are present they must be done properly if they are to clarify and contribute to the narrative rather than detract from it and cause confusion and misunderstanding on the part of the hearer.

The speakers in the cohort we have been studying frequently omit necessary segments from their narratives or include segments that are so ill-formed as to make major portions or even the central point of their narratives incomprehensible (see Kernan and Sabsay, 1979; Kernan and Sabsay, in press). A common area of difficulty is in providing the background necessary to orient the hearer with respect to person(s), place, time, and activity or behavioral situation of the narrative. In other words, the speakers in our study frequently do not provide the necessary linguistic and pragmatic setting for their stories.

Example (6) is taken from a counseling session and is typical of many of the conversations in our data in two ways: inadequate background information is given and the nonretarded interlocutor is finally able to understand the story only through a series of questions and proffered interpretations.

(6)   Richard: *Well let's see last night my dad and my mom's got a bit um little bit of a problem last night. Little bit problem. ((pause)) See they–*

     Counselor: *This with the uh motel?*

     Richard: *No this//is the*

     Counselor: *(   )?*

     Richard: *Apartment.*

     Counselor: *Apartments.*

     Richard: *And um my dad said ((pause)) if they been quit we're gonna move in another apartment adult building. If we be gonna move then.*

     Counselor: *You're gonna move. To–*

     Richard: *No. My mom's my dad's gonna move. 'N' they gonna quit I going along with them.*

     Counselor: *To an all adult apartment?*

     Counselor: *Too many problems with kids?*

     Richard: *That's right. Too many problems these kids and they– the kids uh ruin wreck stomp them or they pee on the pool and– But the time go swimming they gonna, y'know, the kids go an' pee in the pool, ya know?*

Even before Richard gets to his father's announcement (which constitutes the start of the complicating action) the counselor finds it necessary to establish that the "problem" Richard is talking about concerns the apartment building that his parents manage. And even after Richard describes his father's announcement that they might move, it is still not clear what precipitated that decision. From Richard's mention of the fact that his family would move to an *adult* apartment building, the counselor infers that the problem may have something to do with children and that children are the "they" Richard is referring to. His question, "Too many problems with kids?" elicits a fuller account from Richard, including what it is that the kids are doing that bothers his parents.

Speakers also leave out parts of the complicating action (the main part of the story). Example (7), which represents the beginning of a phone conversation, illustrates this point, as well as the preceding ones:

(7)   Researcher: *Hi, Elva, how you doing?*
          Elva: *I just asked this guy where he worked. I threw the paper on the ground. Do you think I should go back for it?*

In reporting on this conversation the researcher commented:

> Needless to say I was totally confused and asked Elva to explain each part. It took a long time to decipher what had happened, and even then I'm not sure this is the whole picture. She had seen a man dressed in a white uniform, like a lab technician, at the bus stop. She thought she knew him from a lab where she once went. She asked him where he worked and he started to write his name down on a piece of paper. She took the paper and threw it on the ground.

Elva originally gave only bits and pieces of the narrative that the researcher subsequently reconstructed with great effort. She left out everything except the information contained in the last sentence of the researcher's summary: that is, that Elva threw the piece of paper on the ground. Although it is difficult for someone reading this story to understand Elva's motivation for throwing away the paper, that is one point the researcher had no problem with because she knew that Elva is frightened of strange men making advances to her. Understanding the point of Elva's question, "Do you think I should go back for it?" is more difficult. At the time this conversation took place, Elva was—as the researcher knew—quite paranoid, and we mean this in a clinical sense. When pressed for an explanation, she explained to the researcher that people were following her and might be able to use the fingerprints on the piece of paper to find her.

One might argue that the confusion in Elva's speech was related to her mental condition, but the same type of confusion was reported as much as a year earlier when she gave no indication of such symptoms. We have used this particular example because it is concise enough to use given the consideration of space allowed here. The same problem is apparent in the speech of a number of other cohort members.

Finally, speakers occasionally omit not only necessary background information or parts of the complicating action, but also entire narratives, presenting only the result of, or a comment on, the omitted story. Elva, for instance, remarked on one occasion with no introduction and not in response to a question: "I only talked because Harold was bothering me." Now it can be reasonably inferred that Elva got into some sort of trouble for talking and is offering an explanation or excuse, but she does not explicitly give that information either preceding or following her statement. Another sample member, asked why she had been expelled from school, responded, "They said it was two boys, but it wasn't." In this case, the story on which the speaker's statement was a comment was eventually elicited by a series of questions from the researcher.

In both of these examples, the speaker omitted the narrative that she was commenting upon, as if the hearer already knew about the incident. The hearer, however, wishing to understand them, was obliged to seek the omitted information by asking a series of questions. Both these examples have the appearance of abstracts or introducers that often and appropriately serve as the opening lines of narratives (see Kernan and Sabsay, 1979; Kernan and Sabsay, in press). Here, however, nothing further is volunteered.

Adequate communicative design involves, among other things, the identification of referents under a number of communicative circumstances and the careful construction of components of discourse units such as narratives. As we have demonstrated, mildly mentally retarded speakers frequently fail to provide their hearers with the information that will allow or enable them to fully understand the speaker's intended meaning.

GIVING TOO MUCH INFORMATION

The omission of information necessary to hearers' understanding of what it is speakers intend to communicate, whether it be in a single act of referring or in the description of an entire series of past events, obviously causes problems for hearers. The inclusion of, or undue emphasis on, unnecessary or irrelevant information can also cause problems, although not always such serious ones. When speakers explicitly mention a particular piece of information, and especially when they elaborate upon that information at any length, they lead hearers to expect that the information will somehow be relevant to their understanding of some point the speakers are or will be making. If that expectation is not fulfilled in some reasonably obvious way, hearers may feel, if not confused, deliberately misled. (See discussion in Grice, 1975.)

We find such problems arising repeatedly in the conversations that constitute our data. Time and again mildly retarded speakers go off on tangents, bring in information extraneous to the points they are making, or emphasize minor details at the expense of major ones, to such an extent that interlocutors find themselves confused. In one conversation, for example, a researcher was attempting to elicit from a cohort member a summary of recent developments in her living situation. She responded by describing one particular development: being called into the office by her counselors at a workshop and offered an opportunity for independent living, which she turned down because she did not like the woman they were proposing as her roommate. She began, however, by going into the details of an incident leading up to that interview: being paged at the workshop while she was in the bathroom (see Example (8) below).

(8)   Researcher: *What's the story of the living arrangement business?*
        Betsy: *A: : :h, It's like weird cuz um (John   ) I didn't know what was going on. He called me. And sometimes he says (so) low that you can't hear it. (Weh– Well when I) was in the bathroom. I think I just got outa the bathroom.*
      Researcher: *He said something so low that you couldn't hear it.*
        Betsy: *No. No. Suh– (A lay–) Well someone called me, and I– when I– I think I was,*

> *I just, just got out of the bathroom and sometimes they talk so low (I can't hear them.) I don't know why they do that. S' a noise in the workshop. And then they go– "Is this–" It's Maryann, and Dennis, and John in there. I go ((laughs)) I "Oh no. What'd I do wrong now?" cuz (they're) all in there. An he says . . . .*

The researcher could not be sure until far into Betsy's account that she was actually responding to his question. His confusion in this instance was complicated by the fact that Betsy did not preface her remarks with any sort of orienting information or with any indication of what was to be the eventual point of the story, that is, with an abstract.

The tendency of mildly retarded speakers to include unnecessary and potentially distracting information is also illustrated by Example (9) below. In the course of this short interchange the mildly retarded speaker twice emphasized minor, irrelevant details (when her cousins came and which phone she called her boyfriend from) instead of directly answering the researcher's question.

(9) Researcher: *And when did you see Luke?*
     You saw Luke yesterday?
       Pat: *Uh ((pause)) no I didn't.*
     Because we were having cous– my cousins over and I wasn't sure what time they were coming over. They came over between one thirty and two.
Researcher: *Uh huh.*
       Pat: *They were//here at two o'clock.*
Researcher: *But I know you– But I know you did talk to Luke about this.*
       Pat: *Yes. I call him up//stairs, my brother's phone, y'know, he's got that button where you can go ((gesture)) this way and this way.*
Researcher: *Oh you called him up?*
Researcher: *Yeah?*
       Pat: *Switch it? And it's okay to call.*
Researcher: *Okay.*
       Pat: *So it called. I say, "Luke . . . ."*

When they give their interlocutors more information than they require, then, mildly retarded speakers are again designing their utterances in communicatively ineffective or inappropriate ways.

FACTORS IN COMMUNICATIVE DESIGN FAILURE

A number of situational factors determine the appropriate linguistic form and semantic content of utterances used in communication. In the preceding three sections we have focused on one such factor, namely, the informational needs of conversational partners, and considered some of the ways in which mildly retarded speakers may design their utterances ineffectively or inappropriately with respect to those needs. We have seen that these speakers may, on the one hand, fail to provide interlocutors with enough information to allow them to identify referents, or omit relevant details of narrative events. On the other hand, these same speakers may give their interlocutors far more information than is necessary or relevant, thereby misleading or confusing them. This failure on the part of mildly retarded speakers to accommodate to the informational needs of interlocutors clearly represents some type of communicative incompetence, but although we can identify both the problem and its conversational consequences, we cannot as readily determine its cause.

From the point of view of current linguistic theory such failures in communicative design may be considered to be purely linguistic phenomena, and it is from that point of view that we have described them. At present, although linguistics does provide a framework for examining the structure of discourse and the conveyance of meaning in semantic units larger than single sentences, it offers no explanation for deficiencies in the production of such units. That is, the relationship of linguistic abilities on this level to the cognitive processes that might underlie them has not been explored nor, to our knowledge, even speculated about. Therefore, no claims can be made at this point about linguistically specific cognitive deficits in the speakers we have studied. Nonetheless, adequate communicative design must rest on social-interactional and cognitive abilities as well as purely linguistic ones, and it is in these first two areas of competence that an understanding of the deficiencies in communicative design by mildly retarded speakers must be sought.

In their most elementary form the inadequacies of communicative design that we have identified here relate to the provision of information relevant to the meaning the speaker is attempting to convey. In the instances we have discussed, either relevant and necessary information is lacking or irrelevant information obscures the point being made. These speakers either do not or cannot make the proper decisions concerning information that particular interlocutors need in order to understand them. But this is not always the case. Although mildly retarded speakers make more errors and errors of greater magnitude in communicative design than do nonretarded speakers, at times their discourse is perfectly well-formed. At these times pronouns are used only in appropriate circumstances, necessary background information is provided, and narratives are clear and to the point. As yet, our data show no discernible pattern of distribution for adequate as opposed to inadequate communicative design. It is not the case, for example, that particular types of referents are identified correctly and others not. Speech situation or setting is not predictive of adequate or inadequate communicative design. Rather, at this stage in our research at least, it seems that an existent underlying ability to do communicative design effectively is sometimes exercised and sometimes not; that the skill exists but, whether through neglect, false assumptions regarding knowledge available to interlocutors, or inability to recognize that the speech situation requires its use, that skill is sometimes not employed by the speaker.

A similar situation has been noted in the cognitive development literature, in which a number of studies have suggested that retarded individuals, although capable of producing the strategies needed to perform a particular task, do not always do so spontaneously (Brown, 1974). Without guidance, such individuals will employ less effective or inappropriate strategies. It is postulated, therefore, that these individuals must possess the requisite basic cognitive abilities, but require guidance to use them effectively in the performance of tasks. Similarly, it seems that communicative design requires not only a complex of underlying abilities, but also some type of strategic organization, and that inadequately designed utterances represent a strategic failure or oversight to include elements of an utterance or discourse unit that the speaker is actually capable of producing and at times does produce.

We do not wish to claim that a ''mediation deficiency'' (Brown, 1974) explains the linguistic phenomena we are discussing here, but to suggest it as a promising line of investigation. In fact, not only do the speakers in our study at times adequately design their discourse, as we have just pointed out, they are also capable, when nonretarded hearers are confused and ask for background information they do not have, question the relevance of some piece of information, seek the referent for a pronoun, and so forth, of supplying the necessary information. That is, they are capable of designing utterances appropriately when given guidance or feedback by their interlocutors.

This last point is interesting in that it seems to reflect what has been identified as a reliance on other-regulation rather than self-regulation (Wertsch, 1979). That is, rather than being concerned with adequate communicative design, mildly retarded speakers apparently rely on their interlocutors to seek the information they need to understand or disambiguate the speakers' messages, and to provide the overall structure for such things as narratives. This happens with great frequency in our data. It is interesting, moreover, that in conversations the mildly retarded almost never ask questions, initiate repair, or use other linguistic means of resolving their own confusion with others' utterances; that is, they make no attempt to regulate the speech of others. This is true even when it is clear from what follows in the conversation that the mentally retarded participant has misunderstood what a speaker has said.

It is not clear why mildly retarded speakers should rely so heavily on other-regulation, but it should be pointed out that conversations are interactions in which one of the participants may easily take control of and direct the course of the conversation. This seems to be the case especially in conversations between retarded and nonretarded interlocutors. Sabsay (1979), for example, pointed out that nonretarded interlocutors direct and control the form and content of conversations with severely retarded Down's syndrome adults. A number of studies of the verbal interaction between parents and their mentally retarded children (e.g., Marshall, Hegrenes, and Goldstein, 1973; Buium, Rynders, and Turnure, 1974), though designed for other purposes, also indicate that these parents regulate the form and direction of conversation more often than parents with nonretarded offspring. It is easy to imagine, then, a lifetime of linguistic experience in which a retarded individual has had most of the verbal interaction he has engaged in controlled and directed by others. It should not be surprising that the result of such experience would be the failure to develop the ability to self-regulate, and a reliance on the regulation of others.

REFERENCES

Brown, A. L. The role of strategic behavior in retardate memory. In N. R. Ellis (Ed.), *International review of research in mental retardation*, Vol. 7. New York: Academic Press, 1974, pp. 55–111.

Buium, N., Rynders, J., and Turnure, J. Early maternal linguistic environment of normal and Down's syndrome language-learning children. *American Journal of Mental Deficiency*, 1974, 79, 52–58.

Grice, H. P. Logic and conversation. In P. Cole and J. Morgan (Eds.), *Syntax and semantics: Speech acts*. New York: Academic Press, 1975.

Gumperz, J. J. Introduction. In J. J. Gumperz and D. Hymes (Eds.), *Directions in sociolinguistics: The ethnography of communication*. New York: Holt, Rinehart & Winston, 1972.

Hymes, D. Models of the interaction of language and social setting. *The Journal of Social Issues*, 1967, *23*(2), 8–28.

Kernan, K. T., and Sabsay, S. L. Semantics in the naturally occurring narratives of mildly retarded speakers. Paper presented at the 103rd annual convention of the American Association on Mental Deficiency, Miami Beach, May 28–June 1, 1979.

Kernan, K. T., and Sabsay, S. L. Semantic deficiencies in the narratives of mildly retarded speakers. *Semiotica*, in press. (Also appears as Working Paper No. 10, Socio-Behavioral Group, Mental Retardation Research Center, University of California, Los Angeles.)

Kernan, K. T., Turner, J. L., Langness, L. L., and Edgerton, R. B. Issues in the community adaptation of mildly retarded adults. In H. Carl Haywood (Ed.), *Living environments for developmentally retarded persons*. Baltimore: University Park Press, 1981.

Labov, W., and Waletzky, J. Narrative analysis. In J. Helm (Ed.), *Essays on the verbal and visual arts*. Seattle: University of Washington Press, 1967.

Marshall, N., Hegrenes, J., and Goldstein, S. Verbal interactions: Mothers and their retarded children versus mothers and their nonretarded children. *American Journal of Mental Deficiency*, 1973, *77*, 415–419.

Sabsay, S. L. The communicative competence of Down's syndrome adults. Unpublished doctoral dissertation, University of California, Los Angeles, 1979.

Umiker-Sebeok, D. J. Preschool children's intraconversational narratives. *Journal of Child Language*, 1979, *6*(1), 91–110.

Wertsch, J. V. The social interactional origins of metacognition. Paper presented at the Biennial Meeting of the Society for Research in Child Development, San Francisco, March 15–18, 1979.

TRAINING
AND PLACEMENT

The Family Setting: Enhancing the Retarded Child's Development through Parent Training

Bruce L. Baker and
Duncan B. Clark

Although the family is probably the most critical environmental influence on a retarded child's development, the family setting's potential has not been fully appreciated in professional practices. In this chapter we begin by noting the mutual impact of retarded children and their families on one another and ways professionals have traditionally approached families. Next, drawing upon our experiences in the UCLA Project for Developmental Disabilities, we consider recent attempts to train parents to be more proactive in their child's learning. Finally, we summarize data on the relationship of family characteristics to successful continued teaching after parent training has ended, and explore the implications of these findings for redesigning training programs.

RETARDED CHILDREN AND THEIR FAMILIES: MUTUAL IMPACT

The discovery of a child's retardation is a trauma for which no family is ever well-prepared. Many theorists and researchers have attempted to delineate the impact of a retarded child upon family functioning. Some have posited psychological "stages" that parents go through, beginning with shock and a feeling of confusion and loss, followed by a period of disbelief that the child might be retarded. With progressive acceptance there is guilt and a relentless search for causes (Solnit and Stark, 1961; Schild, 1964). Many parental reactions, however, are not so much stages entered and left, but moods and mind sets that linger. Questionnaire studies have found that mothers and fathers of retarded children score more negatively on measures of mood, self-esteem, and interpersonal satisfaction than parents of normal or chronically ill children (Cummings, Bayley, and Rie, 1966; Cummings, 1976; Waisbren, 1980).

This chapter is based on the activities of the UCLA Project for Developmental Disabilities, sponsored by grant 1 RO1 HD 10962 from the National Institute of Child Health and Human Development.

There is an impact on family interactions as well. Disagreements between husband and wife over child-rearing, severe restriction of social life, disruption of short- and long-range family plans, disproportionate amounts of time devoted to the retarded child to the exclusion of other family members and excessive financial burdens have been frequently noted (Jacobs, 1969; Schild, 1971; McAllister, Butler, and Lei, 1973).

Parents have echoed these findings of the child's disruptive impact on themselves, their marriage, and relationships with their other children, friends, and neighbors (Greenfeld, 1973; Brown, 1977). Parents have spoken loudest about their frustration, anger, and despair with the service delivery system's unresponsiveness to their needs. Indeed, until recently professional practices seemed to overlook the impact of the family setting. The child was diagnosed, treated, taught or forgotten in special settings—clinics, hospitals, schools, institutions. The family's role was essentially to listen, watch, and wait. Family services, where available, often meant psychotherapy. Professionals, dwelling on the ill emotional effects on the family wrought from the child's birth, focused on enhancing the parents' psychological well being. Parents often found themselves in the role of patients.

To be sure, counseling, especially of a supportive and informative nature, can be welcome and helpful, particularly for parents of an infant, who are still struggling to accept the reality of the child's disability. Much of the negative impact on parents' mood and family interactions, however, seems to stem not as much from the fact of the retarded child per se but from frustrations parents face in living with the child. Each day can bring unsuccessful attempts to cope with behavior problems or to face a multitude of skill deficiencies, where approaches that somehow worked with other children in the family simply fall short. The primary task of parenting a retarded child, as with any child, is teaching. No matter how retarded the child is, society holds parents responsible for some degree of socialization. No one is well prepared to become the parent, and thereby the teacher, of a retarded child. Teaching even the most basic skills in areas such as self-care, communication, or play comes slowly and requires a degree of motivation and ability not demanded by more typical parenting.

In the past several decades some service providers have come to view the family quite differently, both as the setting that primarily influences the development and behavior of retarded children and as the most appropriate place for intervention. Professionals have begun to realize that families especially desire practical advice to meet the daily demands of managing and teaching their children, and that well-trained parents can be significant partners in their children's education. This appreciation of the family's teaching role has led to numerous parent training programs. There is considerable diversity in training aims and approaches, as well as in visions of the ideal family climate for enhancing the child's development. The remainder of this chapter draws on our own experience to illustrate this new form of family intervention.

Parents as Teachers

The primary aim of the UCLA Parents as Teachers program is to enhance teaching and behavior management skills. Our successfully trained family would ideally be better able to objectively observe behavior of the child and other family members, to specify the child's strengths and the particular behaviors to change, and to assess the impact of their own behavior vis à vis the child. Furthermore, they could work together to determine an effective approach to the problem, recognize and create learning opportunities, teach skillfully (in formal sessions and incidentally as the occasion arises) and evaluate progress. Most of all, we would hope the family would hold their child's skill development as an important value and would actually utilize their teaching skills to follow through after training. The Parents as Teachers curriculum and measures are oriented toward these objectives.

Curriculum   The program was developed for parents of moderately to severely retarded children, ages 3 to 13. Training typically involves an initial assessment followed by ten 2-hour sessions, a post-assessment, and several follow-through meetings. It is conducted in groups of eight to ten families, with the child present only in the assessment sessions and one meeting midway through training. The first four sessions focus on teaching self-help skills and on instructing parents in assessment and basic teaching methods, such as setting behavioral objectives, breaking skills down into components, and using guidance, backward chaining and rewards. For the fifth session, parents bring their children and receive feedback on their teaching from trainers and other parents. The next three sessions focus on strategies for behavior problem management, and toilet training if applicable; the final two sessions deal with applying learned skills to the areas of speech and language and play skills. The program advocates regular formal teaching sessions in early stages of learning a new skill and incidental teaching thereafter, to incorporate learning experiences into the child's daily routines.

In preparation for each session, parents read parts of the *Steps to Independence* series, eight teaching manuals covering skill areas in the curriculum (Baker et al., 1976, 1977, 1978). Trainers do only limited didactic presentation; they rely heavily on action-oriented approaches such as demonstrations, role-playing, videotapes for modeling and to generate focused discussion, and consultation with and between parents about progress and problems. A session-by-session guide to this curriculum is available from the authors.

Short-Term Results   In this chapter we focus on measures of parent behavior; child measures have been described elsewhere (Heifetz, 1977). Parent proficiency post-training is assessed in two main ways. *Knowledge of teaching principles* is measured by the 20-item Behavioral Vignettes Test, a questionnaire that poses hypothetical teaching or behavior problem management situations and asks for the most appropriate response from four alternatives. *Teaching proficiency* is assessed by having parents teach their child self-help and play skills in our clinic. The videotape of this session is scored on four main dimensions of teaching proficiency: arranging the environment, teaching strategies, reinforcement, and managing off-task behavior.

We have reported evaluations of program outcome elsewhere (Baker and Heifetz, 1976; Baker, Clark, and Yasuda, 1980; Baker, Heifetz, and Murphy, 1980; Brightman et al., 1980; Heifetz, 1977). Briefly, of 225 families who have begun our program, 92% have completed it. Trained parents have increased in knowledge of teaching principles and in teaching proficiency relative to delayed-training control parents. Moreover, children have increased in self-help skills and decreased in behavior problems. Cost-effective curriculum formats such as training in media-assisted groups have proved as beneficial as more costly individualized formats. Although our results and those of other investigators indicate that a short-term parent training program is effective in helping many parents acquire necessary teaching skills and begin useful programs with their children, the most important outcome question remains: What do families do with these skills after the training program ends?

Long-Term Change   Most follow-up reports of parent training have been with conduct-disordered children and have focused almost exclusively on maintenance of child behavior problem change (cf. Patterson and Fleischman, 1979). With retarded children, gains during training are typically new skills learned, and these will usually maintain if parents encourage their continued use. The more important focus becomes parent behavior after training. Ideally, when parents complete a training program they should not only be equipped to continue with the teaching and behavior management programs begun during training, but also to develop and implement new programs as needs arise.

We will report here on the follow-through of the 83 families who completed our standard training program. Sample 1 ($n=41$) were trained in Fall 1977 and Sample 2 ($n=42$) in groups begun from Spring 1978 through Winter 1979. Six months after training a project staff member who was not their trainer interviewed each family at home. A structured interview format was employed, with specific, detailed questions to make fabrications or exaggerations less likely. Interviews were tape recorded. Interviewers rated their own tapes for the extent of programming and the behavioral sophistication with which it was done, with high inter-rater reliability. Also, Sample 2 completed a questionnaire that assessed the extent to which they felt each of nine potential obstacles had impeded their follow-through efforts.

As might be expected, families varied greatly in their follow-through teaching. Based on the extent of programming reported as well as the behavioral sophistication with which parents seemed to engage in these programming efforts, the sample was divided into high, medium, and low follow-through groups. Generally, the 32 families in the high group had been able to productively continue with the programs they began during training and to independently initiate some new teaching and/or behavior management programs following training. The 31 families in the medium group also seemed to have derived some long-term benefits from training. Generally, they followed through well in some areas and less well in others. The 20 low group families reported little or no continued application of behavioral principles and techniques. From our perspective, it's unlikely that their occasional, haphazard programming efforts had any significant positive impact on their children.

These low follow-through parents reported significantly more severe obstacles than other parents on the total obstacle score and on three obstacle items: major disruptive events (such as death in the family, divorce, or serious illness), lack of time, and daily interruptions (such as telephone calls or other children). (The groups did not differ on these items: lack of patience, lack of encouragement from family, child's slow progress, child's lack of skills, unable to manage behavior problems, not knowing what to do next.) These findings could simply reflect the low group's need to find excuses for not teaching. Alternatively, it could be that these families were more stressed and less well-organized in their daily lives (Ambrose and Baker, 1979).

In summary, for most families media-based group parent training has some long-term benefits. About one family in four, however, evidenced low, if any, follow-through after training. These families reported more obstacles to teaching; however, a variety of other factors might also relate to follow-through. It would be useful for a program to be able to predict in advance which families would not follow through, and to develop alternative strategies for working with these families. For this reason we examined the relationship between characteristics of the family setting and follow-through.

Family Characteristics and Follow-Through

Five types of family characteristics were hypothesized to be related to follow-through: 1) child characteristics; 2) family socioeconomic status; 3) parents' related experience and skills; 4) parent expectations; and 5) parents' marital status and adjustment. The analysis took place in two steps: first, the determination of the relationship between single variables, and second, the derivation and testing of a prediction model. In the first step, t-tests were used to determine variables that distinguished low follow-through families ($n=20$) from the medium and high groups combined ($n=63$). In the second step, variables on which low group families differed were combined by discriminant analysis to yield a prediction formula. Each of the five characteristics is examined separately.

Child Characteristics   As discussed above, a child's retardation strongly influences parents' mood and behavior. Extending this perspective, the degree of the child's disability might be expected to relate to the family's capacity to act positively on the child's behalf. A child who learns quickly, for example, might be expected to reward a parent's efforts, leading to more enthusiastic and extensive teaching. Although there is some limited evidence that characteristics of children have some relationship to parent performance in training programs (Sadler et al., 1976), these results have been neither consistent nor convincing.

This sample was a good testing ground for this hypothesis. There was considerable variability in relevant child characteristics. Skill repertoires ranges widely, ages ranged from 3 to 14 years, and a variety of diagnoses were represented. The most frequent diagnosis was Down's syndrome (31%), followed by organic retardation of unknown etiology (29%), and autism (9%). Some children had very few behavior problems, and others had many severe behavior problems that interfered with teaching sessions. Four child characteristics were examined: 1) self-help skill performance before training; 2) degree of behavior problems before training; 3) age; and 4) self-help quotient, derived by dividing the child's self-help skill score by age.

As indicated in Table 1, none of these child characteristics was related to parent follow-through. Child characteristics, however, may influence whether parents join the training program in the first place. In another study, the Parents as Teachers program was offered to all appropriate families in a large special education school, and joiners were compared with non-joiners (Baker et al., 1980). Parents who joined the program were found to have children with greater retardation and more difficult management problems than children of non-joiners. Child characteristics influenced the parents' decision to seek training, but not their persistence in implementing what they had learned.

Socioeconomic Status   If child chracteristics do not influence what parents do at follow-through, characteristics of the family may be more important than previously suspected. Our family-oriented perspective led to the investigation of the relationship between a variety of parent and family characteristics and follow-through.

Middle and high socioeconomic status families have generally been reported to perform better than low socioeconomic status families in parent training programs. Income,

Table 1. Family characteristics: Low follow-through families ($n = 20$) versus medium and high follow-through families ($n = 63$)

Factors		t	p
1. Child characteristics			
Self-help skills		0.66	0.51
Behavior problems		0.93	0.36
Age		1.33	0.19
Self-help quotient		0.55	0.58
2. Socioeconomic status			
General SES	(M,H>L)	2.36	0.02*
Primary parent's education	(M,H>L)	2.37	0.02*
Family income	(M,H>L)	1.45	0.15
3. Related experiences and skills			
Pre-training BVT	(M,H>L)	2.20	0.03*
Membership in past groups	(M,H>L)	1.10	0.27
Behavior modification experience	(M,H>L)	2.20	0.03*
Previous behavior with child	(M,H>L)	2.45	0.02*
Post-training proficiency	(M,H>L)	5.08	0.001**
4. Expectation of obstacles	(L>M,H)	2.91	0.005**
5. Marital factors			
Marital status	(Intact M,H>L)	3.49	0.001**
Marital adjustment	(M,H>L)	1.40	0.20

$^*p < 0.05$; $^{**}p < 0.01$.

education, and occupation have been used as indicators of socioeconomic status. Rose (1974) studied the relationship between social class and performance in group parent training with parents receiving Aid to Families with Dependent Children, and middle-class families. The AFDC parents took longer to develop adequate monitoring and treatment plans than middle-class parents, and therefore were not able to change as many behaviors. Similarly, assessing targeted child behaviors, Rinn, Vernon, and Wise (1975) found that the "low-income" group in their program obtained a median of 5% goal attainment and the "middle-income" group obtained 93% goal attainment. In a study with only parents of retarded children, Salzinger, Feldman, and Portnoy (1970) found that child behavior change correlated positively with parents' level of education.

Although these studies related socioeconomic status to various measures of child progress, the implication of the finding is that parents of lower socioeconomic status do less teaching and/or less effective teaching. In this study, three socioeconomic status variables were examined: 1) income; 2) education of the parent primarily responsible for teaching; and 3) socioeconomic status, determined by the Hollingshead (1957) two-factor index that combines father's (or, where father was not living in the home, mother's) education and occupation. Primary parents ranged in education from eighth grade to doctoral degrees, with a mean education of 13.8 years. Compared with census data for Los Angeles County, the average education of parents in this sample was just more than 1 year higher than for the population of persons ages 25 or older. Income was also slightly higher than the average family's, even though the program is offered without cost to the family.

Consistent with previous studies, low follow-through families were lower in socioeconomic status (see Table 1). Both the socioeconomic status variable and the primary parent's education showed a significant positive relationship with follow-through. The relationship between follow-through and income, although in the same direction, was not statistically significant.

Related Experience and Skills   It was hypothesized that parents who entered the program already evidencing some of the knowledge and behaviors that the program aimed to increase would perform better at follow-up. Four variables assessed related experiences and skills prior to training: 1) programming knowledge, measured by Behavioral Vignettes Test score; 2) previous membership in parent groups; 3) experience with behavior modification; and 4) previous teaching, measured by a structured interview that assessed the extent of past teaching and its quality from a behavioral perspective.

Three of these variables differentiated low follow-through parents from others (see Table 1). Upon entering training the low group had lower scores on the Behavioral Vignettes Test, reported having less experience with behavior modification and had done less behaviorally oriented teaching of their children. Prior experience with parent groups was not related to follow-through; however, a high proportion of these families had some such previous experience. This was consistent with the results of our study comparing joiners of our program with non-joiners, which found that joiners had shown more involvement with parent meetings in their children's schools (Baker et al., 1980).

A further prediction was that parents who attained proficiency in the program would be more likely to follow through. Each family's proficiency in behavior modification at the end of training was determined by a combination of the after-training Behavioral Vignettes Test score, Teaching Proficiency Test score, and a trainer evaluation of parent performance during training. As seen in Table 1, proficiency in behavior modification was a very strong predictor of follow-through.

Expectation of Obstacles   We have seen that at the follow-up interview low group parents reported having encountered more obstacles to teaching than other parents. Perhaps these parents would also anticipate obstacles pre-training, so that their expectancy would be predictive of their subsequent performance.

To measure parents' expectancy of obstacles to teaching their children, we administered a 12-item questionnaire pre-training. Six items related to expected obstacles: 1) not being able to change the child's behavior; 2) generally having problems teaching; 3) lack of time; 4) lack of encouragement and help from the family; 5) slow progress; and 6) lack of patience. Each of these items was followed by a question asking the extent to which the parent felt she could overcome the problem. Parents showed considerable variability on the total obstacle score, a combination of expected obstacles and expectation of overcoming them.

This total score was highly related to follow-through. We cannot say whether this parent expectancy was an accurate prediction of real obstacles that subsequently interfered with teaching or a cognitive set that reflected lower motivation, confidence, and the like. Therefore, although for practical purposes expectancy of obstacles is a useful predictor of follow-through, additional measures are needed to understand this relationship better.

Marital Factors   We have examined the child's characteristics, the parents' related experiences, skills and expectancies, and the family's socioeconomic status. In this section we turn to the more elusive but potentially very important area of the marital relationship. We consider two marital factors: whether the primary teaching parent has a spouse in the home and, if so, the degree of marital distress. It was hypothesized that continued teaching would be more likely if the primary parent had a partner who provided support and help.

Single parents headed 17% of families in our sample. This is comparable to national norms that presently estimate one in five families to be headed by single parents. Marital status has shown a relationship in this sample with completing the program and attaining proficiency, with single parents more likely to drop out or fail to attain proficiency. Single parents also evidenced less follow-through, as shown in Table 1. In this sample, the likelihood that a parent who began training completed the program, attained proficiency and 6 months later was in the medium or high follow-through group was only 14% for single parents compared with 59% for parents with intact marriages.

Marital distress has often been noted to interfere with parent programming (Bernal et al., 1972). Some professionals even require that parents have a good marital adjustment as a prerequisite to accepting them into behavioral training programs. One study that directly investigated marital adjustment and outcome of behavioral child therapy did not find a significant relationship. Oltmanns, Broderick, and O'Leary (1977) assessed marital adjustment with a scale developed by Locke and Wallace (1959), and found that pre-treatment level of marital adjustment was not related to child behavioral change at the end of therapy or at a 5-month follow-up. Marital adjustment might, however, relate to a more direct measure of parents' behavior.

In order to study this relationship further with parents in our program, the Locke-Wallace Marital Adjustment Test (MAT) was added to our pre-assessment battery for Sample 2 families. Oltmanns et al. (1977) reported a mean MAT score of 103 (S.D.=26.5) for mothers in their clinic sample and 122 (S.D.=21.5) for a community control sample. The mean MAT for mothers of retarded children in our sample of 115.1 (S.D.=24.6) fell midway between these. Overall MAT scores were significantly lower for the low follow-through group ($\bar{X}$=97.4) than for the medium and high group ($\bar{X}$=119.3) (see Table 1).

For a further analysis, we designated a MAT cut-off of 100. Follow-through outcome was contrasted for the seven mothers with a MAT score below 100 and 31 of 100 and above. A chi-square analysis found the low MAT mothers significantly more likely to be in the low follow-through group (χ^2=5.69, df =1, $p<0.01$). Marital adjustment may, then, be predictive of outcome only for especially low scoring families, a relationship that is obscured when the complete sample is examined.

In summary, we found that single parents and couples with relatively low reported marital adjustment tended to evidence little constructive teaching post-training. When these two marital variables were combined, the relationship to follow-through was even greater. Of single parents and intact marriages with MAT below 100, 58% fell in the low follow-up group; for intact marriages with MAT 100+, only 10% fell in the low group (χ^2=8.91, df=1, $p=0.002$).

Prediction Model

Given that a number of characteristics distinguish low follow-through parents from medium and high follow-through families, we attempted to combine these to yield a prediction model. Of the variables previously discussed, the only one that was not considered for inclusion was the MAT, because it was not available for the entire sample. To limit the variables actually used in the prediction equation and thereby avoid the statistical problem of "overfitting" common in prediction research, only variables that were significantly related ($p<0.05$, two-tailed) to follow-through individually were allowed to enter into the equation (see Table 1 for significant variables).

The equation predicting follow-through category was developed by a "forward step-wise" discriminant analysis computer program (Brown, 1977). From the pool of variables previously found to significantly relate to follow-through category, the forward variable selection proceeds by the following steps: 1) the variable most highly related to follow-through category by an F statistic is selected to enter the model first; 2) the partial F statistic associated with each remaining variable is calculated based on a discriminant analysis containing that variable and the variable initially selected; and 3) the variable in step 2 with the largest partial F statistic is added to the equation. This process repeats until no remaining variables have a significant F statistic; at that point, the process is terminated (Kleinbaum and Kupper, 1978).

Another feature of this program is that variables included in the equation in an early step can be removed at a later step. When a new variable is added to the equation, the contribution of each variable is re-examined. The variable with the smallest nonsignificant partial F statistic, if there is such a variable, is removed, and the equation is reconstructed with the remaining variables.

In summary, variables in the final equation must meet three criteria. First, the variable must be significantly related to follow-through category independent of its relationship with other variables. Second, to be initially included in the equation, the variable must add significantly to the variance accounted for by variables already in the equation. Third, all variables in the final equation must each contribute significantly to the variance accounted for by the set of variables in the equation. These criteria provide a substantial safeguard against variables being included in the equation by chance.

The variables included in the prediction formula were parent proficiency, marital status, and previous teaching. This formula correctly classified 15 of the 20 in the low group and 51 of the 63 in the medium-high group. Because this apparent error rate tends to underestimate the rate of incorrect classification that might be expected with another sample, a within-sample "leaving-one-out" analysis[1] was performed to more accurately estimate the expected error rate (Lachenbruch, 1975). The results are shown in Figure 1. In this analysis, 70% of low and 78% of medium-high families would be expected to be correctly classified; this prediction is significantly better than chance.

Summary and Implications

Summary of Predictors   We have seen that a number of parent characteristics relate to the extent and quality of continued teaching after a training program ends. Despite a fairly

---

[1] The "leaving-one-out" procedure, developed by Lachenbruch (1975), is a variant on the "split sample" method of error estimation. In the "split sample" method, half of the sample is used to derive the equation, and accuracy is estimated by applying it to the other half. The "leaving-one-out" procedure is conceptually similar, in that it takes all possible "splits" of one subject in one "group" and the remainder in the other. An equation is derived for this latter group of N − 1 subjects, and the left out subject is classified using this equation. This procedure is repeated for all subjects. For each N − 1 group, a discriminant function is constructed to classify the left out observation, and the error estimate is based on the accuracy of these independent classifications. Thus, a given observation is not used in the construction of the discriminant function used for its classification, and the error estimate is unbiased. The "leaving-one-out" method is superior to the "split sample" method with relatively small samples (Lachenbruch, 1975).

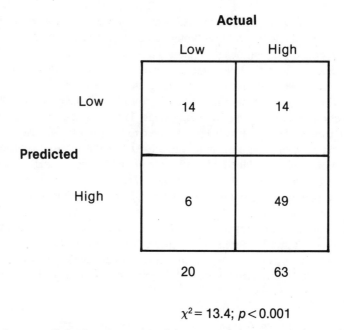

$$\chi^2 = 13.4; \; p < 0.001$$

Figure 1.   Follow-up prediction formula: parent proficiency + marital status + previous teaching.

heterogeneous sample, child characteristics did not relate to follow-through. When they entered training, families that subsequently did little follow-through were characterized by lower socioeconomic status, less education of the primary parent, and greater expectancy of obstacles. They had less related experience and skill, such as behavioral programming knowledge, experience with behavior modification, and previous teaching. They were more likely to be single-parent families or have less well-adjusted marriages. At the end of training, parents who had not attained proficiency were less apt to follow through. These variables are relatively easy to measure, and an equation based upon them (excluding marital adjustment) correctly predicted follow-through status for three of four families. These predictors must now be cross-validated and expanded to include other family characteristics.

There are additional family characteristics that might relate to follow-through and improve this prediction. Marital distress may interfere with teaching; the relationship found was based only upon half of the sample and needs further study. Psychological mal-adjustment of the primary parent would also seem a likely inhibitor of success. Miller and Gottlieb (1974) reported a relationship between MMPI profiles and parent training out-come. We also have begun to incorporate the MMPI into our assessment battery. The family's values and characteristic ways of interacting—referred to as "family cli-mate"—seem important, though difficult to assess. We have begun to employ Moos' Family Environment Scale, a 90-item self-report measure that assesses such dimensions as family conflict, organization, achievement orientation, and moral-religious values. The addition of the MMPI, Marital Adjustment Test, and Family Environment Scale may enhance the predictability of family teaching.

Implications for Parent Training   The ability to predict which parents will benefit from group training has obvious practical significance for agencies. Parents predicted to do well in parent groups such as the Parents as Teachers program can be assigned to this relatively inexpensive intervention, while potential low benefit families can be offered a hopefully more effective, though perhaps more costly, alternative. The relationships we have found with outcome suggest possible training variations. These must be interpreted, of course, with caution because such correlations do not necessarily indicate causal relationships. Nonetheless, these factors that relate to long-term outcome are potentially useful places to begin in considering alternatives, and evaluation of those alternatives should indicate whether our "educated guesses" about causality were valid.

The consideration of predictors to develop alternatives can take two directions: 1) redesigning training in minor ways to change modifiable parent characteristics, and 2) designing very different training approaches that accommodate better to more static parent characteristics. To illustrate changing modifiable characteristics, consider *expectation of obstacles*. This may reflect a negative cognitive set as much as an accurate perception of real obstacles; as such, there is evidence from other areas (e.g. depression) that negative cognitions can have enormous and often unrecognized effects on actions. For example, the parent who automatically says to herself "He'll never learn anything" or "I can't teach well" may abandon the teaching role after the training program ends. It may be that cognitive behavioral inputs in training, aimed at uncovering negative expectations and teaching alternative coping thoughts, would alter expectations and result in changed behavior after training. In this case the parent attribute correlated with outcome has itself been changed.

As a further example, consider the two marital factors predictive of low follow-through: single parents and distressed marriages. These are both modifiable characteristics. We don't suggest arranging for single parents to meet eligible potential mates, but we have had some success with a lesser intervention to reduce these parents' isolation. Single parents have been particularly apt to drop out of training. By encouraging them to attend meetings with someone (e.g., friend, relative) we have practically eliminated dropouts. A follow-through plan that involves another person may be worth exploring as a facilitator of continued teaching. For couples with poor marital adjustment, some form of marital therapy may be a useful precursor for or adjunct to group parent training. In both of these cases, the training plan seeks to modify characteristics associated negatively with outcome.

To illustrate accommodating training to relatively static characteristics, consider mother's education and family socioeconomic status (SES). These are the strongest predictors of post-training proficiency; less well educated mothers from lower SES families are less apt to meet proficiency criteria. Proficiency, in turn, is the strongest predictor of follow-through. To enhance proficiency and eventual follow-through for these families, a different approach to training must be explored. The present curriculum, even though it utilizes media, role playing, and the like, is in many respects like a course. A different direction is suggested by evidence that lower SES persons learn better from action training approaches than didactic ones, but the two modalities are equally effective for middle-class SES (Schneiman, 1972).

One alternative that we have studied is a school-based model with more action-oriented inputs (Brightman, Ambrose, and Baker, 1980). Thus far we have not utilized this model with families predicted to do poorly but have employed it with families who actually completed training and demonstrated low proficiency. Children of nine low proficiency families attended a 3-week mini-camp for 5 days a week (Tuesday through Saturday). Their parents were required to attend for 1 or 2 full days each week. Training for parents involved active teaching and direct supervision; they were taught to monitor their own teaching by scoring videotapes of their sessions with their children. Overall, the inputs were directed toward 1) increasing knowledge of behavioral teaching principles, 2) increasing actual teaching skills, and 3) promoting follow-through. Each training input was developed to be easily exportable to schools for retarded children. By the end of this program, parents had increased in knowledge and teaching skills to about the average level of standard-trained parents. Their proficiency was now significantly greater than a comparison group of low-gain families who did not attend camp. Furthermore, our follow-up results indicate that these families attained higher scores for continued programming than they would have been expected to achieve on the basis of our predictor equation. The success of this school-based pilot program supports the approach of searching out predictors of outcome and then using these relationships as guides for programmatic change.

ACKNOWLEDGMENTS

We would like to acknowledge with appreciation the contributions of our colleagues on the project staff, in particular: Stephen Ambrose, Peggy Henning Berlin, Richard Brightman, Jennifer Carter, Dr. Andrew Christensen, David Donovan, Ann Hazzard, Stephen Hinshaw, Dr. Ron Huff, Mary Prieto-Baird, Patrice Yasuda. We particularly thank Elizabeth Mooney for computer assistance and Dr. Donald Guthrie for statistical consultation.

REFERENCES

Ambrose, S. A., & Baker, B. L. Training parents of developmentally disabled children: Follow-up outcome. In A. Christensen (Chair), *Maintenance of treatment effects following behavioral family therapy.* Symposium presented at the American Psychological Association, 87th Annual Convention, New York, September, 1979.

Baker, B. L., Brightman, A. J. Carroll, N. B., Heifetz, B. B., & Hinshaw, S. P. *Steps to Independence Series* (for parents of retarded children). Champaign, Ill: Research Press Co. *Speech and language: Level 1*, 1978, 82 pp. and *Speech and language: Level 2*, 1978, 106 pp.

Baker, B. L., Brightman, A. J., Heifetz, L. J., & Murphy, D. *Steps to Independence Series* (for parents of retarded children). Champaign, Ill: Research Press Co. *Behavior problems*, 1976, 80 pp.; *Early self-help skills*, 1976, 96 pp.; *Intermediate self-help skills*, 1976, 80 pp.; *Advanced self-help skills*, 1976, 96 pp.; *Toilet training*, 1977, 96 pp.; *Trainer's guide*, 1976, 24 pp.

Baker, B. L., Clark, D. B., & Yasuda, P. M. Predictors of success in parent training. In P. Mittler (Ed.), *Frontiers of knowledge in mental retardation.* Baltimore: University Park Press, 1980.

Baker, B. L., & Heifetz, L. J. The READ Project: Teaching manuals for parents of retarded children. In T. D. Tjossem (Ed.), *Intervention strategies for high risk infants and young children.* Baltimore: University Park Press, 1976.

Baker, B. L., Heifetz, L. J., & Murphy, D. Behavioral training for parents of retarded children: One year follow-up. *American Journal of Mental Deficiency*, 1980, *85* (1), 31–38.

Bernal, M. E., Williams, D. E., Miller, W. H., & Reogor, P. A. The use of videotape feedback and operant learning principles in training parents in management of deviant children. In R. Rubin, H. Fensterheim, J. Henderson, & L. Ullmann (Eds.), *Advances in behavior therapy.* New York: Academic Press, 1972.

Brightman, R. P., Ambrose, S. A., & Baker, B. L. Parent training: A school-based model for enhancing parent performance. *Child Behavior Therapy*, Fall 1980, *2* (3).

Brightman, R. P., Baker, B. L., Clark, D. B., & Ambrose, S. A. Effectiveness of alternative parent training formats. Unpublished manuscript, UCLA Department of Psychology, 1980.

Brown, M. B. (Ed.). *Biomedical computer programs: P-series*. Los Angeles: University of California Press, 1977.

Cummings, S. T. The impact of the child's deficiency on the father: A study of fathers of mentally retarded and of chronically ill children. *American Journal of Orthopsychiatry*, 1976, *46*, 246–255.

Cummings, S. T., Bayley, H. C., & Rie, H. E. Effects of the child's deficiency on the mother: A study of mothers of mentally retarded, chronically ill, and neurotic children. *American Journal of Orthopsychiatry*, 1966, *36*, 595–608.

Greenfeld, J. *A child called Noah*. New York: Warner Books, Inc., 1973.

Heifetz, L. J. Behavioral training for parents of retarded children: Alternative formats based on instructional manuals. *American Journal of Mental Deficiency*, 1977, *82*, 194–203.

Hollingshead, A. B. Two factor index of social position. Unpublished manuscript, Yale University, 1957.

Jacobs, J. *The search for help: A study of the retarded child in the community*. New York: Brunner/Mazel, 1969.

Kleinbaum, D. G., & Kupper, L. L. *Applied regression analysis and other multivariate methods*. North Scituate, Mass.: Duxbury Press, 1978.

Lachenbruch, P. A. *Discriminant analysis*. New York: Hafner Press, 1975.

Locke, H. J., & Wallace, K. M. Short marital-adjustment and prediction tests: Their reliability and validity. *Journal of Marriage and Family Living*, 1959, *21*, 251–255.

McAllister, R. J., Butler, E. W., & Lei, T. Patterns of social interaction among families of behaviorally retarded children. *Journal of Marriage and the Family*, 1973, *35*.

Miller, W. H., & Gottlieb, F. Predicting behavioral treatment outcome in disturbed children: A preliminary report of the Responsivity Index of Parents (RIP). *Behavior Therapy*, 1974, *5*, 210, 214.

Oltmanns, T. F., Broderick, J. E., & O'Leary, K. D. Marital adjustment and the efficacy of behavior therapy with children. *Journal of Consulting and Clinical Psychology*, 1977, *45*, 724–729.

Patterson, G. R., & Fleischman, M. S. Maintenance of treatment effects: Some considerations concerning family systems and follow-up data. *Behavior Therapy*, 1979, *10*, 168–185.

Rinn, R. C., Vernon, J. C., & Wise, M. J. Training parents of behaviorally-disordered children in groups: A three years' program evaluation. *Behavioral Therapy*, 1975, *6*, 378–387.

Rose, S. D. Group training of parents as behavior modifiers. *Social Work*, 1974, *19*, 156–162.

Sadler, O. W., Seyden, T., Howe, B., & Kaminsky, T. An evaluation of "Groups for Parents": A standardized format encompassing both behavior modification and humanistic methods. *Journal of Community Psychology*, 1976, *4*, 157–163.

Salzinger, K., Feldman, R. S., & Portnoy, S. Training parents of brain-injured children in the use of operant conditioning procedures. *Behavior Therapy*, 1970, *1*, 4–32.

Schild, S. Counseling with parents of retarded children living at home. *Social Work*, 1964, *9*, 86.

Schild, S. The family of the retarded child. In R. Koch & J. Dobson (Eds.), *The mentally retarded child and his family*. New York: Brunner/Mazel, 1971.

Schneiman, R. S. An evaluation of structured learning and didactic learning as methods of training behavior modification skills to low and middle socio-economic level teacher-aides. Unpublished doctoral dissertation, Syracuse University, 1972.

Solnit, A. J., & Stark, M. H. Mourning and the birth of a defective child. *Psychoanalytic Study of the Child*, 1961, *16*, 523–537.

Waisbren, S. E. Parents' reactions after the birth of a developmentally disabled child. *American Journal of Mental Deficiency*, 1980, *84*, 345–351.

Severity of Intellectual and Associated Functional Impairments of Those Placed in Mental Retardation Services between Ages 16 and 22: Implications for Planning Services

Stephen A. Richardson, Helene Koller,
Mindy Katz, and Janice McLaren

The impact of specific settings on the development and behavior of retarded persons needs to be considered in interactional rather than cause and effect terms. The setting, defined in terms of a social and physical environment, influences the retarded person. The characteristics of each retarded person influence the placement in a particular setting, however, and also influence how the individual behaves in each setting. Although this may seem obvious, it was not realized at the time therapeutic communities were being organized for psychiatric treatment, on the premise that all aspects of daily life in a psychiatric institution could contribute to the therapy of all patients. Experience with these programs showed that any given therapeutic milieu would have varying effects on different patients ranging from beneficial through harmful, depending on the prior history, personal characteristics, and needs of the patient (Rapoport et al., 1961). The results of this experience do not seem to have been taken into account in the care of persons who are mentally retarded. Perhaps this is due to the mistaken belief that the characteristics and backgrounds of persons in mental retardation settings are sufficiently similar that less concern is needed for individual differences.

Although it might seem reasonable that a residential facility for persons who are mentally retarded would be organized to meet the various needs of those who were to be

This study was supported by the Foundation for Child Development, The Grant Foundation, The Easter Seal Research Foundation, The National Institute of Child Health & Human Development Grant No. HD07907, and The Social Science Research Council of the United Kingdom.

served, in fact, the physical and social environments were copied from hospitals providing medical care. Growing awareness of the inappropriateness of the hospital model of care led to major reorganization efforts in the directions of deinstitutionalization, community centered care, and mainstreaming, shifting the major emphasis away from bodily care to the development of social and intellectual skills and training for everyday life in the community. With the current emphasis given to psychosocial factors, other needs and characteristics of the mentally retarded have been given less attention. The diversification of programs and settings that has been initiated by these recent changes has had many beneficial results, but has taken place without good evidence about the numbers of mentally retarded persons in a population and the variability in the characteristics of these people, factors that should be taken into account in planning kinds and size of services and settings.

In general, an individual is placed in a particular mental retardation service because he or she has needs that cannot be met elsewhere, and there is an opening avaialable in the setting. In part, the placement may be the consequence of the inability of other settings to cope with or tolerate the individual. We have selected characteristics of the individual that indicate specific needs that may be difficult to meet, and problems that may make it difficult to deal with an individual in the customary socialization settings—the home, formal educational facilities, and the world of work. The characteristics selected are degree of intellectual impairment, physical impairment, seizures, and behavior problems.

Sometimes the entry into a mental retardation service is precipitated by a change in the setting or home environment of the mentally retarded person. For example, a family that has been able to manage a mentally retarded child at home experiences the onset of a chronic illness of a parent, the addition of another child, or breakdown of the family due to separation, divorce, or death.

At any phase of a person's life, the individual may be exposed to several different settings; for example, a mentally retarded person may live with parents and attend a day program, or may reside in an institution and go to another setting for the day. The effect of any one setting on an individual has to be viewed in the context of the other settings the individual is experiencing. Some of the settings may be mental retardation services and others may not. Even within a total institution there is some variety of environments, and residents will generally experience some of this variety during the course of the day.

The characteristics of individuals are also influenced by the history of the settings with which they have interacted, so it is necessary to view individuals at any point in time in the context of their previous experiences. For example, two persons in a residential facility for the mentally retarded may differ considerably if one has been in institutional care since early childhood, and the other has lived within a family and community, and has only recently been placed in the institution. It is important, then to consider the career course of retarded persons in the context of all the settings they have experienced as well as in the present setting.

Most studies of services for the mentally retarded have focused on the structure and functioning of the service and its staff at a particular point in time. The study discussed in this chapter focuses on the individuals for whom services are provided, and follows them through their experiences with services up to age 22. It provides a perspective that complements the other type of study.

The purpose of this chapter is to identify and examine some characteristics of a total population of young people in a city who were classified as mentally retarded. We examine the kinds of mental retardation services that were available, and describe the subsets of mentally retarded persons who were in the various settings. By examining the reasons for entry into the different services or settings, we can determine some of the individual needs the different settings have had to deal with. The settings that have developed in the geographic area of the study are to some extent unique and the product of local history, legislation, politics and administrative style, but it is likely that the range of individual characteristics of those who are mentally retarded will be more general across a variety of geographic areas.

DESCRIPTION OF THE STUDY

Data for this chapter come from a study of mentally retarded individuals in a city in Britain whom we have followed from childhood up to age 22.

The numbers of persons in a population who are mentally retarded and the proportion with associated impairments will vary depending on how mental retardation is defined, and how cases are identified and classified in the community selected for study. Furthermore, the frequency of mental retardation may be influenced by the characteristics of the community. A brief description of these factors is given for the population in this study to provide a basis for considering the relevance of the results for other communities.

The study population is derived from all those born in 1951–1955 who resided in the city in 1962. This constitutes the population at risk of mental retardation. A child was considered mentally retarded and included in the study if at any time before or during the school years he or she was classified and placed in a special facility for the mentally retarded. A systematic set of procedures was used by the local authorities for screening and evaluating cases. These procedures are described in detail elsewhere (Birch et al., 1970). The decision for each child was based on a clinical judgment, taking into account school performance, IQ, social competence and the findings of a medical examination. IQ was not the overriding determinant as is found in some communities. In 1962 a research team from the United States independently evaluated all persons born in 1952–1954 who had been classified as mentally retarded by the city authorities. They concluded that proper placement had been given to every child who was in a mental retardation facility.

At the time the study population was growing up the city had a wide range of industry, was the center of an agricultural area, a seaport, a summer resort, and had a university. The city had a stable population with no sizable minority or recent immigrant groups. The various mental retardation services were of good quality and services were, in general, available to all who needed them. These, together with health, education, social work, and welfare services available to all, were financed from tax revenues and not on a fee-for-service basis. A fuller description of the city can be found elsewhere (Birch et al., 1970). In recent years it has experienced a low unemployment rate among young people.

A variety of mental retardation services were available for the study population. During the school years special classes were available for those considered as educable mentally retarded (EMR) or, to use the British term, educationally subnormal (ESN). An alternative placement was a school for children considered too severely retarded to benefit from ESN classes, where the main emphasis was on training in self-care and social skills. These are called classes for the trainable mentally retarded in the United States and Junior Occupation Centers in Britain. A third service was a residential institution mainly for children. After the school leaving age of 16 years, two general types of services were available: day care programs that operated 5 days a week and residential institutions.

Most of the day care programs provided training in social skills and activities of daily living, recreational activities, and some vocational activities. There were also some programs where more emphasis was placed on vocational activities and training.

The residential institutions available were a large regional facility for the mentally retarded, farms where young men were housed and supervised in simple farming activities, a small residential facility and a hostel located within the city. There were also psychiatric hospitals where members of the study population have been sent.

The focus of this chapter is on the post-school years between ages 16 and 22, and the characteristics of those young adults placed in the settings just described.

METHODS

The data used in this chapter were obtained from comprehensive life history interviews with the young people, separate interviews with their parents, and observational ratings made on each young adult at the conclusion of the interview. The data, for most cases, were cross-checked against school, social work, and hospital records, and an independent medical survey of some of the more severely retarded cases. For the cases for whom interviews were not obtained, records were our only source for information on their life histories. In fact, there are a few cases for whom information is still outstanding. Addition of these cases may result in small changes in data presented in future reports.

A summary description of the numbers of cases in the study and post-school services they received is shown in Table 1. For comparative purposes it is valuable to know the prevalence of mental retardation in the total population. There were 222 cases out of a population at risk of 13,842, yielding a prevalence rate of 16 per 1,000. Clarke and Clarke (1974), in a review of mental retardation, suggested a prevalence of 20 per 1,000 as "a proportion of the population 'at risk' of needing special services at some time during their lives" for Great Britain (p. 22). They also cited a prevalence of 30 per 1,000 given by Heber based on studies in the U.S. In the U.S., IQ results seem to be given heavier weighting than in Britain in the administrative classification of mental retardation, and this difference may account for the somewhat lower prevalence in Britain. In an earlier study (1962) of the 1952–1954 birth cohorts in this study, the prevalence of those administratively classified as mentally retarded was 12.6 per 1,000, but when children in regular classes who on psychometric grounds could be considered as mentally retarded were added, the prevalence increased to 27.4 per 1,000, close to the 30 per 1,000 prevalence rate frequently cited in the U.S. (Birch et al., 1970, p. 30).

Ten study cases died between the ages of 8 and 22 years. Of the survivors, 55% received no further mental retardation services after leaving school. (A preliminary report of what happened to this subset in the post-school years is given by Richardson, 1978.) These rates correspond closely with an estimate made by Gruenberg (1964) based on a

Table 1.   Receipt of mental retardation services between ages 16 and 22 for study population

	N	%	Prevalence/1000
No mental retardation services			
since leaving school	117	55	8.5
Day services only			
Entire post-school period	38	18	2.7
Less than entire period	16	7	1.2
Total in day services only	54	25	3.9
Residential services only			
Entire post-school period	19	9	1.4
Less than entire period	10	5	0.7
Total in residential			
services only	29	14	2.1
Both day and residential services	8	4	0.6
Unknown whether post-school			
mental retardation services	4	2	0.3
Total survivors to age 22[a]	212	100	15.3

[a]There were, in addition, 10 who died between ages 8 and 22. Inclusion of these cases raises the prevalence rate to 16/1000 for the total population.

review of age-specific prevalence rates from studies of mental retardation, that about half of all children classified as mentally retarded during the school years disappear from mental retardation services after leaving school. These figures suggest that this study population is similar enough to other populations that some generalizations can be made.

The remainder of this chapter deals with those in the study who received services after school-leaving age. They constitute 43% of the survivors. Table 1 shows that there were almost twice as many who only received day services compared to those who were only in residential services. Very few (4%) of the survivors, experienced both day and residential mental retardation services after school leaving age. For those in either day or residential services only, a stay throughout the period from 6–22 years is about twice as common as more limited periods in these services.

Types of Functional Impairment in Young People
Receiving Post-School Mental Retardation Services

Although the severity of intellectual impairment as measured by IQ tests is indicative of some of the needs of young people who are mentally retarded, it only provides a partial picture of the individual. This picture needs to be filled out with knowledge about impairment in other functional modalities—physical and behavioral. In some cases it is the presence of associated impairments that presents the major problems of care and management. By examining the various forms of functional impairments of those in different services, we can learn more about the needs that the services have to consider in their structure and functioning. To do this it is necessary to first determine measures of functional impairments used in this study.

IQ classification has long been used as a means of measuring intellectual impairment, but the classifications of other functional modalities have generally been developed for purposes of making inferences about the cause of the impairment, or for medical diagnosis. We have used classifications of physical impairment, seizures, and behavior disturbance in which a case was judged impaired only if the disability would be expected to interfere with activities of daily living, or with interpersonal relationships.

IQ   All subjects were given intelligence tests at various ages during their school years. We have used the scores of tests taken between the ages of 7–10 years, the period when the children were most often assessed. Primary weighting was given to the WISC. We are here using scores of below 50 to distinguish the more and less severely retarded. In general, IQ tests given at ages 7–10 predict level of intellectual functioning into early adulthood. There are two cases for whom there have been marked changes. One has suffered severe degeneration of intellectual functioning and the other has shown a marked improvement in the intervening years. For these cases, an adult test measure was used.

Physical Impairment   The forms of physical impairment vary widely within the study population but are contained within the following classifications: speech, vision, hearing, impairment in the use of limbs, heart defects, and incontinence present at age 22.

Seizures   The term *seizures* is used in order not to have to judge what seizure manifestations constitute epilepsy. The classification was of four degrees of severity and was based on criteria of frequency, proportion of time when seizures occurred, type of seizure, use of medication, and side effects. Severity was assessed for each of four time periods up to the age of 22, and an overall classification of severity was evaluated, taking into account all four time periods. (See Richardson et al., 1979, for a full description of this classification.)

Behavior after Age 15   The following three forms of behavior disturbance were identified within the study population:

Neurotic   Any indication of disturbance of emotions, for example, misery and unhappiness (i.e., depression), "nervous breakdown," problems with "nerves" and anxiety, need for tranquilizers on a regular basis, and suicidal and other self-destructive acts. Other indicators used were admissions to a psychiatric hospital or attendance at an out-patient psychiatric facility.

Conduct   Mostly unsocialized aggressive disturbances: quarreling, fighting, aggression, destructive or impulsive behavior, temper tantrums, inappropriate sexual behavior, and generally difficult to handle.

Antisocial   Delinquent behavior evidenced by fines or imprisonment for stealing, assault, breach of the peace, arson, and other illegal acts.

Behavior disturbance after age 15 has been difficult to assess for the group in residential care since childhood; it is not clear the extent to which institutional management may have affected the behavior of these individuals. We are still in the process of evaluating the institutional records; therefore, any findings of behavior disturbance among this group should be considered tentative, and probably an underestimate.

Characteristics of Those in Day or Residential Care Only

The two general types of mental retardation services in the post-school period are day and residential care. The majority of young people received care in either day or residential services only, so we first examine the kinds of functional impairments of those in these two forms of care. Table 2 shows that in both day and residential care, the young people, in addition to being moderately or severely retarded, have sufficient frequency of physical impairments, seizures, and behavioral disturbances to require mental retardation services to

Table 2.   Percent frequency of IQ <50, seizures and physical and behavioral impairment among young adults in day and residential facilities for the mentally retarded between ages 16 and 22.

| | For period between ages 16 and 22, percent of young adults who received mental retardation services | |
Type of impairment	In day care only (n=54)	In residential care only (n=29)
IQ less than 50	43	48
Physical impairment[a]		
Single	24	31
Multiple	17	28
Total	41	59
Seizures		
Moderate	13	17
Moderate-severe	7	17
Severe	7	7
Total	27	41
Behavior disturbance		
Neurotic	24	7
Conduct disorder	2	21
Antisocial	2	3
Conduct and antisocial	0	14
Neurotic and conduct	4	7
Neurotic and antisocial	2	3
Total	34	55
None of above impairments	11	7

[a]Nine percent of those in day care and 36% of those in residential care had such severe speech impairments that interviewing them was not possible.

make provisions in their programs for dealing with these impairments. In addition, service providers in both day and residential facilities should recognize their clients may more often have multiple rather than single impairments (Table 3).

Returning to Table 2, as might be expected, the frequency of impairments is somewhat higher among the young adults in residential care in each of the four functional modalities than among those in day care. There is a significant difference in the types of behavior disturbance found in the two forms of service, with those in residential care having more

Table 3.   Number of functional impairments, considering IQ<50, physical impairment, seizures and behavior disturbance, for young adults receiving mental retardation services in day care only and residential facilities only for the period between ages 16 and 22.

| | For period between ages 16 and 22, percent of young adults who received mental retardation services | |
Number of impairments	In day care only (n = 54)	In residential care only (n = 29)
0	13	7
1	32	18
2	34	43
3	17	29
4	4	4

Table 4.   Percent frequency of IQ<50, seizures and physical and behavioral impairment among young adults receiving only residential mental retardation services for all and part of the period between ages 16 and 22.

Type of impairment	For the period between ages 16 and 22, percent of young adults in residential mental retardation services only for:	
	The total period (n=19)	Part of the period (n=10)
IQ <50	68	0
Physical impairment		
Single	26	40
Multiple	42	0
Seizures		
Moderate	16	20
Moderate-severe	26	0
Severe	11	0
Behavior disturbance		
Neurotic	0	20
Conduct disorder	21	20
Antisocial	0	10
Neurotic and conduct	11	0
Neurotic and antisocial	5	0
Conduct and antisocial	0	20
None of above impairments	0	20

conduct and antisocial behavior and less neurotic behavior than those in day care ($\chi^2 = 11.89, p < 0.005$). This suggests that one reason for placement in residential care may be the inability of the day care facilities or the parents or parent surrogates of the young adults to manage conduct disorders, or of the community to tolerate antisocial behavior. It also suggests that neurotic behavior, if not too severe, can be dealt with by the day centers and by parents or guardians outside of the day care facility.

Duration of Care

By obtaining information about the career paths through mental retardation services, which are followed by the study subjects, we can distinguish between those who remained in a service between the ages of 16 and 22 years and those who were in service for only part of this period. These two subsets would be expected to differ in the kinds of impairments they possess, and in consequence, the kinds of needs to which the services must attend. This distinction would be lost in a cross-sectional study.

Of the young people in residential service, those in care for only part of the post-school period are markedly less impaired in intellect, physical impairment, and seizure history than those in residential care for the entire period (Table 4). The amount of behavior disturbance among those institutionalized for the entire period may, as stated earlier, be underestimated; therefore any apparent differences on this modality should be discounted until further examination of the behavior of this group is completed.

In day care facilities, those who received services for only part of the post-school period have a lower frequency of severe intellectual and physical impairment than those in day care for the entire period, but the two groups do not differ on seizure histories. The

Table 5.   Percent frequency of IQ<50, seizures and physical and behavioral impairment among young adults receiving only day mental retardation services for all and part of the period between ages 16 and 22.

	For the period between ages 16 and 22, percent of young adults in day mental retardation services only for:	
	---	---
Type of impairment	The total period (n=38)	Part of the period (n=16)
IQ <50	61	6
Physical impairment		
Single	24	25
Multiple	45	13
Seizures		
Moderate	13	13
Moderate-severe	8	6
Severe	8	6
Behavior disturbance		
Neurotic	16	44
Conduct disorder	3	0
Antisocial	3	0
Neurotic and conduct	3	6
Neurotic and antisocial	0	0
Conduct and antisocial	0	0
None of above impairments	8	19

subset in day care for only part of the period have a higher frequency of behavior disturbance, manifested primarily in neurotic behavior (Table 5).

The marked differences in the individual characteristics of those in care for the entire period from 16–22 years and those in care for only part of this period indicate that both day and residential services must deal with a wide diversity in the young people they serve.

Those in care during the entire period, whether day or residential, have a higher frequency of multiple functional impairment than those in care for only part of the period (Table 6). This difference is significant for the group receiving day care, and nearly so for those in residential facilities ($\chi^2 = 3.91, p < 0.005$ for day services; $\chi^2 = 3.32, p = 0.07$ for residential services).

Table 6.   Number of functional impairments, considering IQ<50, physical impairment, seizures and behavior disturbance, for young adults receiving mental retardation services for all and part of the period between ages 16 and 22.

Number of impairments	In day mental retardation services for:		In residential mental retardation services for:	
	Part of the period (n=16)	The total period (n=38)	Part of the period (n=10)	The total period (n=19)
0	19	11	20	0
1	44	26	30	11
2	13	42	40	42
3	6	21	10	37
4	6	3	0	5

Reasons for Entry into Services

The nature of functional impairments of individuals in the various forms of post-school mental retardation services provides evidence of the kinds and variety of needs that service providers should take into account in considering staff skills and programs. We can obtain further clues about individual needs by examining the reasons why individuals were initially placed in particular services.

Residential Placement   The reasons for placement in residential services are summarized in Table 7, which also gives the numbers for whom these reasons apply. In subset A, the reasons are related to age of placement. For the seven placed between the ages of 1 and 4, the reasons seem to be a combination of: 1) early evidence of severe intellectual impairment, and 2) medical diagnosis of mental retardation, Down's syndrome and cerebral palsy, and the beliefs and values of some doctors and acquiescence by parents as to the most appropriate forms of care. That not all doctors and parents shared these views is suggested by the fact that most children with Down's syndrome (72%) and cerebral palsy (77%) were not placed in residential care. One additional person with cerebral palsy was placed in residential care at age 13, but the reasons were a combination of severe behavior problems and epilepsy.

For the children placed between ages 6 and 15, the reasons for placement are largely related to the severity of the burden of care that the children's behavior placed on their parents, particularly on the mother. The characteristics of the children that seemed to

Table 7.   Reasons for placement in residential mental retardation facilities

A.	In residential care for entire post-school period[a] ($n=19$)
N	Reasons for placement
7	Placements between ages 1 and 4: Three with Down's syndrome, two with cerebral palsy. Placement advised by doctors on basis of mental retardation. Rejection by parents based on feelings about mental retardation. (In one case placement due to broken home.)
12	Placement between ages 6 and 15: Except for one case, severe problems of child management: incontinence, seizures, behavior problems, need for constant supervision, and mother under such stress that physical and emotional breakdown occurred or likely. (In two cases broken homes.) For the other case, frequent moves of family to and from a foreign country were disturbing to child, and led to decision.
B.	In residential care for only part of post-school period ($n=10$)
4	Severe behavior problems: running away, wandering; violent and destructive behavior; problems of sexual management. Decision made by doctors, social workers, and parents. (In three cases broken homes.)
4	Placements made by courts under legal discretion to place in mental retardation facility rather than prison or fines. (Three cases broken homes.)
2	Placements made when parents died and no other placement available.
C.	In day and residential services during post-school period ($n=8$)
	a) Mainly day and short-term residential care
3	For psychiatric treatment for severe depression, nervous breakdown, and behavior—difficult to manage at home and in day care. All cases returned to day care. (No broken homes.)
	b) Miscellaneous patterns of jobs, day and residential care
4	Severe behavior and management problems.
1	Residential placement recommended by social workers because of breakdown of family and no other placement available.

[a] All cases in this subset entered residential care before age 16.

cause undue parental stress were failure to control emotions, impulses, and bodily processes rather than inability to perform the kinds of tasks that are measured by psychometric tests. As we have seen, it is not level of intellect that mainly differentiates those in residential from those in day care for the entire post-school period. Of course, parents differ with respect to the amount of stress they can withstand. In the cases where there are single parents or broken homes, it may well take a lesser degree of stress before the parent or substitute arrangements break down. Furthermore, the stress caused by the mentally retarded child must be seen in the context of the overall burden of stress the parents experience both within and without the immediate family. This might include the number of children to be cared for, the presence of illness or handicaps among family members, or work that is stressful or takes the father away for long periods. Stress may also accrue from the lack of material resources that are available to the family. In one case, where the child had bowel incontinence, the absence of a washing machine and hot water were included in the mother's reasons for her inability to cope with the child and placing him in residential care.

The reasons for residential placement of young people for only part of the period from 16–22 (subset B) are also largely related to difficulties in management. Eighty percent were placed because of behavior problems. Half of these cases were placed in a residential facility by court order because of antisocial or illegal behavior, and for the other half, decisions to place the young adult were made by doctors, social workers, and parents. In some of these cases, fear that continuation of the behavior would lead to arrest and legal action contributed to the decision. In the city where the study was carried out, the courts are required to obtain a social work report on young offenders, and if there is a history of mental retardation, the court has the discretion to send the offender to a residential institution for the mentally retarded rather than using the normal penal sentences. Seventy percent of those in subset B compared to only 16% of those in subset A came from broken homes. The degree to which knowledge that the young person had come from a broken home contributed to the court's decision, and the degree to which the home conditions or the experiences after the break up of the family may have contributed to the behavior disturbance are difficult to determine, but both are possible contributors to placement.

There are eight additional persons who received a combination of both day and residential services (subset C). In three cases, residential placement was for short-term treatment of psychiatric symptoms that developed while the young people were living at home and attending a day care center. In these cases, rather rapid improvement in behavior occurred after residential treatment, and the young people were able to return to their homes and a day care setting. Each was in day care for the entire period of 16–22 except for the short stays at a residential setting. Four other cases in subset C were placed in residential settings for longer periods because of behavior and management problems. Of all 37 cases who received some residential care, only four were placed primarily because of difficulty in finding any alternative caregiving arrangements.

This review of reasons for residential care makes clear the diversity of individual characteristics and problems that residential care providers must take into account in planning residential environments. It also suggests that many of the problems with which the residential settings have to deal are of a magnitude greater than those that can be dealt with by the combination of parental care at home and a mental retardation day service. This can be better judged after examining the reasons for placement in day care settings.

Day Care Placement   Of the 62 cases who received services in day care settings, 61% remained in day care throughout the period up to age 22. For almost all these cases, their level of functioning during the school years had made it apparent to parents and educational authorities that as young adults they would not be able to work in open employment, and that some form of service after leaving school would be essential for the well-being of both the young person and the parents. In a few cases attempts were made to find jobs, but a very brief trial made it apparent the young person could not manage. In no case, however, did their behavior present problems of management.

Twenty-six percent (16 cases) were in day care for only part of the post-school period. Half of these went into day services after unsuccessful attempts to find or to hold jobs in open employment. Seven persons went into the day services immediately after leaving school, but left to become housewives, to seek open employment, or to remain at home during the day. The remaining person had a short period in a day center that terminated because the staff there could not cope with his frequent severe seizures. At 22, he had been in another day care facility for about a year, after spending several years at home with no respite for his parents. No cases in this group manifested unmanageable behavior.

The remaining eight persons who received some day care during the post-school period were those who also received some residential care, and were discussed above, under that heading (Table 7, subset C). Most cases in this group did present management problems, resulting in the institutional stays.

DISCUSSION

From a longitudinal and ecological perspective, the care of mentally retarded children and young adults needs to be considered in terms of the interrelated roles played by the parents or parent substitutes, the formal and informal supports provided by relatives, neighbors and friends, the more formal supports of human services in the community and those services that take specific responsibility for the mentally retarded. Any of these support systems may provide the human and material resources necessary for the upbringing and socialization of a child. By studying the life histories of a population of young people who were initially designated as mentally retarded during their school years, we have gained a picture of the factors that influence their career paths through mental retardation services, and the demands their needs place on the social system of the community of which they are a part.

Approximately half of the young people who were in special mental retardation services during the school years had no further contact with mental retardation services after leaving school. The extent to which they were able to manage their own affairs, the support services they received from other agencies and from informal services and the quality of their lives are issues that are dealt with in separate publications. Here the focus is on those who continued to receive mental retardation services in the post-school years. Although the school ends its contributory role during the mid-teens, the family and the informal social network of those significant to the young person continue to provide a supportive role. We have a number of cases where, due to some form of family misfortune, a breakdown occurs and they no longer can or will care for the child outside of school hours. Sometimes breakdown is in large part due to the severe stress imposed by the problems of managing the behavior disturbance and/or seizures of the child, and in other cases the child makes little or no contribution, for example, in cases of death, separation, divorce, abandonment of the child, or removal of the parents from the child for a variety of reasons. Where the child does not have severe management problems, substitute forms of parenting and care can often be found for the child outside of mental retardation services. These include care by relatives or neighbors, foster care, or placement in a residence whose purpose is to care for orphaned or abandoned children. Provided the substitute parenting arrangement was in the city, the child would be able to continue at the special school. Where the management problems are beyond the capacity of the substitute parents to deal with, the child is then placed in an institution organized for the care of the mentally retarded. In the study population, with one exception, every child placed in a mental retardation institution during childhood has remained in institutional care until the time of follow-up at age 22. The majority of those who were cared for by substitute parents have not received mental retardation services after leaving school. In a few cases the overall upbringing and care system for the child has broken down because the special school is unable to cope with the child. Expulsion of the child was in almost all cases due to the failure of the school to manage the behavior problems of the child. This led to placement in residential facilities, which were sometimes mental retardation residences, and sometimes residential programs for delinquent children.

In the post-school period, the young person's placement in a mental retardation day service is, like earlier school placement, dependent on the presence of a parent or parent substitute, who is responsible for the young person outside of the hours of the day service. For the young people in the study, the large majority of those in day care are still living at home with at least one parent. The number for whom substitute parents and homes will be needed will increase as time passes and the parents become infirm or die. The almost universal hope expressed by parents in our study is that a substitute parent and home can be found in the city so that the young person may continue at the day service with the company of those he or she knows at the day care center and often knew in childhood-when they attended the same school for TMR children. The alternative of placement of the young person in the regional mental retardation residential institution outside the city is a dreaded alternative. So far, only three have gone to the residential mental retardation service from day care centers, and this was because their behavior became unmanageable and they developed such serious neurotic symptoms that residential placement was made to allow for treatment. In all cases, the treatment was sufficiently successful to enable return of the young person to the day service and their homes. In a few cases the young persons decided they did not want to continue at the adult day service and stayed home, placing the full burden of care on the parents and the informal social support network of the parents.

Institutional care can be viewed as the end of the line of alternatives available, and these institutions play a wide variety of roles. Among these we have identified the following:

1. Taking responsibility and providing programs for mildly retarded young adults who have gotten into trouble, came to the attention of the courts and have been committed to the institution for custody and rehabilitation. In all cases in our study, a major effort was made in the social rehabilitation of these young people, and they have returned to the city with attempts made to provide a transition back to community living using various formal human services in the city with which the institution has close liaison.
2. Some of the residents live at the institutions and go out to jobs in open employment during the day. These patterns developed to provide a first step in outside experience

before returning to the community, or followed unsuccessful trials living away from the institution.

3. Some residents hold jobs within the institutions.
4. Some residents hold no jobs, but are involved in daily programs of training in social and physical skills and in recreation activities.
5. The most severely and multiply handicapped residents are given largely nursing and custodial care.
6. Cutting through these categories, the institution has to deal with the severe management problems that no other combinations of care have been able to cope with.

In our study there was some interchange of residents between institutions. In some cases the regional institution that provided most of the care made sufficient progress in rehabilitation that they moved the young person to a smaller residence that played a half-way house role and enabled the young person to try out jobs in the city and aided in the transition back into the city. In other cases the large institution was unable to cope with the severe behavior problems of the young adults, and transferred them to special psychiatric facilities that deal with people whose behavior is viewed as a grave threat to themselves or others.

It has already been shown in the reasons for admission to residential facilities in the age range of 16–22 that management of behavior disturbance was the major task confronting the institution.

An important contributor to the effectiveness of mental retardation services is how well staff can work and communicate within their own facility, between the different mental retardation services and with social and medical services outside of the mental retardation system. We have emphasized their role in dealing with behavioral problems, but they also have to deal with seizures, physical handicaps, and in some cases chronic and degenerative diseases.

The number and kinds of people who enter and leave the mental retardation service system are influenced by the extent to which parents are able to rear their children, aided by the informal social network in the community to provide the human and material resources to assist parents and take over their role when necessary. They are also influenced by the overall structure and functioning of the more formal agencies in the community that provide support and human and material resources. After school-leaving age the number and kinds of jobs available will also be influential, together with the quality of liaison between mental retardation and employment services.

Given even a fairly wide variety of social and economic conditions in the society, the requirements for mentally retarded services for those who are more severely retarded should remain fairly constant in terms of the prevalence of those needing services and the needs of those served. It is the prevalence of the less severely retarded that is likely to increase in terms of mental retardation service demands as the social and economic conditions deteriorate.

The prevalence of mildly retarded individuals who have behavior disorders and enter adult mental retardation residential services is also likely to vary, depending on the overall social and service system of the particular community. The variation will be due to the extent that psychiatric and mental retardation services are used as the setting for treatment and the extent to which the courts refer those who come before them to psychiatric or mental retardation services, or use the penal options of fines or imprisonment.

At this time in the United States, a major focus of attention in residential care is the transfer of persons from large institutions to small community facilities. Because of the lack of experience with social skills and community living of those who have had long stays in large institutions, great emphasis is being given to providing training to help remedy this deficit in experience. In the study reported in this chapter, the system of services for young adults is one where there has been relatively little institutionalization and long-term stays and where, when it has happened, it is of those with severe and multiple problems. The distribution of those in post-school services of this study is likely to resemble the pattern of services in the U.S. where the problems we have inherited of a large and long-term institutional population has been dealt with through the present programs of de-institutionalization. This study population shows that plans for the organization of services for young people must take into account the need to deal with physical handicaps, seizures and behavioral disturbances, which separately and often in combination create serious management problems that will require highly skilled professionals from a variety of disciplinary backgrounds.

For residential care to take the form of small community residences it will be essential to provide a variety of settings to meet the widely differing individual characteristics described in this chapter. Unless special arrangements are made to meet the needs of those with severe management and behavior problems, the presence of these young people in residences not prepared to meet these special problems can create severe strain on those responsible for and those served in the residences.

ACKNOWLEDGMENTS

The authors wish to thank Professor Raymond Illsley and Gordon Horobin of the MRC for their help and support.

REFERENCES

Birch, H. G., Richardson, S. A., Baird, D., Horobin, G., & Illsley, R. *Mental subnormality in the community: A clinical & epidemiologic study.* Baltimore: Williams & Wilkins, 1970.

Clarke, A. M., & Clarke, A. D. B. Criteria and classification of subnormality. In A. M. Clarke and A. D. B. Clarke (Eds.), *Mental deficiency: The changing outlook.* London: Methuen, 1974.

Gruenberg, E. M. Epidemiology. In H. A. Stevens and R. Heber (Eds.), *Mental retardation: A review of research.* Chicago: University of Chicago Press, 1964.

Rapoport, R. N., et al. *Community as doctor: New perspectives on a therapeutic community.* Springfield, Ill.: Charles C Thomas, 1961.

Richardson, S. A. 1978. Careers of mentally retarded young persons: Services, jobs and interpersonal relations. *American Journal of Mental Deficiencies*, 1978, *82*, 349–358.

Richardson, S. A., Katz, M., Koller, H., McLaren, J., & Rubinstein, B. Some characteristics of a population of mentally retarded young adults in a British city. A basis for estimating some service needs. *J.M.D.R.* In press.

Index